MINE HOST, AMERICA

OTHER WORKS by LORD COTTENHAM

Novels

ALL OUT : The story of Thomas Furness's
adventure.   1932

SICILIAN CIRCUIT : Some further adven-
tures of Mr. Thomas Furness and
his friends.   1933

Motoring Books

MOTORING WITHOUT FEARS: A simple text-
book of driving, with an introduction
by the editor of the *Autocar*.   1928

MOTORING TO-DAY AND TO-MORROW : A
discussion of some motoring problems
of the time, with a preface by John
Buchan, Lord Tweedsmuir.   1928

STEERING WHEEL PAPERS : A collection
of radio addresses, articles and
speeches.   1932

In Preparation

SEGRAVE : The life of the late Sir
Henry Segrave.

MINE HOST, AMERICA

BY
MARK PEPYS
6TH EARL OF COTTENHAM

" From quiet homes and first beginning
Out to the undiscovered ends,
There's nothing worth the wear of winning
But laughter and the love of friends."
HILAIRE BELLOC.

COLLINS
FORTY-EIGHT PALL MALL LONDON
1937

THIS BOOK IS SET IN FONTANA, A NEW TYPE
FACE DESIGNED FOR THE EXCLUSIVE USE OF THE
HOUSE OF COLLINS, AND PRINTED BY THEM
IN GREAT BRITAIN

COLLINS CLEAR-TYPE PRESS · LONDON AND GLASGOW
COPYRIGHT 1937

IN exact, individual degrees of gratitude, intimacy and pleasure

TO

each and every one of my American friends and acquaintences, of whom none is forgotten, although space forbids the mention of them all : especially to Dotty, Cordie, David and Margey, her mother and Anne, and the blithe memory of Babs, to Maeve, Harriet, Bill, Effingham and Mrs. "Effingham," and to Cordie's mother, to Floyd and Lenore, Lester and Mrs. "Lester," Bob and Reba, and Cy and Phil; to my compatriots—the "open air girl," Hugh, then sojourning hospitably in Hollywood, and Liz, also joyously there; to Donald and Mrs. "Donald," Eddie and Mrs. "Eddie," Bill and Lenore, Clark and Helen, and Al and Dave ; to two kindly inspectors of the San Francisco Police Department, Mrs. Cotton—my most helpful temporary secretary in Los Angeles, and George V. Koyse—for a week my patient driver by day and night in New York; to the Chrysler Corporation, in particular to Ledyard Mitchell, Byron Foy, Glenn Mooney and Toby Couture with renewed thanks for their entertainment, forethought and great kindness, and to Louis Skinitzero, best of amateur *couriers*, for his merry companionship, forbearance towards my haste, and performance of innumerable acts of grace during about five thousand miles of fast touring; to Metro-Goldwyn-Mayer, Fox 20th Century, Universal and Warner Brothers, with the happiest recollections of being a guest in their respective motion picture studios; to United Air Lines Corporation and its President, through the good offices of Mr. Don Black, with grateful recollections of an interesting afternoon's inspection and a swift journey to San Francisco and back; to Transcontinental and Western

3

Air, Incorporated, and its President, through the careful organisation of Mr. T. Park Hay and Mr. Clancy Dayhoff, with added appreciation of the remarkable care taken to provide for me an instructive transcontinental flight, apart from its usual efficiency; to the respective Chairmen and Committees of the Union, Knickerbocker, University, Racquet and River clubs in New York, the Athletic club in Detroit and the Pacific Union club in San Francisco, with an assurance of my sincere appreciation of being granted the honour of temporary membership; to the Management and Staff of the Weylin Hotel, New York, and the Ambassador, Los Angeles, with most thankful recollections of their untiring efforts for weeks on end to promote my every comfort and strictly to preserve my privacy; to numerous restaurant proprietors, shopkeepers, clerks, waiters, chamber maids, bell-boys, elevator men, white and coloured, many of whose names I know but have no room to record here, to the police, rangers, service station attendants and porters, whose names I never knew—to all these, their faces still in my mind, as well as to my closer friends, old and new, I tender my warmest thanks for all they did (and it was much) to make me feel welcome in the great country of America.

They as greatly succeeded. Next to any place in the British Commonwealth, I shall always regard America now as my second home, and look upon as truly friendly the peoples who live there—polyglot no doubt, indeed no more a single race than are the peoples of the British Commonwealth itself, but harbouring in their heart of hearts fine and good ideals for their united communities—their destiny to be even more blessed with the fruits of endeavour, their eyes always looking to the future.

CONTENTS

List of Illustrations and Map

PROLOGUE

A Gale and an Arrival

PART I

Mainly of Motoring—especially from Atlantic to Pacific

5

INTERMISSION

Moonshine in sunny California

PART II

Chiefly of Flying—particularly from Pacific to Atlantic

EPILOGUE

A Pause and a Departure

APPENDIX : Some notes on the cost of motoring across America

INDEX

LIST OF ILLUSTRATIONS

7

AUTHOR'S PREFACE

BROADLY, THIS IS LITTLE MORE THAN A DESCRIPTIVE ACCOUNT of a drive from New York to California and of a flight back; both seen through the eyes of an Englishman with a working knowledge of motoring and aviation but possessed of no previous, practical acquaintance with American conditions, social, political or economic. A certain historical background, self-admitted to be inadequate, and a bookish approach to recent developments, both acquired since a youthful semi-education ended, may be taken for granted as colouring—not, perhaps in the correct shades—such comments as may be found herein. The privilege of close friendships, some of many years standing, with Americans, may also legitimately be pre-supposed by readers, though naturally I myself am differently situated in respect of this, and would not commit the personal mistake of treating impersonally or taking for granted such highly-valued relationships—a consideration not always given due weight in the perusal of a non-fictional work. Thus, where names are withheld, or conversations patently edited, the explanation is not far to seek.

Likewise, no notable people, known or unknown, are dragged into these pages merely on account of notability. In any event, they might be notable to me for some other reason than that which the world's press, their contemporaries or their own primary activity has attached to them: for personal estimates depend as well on individual dealings. So there are purposely few referred to by name, although a number were met; and those who are mentioned enter naturally as participants or accurately to colour a scene or assemblage.

Moreover, being only an amateur newspaper correspondent, a "story" means nothing to me—and never will. Life is sufficiently remarkable in all its permutations and commutations; I see no reason to garnish facts with fiction, but only to relieve the sterner happenings or probabilities with humour lest the human frailties of fear or tears gain sway. That the editors of certain newspapers and a journal saw fit to publish some of the matter now forming this volume, is therefore a credit to them rather than to me, who simply recorded facts. For facts by themselves are often held to be poor fare for the public: which is the public's loss, and, where certain matters (naturally of more importance than those treated in this book) are concerned, is a loss which modern education will rightly urge them not to tolerate much longer.

Unless one is reading or writing fiction for relaxation or profitable interest respectively, facts remain the most suitable staple diet; and such theories as will best accord with them in our reasonable rather than conservative judgment. Granted a decent motive, each of us, with lesser or greater ability, can only truthfully record our own impressions, the visible or audible impressions of others, and facts as we encounter them, or take perhaps an unfashionable degree of trouble to read them up, pre-historical, historical and contemporaneous. This is progress, this is learning, this is understanding—whether of science, of world affairs or merely, as in this book, of a cross-section of a country quickly viewed. Without progress, learning and understanding, we can only look forward to remaining, *en masse*, as ignorant of fundamentals, as superstitious and as intolerant or ineffective as the generation that brought about the world war.

Such a remark seems to portend a drift towards politics. Actually, there are few serious political conclusions hereafter, and those only of the broadest kind, induced by conversations with acquaintances or chance passers-by, some of which were enlightening and have inspired a paragraph or two, others profoundly dull and limited. Such sense as I have, will not allow me to visit the United States for ten weeks and then come home to air fixed theories of the political situation, with a lot of impertinent wisecracks thrown in about the general characteristics of various Senators and Congressmen or even of the President himself. I know it is fashionable to do so, but again I plead a preference for the older standards of accuracy, (even at the expense of spurious interest), and of courtesy towards one's hosts and hostesses. Sometimes I have quoted opinions, but they are American opinions. When I have discussed, it has been in general terms and upon matters of which I know something; and any criticism also relates to familiar subjects and is limited to a kind welcomed over there.

Many of us have read much about America, in genuine admiration and for love of our friends. But surely only when an author has read a great deal and paid several extensive visits to a country, is he justified in embarking upon the analytical commentary which, in a *pseudo* form, seems to result all too frequently from one hurried tour.

This itself being a personal account, it must suffer from the same disadvantages as a detailed part of any memoir. The "I's" must be overlooked and the book viewed as a whole—for the general impression it gives of what was seen, heard and done. Furthermore, any conclusions drawn by readers, or by the writer, will inevitably be qualified by the age-old query: "What is truth?"

Here, then, is merely a tally of simple happenings during a journey planned long ago as a holiday and frequently deferred; one which was badly needed when at length it materialised, but, being subject to the usual circumstantial changes, turned out to be as physically strenuous as it was mentally stimulating. Once landed, nearly eleven thousand miles in fifteen days, over half of it by car, a few hundred by train and the rest by air, was a programme productive of sights, sounds and sensations almost too bewilderingly numerous to catalogue. Had it been consecutive, my notes would have proved even scrappier than they were. Fortunately, the journey could be divided into two main parts: a racking, eight-day drive from New York to Los Angeles, and a day and a night flight eastward again, purposely in the stopping 'plane rather than the express. I remained on either coast for periods of about a month and, during those times, drove or flew the remainder of the mileage.

The westward drive at the rate of about four hundred miles a day for eight days, meant that my impressions, jotted down each night for elaboration in the morning, became more sparse and laboured as I neared the Pacific. Still, the haste was inevitable, for I was due in Los Angeles in a matter of days, yet wished to see much on the way. When I arrived there, the production of forty-five thousand words in twenty-one days, interspersed with much sightseeing, the reception of many kindnesses and two week-ends away—one yachting off Santa Catalina Island and the other in San Francisco, afforded me scant opportunity for physical regeneration. The transcontinental flight westward, although a straightaway effort amounting only to hours, was nevertheless another severe test of note-taking; I slept unashamedly at short intervals during the night, having been in the pilot's cockpit all morning. During ensuing weeks in New York, relieved by week-end visits to Long Island, Washington and Virginia, the generosity of my friends and the night life to which I was gladly tempted by them, took further toll of good intentions where rest and a little milder work were concerned.

Inevitably, therefore, there are signs here of sketchiness resulting from fatigue, of errors of omission which may not now be rectified without a more leisurely return to the

14

scenes in question. No doubt, too, there are errors of judgment. For these, though I am unconscious of them, I apologise in advance. But as a charcoal drawing, made with a few quick strokes, presents at a distance some indication of what a finished painting of the same subject might be, so these pages may afford my English friends a passing glimpse of some aspects of America, and my American friends a revelation of the effect of their inspiring land upon at least this stranger.

What I have written is, in effect, my bread-and-butter letter of thanks to the United States for their hospitality. Although "it is not all who fulfil the duties of gratitude who may on that account flatter themselves that they are grateful," my lengthy epistle is aimed throughout at expressing a sincerity incapable of misunderstanding. In this, at any rate, I hope it succeeds.

It only remains for me to acknowledge a debt to four friends: Frances Davis, brilliant as ever with her typing and humorously patient over my handwriting; David Grant, editor of the *Sunday Pictorial*, in which paper extracts from my motoring diary appeared; Collin Brooks, editor of the *Sunday Dispatch*, who serialised part of my Californian notes; and Charles Grey, editor of *The Aeroplane*, who allowed me to incorporate here certain of my material published originally by him.

Each borrowed illustration is individually acknowledged. My old No. 1 folding Kodak, battered by nine years' travel and possessed of no filter, cannot adequately compete with such pleasing work. But that in some instances it makes a gallant attempt to do so, is largely due to the unfailingly careful preparation of my prints by Will R. Rose, Ltd. of Oxford.

C.

TRAVELLERS' CLUB, LONDON.
October, 1936.

PROLOGUE

A GALE[1] AND AN ARRIVAL

LONDON IN SEPTEMBER: SLIGHTLY CHILL DAWNS FOR THOSE at Covent Garden market; bright warm days from Highgate to Mitcham, Barnes to Bow; evenings with a hint of vapour in the distant view up-river to Westminster, downstream to the Tower; nights bringing brisker steps to theatre-leaving crowds in Piccadilly Circus, to dance-club strollers in Mayfair, to the shoving chattering throngs and yelling hawkers in the glitter of Commercial Road. The prim trees in the parks, like girls in green school linen, still make a show of modest uniformity at the end of term, before gaily emerging one by one into *débutante* adolescence during succeeding weeks and donning in celebration the tempting frocks of autumn.

Sombre Euston station: a long train waiting at a long platform; a locomotive steadily spewing a hissing jet of steam; porters with bent knees pushing piled barrows of luggage at a half-run—luggage with gaudy shipping labels on it; restaurant car attendants standing waiting by their

[1] The side-lights of a sea voyage, its human contacts or avoidances, comforts or discomforts, the sights it reveals and the varied thoughts which a bundle of books may provide as companions, will naturally pall upon many. These first pages deal mostly with passing considerations of English or American society, gulls, the Clyde, the partial renaissance of aristocracy in Italy and Germany and its death in France and Russia, prehistoric races, Christianity, espionage, lifebelts, stormy weather, Spiritualism, God versus dogma, health, education, divorce, political competency, icebergs, the St. Lawrence, trees in autumn, Wolfe's cove, Canadian mining, aviation as a means to natural development, immigration, obtrusive sentimentality, some people's philosophy of self-defence, privacy lost and privacy regained. Consequently, those who wish straightway to read of America are recommended to skip most of this prologue and start at page 73.

cars; passengers for Canada already eyeing one another even as they part from relatives; a boy trailing a rubber-tyred, mobile stall of magazines and papers, and calling "Pa-apers 'nd Ma-agazines." A jaded man in a corner seat with a book he wants and several publications that he doesn't: myself.

. . . .

A warning passed from official to official down the platform. A slim young woman said good-bye to a spare, fit-looking man, entered the train and stood for a moment at the corridor window for a last word with him; I guessed he was her father or her uncle. The train made one of those smooth, gliding starts upon which our crack engine drivers pride themselves. The girl gave a final wave, turned away and came into my carriage. A Cairn terrier puppy made its appearance behind her; pattering perkily at the end of a leather lead. The girl sat down, lifted the little tyke on to the seat beside her, and proceeded to look out of the window. But the dog, its head on one side, regarded me quizzically with a pair of bright eyes—a sort of mutual, man-to-man inspection.

"You're a genial little devil," I thought, "and your mistress is extremely nice looking." And, indeed, she was, with her trim tailor-made costume, neat hat, well-chosen shoes, and the softly healthy complexion which comes from rain as well as the sun. Without being observed, I had noticed a more than usually thoughtful brow, well-spaced eyes, a humorous little nose, generous but firm lips and a stiff enough chin. And I liked the appearance of her hands, brownish, capable, adequately but not over manicured. I concluded that she was almost certainly quite delightful, and started to pay some real attention to the first of my fashionable journals, behind which I had been taking cover while conducting this reconnaissance.

One by one, I went lazily through them, journals of the kind one idly studies at the club and occasionally buys, cruelly described by some as unconscious propaganda for communists, patterns for self-conscious socialists and climbing bulletins for socialites, but which are to more normal, less intense people just amusing pages of snapshots among which we may sometimes spot old Tom, Dick or Harry, or possibly dear Anne, Joan or Betty, looking far more half-witted, knock-kneed or splay-footed than any of us ever do in real life.

Among the portraits of the monied clowns which nowadays crowd these pages—fair game for labour brickbats—being the first or second generation from some able working man who would sooner have failed to make a pile than see his descendants spend it as they do, it is indeed a joy to spot old Tom, Dick or Harry, dear Anne, Joan or Betty, who, in the cause of charity, graciously mingle with these money-spiders that their ambitions may benefit some hospital.

My tired glance encountered a photograph of a couple of the new and selfish rich, a remarkable blonde female in check bathing drawers and *brassière* reclining on a striped mattress under a quartered sunshade at some balmy Mediterranean *plage*, whose only possible excuse for ever being photographed could be quintuplets, just as her escort's sole legitimate reason for being so blackly unfit must have been that he planned to leave his body to a hospital or to a blubber factory. I was starting to reprove myself anew for trying to induce the holiday feeling by purchasing four papers of this kind, when a cold nose came nuzzling at my right hand, and I looked down to see the Cairn puppy on his hind legs and wagging his tail, and looked up to meet the eyes of my travelling companion as she leaned forward to reprove him.

"Rascal," I said to the puppy, rubbing his ears and, to his mistress, "How old is he?"

"Six months," she replied.

"Are you taking him to Canada?"

She said she was. The restaurant-car attendant now

intervened with two tickets which he made to give to me. The girl protested. I protested. The man apologised. Then I laughed. Then she laughed. The man went away grinning. And the dog again wagged his tail.

From that point, we were so deplorably un-English as to read each other's newspapers for long periods and at intervals to chat of hunting and flying, and of Scotland—apparently a mutual joy, and to feed in one another's company in the restaurant car, until, four and a half hours later, the train slowed to a walking pace and started passing literally through Liverpool warehouses during its final ponderously reverberating approach to the boat. As it emerged clanking from one warehouse and curved sharply into another, it afforded me a glimpse down the long vista of the eight-mile dockside road, reminding me of a hurried tour which I had made of it three years before by taxi, on the morning after the annual banquet of the Chief Constables' Association at the Adelphi Hotel, where I had risked the nervous indigestion of an excellent meal by making what seemed to me afterwards a singularly ineffective speech.

Presently, the train stopped. My companion and I went our several ways; she with her porter, I with mine. A man wearing a dark suit and a bowler hat glanced at my luggage as it passed, and fell into step beside me; politely expressing the hope that I would find my cabin comfortable and experience a good voyage. In such matters, the un-ostentatious efficiency of British transport companies is beyond all praise. Like the justly great Miss Garbo, I had expressed a desire "to be alone"; at least as much as I liked, although not perhaps for the same reason. Abroad, there would have been a song and dance, all very kindly intended but annoying in the extreme.

Here, to avoid a thoughtless charge of inverted snobbery, the well-known fact should be re-stated that it is easier

"*A thin crowd watched, too, from the dock. . . .*"

"*. . . the Birkenhead side of the estuary.*"

for a camel to pass through the eye of a needle than for any person whose name is beset with prefixes, as a ship's keel with barnacles, to enter quietly the greatest democracy on earth. Plans to make such an entrance have to be laid before starting and are then not always successful. Frank Sullivan has delightfully expressed such a need in *Morrow's Almanack.* "The Japanese," he writes, "do know how to do things on a big scale. Take these kimonos, or men's dressing-gowns, they make.

"If a man is tired and wants to get away from it all, and is lucky enough to own a Japanese dressing-gown, all he has to do is retire from the main body of the dressing-gown and lose himself in one or the other of the sleeves. Nobody will ever find him."

Alas, I had no kimono. But the purser was introduced to me, and I was reassured that my name was not on the passenger list. This left me free to go to my cabin, light a pipe, unpack my light kit-bags as they came down one by one, and start to make the acquaintance of a helpful middle-aged steward. Soon, the latter returned with some packages: enough cigars from my brother to last me to Montreal, red roses from my sister-in-law, a book, a note or two and some telegrams from other thoughtful friends. Having rewrapped the cigars to avoid the effect of sea air upon them, I sent the roses to my secluded table in the saloon and went up on deck to watch our departure.

A thin crowd watched, too, from the dock, and continually looked up at friends and relatives on the liner; uncertain quite how much to wave. As the tugs slowly pulled us clear, there were one or two of the usual wistful faces, infinitely touching to see. A fresh-faced man came and leaned on the rail beside me; he asked with a Canadian accent which was the Liverpool and which the Birkenhead side of the estuary.

While having tea in an alcove in the lounge, I observed

23

the inquisitive types summing up each other—probably wrongly. On deck, the peregrinations of sea-going life had already begun. Two Dutch parsons, immense, bespectacled and speechless, lumbered heavily round and round. Their garments, seen from the rear, creased sharply in the same folds at every pace, like the tough hides of elephants. Twice as fast as they, two serious voluble young men strode manfully along. Dressed in black coats, striped trousers, and wearing metal badges in their buttonholes, they kept their heads down, their hands clasped behind their backs and their feet in step. Obviously, they bore upon their shoulders the sins of an afflicted world. I could not obtain a close glimpse of the insignia at their lapels, but a study of their blank, earnest faces led me to suspect that they were weighed down with the responsibilities of furthering some " movement " for the well-meaning propagation of a sentimental fallacy of one kind or another. The demon of unrighteousness made me hope, vainly, I'm sure, that they might later be relieved of any such intention, possibly with their dinners, by the more natural movement of the ship.

Gradually, the smoky haze of the great Mersey port died away astern, and gave place northwards to sands, clean in appearance at this distance, and southward to the hills of Wales. Most of the passengers were below, settling in, and some would join us to-morrow in the Clyde. So the decks were as yet practically deserted. Rounding a corner of the boat deck, I came upon a tiny woman in bright blue tweed, a sweet faced, merry little soul, tripping along and calling gaily over her shoulder to an astonishingly fat boy of about twelve, who trailed her in laggardly fashion while inspecting each successive lifeboat and bidding fair, I reckoned, to split his pants upon the slightest exertion. He was as overgrown as she was undersized. It seemed beyond the bounds even of Nature's sense of humour that she should be his mother.

24

But she was, for he so addressed her. Over my shoulder, I watched his querulous, lolling pursuit, and marvelled. Returning on the leeward side, I discovered the "open-air girl," as I mentally christened her, and her dog; whereupon my faith in our human species, momentarily disturbed, was restored by her cheerful normality.

She was alone, for her travelling companions were not coming aboard till next morning at Greenock, so she kindly dined with me. Across my sister-in-law's scented roses, we talked of this and that, as new acquaintances do. By ten o'clock, in the observation cabin above, we had somehow reached religion. She was apparently no churchgoer and had for some time questioned the existence of an orthodox Deity as such; having been put off, as are many who allow their intelligence full play, by the uneducated expositions of ignorant preachers. But she had none of the despair or assumed indifference common to many of her age—she was twenty-three—in these days. She was as thoughtful as her appearance had led me to believe, and a brave thinker, too, out to explore any line of knowledge or reasoning which would render understandable the obvious Power in the laws of Nature.

I remarked cheerfully that I also felt the same; that sense from a book meant more to me than nonsense from a pulpit, a sunset more than forty allegorical paintings, and that the blossoming of my roses, like those on the dinner table, in strict accordance with my care and pruning of them, was in itself a truer sermon than most; that, in fact, the only sermons I ever remembered liking in years and years of churchgoing were common-sense talks on modern problems by a few clergy who confined themselves only to such matters (recognising their own and their hearers' limitations), and that even those would have been easier to listen to in a barrack-room, or comfortably in a library arm-chair, than on a hard pew during

25

one of the intervals of automatic chanting and lengthy appeals for mercy to a supposedly frightening Being. Upon this, we were agreed.

I instanced the age of the world, now established with sufficient accuracy at millions upon millions of years. And together we were as fogged as any one to know why the majority of respected theologians persisted not only in confining their thoughts to the mere 6000 years of Hebrew chronology, but blandly assumed that any one born B.C., i.e., 1936 years ago, hadn't a ghost of a chance; that the bulk of the modern world, followers of Mohammed, believers in Buddha, etc., were heading for damnation; and that even their own flock, divided over the doctrine of Rome, were most of them miserable sinners—according to which view they held to be right. It sounded bad, we thought, for the entire Neanderthal race, plentiful in Europe 40,000 years ago, and for the Cro-Magnon type that predominated 24,000 years later. And when we added the numberless millions of past and present members of these sub-species forming the majority populations of Europe, the Nordic or Baltic, the Mediterranean or Iberian, and the Alpine with its sub-division of Armenoids, we concluded with a certain amount of amusement that the housing problem in hell must long have been acute.

At this point, we decided it was also pretty hot where we were, so we went out onto the promenade deck.

Religion, after all, only means a binding—a code, if one puts that construction on it. And a good code, for instance, is that of efficiency in living. It sounds simple at first; indeed, so simple as to be worthless. But is it? After all, it includes efficiency in kindness, efficiency in settling motives, efficiency in seeking, speaking and writing truth, efficiency in facing hard facts, efficiency in condemning harmful or useless traits and tendencies, efficiency in occupation and health, efficiency in all the deeper thoughts, works and studies as well as efficiency in golf, ski-ing, flying, driving a car or whatever you like.

We agreed that it called for a high standard of concentration but was nevertheless the best possible target at which to aim. To expect a bull's-eye every time was ludicrous, but those who practised consistently would probably score a few, and a large proportion of inners and outers. Among our circles of acquaintances, we both could think of more and more people trying to lead useful lives along these lines, convinced that to whatever Deity there is, a closer approach may be made solely along the path of sustained effort in all instinctively right things: for instinct is our greatest heritage. Nothing, we concluded, could be more like burying a talent in the ground than blind adherence to forms of words written by ignorant men in mediæval times and now found, upon examination, to be almost meaningless when measured by the yardstick of present-day knowledge.

Whereupon, we changed the subject and talked for a time of other things; she had been to India and so was used to ocean-going liners.

Presently, she said good-night and went below. I lit a last pipe. The ship was forging steadily through a calm sea towards Ireland. Far ahead, I could see the twinkling lights of Belfast.

. . . .

Next morning, Saturday, I awoke to find the ship lying in the Clyde, off Greenock. Everything was still. The river itself was glassy. A few white, cumulus clouds, bulging in a blue sky, made slowly changing patterns across the distant hills of Argyll where the last bloom was on the heather. Smoke from the housewives' fires in Greenock rose vertically into the air. Languid sounds from the quay seemed magnified and close. A few cargo boats could be seen in mid-river;

some at anchor, their decks lifeless, others just under way, like sleep-walkers, on the tide.

The first sign of real activity was the appearance of a small Cunard liner, in from Montreal, whither we were shortly sailing. Heralded by a deep melodious hoot, she came very slowly past us to anchor. To her, and to our vessel, the gulls came in scores, suddenly aware that breakfast for us meant garbage thrown overboard for them. Many were youngsters in their first, mottled plumage. Kittiwake and herring gulls predominated, though I saw one or two of the larger, black-backed variety, squawking harshly at the others and lazily robbing them. With the coming of the Cunarder and the gulls, the Clyde awoke to life.

Having written and posted my letters of acknowledgment for the gifts and telegrams of the previous day, I stood leaning on the rail in the sunlight; talking to the "open-air girl." Her friends were coming in the tender, so she would now have regular and more familiar companionship for the voyage. Soon we saw the tender approaching, and she went below to meet it, while I moved to a position of advantage from which to look down upon the newcomers.

One in particular drew my eyes like a magnet: a large, elderly woman, outstandingly clad in a tweed skirt and cape of squashed strawberry hue, black lisle stockings, stout shoes of black kid and a black velvet tam o' shanter ornamented by a feather. Walking with the aid of a sturdy ash-plant, she carried in her other hand a huge handbag, as big as a saddle-bag, covered with close-stitched embroidery, like the upholstery cover of a Jacobean chair. Indeed, I vowed to myself that such it really was; that having often supported, in a long domestic career as a piece of furniture, innumerable well-tailored pairs of bags, occupied doubtless by the seats of the mighty, it had now itself become a bag, though of a different sort—a regrettable if appropriate fate in these democratic days.

Many Canadians came aboard. Their accent became the one most commonly heard. French-Canadians formed the bulk of the remainder; dark, vivacious women, swarthy, beetle-browed men, and quantities of children, staring or talkative. I had just finished my after-luncheon coffee when the siren sounded, and we slid majestically away.

As we steamed slowly down the Firth, I stood watching the hills, engaged with memories of my first journey to Loch Fyne which had been made this way many years ago. But now, instead of circling Bute, we passed on by Arran, by Ailsa Craig, round the Mull of Kintyre and westward by Northern Ireland, with Islay on the starboard bow. Green isles there were in plenty. All afternoon, I watched them; not with sadness, for I was glad to be going for a time, but with the searching regard that voyagers reserve for their own land, conscious of the uncertainty of their mortal tenure anywhere.

At dinner, with a carnation, provided by my thoughtful steward, in my buttonhole, I finished *Farewell to Fifth Avenue* by Cornelius Vanderbilt, Jnr. Perhaps the carnation ranked me subconsciously with those whom he criticised, for I could not like the book, although I was amused by it. One may admire a working class and see the huge value and worth of it without damning the more fortunately born, or admire an aristocracy without despising a proletariat. Both views are extreme and ridiculous. No labour leader has ever got himself or his party anywhere by the first method. No king has ever profited for long by the second. We find that mutual affection or esteem works better; moreover, it is genuine on both sides.

Of the older countries now firmly established in undoubted majority rule by unity of heart, Britain, Germany and Italy afford patent examples of a progressive aristocracy and an adaptable proletariat combined in aims. Our system is well known as one of gradual change on behalf of all classes

29

in accordance with the march of events. In Italy, where a sharp regenerative process became necessary, the Royal Family and a number of the noble families collaborate effectively in the Fascist regime; many scions of the latter fought well in Abyssinia and some were leaders. In Germany, similarly situated, the well-born support the Nazi regime in huge numbers, and several occupy positions of great authority. But Russia, under minority rule, by the wholesale deliberate murder, starvation or banishment of most of its aristocracy —including the young, from whom much might have been expected with wiser handling—and vast numbers of its proletariat (the liquidation of the Kulaks) has suffered a loss which only succeeding generations will fully make plain, and faces the world so blooded that, whether any can bring themselves to agree or not with the long view of her people's betterment, the Fascist and Nazi purges, admittedly as deplorable in principle, are by contrast the skirmishes of an afternoon.

Born and bred in America, Vanderbilt must have known that many of those who may be described as America's aristocracy work hard and unselfishly. But perhaps he didn't meet them much, or they him? His book, I noticed, rightly condemned "playboys." We have "playboys" too. We regret them in some ways, but do not take them too seriously. In peace time, they circulate money and support amusement; in war, they usually die gallantly. Likewise, we know the innate sense and value of our artisan and labouring classes, just as he waxes enthusiastic about corresponding sections of the United States communities. But I saw no reference to the fact that America's criminal classes proportionately outnumber ours by hundreds to one—a fact which I was subsequently to discover is a source of shame to the American working man.

I dropped the book in my cabin on my way aloft. I felt it to be a pity that such a volume, certain to be read because of the author's name, and with enjoyment by reason of the intrinsic

30

value of its humour, should yet be marred by apparently vindictive criticism of his own stock, when balanced comment from a man in his position might have been highly valuable. Butted by their emotions from one to another of the many sub-political enclosures of to-day, too many men and women are writing with their spiritual eyes obscured by the fleece of unreason.

The evening glow drew me out for a moment on to the promenade deck for a last look. Along a golden track, we were passing a mauve island set in a rose-strewn sea. By morning, there would be nothing but wastes of water, the hiss of the prow cutting through them, the song of the wind in the rigging.

A selection of funny films was being shown in the saloon, but by a faulty decision I retired to the observation cabin with another disappointing book, *Hollywood by Starlight*, by R. J. Minney, one of the joint authors of *Clive of India*—which I had greatly enjoyed. True, I had bought the book because of hearing it angrily condemned by people I knew in Hollywood, but this had seemed no reason why I should not glean something from it to add to what I had already read about that apparently glamorous place. I did glean a lot from it. It proved to be good light journalism, and most amusing. But, as with Vanderbilt's book, I could not swallow what appeared to me patent exaggerations. Weeks later, after my own experience of Hollywood, they still seemed to be exaggerations. Few of us, of course, attach the same measure of importance to the same things. Because ignorance, adultery, drunkenness, crudity and the peculiarly modern pursuit, occupation, talent or whatever it is called, "blurb," are common in greater or lesser degree to the bulk of the human race, I saw no point in stressing their application to America, in particular to Hollywood, however wittily. Perhaps wrongly, I gathered there was much over there that Mr. Minney did not like—perhaps rightly. Yet, I could not help wondering to what extent the people over there would now like Mr. Minney. No broad principles were expounded or criticised, which can legitimately be done in a book of that nature. It seemed to me to be simply gossip for effect, better left unwritten: matters of no importance masquerading as a portrait of contemporary life. Such books do not lead to a better understanding between two peoples possessing a special need for it. I put my watch back an hour and turned into my bunk at a quarter past ten.

．　．　．　．　．　．　．　．　．　．　．

Movement of the ship awoke me at two-fifteen on Sunday morning. A moderate to rough quartering sea had started her rolling. After dosing uneasily till six o'clock, I watched from my porthole a reddish, rainy sunrise. The water was sombre and threatening, the waves rising. We were obviously in for it. I took a precautionary tablet of Vasano and read *The Aeroplane* with my early tea; finding Charles Grey very interesting on the subject of air racing.

Few people were in the saloon for breakfast, doubtless on account of the movement. But, thanks to my dope, I ate heartily and felt extremely well. I started reading *The Dark Invader* by Captain von Rintelen—a gentlemanly account of most difficult and anxious intelligence activities on behalf of Germany during the war. One experiences a great feeling of satisfaction at finding such a man on good terms with us now. Continuing with him for an hour or more under cover on deck, for a drizzle had set in, I abandoned him with regret in order to pace the lee side energetically for forty minutes. None of us yet had our sea legs, and walking was a difficult matter. The two Dutch parsons were out, unconcernedly puffing cheroots and tacking heavily. I gave them a wide berth in passing, knowing that, although more active, I must get the worst of any chance collision. Several hearty young

32

women were laughingly making the most of their male escorts' willing arms. A few other ladies, more elderly, some a trifle acid in appearance, lay under rugs in chairs, their mouths pursed in expressions of saint-like endurance, their eyes closed, their spectacles rammed well home on their noses. Prepared for the worst, hoping for the best, only a lifetime of self-discipline in all things had brought them on deck at all.

I stalked a bird that landed on a davit, and found it to be a small dove. It had probably come with us from one of the islands near the north of Ireland, which we had left at ten o'clock the previous night. In the afternoon, the sun won through, the sky cleared, and it was possible to see a great distance.

Tea brought me to the end of Rintelen's personal chronicle, so in some attempt at continuity I read a much-discussed pamphlet in defence of recent German policy. I found the case well put and with a complete absence of hysteria. The figures quoted seemed unlikely to be faked, being drawn from sources available for checking. If they were correct, they constituted a bad show-up of the foreign correspondents and the policy of some of our more irresponsible newspapers with interests to preserve which do not always prove upon examination to be as humanitarian as the leader writers claim. Certainly, a number of friends with business interests in Germany had repeatedly told me during the last year or two a different story from those common in the English press,[1] and the inside of a week which I had spent the previous Summer in motoring observantly from one side of Germany to the other had enabled me to confirm their reports of the huge progress made, the general betterment of the workers' conditions and the growing happiness and unity of the majority.

[1] The tone of the British press afterwards became progressively favourable in general terms, towards Germany. More of the truth was allowed to appear, and we concluded a Naval Agreement with her.

I finished reading the pamphlet and went for a walk on the boat deck before dressing for dinner. There I found the "open-air girl," not quite at the top of her form, having been seedy all morning. I gave her a Vasano tablet, so that she could later eat a good dinner, obviously needed. Myself, finding oysters on the *menu*, I mentally turned a deaf ear for that evening to my doctor's last instructions, and ordered half a bottle of Chablis instead of the whisky and soda which he had ordained as more suited to a momentarily fatigued and suspicious duodenum. Propping a new book against the bottle, I started reading it. It was *England*, by Douglas Jerrold, a determinedly knowledgeable thinker, succinct writer and understanding person.

Alas, Vasano had not had time to be of much service to my acquaintance; she couldn't stick the dining-saloon and feeling a little forlorn, came up on deck. We talked of the wider recognition nowadays of a frank sense of values in the age-old problem of the relationships between men and women; particularly, between some, of the intangible affinity of spirit upon which confidence and respect comes to be founded, which in turn leads, in those capable of recognising it, to normal, efficient and contented mental reactions in all other respects; a companionship glowing with a steady warmth instead of flaring up only to die away. We could not recall many instances among those we knew, but could pleasurably remember at least a few, mostly late marriages, second marriages or intense friendships with or without a suspicion of romance. The actual causes of discord, being often physiological as well as psychological, and interacting, naturally set limits to such discussions, particularly between laymen as distinct from members of the medical profession in its widest sense. But if clearly faced, they usually end in some conclusion based upon three facts: marriage is too easily available to the young, divorce is still too difficult in certain countries, and sensible education is too restricted in all matters pertaining to marital life.

I lent her *The Dark Invader*, gave her another tablet of anti-seasickness dope and sent her to bed at eleven o'clock. It was not really so late, because clocks and watches were put back the usual hour.

A big sea running on our beam awoke me at six next morning. A lot of poor folk, I foresaw, were going to spend a miserable day. I rang for my tea at seven. The rolling increased steadily. Hair brushes and bottles began falling about. Getting up to wedge them, I myself nearly fell. From my porthole, the Atlantic presented an appearance as awe-inspiring as it was disgusting, so I went back to bed with Jerrold's *England*. Later, I shaved somehow without cutting myself, and found a miniature swell disturbing the surface of my bath water. The necessary formality of standing on one leg to dry the other, involved the risk of a toss, highly undesirable in view of pipes, taps, corners and edges which would have been certain to hit one where one would have preferred they didn't.

Later in the morning I determined to attach myself to some firm part of the superstructure and take a photograph. The ocean would certainly be worth it.

The ocean was more than worth it! From being heavy, the seas now became precipitous, the swell higher than ever. The whole boat was made violently aware of the fact. There was a long, sickening roll, worse than any. A stout, grey-haired woman shot bodily forward, chair and all, into the scuppers, where she was tipped out onto her face, the chair folding up on top of her. A girl of about twelve, sitting with her flew several feet through the air, landed heavily near the rails, and, thoroughly scared, began to whimper piteously.

"Lie still," I yelled, unable to do more at the moment, for only by dropping both rubber-shod feet to the deck and bracing my legs had I myself been able to remain stationary.

My left arm just managed to withstand the wrench of grabbing and holding my next door neighbour, chair and all. It seemed a hour before the vessel started to right herself.

When, at a sort of crouching run, I reached the old woman some seconds later, she dropped her head on to her arms and groaned. But I guessed it was fright, not injury, that made her do so, for I had seen how she fell.

"Come on now," I holloaed briskly, "get up." If she did not do so before another such roll occurred, we would all be in a heap, with more chairs; staring down through the rails into what looked like the bottom of the Atlantic. A bo'sun arrived, also at a slanting run, picked up the child and then turned to help me with the old woman, who must have weighed quite sixteen stone.

"I think I'll go into the lounge," she murmured gratefully. She had a Scotch accent.

"You'll go nowhere else," I assured her.

There, we handed her over to a swaying steward, who took her below to her cabin. Half the furniture in the lounge was piled up in a heap.

We had just had "elevens"—a cup of beef tea and a biscuit. Fragments of these cups were clinking about the deck. Later, the deck steward told me that nobody on the other side stayed in their chairs at all; the whole lot slid into the scuppers. Fourteen were injured. One old American judge had to have several stitches put into his scalp. The steward, his assistant, and their trays of "elevens" had added to the general *mêlée*. Later still, the captain told me that the big roll registered $37\frac{1}{2}$ degrees, the worst he had experienced for years, and that the maximum for the ship was 44 degrees.

I obtained my photograph all right by making a leaning approach to the after end of the promenade deck and hooking my arm round a stanchion. But I took four very bad snapshots in order to get one reasonably fair one. The sea was still

36

getting up, incredible as it seemed. In a further hour, it had become tremendous. The high-slung lifeboats on either side dipped alternately until their gunwales appeared many feet below the horizon.

All afternoon, conditions grew worse. A woman, seeing me with my camera, staggered up to ask me what stop and exposure I was using. I told her, and she decided to fetch her own. For a moment, she sat down next to me. I judged her to be forty-ish. She was slightly weatherbeaten, had grey eyes charmingly wrinkled at the corners, broad hands on one of which was an ornamental ring, probably of Indian workmanship, and spoke with a Canadian accent. She presented an attractive figure in her blue gabardine raincoat, small blue hat, good stockings and almost as good shoes. When the skirt of her serviceable two-piece costume blew back over her knees, revealing a lace-edged Celanese petticoat, the revelation concerned her not at all, for she did nothing about it. She was staring out to sea; defying the wind with a cigarette held firmly in the corner of her mouth. A friendly, natural person. I disliked only the petticoat. Dressed as she was, I wondered casually why she wore a petticoat at all, particularly one so unsuitable.

When she returned with her camera, a huge affair, she chattered gaily on. A Mr. Smith had waylaid her to ask if she was going down to her cabin, which was apparently on the same deck as his; he said a steward had told him it was a foot deep in water, having shipped a sea through the open port. Actually, of course, everything had been battened down for hours. This was merely Mr. Smith's idea of a joke.

"Who," I inquired, feigning interest, "is Mr. Smith?"

She told me. It conveyed nothing, save that he, too, was a good sort. Apparently, she already knew half the people on the boat (we were but three days out from the Clyde). I became politely monosyllabic, so she lurched away to take

37

a photograph. Instantaneously, I appeared to be asleep. She probably thought me dull anyway. I certainly felt it.

The wind increased in intensity towards evening. It mounted steadily from Force 7 to Force 10 of the Beaufort Wind Scale, denoting respectively a moderate gale, a fresh gale, a strong gale and finally a whole gale. To me, it was just a gale!

The few passengers who could stand, gathered in swaying groups behind the heavy glass windshields at the for'ard end of the promenade deck to watch the gigantic rollers bearing down. At intervals, there was speculation as to whether the ship would dig her bows into one. She was a grand sea-boat.

The sun had long since gone. It was raining, if water blown horizontally can be called rain. The sea was magnificent, and hideously uncomfortable. The lady of the camera, Celanese and cigarette came up, saying she was cold and did I think the bar would be open. I grinned amiably but, appearing not to understand, said ungallantly "not in this sea"—a quick, nautical version of the music hall *riposte*, "not in these trousers." I saw her glance round, and presently she drifted off—perhaps to find Mr. Smith.

Dinner came. The same handful of people zigzagged in to eat it. In the smoking-room afterwards, where I went for a cigar and two more chapters of *England*, I found the sofas and chairs wedged end to end in line across it, so that they should not be broken. Shutters were being put up outside, deck chairs lashed and everything made secure. The captain walked past, issuing some order or other and pointing. I had gloomy prognostications of a filthy night.

And so it proved. I stiffened myself diagonally across my bunk and lay sleepless for hours; listening to the vast, regular creaking of a great ship under dire stress; putting out a weary hand occasionally to the switch to illuminate my watch, hung on its hook, and seeing, as I rose on one elbow,

38

my coats and caps and the curtains over my porthole standing out from the wall—a comforting reminder that the law of gravity still functioned and that sometime this savage lurching, by now intolerably wearisome, would cease and all of us stand level on our feet.

. . . .

When I awoke in the morning—I had not slept for long— I felt at once that we were going full speed ahead again and pitching more than rolling; which implied a change of wind and possibly of sea. This proved to be the case. The sky was grey and weeping, the ocean leaden and heaving, but conditions in general were distinctly less violent.

My steward looked worn but triumphant.

"We dinna get the same type comin' tae sea in these days, sir-r," he remarked with justifiable superiority; referring to the fact that several of the ship's company had succumbed. "Man and boy, I never remember abandonin' m'duty on account o' dir-rty weather these thir-rty years."

Upright as a ramrod and moving easily with the ship, he took my order for breakfast as though he was *mâitre d'hotel* of the smartest haunt in London.

Large numbers of people, mostly women, had been dreadfully ill during the night. With profound sympathy, I had heard the talking and the coming and going of stewards and stewardesses. For nothing, as I had previously known to my cost, is a more lowering and miserable experience than seasickness or airsickness. Mercifully, I seemed to be acclimatised; I had not taken an antidote for twenty-four hours during which a full Atlantic storm had raged.

Lying in to rest, I lit a pipe after breakfast and started on *Divorce and its Problems*, by Haynes and Walker-Smith. It seemed a reasonable, well-balanced *exposée* of the present practice, which I have always considered uncivilised in its essentials judged even by the low general standard of educa-

39

tion, although humane judges do their best, patently at some cost to their legal consciences, to temper the wind of parliamentary indifference to the shorn lamb of the unhappily married. As for the enlightenment of those who regret the emancipation of women, and oppose any measure of divorce reform, even a lifting of the burden in cases of insanity, life-sentences, moral perversion or habitual drunkenness—well, the word enlightenment scarcely applies. Most of such opponents are now elderly, so their youthful curriculum may be regarded as having anyway been insufficient to meet the needs of to-day, unless since augmented with a regularity which we know to be the exception rather than the rule; augmented, that is, by broad study as opposed to mere experience which, although inevitable, becomes valuable only when accompanied by the will to learn. Not that their lack of mental background is altogether their fault; a similar disadvantage has applied to the bulk of the old in every era; and particularly in this one may excuse be made for them by reason of the huge amount of varied knowledge, bearing upon human destiny, unearthed during the immediate past.

Of the creative minority among the old and late middle-aged, it is impossible to think too highly. In every age, they constitute an aristocracy of mind. Though stiffening in body, they have remained flexible in outlook, and bring their mature judgment to the weighing of new facts and the assimilation of fresh experience, whether personal or universal; thus remaining in advance of their juniors despite the latters' now greater initial advantages attendant upon growing up with modern science. It is apposite to recall with admiration the forthright, brilliantly phrased sense expressed by the late Lord Birkenhead in the House of Lords when attempting to bring about divorce reform of a kind urged again and again by the most experienced magistrates in London, by the bulk of the medical profession and by humane thinkers in every walk of life. That such efforts should twice have been buried with contumely in the Commons, is yet another reason of many why the standard of those returned to that House as representatives of the people is increasingly considered by the thoughtful to stand in need of alteration for the better. But the main responsibility is traceable to the Church. Not for nothing did the *Daily Telegraph* roundly condemn the failure of a meeting of the Lower House of Convocation to show itself in an understanding light when again discussing this problem:

"The general public conscience," ran this dignified reproof to the bishops, "is shocked and revolted by the law which condemns to lifelong unhappiness, and often to acute misery, thousands of persons who are fast bound by chains from which they cannot escape, and the justice or necessity of which they deny. There is, moreover, a growing impatience with the stubborn ecclesiastical conscience which refuses them relief, on a point of dogma, or on the interpretation of a text. The Primate said that the idea of a bargain between Church and State was repugnant to him . . . the answer, as many see it, is that while the Church should continue to uphold the highest standards, her administration should ever be guided by the law of charity."

Indeed, the gravest fault does lie at the door of those whose opinions of things humanitarian and biological, such as divorce, birth control, etc., are shaped by their leanings towards things superstitious and falsely pious, especially when the majority deliberately remain unaware of how shifting are the sands upon which their superstitions have been erected. Into this category, alas, fall all too many clerics, virtually under oath not to think for themselves (which is possibly of little account with a number of them, though the more enlightened do magnificent work in a quietly unorthodox way) but forced by self-interest, and

41

for the sake of peace and a quiet life not to differ except with discretion, and an eye open for retreat, from the leaders of the organised churches; those great trade unions, used as political pawns, whose utterances now bear so little relation to the simple principles and kindly humour of the original exponent, as mined with scholarly devotion by painstaking men of all nations from the mass of mythology, tribal history, hearsay and doubtless fairly accurate reporting that constitutes the once infallible Bible. Although referring to a different breakdown in wisdom, (the continuance of wars), the words of Dr. W. R. Inge held a deeper significance: "——we have known of Christianity for nearly two thousand years and have never tried it." Dr. Henson, the Bishop of Durham, has also admitted that the Nation has outgrown the Church; that the Church has become "exceedingly inefficient."

Now, of course, we shall never try Christianity as commonly interpreted by the churches, because to modern eyes their brand is at once too material in respect of tithes, land ownership and the burdensome, wasteful upkeep of bishops' palaces (with notable exceptions such as the late Bishop of Exeter who preferred to live in a modest little house), and too unenlightened where social problems such as those mentioned, namely, divorce, birth control, etc., are concerned.

It is only a year or two ago that the Church of England officially condemned birth control. Yet within a month or two of its edict, a ball was held in Park Lane to raise funds for the proper propagation of such knowledge along right lines among the poor. The ball took place under the patronage of an "Important Personage," the guests were received by one of his Majesty's judges, and the leaders of the medical profession were well represented. Out of this Gilbertian, if pathetic, conflict between church and people, we may extract a certain cynical amusement, at the same time sincerely regretting that it is possible to do so. That the Churches of England and

Rome can claim as adherents only such a small proportion of the population of the country points to the verdict of the people upon these institutions as now conducted: likewise, it indicates that unless the Churches soon show a change of heart, of mind, and, above all, of spirit, to meet the spiritual needs of men and women to-day in the light of new knowledge of all kinds pouring upon the earth, even the obsolescence of the present will be denied them and they will become, in a generation or two, entirely obsolete. That they comfort a few millions (if they really do comfort them) is not sufficient when many more millions revolt from their absurdities.

It was a dull day on board, even duller than these last few paragraphs will have been to many readers. A moderate gale, wind velocity 7, still persisted when evening came. But now it blew from the south; we kept purposely a little off our course to meet it; and so pitching instead of rolling was the order of the day. Passengers, as usual, preferred this movement. More of them, pallid-faced, had emerged from the bowels of the ship. On account of driving rain, the canvas screens were rigged all round the promenade deck. Behind this shelter, the tired voyagers took unsteady exercise in depressing obscurity, their long suffering conversation torn from their lips by raging draughts and lost in the howling of the wind.

After reading, dosing and walking at intervals till tea time, I subsequently did indifferent tricks with pennies and a toothglass to amuse a red-headed boy of eleven, one of the same party as the "open-air girl." Known all my boyhood as "Ginger" or "Coppertop," it is now with a mild pleasure, albeit sharply conscious of the passage of time, that I, the pot, insultingly call such kettles black.

Not feeling like talking, I successfully avoided all other contacts, though I watched the talkie, *Cleopatra*, in the dining-saloon after dinner; entering stealthily after all the lights were out. It might have been more enjoyable if it had been a good picture and the few onlookers murmuring excitedly had not had to cling at intervals to their chairs. The one bright spot was the star, Claudette Colbert, enchanting as ever in movement and expression. But as the sound apparatus had gone wrong, I naturally could not hear a word she said.

· · · · · · · · · · ·

Fewer white-caps to the waves greeted my eyes next morning, but the interminable pitching went on, now allied again to a slight roll. If this weather continued unabated for the further three days still separating us from the haven of the St. Lawrence, I reckoned it would be indeed a shaky boatload which would lie about recuperating as we steamed up the river. The last chapter of *Divorce and its Problems* left me longing for the simpler problem of not divorcing my early morning tea from its cup on the way to my mouth; so I rang for my tray. Reassured as to my juggling capabilities, I tackled Lord Merrivale's interesting, sixty-seven page pamphlet, *The House of Lords, its record and its prospects*. This short reference book should be of interest to all. I found it particularly so, as it put my own preliminary ideas on the subject (published by Douglas Jerrold in the *English Review* in 1934) in their proper and by no means high place. But it is surprising, and a cause for anxiety, to note that few, in considering the reform of the House of Lords and the part which the Commons must play in it, draw attention to what seems to me an interdependent factor, namely, that changes in personnel and in certain procedures are badly needed in the Lower House as well. I make no apology for mentioning this again.

"Not enough of the best people go into politics," is a remark often heard. We know what is meant by this parrot cry. Nevertheless, the short-sighted interpretation usually placed upon it is the wrong one.

Who are the "best people"?

They are those with the best minds: so much is obvious to any one who thinks. Some were born with ponies to ride, and now perhaps wear the ribbon of a distinguished order. Others started life with scarves instead of collars round their necks, and now are councillors. Like horses, some were well bred, others not so well; in neither case through any virtue or fault of their own. But unlike horses, their minds have raised them, or lowered them, or made them equal in usefulness.

Compare, for example, the careers of the talented but wild Lord Byron, head of a long line, with the great Lord Salisbury, head of another; or of Thomas Masaryk, born a peasant, until recently President of Czechoslovakia, "father" of his people and one of the most respected figures in the world, with that of the anarchist oaf, also of lowly birth, whose bullets at Serajevo precipitated the world war. From castle or cottage they come, inevitably, these best minds, but how to ensure a greater proportion of them in politics is a very difficult matter. By stages, we enfranchised years ago the too-young of both sexes, and gave them a vote while still inexperienced or irresponsible—a vote which should really reward budding ability or instructed maturity, thus putting a premium on dignity in manhood and womanhood. Now only by almost inconceivable concensus of opinion between political schools of thought could this privilege, still obviously lightly regarded and to some extent unexercised, be once more curtailed.

Probably, this will not happen in our time: the thinkers will have to wait perilously upon the education of the thoughtless. But that some intermediary measure should be introduced to better our system of representation in Parliament, becomes increasingly apparent; and I hope it will not be long delayed. It is preposterous that in the twentieth century the floating votes of an irresponsible section of the British community can exert influence one way or the other upon the destinies of the much larger section of steady-going people, whether Conservative, Labour, Liberal, or simply Nationalist. Painstaking mass education, the *realist* application of *facts* to form well-founded improvements in living and the constant open-minded search for further facts —however hard to envisage—is the supreme need of our time. Indebted though we are to H. G. Wells for his brilliant pictures of a Utopian State, painted on a canvas well-woven from the threads of wide knowledge, Kipling was the man who sang the praises of cheerful common sense and dogged lust for work by which alone we may save up to buy such masterpieces.

And is it not remarkable how uncommon is common sense? A little thought on this subject is as beneficial for mental complexes as an astringent lotion is for facial complexions.

Most of us, at one time or another, have been caught in the snare of saying or thinking, "Oh, old so and so; he can scarcely write his own name, but he's bung full of common sense."

Of course, this is really absolute drivel. If old "so and so" had as much common sense as we loosely claim, he would certainly have learned to express on paper something better destined to help him in civilised intercourse with his friends and business acquaintances than a series of shaky, rather illegible signatures. What we really mean is that he has practically no knowledge of calligraphy, but, on the other hand, is possessed of a sound, working acquaintanceship with most normal aspects of life: he will refuse to pay a shilling for a loaf of bread, will refrain from trying to put out burning oil with water, will counsel his daughter not to be too free with her kisses on the way home from dances with attractive young men, and will deal wisely, firmly and humanely with

46

the situation if, as so often happens, she doesn't take his advice and finds herself successively and rapidly in love with Alf and then Bert and then Sid. In other words, he knows his way about.

Common sense, then, is the right application, as far as it goes, of knowledge however sparse. A man or a woman may have acquired a heterogeneous mass of knowledge and be almost totally lacking in the common sense to correlate it. Such are learned fools; a genus that gives rise to cranks of all shades who do a great deal of harm with the best intentions—allowed to do so because their apparently instructed chatter renders them superficially normal. By contrast, the standard model fools are infinitely preferable, being too idle or incapable to acquire the knowledge which their lack of common sense might put to tiresome uses. As a rule, they are harmless, kind and happy. When they prove to be harmful, they are locked up.

People, otherwise normal, who have lacked opportunities for gaining knowledge and have, therefore, a proportionately small amount of common sense, can be said to behave well by instinct: their souls come through. And they, like those with much knowledge and the common sense to go with it, are the salt of the earth—whatever their origin. The only difference between them is one of opportunity, which the former are instinctively too wise to resent (though they may regret it) and the latter are instinctively too wise to flaunt (though they may be grateful for it). What is plain is that without an evolved instinct there is little desire for real knowledge, even granted the opportunity; and without knowledge there is no common sense. (In this I am at variance with Reid's philosophy). Only experience of living and dying is common to all, and doubtless as many will fail to do well in the fleeting examination of dying as have neglected to profit by their years in the school of living. I am confident that those with the right instinct, thwarted or not, will be promoted, provided that theirs has been a constant effort; while the others, I expect, will settle down to cram—perhaps back here again, but in different circumstances.

Granted, this sounds similar to those grand conundrums, "When is a mouse, if it spins?" or "Which would you sooner do, or go fishing?" But if we apply this definition of common sense to the everyday actions of any one, or to the collective actions of those responsible for the trend of world affairs, our estimates are afterwards likely to be, if not revised, at least clarified.

Later, I read Doctor Dearmer's[1] Essex Hall lecture for 1935, entitled, "Christianity as a new religion." In it, he hit the nail pretty squarely on the head. What he said must have annoyed some of the church pundits, but Doctor Dearmer was well able to take care of himself.

It is a pity that more of the bishops do not speak their minds, like Henson and Barnes. They may encounter agreement or not, but at least they are trying to point the truth as they see it and not deliberately to bolster up ignorance and inaccuracy. It is, I suppose, asking too much of human nature to expect the average bishop, having reached the top of his material tree, to risk his perch by being a real leader, boldly in the van of contemporary thought, rather than a dignified guardian of purely illusory if still legal clerical privileges. Still, that is what they will have to do or gradually lose the remnants of their influence. Disestablishment would undoubtedly ease the situation, provided that they then adhered strictly to the Christian code, sensibly modified for application to things contemporaneous, and ruthlessly pruned of the deplorable trimmings added in the dark ages and since.

Some one turned on a radio a few cabins away, receiving

1 Percy Dearmer, M.A., D.D. Canon of Westminster, Professor and Fellow, Kings College, University of London; since deceased.

apparently from an American station. This disturbance, if nothing else, drove me to seek refuge in my bath.

It was cold and bleak on deck. The promenade deck still gloomed behind its canvas screens. One look was enough; I immediately went below for luncheon. Afterwards, some hearty Scotch Canadians amusingly making whoopee near my chair, eventually made too much whoopee for me. A consultation with the deck steward resulted in a removal aft, to the vacant chair of a crotchety judge whose painful rheumatism, poor old chap, was keeping him below. There I stayed till tea, and waded into Arthur Findlay's *Rock of Truth*, a review of past and present religions and their largely shared doctrines, and a forthright statement of the case for Spiritualism.

Mild aggravation caused occasionally by the style of writing was quickly smothered by evidence of Mr. Findlay's amazing industry. He had read and thought enormously about the whole subject—so much was patent—and I liked his quiet corroborative references to great works by authors of unquestioned authority, with some of which I was familiar. His review rang very true, and I trust it will have great effect. For me, knowing after thirteen years something of psychic happenings, the research into them and the possibilities connected with them, the book was not startling—merely satisfying. But it must have shaken a lot of people into thinking for themselves, and will, I hope, shake more: I noticed that it had already run into eight editions in two years.

Because books like this, and the accredited volumes to which it refers, are rightly available to the public, the corner in which orthodox theologians find themselves is indeed tight. Their present appeal is limited more and more to the ignorant and sentimental. There are always thousands of the latter, but the numbers of the former are progressively decreasing. The

49

dissemination of fallacies and the withholding of facts by occupants of pulpits is now widely known to originate in two causes: ignorance and fear. Both are to some extent excusable, but the excuses are becoming threadbare. The repair of ignorance is a matter of time and opportunity. Fear, in this instance, is based upon the economic necessity of holding down a job or upon an instinctive shrinking from the disapproval of even more ignorant colleagues and parishioners. I sympathise greatly with those who find themselves affected by the latter. The whole situation of orthodox priests in the world to-day is parlous in the extreme. Even in our lifetime, there will be striking changes.

This firm conviction caused me, a few years ago, to hand back to the Church of England the last "living" in my gift. The patronage was of a parish with which my family has had no personal connection for many years. But on the resignation of the previous incumbent, various appeals were addressed to me by the local inhabitants, imploring the appointment of some one more suited to their own way of thinking than the last man had been. After a number of interviews with applicants, I appointed one who seemed likely to satisfy the religious desires of the majority, and, feeling my immediate responsibility to be ended, instructed my solicitors to transfer the patronage forthwith. To adopt any other course appeared to me unjust, for I did not, indeed, have never, lived in the place, and so could not fairly use an old privilege to impose advanced views upon those with whom I was not in frequent contact. Had I resided there, or nearby, I should certainly have sought a younger, broad-minded cleric and given him my personal backing in the gradual propagation of up-to-date ideas. Doubtless the bishop of the time, a charming person, was devoutly thankful that I didn't.

After tea, I walked a good deal, but with the usual discomfort despite having had my sea-legs for a full three days.

The boat still pitched incessantly. Needless to say, there had been no flowers on the dinner tables since we passed Arran. Nevertheless, we pushed along well that day, and logged 423 miles as against 297 and 365 on the days when the gale was reaching its climax and beginning to abate. If we kept hard at it, we would only be less than a day late at Montreal instead of a day and a half, and I would just catch the night train for New York in two days' time.

I could not resist oysters at dinner, and fell to a half-bottle of German wine. Thus I broke my diet for the second time on the voyage, but only in a detail easily offset by a dose of the right medicine. Misfortune in health provides compensations unknown to those with trouble-free interiors. Physical limitations, by being familiar companions, can direct attention to intellectual boundaries. Realisation of either, if frankly faced, may not be exactly a matter for happiness or pride; but at least it constitutes a source of strength. Because of it, watch may be kept to prevent a too swift closing in of the former, and a patient effort made to extend the latter. In these days, we should certainly be able and willing to nurse our own engines like those of the boats we steer, the cars we drive, the aeroplanes we pilot. A little intelligence, a slim bundle of prescriptions from a good doctor and a certain obstinacy are all which we can furnish to this end. What else is needed is the serenity that comes from a knowledge of having genuinely tried; and to this, although with difficulty, we can train ourselves in opening our minds. After an hour of Findlay's book, I went to bed at a quarter to ten. With the clocks put back the usual hour, this became a quarter to nine; and I hoped for a long sleep.

.   .   .   .

By waking at six-thirty next morning, I had achieved nearly ten hours—a good three more than I usually get at home, so I felt I had done well. For the first time since leaving

51

Scotland, I was able to unscrew my porthole and fill the cabin with fresh air, almost intoxicating after the artificially circulated atmosphere of the past six days. Under a tattered, somewhat overcast sky the sea was now cheerfully ruffled. It stretched, sunlit in rare patches, to a far horizon. And there was a chill snap in the air—a brisk vanguard well in advance of winter. I could see Belle Isle ahead, guarding its straits between Newfoundland and Labrador.

Returning from the bath, I found my steward at a porthole. Just then the ship's siren boomed a signal to the coastguard station as we drew level with it.

"They will telegraph to Montreal, giving the time we passed here," he explained. "Bleak, sir-r, is it not?" he added indicating the coast.

I remarked upon its likeness to Caithness.

"Ay, I've heard o' that pairt, sir-r," he replied, "but ah'm frae Dumfries mysel'."

I reached the deck in time to look back at Belle Isle. The coast of Labrador would be with us some time. Crossing the ship, I stared at the distant shore of Newfoundland.

The chief deck steward joined me. He sniffed the keen air. "Winter is beginning, sir," he remarked. "They've only had about a month of really warm weather here this year. As we came across to Liverpool last trip, there were icebergs here— one or two of them." He bustled away.

I went below with a tremendous appetite for breakfast, and afterwards turned for half an hour to the tiresome chore of writing luggage labels. We were now within ascertainable reach of our port of landing.

After the days of savage storm, bitter winds and flying spray, there was a feeling of great peace here in the Gulf of St. Lawrence; as though this old, tough and sinewy land could now reach out sufficiently to press back the Atlantic, and give tardy refuge to what seemed to us a liner but to it no more than a determined insect of man's brave fashioning. The sea had become like a flat silver dessert, slightly rippled. Patient cloudscapes stretched above it, still more delicately formed. Dark blue coastlines rose to port and starboard, and the decks became crowded with people looking thankfully at them. One realised for the first time how many must have been hiding in their cabins, victims of nausea and nerves, and quite unable to shake off either one or the other. Previously, one could judge only by the hollow-eyed, tired appearance of the stewards.

As I sat in my deck chair after luncheon, in bright sunshine and a sharp breeze, the "open-air girl" joined me; bringing a copy of a well-known art journal. We spent an interesting and amusing hour over it, for it contained some good matter and a number of illustrations of excellent engravings. Thus the interest. The amusement came from certain other pages packed with pseudo-intellectual nonsense treating of what is known as modern art, which in itself is an impertinent term because normal modern people do not really visualise things distorted out of all likeness to beauty. Crude colour grouping surely does not conjure up in their minds a plantation, two ploughed fields and a hen coop, or the "spirit of song" as expressed in terms of Spring impulses forming a background for a speeding Jason without his fleece, all according to which way you hold up the damned thing! If it did, the recent success in London of the Chinese exhibition of ancient art, meticulously fine, becomes quite inexplicable.

Neither, in my opinion, does Epstein for all his first-rate bronzes—much to be admired—succeed in producing in stone anything that a healthy-minded person can fail to regard as crude examples of chisel work with an unpleasantly bestial air about them. As for all but the most ingenious surrealists, their own behaviour, quite apart from their hotch-potch daubs, is enough to convince any sane man that they are *poseurs*. Some

53

modern art, genuine in its pretensions to beauty and taste, is finer, we know, than certain older examples now being viewed with more accurate appreciation than their creation originally called forth. But my acquaintance and I felt we could legitimately chuckle over many of the formless or slipshod illustrations and much of the meaningless verbiage in the journal: which we did, feeling better for this innocent form of enjoyment. Few things to-day strike one as more important than the condemnation, absolute and complete, of crankiness in all its manifestations, for it is the chief disadvantage attendant upon education . . . yet education must go on, urgently.

The term æsthete became a reproach in Oscar Wilde's day; for to love beauty it has never been necessary to slip the moorings of manliness, womanliness or of the standards of dress, deportment and conduct expected of both sexes as members of civilised races in cultured intercourse with each other. To-day, young men at the Universities who get themselves up like Autumn sunsets and pass ebullient resolutions binding themselves not to fight for their country are happily ridiculed.

Likewise, a revealing searchlight of ribaldry directed in the past on our more obtrusive intelligentsia has put paid to its account. All but a few now understand that, to read selectively, to write good English and practise what intelligence is possessed, it is not necessary to wear long hair and rubber over-shoes, or to live in Bloomsbury. Again, "pacifist" is a label now being shown up in its true colours. People are realising that all sensible men and women are lovers of peace, none more so than those whose acquaintanceship with the military, naval and air arm techniques gives them a close understanding of war. "Pacifist" has come to mean a well-intentioned ignoramus of the worst kind, who talks interminably, pushes ballot papers through his neighbours' letter-boxes, holloas the need of national prayer for intercession (to a God who, did he or she but think it out, has plainly ordained the fruits of peace for responsible-minded realists), and, in general, influences hundreds of the thoughtless to reduce their country to a state of ineffective weakness in a still far from civilised world; in other words, a thorough going war-monger. Against such, the true lovers of peace in England, experts and thinkers, out to keep order, have recently won a laggard victory.

Any pursuit too ardently pursued makes a crank of the pursuer. We are all familiar with cranks. Some are, or should be, in asylums, where repose behind bars is doubtless of value to their one study, although a sore expense to us ratepayers. Others, harbouring the useful or harmless crazes, and still at liberty, might be of so much more worth as citizens could they bring themselves to touch life at other points as well, and so see their hobby in its true perspective.

We all have our foibles, harmless, silly, even a little regrettable, for which toleration is shown us more often than perhaps we know—which, indeed, are sometimes of a kind to endear us one to another. But as more education reaches more people, and the danger increases of a proportion of them fastening upon one subject and becoming cranks, so must we be readier than ever to apply the healthy vacuum sweeper of mirth.

Where other, too extreme, nations exile their cranks or shoot them, we, thank God, have always been able to laugh at them. And so, I was to discover, has America, although she is cursed with hoards of them. Neither of us must abandon this estimable habit, as we have both shown signs of doing: for cranks to-day hatch out like bugs. We have only to look round to find plenty of little communities badly in need of the antiseptic glee which they occasion in their more normal compatriots.

Presently, the deck steward brought tea to the "open-air girl," the red-headed boy and myself. The boy ate more macaroons in a shorter time than I remember seeing accomplished since I left school; he was only bunkered by half the last one, which he threw overboard with palpable regret.

Half an hour later, the forthright, forty-ish woman came to anchor by my deck chair. Talking, rather unreserved talking, was obviously a habit with her. But she was sound and humorous, and I liked her. We chatted aimlessly, she against the rails some feet away, I in my chair. Presently, leaning backward over the side, she called my attention to a large cumulus cloud immediately above the ship.

"Do look," she exclaimed, "the sun's on it."

I thought maybe it was, but not having Röntgen ray apparatus in my sleepy skull I was quite unable to see through the boat deck above me. This deficiency should be supplied, I felt, for those let in for living through the dawn of a brave new world.

"Do come," she implored.

Cursing inwardly, I emerged from my rug as from a chrysalis, and joined her. What I saw lasted only a few minutes, as would the end of a film, but it was enough to make me regret my churlish thoughts and be grateful for her insistence. The steely waters of the gulf ended everywhere in a black barrier dividing sea from sky. Heavy clouds massed themselves carelessly round half the view, their lower contours dark as pitch, their upper curves turned to lumps of coral. Through gaps in them, a pale jade backcloth glimmered, and over one the lemon moon was rising—full this evening. But a curtain of grey murk slid quickly across from the east to cut short the day's farewell, and once again the ship forged powerfully into another night.

The "open-air girl" joined us. We strolled aft, down a companionway and across the tourist class deck to the stern, where the three of us stood on the counter to watch the ice-green wake with its milky froth on it. For some imaginative

56

" *The steely water of the gulf (of St. Lawrence) ended everywhere in a black barrier. . . .*"

" *Heavy clouds . . . through gaps in them, a pale jade backcloth glimmered. . . .*"

people, there is a hypnotic effect in the welter of water fiercely churned up by a swift ship's propellers, as there is for others in the downward view from heights towards the hard, stark terror of a rock or pavement. Only by staring at such things, deliberately loose-muscled and at ease, are they to be relegated to the age of fearsome gods, and self-respect endorsed in those who stare.

Soon the girl went to dress for dinner, and the forty-ish woman went to extremes in expounding her philosophy of life. It had its points, and despite her exaggerations I listened with attention. She believed in a ruthless elimination from her life of inessentials, whether beliefs, people or things, and boasted a little of being selfish: a rather *naïve* policy of isolation, self-ordained as to degree; just what certain not very profound newspaper proprietors and business men are clamouring for on Britain's behalf—as though any individual, other than a *yogi* in a cave, can be independent of others or blind to the effects of the actions of others on himself, and as though a small island a few minutes' journey by air from a hive of huge European countries can squat behind a twenty miles trip of channel, even though she be the centre of a far-flung Empire, and say, "Yah, don't speak to me. I'm an honest woman, I am—and in *purdah*!" Britain doesn't have to strike a series of indiscreet bargains with her wooers, but she cannot help sitting in the bazaar if only because she has long been a respected figure there and because her humane views have, in fact, led to the gradual abolition of the *purdah* system in International and Empire affairs, and her reputation has helped to keep order while it was being done.

But to return to the stern of the boat and my declamatory acquaintance: there was no time in this life, she said, to get alongside people and ideas that did not accord with ourselves. This contained some truth, but I doubted if she was as selfish as she made out; and said so. Although she maintained that

57

she was, I could see she was pleased. After her circumfluent indifference of a moment before, this return to more human traits was becoming. But I had to concede that at least rigid selection, if not her intolerant elimination, forms the basis of efficient living.

We passed to books. Rather to my surprise, she produced the trite excuse of not having time to read enough; which gave me an opening to suggest that she had not carried her process of elimination sufficiently far, or she would have cut out something in order to find time for studying the writings of at least some of the world's cultivated thinkers, past and present. She asked me who they were (as though any one the right side of fifty knows more, comparatively speaking, than a few!). I tossed the ball back by saying that, in reading as in all else, the rigid selection of which we had spoken was a matter for each individual, and that I couldn't answer her question in so many words, or names, because I did not know along what lines she was seeking knowledge.

She changed the subject, and tried to draw me: where was I going in America, what was I going to do, etc.? But beyond the bare statement that for the good of my mind I was going to drive myself across America and fly back, I hedged. She regarded me quizzically. The next question, I felt, was going to concern my identity; I was going to be pigeon-holed next to Mr. Smith and the other Misters met on a certain boat, during a certain voyage, in a certain year. Not if I knew it! With the salvatory prescience of a maiden sitting out with an ardent swain in a dark corner at a dance, I pleaded hunger as an excuse for moving. Mercifully, the dinner bugle backed me up at that very moment; so we went our several ways to change, both obviously to be late.

Afterwards, Findlay's book, my cigar and I found ourselves again in peace in the for'ard observation cabin. Thus I avoided the ship's concert, but "saved face" by sending a

58

modest subscription towards the excellent charity which it was designed to aid. And later I discussed fishing, yachting, child education and, profitably, Canadian immigration and mining with the wife of a famous business man, to whom I had been introduced by the " open-air girl."

She held the view that mining in Canada had become somewhat discredited by reason of the speculative appearance given to a number of its manifestations by get-rich-quick brokers. And we agreed it was a pity that the English are not as enterprising about emigration as the Scots. I ventured the opinion that this lack of enterprise, which is very real, will only be overcome by education (again education!). The English working classes have only occasionally thrown up pioneers; *en masse*, they want to know a good deal of the conditions obtaining in a country before they move to it. Whereas, the Scots take it for granted that the conditions are probably tolerable but capable of improvement, and set out with a passionate desire to take some part in the improving.

This, naturally, as a general principle, is applicable (as history records) to other countries as well as Canada. Which is mildly astonishing when one considers that England and Scotland share a lot of Norse blood, superimposed upon the Mediterranean, which was itself mingled with Goidelic and Brythonic. Doubtless, the lack of opportunity in Scotland provided the solution. The land could not support the people.

Certainly, we must strive to bring about a greatly increased development of this partner-Dominion in our lifetime, for so many problems depend upon it for a sound solution. Canada should be the happy, profitable home of many more millions than those who now so regard it. Its rugged, wooded terrain, inland waters and hard winters militated against easy development until the recent advent of reliable, all-winter aircraft.

59

To-day, these natural features, formidable still, no longer constitute quite such an obstacle as they did.

The situation is changing. Take Mackenzie Air Service Ltd., for instance, which has done and is doing such important work in the development of mining. Hitherto, when the waterways were frozen over—and they afford slow transport anyway—a dead season ensued. Now, aircraft alternatively ferry heavy loads of concentrates or passengers and supplies between mine and railhead in temperatures varying from 90 degrees above zero in Summer to 70 degrees below zero in Winter; landing on floats or skis according to the time of year. And these successful services are on the increase. Great Bear Lake, Lake Athabasca, Great Slave Lake, the Barrens, even the Yukon, have all had their frozen defences stormed by the onslaught of civil aviation. A trans-Canadian air service on a businesslike basis is a development now on the way to realisation despite the difficulties of the past.

Canada has her budding airlines all right, but still awaits her Rhodes. We have not, I consider, made nearly enough use of the cinematograph—of "talkie" exposition—in connection with land development over-seas, nor of state-aided tourist facilities for acquainting English folk with Canada and thus popularising the theory of cheerful "group" as distinct from the lonely and unpopular "family" emigration. The matter, of course, is not one to be rushed. Aviation has still much opening-up to do, and the first to be absorbed into new settlements should plainly be the Canadian unemployed, of whom there are many; some at present employed in the completion of the coast-to-coast highway, on harbour developments, public buildings, the establishment of small-holdings, or upon the 118 aeroplane landing grounds made or the process of making at the end of 1935.

Such sections of the community stand in need of a graded measure of financial support while they are making good.

Consequently, it is only the emigrant farmer, for example, with some capital of his own, or a skilled technician with special knowledge to sell, whom Canada is likely to welcome for a time—but to welcome the more because they, themselves, are potential employers of labour. It was for their eventual protection, I imagine, no less than to safeguard those already living there, that the Canadian Government passed the Housing Act; which provides that where a prospective householder can furnish 20 per cent of the cost of building his home, loan companies will lend the other 80 per cent, of which 20 per cent will be supplied by the Government.

There is no doubt that the adequate, feasible populating of Canada is a Commonwealth necessity of considerable magnitude. A scheme should be framed for meeting it, progressively, over the next fifty years. Meanwhile, incongruities persist such as the fact that some Canadians find American coal cheaper and easier to obtain than Canadian coal, of which there is plenty.

On my way to bed that night on the ship, the library steward regaled me with his version of the storm. According to him, one lady had collided with a light table after an involuntary run of some yards and entirely removed the top from the legs (the table's, fortunately, not her own!). Likewise, a man in the smoking-room was forced by the inexorable law of gravity to sit suddenly on another table, which forthwith collapsed; and several of the crew regretfully damaged various other items of the ship's equipment or, more regretfully, were themselves damaged. Altogether, I seemed to have got off lightly by reeling to the rescue of a sixteen stone, well-padded female and one scared child.

. . . .

As we were now using Montreal daylight-saving time, our clocks and watches were not put back. Thus, at 7.30 next morning, I only appeared to have slept longer. It was brilliantly sunny, but whether by reason of an unusual amount of talking the previous day, or because, like some of us, I was still being internally resuscitated from the effects of keeping about during the gale, a depressing fatigue kept me in my cabin for breakfast, followed by two pipes and a concluding dose of *The Rock of Truth*.

That book seemed to me a good follow-on to the author's first, *On the Edge of the Etheric*, and I determined to read the third of the triology, called *The Unfolding Universe*, which I had with me. In between whiles, a change was indicated, and I fetched out Nigel Tangye's symposium, *The Air is our Concern*. He had got some knowledgeable men to write for him, and I hoped to have learned more when I had read their views.

Findlay's books are monuments to his industry and obvious sincerity. If they have weaknesses, they are those of reiteration, which becomes noticeable in places, and of undue optimism regarding the future. I cannot conceive of a society as mild as he trusts ours may become, without simultaneously fearing it ineffectiveness. Though any vision of the sort obviously applies to generations whose great-grandparents are yet unborn, even then I would postulate the need for progressive government and strong leadership. Are there not, indeed, more strong leaders than ever before, and, national prejudice apart, is not much of the world better fed and more self-respecting because of them?

Who but the Comintern, and its internationally burrowing agitators (for whom, incidentally, our lice powder consists of a national sense of the ridiculous, and, should it fail, a bench of judges whose sentences are anything but ridiculous) will doubt that the Commonwealth, indeed, every lover of law and order, whether of the new or old brands, views the future with transcendent confidence and an uncompromising determination to alter what needs to be altered in our own way?

Yet, it is tremendously worth while to work through

62

Findlay's pages, from a historical as well as a philosophical stand-point, and to confirm his footnotes. He is a little apt, as are most sincere people, to impute his own motives to all connected with the development of Spiritualism. I have not quite his high opinion of some, although the majority I have met typify in every way a more truly Christian conception of daily life than many of those who, thoughtlessly optimistic of having unloaded their trespasses once a week, along with their best hats and prayer books, set out for home and the roast beef of England with a hearty, audible or inaudible, but quite understandable, "Thank God, that's over." After which, bless them (we are pretty well all the same) they sin cheerfully, harmlessly, seriously, fearfully, with or without malice aforethought until next Sunday comes round; in other words, just what they've always done and always will do, unless, one day, they suddenly *think*, realise the funny side of this weekly routine and rigmarole, burst into roars of laughter, sober down and decide it might be a good plan to learn something about real religion and the doctrine of personal responsibility.

Psychic phenomena, though studied with devotion by men of the calibre of Sir Oliver Lodge, Doctor Gustave Geley, the late Professor Richet, the late Sir William Crookes and many others, still remain as little understood by the public —apart from some of the considerable number of Spiritualists themselves—as were once antiseptic surgery, the culture of bacteria, anæsthetics, radio, colloidal chemistry and so on. But the study will undoubtedly continue because there is plainly much to be learned from it. Now that Alexis Carrel, the French biologist and surgeon, has kept a piece of heart healthy and beating in New York for twenty-four years and, with Lindbergh, has devised a robot heart and lungs, now that Voronoff and Steinach have done successful rejuvenation operations, one by the knife and the other with rays, and Doctor Fell, near Cambridge, watches over such curios as an isolated eye grown in a bottle from the incipient retina of an unborn animal (to quote four apparent "miracles"), only the genial battalions of the uninterested would rule out the possibility of ultimate success in disclosing further the secrets of the etheric.

That afternoon, the southern shore of the Gulf of St. Lawrence started to protrude towards us till the Notre Dame mountains were but a bare mile away; grassy braes, like those of Morayshire, marked with lines of firs and plantations of them, and backed by farther hills, quiet and dreamy. A string of pearly clouds shunning the estuary, lay motionless above them. Borne to us on a gentle off-shore breeze, the welcome smell of aromatic land killed in our nostrils the weary tang of salt. We passed a sister ship, outward bound; her foghorn gruffly greeted our arrival. Ours hoarsely echoed, wishing her God-speed. At Father Point, a pilot waited. On taking him aboard, we dropped our mail.

Heavy-headed through lack of exercise, I started Tangye's book at dinner. I read the first two chapters: "The Development of Civil Aviation in Europe" and "Air Transport To-day" both by Charles Grey, the editor of the *Aeroplane*. In them, he was plainly preaching to the layman and so confined himself largely to recitation of past developments and statement of general tendencies. His gift of specialised analysis was thus hampered, which personally I regretted, admiring it as I do. Chance readers of the *Aeroplane* must often have been surprised to find in its pages so much erudition, such a display of encyclopedic knowledge, where doubtless they expected only technicalities. Yet Grey must also be one of the most able technical journalists in the world (and the rudest critic I know).

Afterwards, I was well into "*The Training of Air Transport Personnel*, by Group-Captain R. J. Barton, the Commandant of Air Service Training Ltd, when the "open-air girl" carried me off to the talkies. We saw a first-rate film, all too short, about the discovery of Lake Louise and Emerald Lake in the Rockies. Apparently, the frontiersman who first came upon them is still living, and has watched them grow from wilderness beauty spots, known only to the Indians, into vacation resorts of annual benefit to scores of people. What splendid memories that man must have! For him, Fennimore Cooper's stories came to life.

I could not sit through the second film, featuring Shirley Temple and that fine actor Sir Guy Standing. True, I had seen it many months before in London. But, sweet though she is, I was not in the mood for little Shirley's precociously clever presentation of the "poifect kid." The usual appeal of such pictures is, I imagine, mainly to childless women or children themselves. A lot of other people need to get specially set for them.

. . . .

Misled by a notice stating that those who had to pass the Canadian immigration officer need not do so until eight o'clock next morning instead of seven, I missed Quebec: a maddening error. My steward, possibly because I had told him to call me at six, suggested that the notice also applied to prospective visitors to the United States; and I was foolish enough to concur. Consequently, I paraded at eight o'clock, and although the purser's clerk was able to accelerate the formal process, and the authorities kindly put me to the minimum of trouble—alas, I could not get ashore. The ship was late, and nobody knew quite when she would cast off; so they feared to let me leave. And I could not see the city, for the quay, situated in Wolfe's Cove, is upstream of it and round a headland. Had we not been held back twelve hours in the Atlantic, I should have come to Quebec as I would have liked to come, in the evening of the previous day, with that magical coral glint warming the Château Frontenac.

As it was, I had to content myself with staring at the cliff up which General Wolfe's force clambered silently one night to the Heights of Abraham. This cliff was my second disappointment. A moderately skilled deerstalker would have made nothing of it. It was even hard to visualise the difficulty of getting fully equipped men up it in a bad light until one remembered that probably few, if any, of them were used to climbing. On the strength of that supposition, I retained my respect for what was undoubtedly an enterprising feat of arms, now visibly commemorated by a museum on the cliff top which I determined one day to visit.

The tugs pulled us clear after breakfast, and we gathered way. Emerging from astern of the *Empress of Britain*, berthed for'ard of us, we steamed up-river round a long curve and under the great railway bridge. Shooting the latter—although a comparatively moderate speed hardly justifies the term—produces a quite exciting illusion: the mast-head seems inevitably due to be snapped off. Until the very last second, at least ten feet of it look like fouling the girders; and in actual passage the clearance appears to be no more than a foot. The real gap, so the captain told me later, is about sixteen feet.

All day, we moved sedately up this magnificent waterway. At first, either shore consisted of steep inclines, on which timber grew almost with the regularity of an afforestation scheme. Here, the already scarlet maples patterned the sombre woods like figures in a tapestry. The banks later sank down to the water meadows, where cattle mooned; and ever so often, grey and white houses, some with bright green roofs, clustered about the spire of a small church to make a hamlet. Despite the immensity of the river, the channel in places was very narrow for big vessels. A sister ship passed us coming down, and I could have chucked a cricket ball aboard her. One or other of us had to get by a lighter before we met. Our captain consequently reduced speed, and wirelessed to the

"... the Heights of Abraham. The tugs pulled us ... from astern of the 'Empress of Britain' ..."

"... the mast-head ... at least ten feet of it look like fouling the girders. ..."

other to pass first—just as two good drivers play for safety on a road, and refuse to cut in.

Thereafter, the river displayed a certain sameness, so the captain invited me to his cabin under the bridge where we swopped yarns. It was then that he told me the extent of the bad roll we had made the previous Monday morning, and also that he had subsequently turned the ship forty-five degrees off her course for many miles, so as to meet the mountainous seas head on until they had sufficiently gone down.

During dinner, served at six-thirty on account of our impending arrival, a number of good-byes were being said—and apparently celebrated: a conventional contradiction particularly, and humorously, suited to many ship's passengers in each other's estimation. *Auld Lang Syne* was played by the orchestra, and many on board, indeed about two-thirds of the diners, stood up and sang half-way through the serving of the *entrée* course. Inconspicuous in my corner, I battled on, slightly deafened, with Doktor Hugo Eckener's chapter in Tangye's book; it put the case for "lighter-than-air" craft. Massed choirs can be ineffably fine, marching songs stirring, community singing either horrible, awe-inspiring or at times useful for directing herd instinct in a given direction (see the Mussolini and Hitler technique—also American ball games), but why will people burst into sentimental caterwauling upon the slightest provocation—in this instance, the conclusion of a few infernally uncomfortable days at sea? Perhaps it was pleasure? But no one could have said for certain! The urge to vocal expression produced by certain tunes in concert with partially loaded stomachs is probably a result, as our scientific friends would doubtless term it, of an even more comprehensive group of interacting stimuli.

The effect, at any rate, was a depressing noise. One trusts that this is another custom which the frank sense of values of the present generation will confine to its proper, and comparatively rare, occasions; for sloppiness is catching. Besides, singing under such ordinary circumstances is a most inconsiderate form of self-indulgence. Quite half the people standing up had doubtless no wish to do so, but, though equally inconvenienced, lacked the disapproving unselfconsciousness of the twenty or so of us who remained immovable.

By seven-thirty, it was dark and raining heavily. But so impressive was our approach to Montreal under those conditions, that I was reconciled to not seeing the city in a way that I certainly had not been reconciled.in the case of Quebec. There came into view a maze of lights, flanking the broad black river which apparently slipped towards us rather than we along it; an illusion heightened by the teeming rain, drowning all sound of our passage through the water. Long sheds reeled past on either side. The torrents streaming from their sloping roofs were caught and turned golden by the rays of many lamps. Behind these sheds were dim houses with lighted windows. Our siren reverberated again and again over the whole place. It was odd to feel a city quickly engulfing a big ship and yet not clearly see the tall surrounding buildings. Moreover, rather disturbingly, one knew it was really the liner that was moving, and still at a pace to surprise landlubbers.

High and bright-faced, the harbour clock grew in size, suspended in the void ahead of us. Once more we boomed notice of our coming; one, two, and then a third prolonged signal, like a giant shouting through an organ pipe.

Now I caught glimpses of bay after bay harbouring cargo vessels, and coldly lit by arc lamps. Beautifully handled, our ship at length slowed down, turned majestically and very slowly into one of these bays, and was gradually warped alongside. As we drew near the puddled quay, the splashing of the rain became still more obtrusive. It was literally pouring.

68

A glittering curtain of water shimmered down in front of the door of the vast illuminated shed in which a crowd awaited the placing of gangways against our side. And we, like passengers the world over, were all on deck too soon, huddled like sheep.

Leaning on the rail and hit by occasional in-blown spatters of wet, I talked nonsense to the "open-air girl"—a trifle homesick, I suspected, and concerned over the whereabouts of her dog, which the ship's butcher, who had been looking after it, had promised to produce at the right moment. Finally, we docked. Remembering I had a train to catch, I said good-bye to my three or four acquaintances and slipped below to take up a position near the gangway. For some minutes, a double column of stewards stamped up and down it; carrying our luggage ashore. Then at last we were allowed to emerge under a canvas tunnel into the orderly confusion of the Customs shed.

My stuff, destined for the States, went through with comparative promptitude, and soon I found myself in a roomy American-built taxi, driven by an inarticulate gum-chewing French-Canadian. We agreed that the night was horribly wet. His car certainly was; it had water on at least two plugs out of six and was half stalling all the way to the station. Thus my sole impression of Montreal was one of dark secondary streets, running with water, and of traffic lights foreignly flicking straight from red to green; and of nothing else at all. It was too bad.

The station, much less impressive externally than Marylebone station in London, turned out to be ten times as well laid out and kept. It was large, clean and rather empty. Here, I was faced with the Customs' inspection of the heavy bags checked through to New York. Each one had to be opened, but all the inspector wanted to see was a presentation copy of T. E. Lawrence's *Seven Pillars of Wisdom* which I had declared.

This was passed without duty; and I was politely helped to re-pack. Buying an American comic paper and deciding against an ice-cream soda, I followed a negro porter to my sleeping cabin on the New York train, where the attendant, also coloured, brought iced water in response to my bell.

At that point, I was unfortunately run to earth by a reporter who had missed me at the boat (some one apparently had given me away). Primed with a disconcerting knowledge of my past, he stood ingratiatingly in the doorway to inquire my views on English highways, traffic courts and police, the Pepys family, National Government and wayside garages—in that order. I told him; because he was a decent soul, and because it was a filthy night to be out chasing stories. Invited in, he sat on my bunk, but refused a cigarette on the ground of possessing other, compensating vices. I did not inquire what they were.

Of English highways, I said with not unnatural feeling that they often passed through unforgettably lovely country with the air of peace which lies upon Britain, but that the idiotically smooth surface of many of them was dangerous in the extreme, and destroyed all sense of peace when it was raining; that only now, having let hundreds of thousands of our people be killed, were we slowly ruminating upon the chances of a successful combat with the lethargy and vested interests responsible for this disgraceful state of affairs; and that just as we had not yet reached the stage of having a modern road system, so we had not yet taken adequate steps to ensure the proper use of the existing one.

Respecting my family name, I merely tried half-heartedly to contradict the usual ridiculous pronunciation "Peeps" and caused my interviewer to open his eyes by telling him there are seventeen known ways of spelling it but that probably a sporting chance at least existed of my knowing the right way and the right pronunciation.[1]

Regarding National Government, I ventured to record my opinion that its advent in England would one day be looked back upon as the first glimmer of dawn after the darkest political hour to which an out-worn three-party system, too long sustained by *clique* ambitions and intensified in its

[1] A tradition exists that the family came from Italy to Languedoc in France, and that certain members moved on northward and settled in Cambridgeshire in England. The name unquestionably exists in Italy, the two well-known authors, Guglielmo Pepe or Peppe, 1611, and the Baron Antonio Pepi, 1750-70, testifying to the fact. So far as the French version is concerned, the name "Pepyons" occurs in the *Armorial General de la France*, Hozier, Paris, 1768, Registre 6, in an ancient contract of marriage in the Province of Languedoc dated 1292; and in *Le Cabinet Historique*, iii, p. 12, also by Hozier, in the Bibliotheque Nationale at Paris, the name "Pepie" occurs.

In England the name has been variously spelt as follows: Pepis, Rolls of the Hundreds, 1273; Pepy, Inquisitiones ad quod damnum, 1439; Pypys, Will of Laurence Pypys, 1511; Pipes, a mis-spelling in the same Will; Peppis, Will of John Peppis of Branktre, 1518; Peppes, Will of Margaret, wife of the same John Peppis, 1519; Pepes, Will of Thomas Pepes of Cottenham, 1520; Peppys, Will of John Peppys of Debden, 1552; Peaps, Will of John Peaps of Cambridge, 1636; Pippis, Will of Anna Peppis of Cambridge, 1639; Peapys, Magdalen College, Cambridge, Records, 1653; Peps, Samuel Pepys, marriage register, St. Martin's in the Fields, 1655; Pypes, Admon. of Wm. Pypes' estate, 1656; Peypes, Letter of Edward Montague to Chief-Justice Pepys, 1656; Peeps, Extract from "Coffee House Paper," Samuel Pepy's diary; Peepes, Marriage Licence, John Peepes and Mary Gibson, Apr. 1683; Peyps, Burial Register of Samuel Pepys, St. Olave's, Hart Street, 1703.

Samuel Pepys, the diarist, a younger son of a younger son of a younger son of the Cottenham branch of the family, who died childless, may of course have pronounced his name "Peeps." But if so, it would be hard to say why, for in the earliest known writing it is spelt "Pepis" and the French form of the name is "Pepy"; and presumably he knew how his immediate forebears spelt their name even if he remained in ignorance of the French connection.

The accepted spelling of the name "Pepys" was adopted generally about the end of the seventeenth century, though it occurs many years before that time. The main line of the family pronounce it "Peppis": which is correct.

(The records from which certain of the above quotations are taken and linked, were compiled by Walter Courtenay Pepys in 1887.)

71

ill effects by Communist International propaganda, had brought a hard-working country; that the breaking of dawn had been largely due, not so much to a renascent patriotic wisdom in politicians, but to the steadfast instinct and personal influence of His Majesty, King George V.; that its slow transition from a cloudy, overcast beginning into a day brighter than past days was in effect the birth of dictatorship in Britain—the British form of dictatorship, which should resemble a cricket team drawn from all parties with a useful contribution to make (when we learn to pick men for character, broad-mindedness and appropriate knowledge, rather than often for sycophantic adherence to fixed ideas in a changing world), the kind of dictatorship some of us had desired for years and had been laughed at for desiring by superficial reactionaries who thought we had coloured shirts in our minds; a dictatorship by a cabinet which should represent the majority of the nation for main issues whatever minor differences of opinion there might be; a dictatorship which should gradually and Britishly adapt for use the best of State Socialism while retaining the best of individual Capitalism, and suppressing the worst of both (our genius for compromise!); a dictatorship destined to become stronger rather than weaker with the growth of general education and understanding, a leadership almost unrecognisable as a dictatorship but nevertheless on the way to constituting our version of the latter in a world returning to dictatorial leadership and strong national spirit, which in turn tends to international balance and respect when in the hands of sane men; a dictatorship by the balanced bulk of British men and women as expressed through a small group of their countrymen for whose actions in the final instance a constitutional and human King stands trustee.

That settled my interviewer (it had very nearly settled me) and presently he took himself off. So did my train. And truth compels me to admit that my earnest peroration, delivered in the intervals of laying out my pyjamas and rummaging about for a sponge and a tooth-brush, was reduced, when I saw it long afterwards as a newspaper clipping, to a few lines, stating that in my view National Government was "about the best administration in the present century": which I cannot flatter myself was of any more interest to the people of Canada than it had apparently been to the editor of the paper.

The American Customs officer and the immigration officer appeared in quick succession. The first politely accepting my word that there was nothing but personal effects in my unchecked dressing-case, and the second made a note or two in respect of my identification papers. Upon my expressing envy of his ability to write standing up in a swaying train, the immigration officer grinned boyishly. He said that he had plenty of practice, did his best, but doubted if any one could ever read what he wrote. Then I switched out the light, but with no great optimism, for deep sleep is elusive in trains.

Getting up before I was called, I went to the parlour car for coffee. The train was running beside a stretch of water like Loch Ness. This was the Hudson. Westward, across the broad river, steep cliffs lifted their tree-crowned summits towards the morning mist. The East shore, where we were running, consisted of a slight embankment planted with firs, among which little suburban houses nestled, partially hidden. These, built squarely of wood, belied their quaint appearance of flimsiness. We flashed through a larger place, where factories and trolley cars accorded ill with the placid river. More embankment followed and, beyond it, some nice park-like land. Then trees closed in again: acacias, willows, poplars and oaks. On the riverside, a length of sand suddenly widened, narrowed, ceased and gave place to a sharp brink, backed by a

73

view of rocky islands. Finally both vanished, their place being taken by the usual ugly buildings fringing a city. And now, too, we were hurrying into rain.

The coffee had been excellent and served with as much cream in a jug as one gets milk elsewhere. The train ran splendidly, smooth and well-sprung, on a first-rate track; for this was a much used line. The coloured attendants were quick and pleasant. Their backchat, issuing from a beautifully arranged galley, rivalled that of Amos and Andy, the well-known comedians.

Unlike the waterfronts of New York, the northerly approach to it by train from inland is characterised by an ugly monotony. No graceful skyscrapers are visible, only dingy cubes; and I caught an appalling glimpse of a workmen's tenement in sham, very sham, Tudor. In such a district of sidings, our English backyards would be barren patches or gallant attempts at gardens. There, I saw them to be full of motor-cars, either discarded or else the cheap junk in which workmen drive to their jobs. High up, the clouds that lay above the city were breaking. The day would be fine, I decided, after all.

I had forgotten being told that trains entered New York more or less on sufferance. So the terminus platform, gloomy and subterranean, was a disappointment. Still, as delightful an old cove checked my five pieces out of the baggage car as had checked them in at Montreal. This man, like the other, wore a venerable air and steel-rimmed glasses. Both had looked surprised when I thanked them, but readily replied, "You're very welcome." Acknowledgment of such services is widely taken for granted in America. If a stranger expresses his gratitude, the answer is just as likely as not to be an embarrassed grunt. But more frequently it is just, "You're welcome"—a delightfully old-fashioned custom in what is still looked upon, wrongly now, as a new country.

74

I had a poor thin lath of a porter and had to help him push the barrow up a brilliantly lighted slope to the reception hall at ground level. On this slope, the far-famed tidiness of American railroad termini began. It was spotless. The hall to which it led was like the foyer of a gigantic theatre, or some enormously wide and clean arcade of glittering restaurants, reading rooms, stalls and shops. Outside, the queue of taxis —large, high-powered sedans—was ordered about in no uncertain fashion by some official, apparently attached to the station. In England, a policeman does it in leisurely fashion. But this fellow, pleasant enough unless angered, turned like a flash and gave a driver hell for jumping his place in the line. Thus, I encountered at once the zip of the American tempo, very different to a ponderous rebuke at Euston or Paddington: "You can't do that there 'ere."

Within two hours I had bathed, changed, unpacked and settled in; within three I was on my way by road to Long Island for the day. There, at Bayside, I visited a house which, from previous descriptions, I knew as soon as I set eyes on it— a low white wooden building in the old veranda'd style, itself by no means young in years but standing where the forebears of the family who own it had built their first house in 1645. A garden and a small piece of grass land still saved the house from serious intrusion by its modern neighbours. And a number of tall, gracious trees gave it shade and shelter; one generation of trees to every two or three generations of its owners.

Inside, the house was low and rather dim. The general impression was one of solid, dignified Victorianism, but with an intangible difference—the original English tradition had been overlaid, with sturdy independence, by one that was American. To mount the steps to this wide porch and cross the threshold into the cool order of the mellow rooms, was to step softly into a small part of America's past, there to read more

75

than one chapter. If the written pages had faded at all, well, the ink had gained in tone what it had lost in depth, and the vellum glowed more golden for the passage of the years. Here was a sideboard, a part of the tale; there were some chairs of another era; china of yet a different period; prints and pictures, each a phrase or a paragraph; and now before me in one shape or another was evidence also of our own day and age. No other collection could furnish this house half so well. Attuned, too, was the gentle courtesy of the customs obtaining: the wit, the conversation, the quiet hospitality that greeted me. There was a Quaker meeting hall near by, in which the great-grandfather of my friends was solemnly "read" out of the community for the deadly sin of owning, not necessarily of playing upon, a piano.

By contrast, not far up the coast of Long Island Sound, Mr. Pierpoint Morgan owns a mansion. Massively built by the shore, it rears up as though to challenge every gale. I do not doubt that it is all a house should be, its appointments as splendid as its situation. But neither he nor any man, wealthy or poor, could reproduce other than an outward similitude of that older American home, or those like it, where an intimate and consequential symposium of furnishings, charmingly in league with the house, are themselves united by the echoes of laughter and tears, by the doings of successive sons and daughters in sickness or in health, and by the pervading sense of being the ancient background of a family and so a small part of what is most gracious in the history of the States.

None but that kind of home could have given me quite the same welcome; or one which I needed more to feel. I counted myself fortunate to have gone straight there.

At Piping Rock Club, where we arrived after a drive of twenty minutes, a scene of friendly vociferation presented itself in the hall and by the bar, and later in the dining-room where one of the Club's famous Sunday luncheons was in full swing.

On these occasions, the world of fashion and of form helps itself from a long buffet with a great joint of roast beef at one end and salads at the other. In between, there are all sorts of delicacies and vegetables, from cunningly cooked clams, chicken cream, lobster and crisp lumps of sausage meat, to succulent peas and browned cubes of apple.

The technique consists in taking a plateful of what you fancy, and transporting it unspilled to your table before going back, like Oliver Twist, for more. Watchful waiters remove empty plates like magicians, but they bring only drinks. The members themselves and their guests pick up clean plates as they regain the buffet, cold plates from a pile in front, hot plates out of a heated oven at the end; and all the time the crowd is jostling good humouredly. Snatches of conversation fly about like shuttles on a loom. "Hallo," is said with a helping of sweetbreads in one hand and a platter of green stuff in the other, and possibly with some lovely lady's indelicately-sized slices of roast beef barring all further progress to one's table till two affectionate friends behind have said their say to each other while respectively balancing fruit salad and oysters, or an elderly gent in inch-thick pince-nez has worked through the pack, while juggling painfully with a hot potato and obviously recalling the days when he played for Harvard.

From outside on the terrace where we sat drinking coffee, there was a view—as it might be—over a sweeping English park in Norfolk. Before luncheon, we had fallen in with Mr. James Gerard, American Ambassador to Berlin during the war. He had generously offered us seats in his box at Meadowbrook for the afternoon; several international players were going to take part, and a hard game was expected. For a while, until we started, the conversation turned to politics, the next Presidential election, Germany in 1914-18, the chequered history of certain American States, and my forth-

77

coming motoring and flying itineraries. The coffee cups clinked, a fallen leaf or two rustled across the stone flags, our cigar smoke drifted slowly in the warm sunlight.

Piping Rock Club, itself, I found to be a delightfully planned building, consisting of long, well-proportioned rooms, built round an open courtyard where a fountain trickled cheerfully in a formal bower of roses. On this, the opposite side from the terrace, a sweeping gravel approach led past shrubberies, lawns and a group of mighty trees. Its firm surface was crunched by car after car, setting down and picking up at the broad porch, from which there was also a view, this time into a shallow, dipping valley where part of a well-kept golf course formed a wide emerald vista between rising woods (then just assuming their autumn tints) which closed in across the sky-line, a mile distant, with a conscious air of privacy.

Meadowbrook, lying in flatter country, revealed no beauty to recommend it except the excellence of its polo grounds and its general appointments, such as the huge stands, painted a pleasing blue-green, from which we watched. The attendants, I noticed, wore yachting caps, blue serge jackets, white flannels and buckskin shoes—a smart, if somewhat surprising, get-up.

The first match proved the closest and keenest I had ever seen. The players were famous not only as players but as horse-lovers: Hitchcock, Balding, the two Whitneys and such-like. Hitchcock's game was magnificent; he had the crowd clapping again and again.

Between two matches, we wandered down to drink orange-ade at a refreshment bar under the stand; and there again the conversation beat round one's ears. Back in the box, the second match being for the moment not so exciting, the ambassador drew a map of New York and Long Island on the back of my programme, and kindly explained to me this and that approach to the city.

78

"Meadowbrook . . . the first match . . . Hitchcock, Balding, the two Whitneys and such-like."

By tea-time, I was in another of those delightful old wooden homes, this one perched high on a bluff overlooking Oyster Bay—a house, as one of the family rightly said, spacious enough but not too big. Seen from its broad window-seats, the distant water was framed in almost Mediterranean blueness by the feathery foliage of the garden. Below the house, two hundred feet or so, there was the village; but we looked over it, and the trees hid it.

Indoors, books in leather bindings filled tall sections of the room in which we sat. Elsewhere, the walls were painted, harmonising quietly. An air of restraint, of being well loved and lived in, characterised it all. A grand piano stood crosswise to a corner, in the light from two windows. On it, some flowers in a vase displayed their elegance and beauty against the background of the deeply-tinted walls. When a lull came in the talk, an old silver kettle on a table by the broad hearth could be heard softly singing.

There is something about these venerable Long Island houses that is unique. The families who have lived long in them are up-to-date enough, but their roots go down deeply and happily into an older America. Weeks later, I was to encounter this same charm again in Virginia.

Motoring back to New York in the evening from Oyster Bay, I passed along narrow country roads that might have been English roads. Behind me, Long Island Sound, where the great yacht races are held, had turned to a silvery blue with so much pink in it that its surface seemed almost a part of the sunset sky above.

But such a sight was quickly driven from my mind when we emerged onto a main road.

Cars passed, or could be passed, on either hand. They did not go over the centre line painted on the road, and most of the slow ones kept closer to the near side than do our drivers; but the sudden swerves of some of them, pushing through, reminded me of the flight of snipe. From twenty miles away, the lights in the highest buildings of New York shone like coastal beacons. Yet, to get there took an hour and fifteen minutes!

Indeed, the week-end traffic between New York and Long Island seems, if there is such a thing, like a dull nightmare. Boredom is the paramount sensation. One drives in an endless stream of automobiles, although on roads wider than many roads out of London. (We ourselves are only now starting to take this warning.) In consequence, a new bridge has been built over the East River to relieve the congestion of Queensborough Bridge, itself a six-car bridge with an over-road. And new roads have, and are, being built on the Island itself; they cross one another like the ivory slivers of a game of spillikins. The local official responsible for this is a certain Mr. Moses. I heard his name mentioned everywhere in terms of praise and gratitude; he had almost halved the time taken two years ago to reach this Promised Land. But he is still going to be busy for a long time.

Long Island really is something of a promised land, rich in variety. Except for hills of any height, which it lacks, there are to be found glimpses of the beauties contained in all the southern and eastern counties of England: the wooded lakes of Surrey, the steep, enclosed meadows and copses of Dorset, the bracken-clothed heaths and forests of Hampshire, the coves of Devon, the market-gardens of Essex, the rolling parklands of Norfolk and Suffolk.

But, as in many thickly-populated districts of America, a close and cautious watch has to be exercised when driving, or traffic lights are missed; especially as successive ones are not always located in the same position relative to the road. In addition, there is a dire confusion between official signs and trade advertisements. This is most noticeable, and it is hard to understand why drastic action is not taken to prevent it.

Trying to pick out a "warning" or "stop" sign, or a road number, is like looking for a needle in a haystack. I have seen even experienced American drivers stop and stare round anxiously for the information they seek while a chorus of impatient horns breaks out behind them. In my opinion, every road junction, in fact the roadsides generally, should be free from any signs except official signs. This will eventually have to come.

The day after my arrival, the maelstrom which New York can be to a stranger, engulfed me. My notes relating to the first week are just a series of brief entries: "I" did this, or "I" did that. This was inevitable and remains so in this book. Only upon my return from California, did I have time to see New York at my leisure.

During the days immediately following my Sunday on Long Island, I lunched twice in the Cloud Club at the top of the Chrysler Building—where the membership is limited to a hundred and fifty well-known business men. The subscription alone is three hundred dollars a year and the entrance fee enormous. From a table in one of these club windows, a wonderful aerial view of New York is obtained, both up and down the East River. The club kitchens, through which I walked later, are a symphony in shining tiles and stainless steel, as spotless as the day the equipment was installed six years ago.

And the cooking, as might be expected, is first rate. I think it was Byron Foy, Mr. Chrysler's son-in-law, who told me as we fed together there one day, that a widely-travelled epicure, eating a specially ordered pudding, had remarked that he knew only one other *chef* who could make it so well—a Belgian in some favourite restaurant in Paris or Brussels (I forget which) where he was once an *habitué*. Visiting the club kitchens later, to congratulate the cook who made his pudding, he had found him to be the

81

same man. Food of this excellence is more easily digested than forgotten.

Again, from the Rainbow Room restaurant at the top of the Rockefeller Building I looked down upon New York at night: a fairyland of myriad lights arranged in neat rectangles and then carelessly bespattered with multi-coloured Neon signs, as though some giant, from the high building where I was supping, had thrown down a huge handful of fireworks which burned each night perennially. A few hours afterwards, having been driven out there, I was sleepily flying a Fairchild three-place cabin monoplane in from Long Island to the river airport of the city; a nice type of touring aeroplane, typically American and new to me. And for the first time since my arrival, I really *saw* New York, a sight to banish weariness: symmetrical towers of every shape, decreasing in bulk as they mounted in height, severe and strong, chaste and palely beautiful, looming mysteriously through the morning haze and suddenly catching the sunlight so that I could steer the plane on one; buildings symbolical of the age of crowded progress in which we should be grateful to live rather than fearful—a sight which, marvellous in itself, became more marvellous when, approaching from the air, one realised its inherent prophecy of still greater things.

I refused, with genuine regret and as good a grace as I could muster, an invitation to be a guest of honour at a luncheon given by the Advertising Club to Miss Laura Ingalls, who had just broken the Woman's Trans-Continental air record; because I wished to escape the kindly but businesslike attentions of the New York press. I fed, too, by daylight in the lovely roof room at the St. Regis Hotel and by night in the Persian dance-room at the Plaza; and, for contrast, spent an hour in a real jazz dive where there was no room to dance even if people wished to do so, but where the regular customers merely sat at little tables along the walls of a narrow room,

82

and drank, smoked, talked or listened at close quarters, until 3 a.m., to a fiendishly noisy band with a marvellous rhythm, conducted by a restless comedian called "George," or alternatively to five coloured boys in white suits whose constantly changing expressions formed an interesting study in sheer *joie de vivre*. There are no places in London quite the same as this. There could not be, for the same spirit is not in our national make-up. Our corresponding pleasures are supplied in a different way by an accordion in a tap-room, a penny whistle outside or a jangling piano in a Soho *café*. But here, in this dive, all sorts and kinds of people could obtain relaxation, outrageous merriment, quite good drinks and be entirely deafened for only a few cents.

I was instructively entertained in a private room high up in the stately building of the National City Bank on Wall Street. From the back of it one looks over the harbour towards the Statue of Liberty, on guard at the entrance beyond which the Atlantic rolls. I watched a sunset from Central Park—the tall buildings above the trees soon became dark against a glowing evening sky, and then one by one lit up.

Not long before, a friend and I had foregathered with a drunken man near the smaller of the two zoological gardens. Hailing me, he hiccoughed a request for a match, and subsequently made immense efforts to stand still while I helped him to light the cigarette he waved. This being accomplished at length to our mutual satisfaction, he raised his hat politely after three attempts and turned towards my companion, who straightway attempted to assume a serious and sympathetic expression. But it was to me that the man addressed himself.

"Guesh you're—a—Britisshher, aren't you? he observed, taking a sudden involuntary pace to the right.

Following suit, I lined up opposite to him again: it made the conversation easier.

"I am," I replied.

He rippled momentarily from the knees up, like a reed, but with a noble attempt at concentration became still again, and focussed a glassy stare upon the lady with me.

"Is shee-e—Britisshher too—*hup* ?"

"No," I admitted, "she's a countrywoman of yours."

He made a grandiloquent gesture of both hands, as though he forgave her.

"S'alright," he pronounced, "I don' care; does'n matter. I'm all for her just the same, left, right and centre."

Suddenly, a look of horror came into his face, and he replaced his hat with exaggerated caution on the side of his head; the thought had just occurred to him that we were all standing on the edge of the sidewalk, with cars passing near by. Together, we made a convoy of three and crossed—without a car in sight. Subsequently, he tacked after us into the zoo, where from a distance we heard and watched him directing his loud remarks to the seals.

I spent an interesting half-hour next morning explaining to the officials of the Department of Taxation and Finance just why it would be advisable for them to enter the rather lengthy description of me on my prospective driver's licence in just the same form as it was entered on my passport, and further staggered them the following morning, when I went to collect the licence, by pretending that I had forgotten two of my names and asking them to add them to the list. This finally convinced them of my eccentricity, although they took it very well. Such complications as titles were almost beyond their comprehension. And who shall blame them? I had to deliver what I hoped was a nimble lecture on the subject, and to explain that, much as I would like to oblige them, I could not discard the identity associated with Cottenham although my family name was Pepys. They scratched their heads and gave it up. I replaced my hat on mine and paid them a dollar. After which, I was licensed to drive in the United States.

PART I

CHAPTER I

NEW YORK TO BUFFALO

THE CROWDED FIRST DAYS OF MY VISIT WERE BEHIND ME. I had seen my old friends in New York, and among their friends had made many new acquaintances; some, I hoped, themselves to ripen into friends. I had paid my calls and kept my business appointments as punctually as the traffic and my comparatively sparse knowledge of the city would allow.

All this and more was accomplished in five days. Now, in a big Chrysler "Airflow" car most kindly placed at my disposal by the parent Corporation in Detroit, and accompanied by a charming executive of theirs, Louis Skinitzero, who knew America pretty widely, I was on my way out of the city; heading for the west. To leave, we made use of Riverside Drive, a raised thoroughfare that runs along what one might term the back of New York, from north to south. This is the quickest way of traversing the city in either direction. We kept a close look-out for "cops," but only saw the parked motor-cycle of one; he himself was not visible.

While in New York, I had frequently availed myself of the services of a chauffeur, George Koyse, who had been loaned to me by Mr. Chrysler, so that I could have time to look about me and watch the traffic. Koyse used also to buy my tobacco for me. He appeared to sense which shops would stock the particular brand of English pipe mixture that I wanted; and no night-club, however new, no restaurant, however obscure, seemed unknown to him. When I needed him, he drove me about that deep warren of steel and concrete and brick with certitude allied to a neat competence. I was sorry when, being California bound, I had to deprive myself of such an obliging and knowledgeable factotum.

Only on one occasion had we started to run foul of a police officer. Koyse had apparently neglected to draw sufficiently quickly to one side of a special temporary sign erected, to obviate congestion, in the middle of one of the narrow streets running past the side of the Grand Central Station. The policeman happened to be standing beyond this sign—supervising. The traffic was moving slowly and quietly at the time, so that I could hear his determined drawl issuing from a point several yards ahead.

"Is there any particular reason for driving there?" he demanded.

"No, no reason at all," my chauffeur was forced to admit.

"Then snap out of it," remarked the officer tersely, and grimly watched us do so.

Apart from this mild encounter, no examples had come my way of the cavalier treatment supposed to be meted out to motorists by the American police. All the same, I was determined to take no chances on my transcontinental trip, though I had been assured that every courtesy was usually shown to foreigners driving in America, and even to Americans themselves driving in an unfamiliar State, where the traffic laws might be different to those they knew; exceptions only being caused by a few young police officers over full of their new authority. True, the police officer in America, elderly, middle-aged or young, does not as a rule frame his remarks and replies to questions in the same remarkably polite tone insisted upon in our English police. But little criticism, I feel, can be levelled at them on this score, for the general relationship in the United States between Federal or State officials and members of the public is different; it is more of a man to man affair. On the surface there is little of the "public servant" spirit about it, although such is doubtless felt at heart.

88

Still, I am not sure that I am qualified to express an opinion on this. I only motored something over five thousand miles in America and experienced no untoward incidents of a character likely to involve me in close contact with the police. Those I heard answer questions, did so with a ready blunt friendliness. This led me to believe that the young, self-conscious American policeman might be no more difficult to handle than his opposite number in England, except that his training in the art of dealing with a less orderly public might have given him a more exaggerated idea of his own importance and a tendency to express himself more forcibly on many occasions than would be strictly necessary. Yet, I felt that both these latter contingencies would doubtless be resolved by reason and common sense. Myself, I liked every policeman I met and was welcomed lik- a brother one night in Times Square by a stocky officer who fought beside the British in France. We must have stood talking on the sidewalk for fully half an hour.

It is not really difficult to pick the right road out of New York. Skinitzero and I only asked our way twice; once of a helpful police officer and once of a truck driver (we should call him a lorry driver) who, seeing our Michigan number plate, kindly pulled up to direct us. This last is a friendly custom prevalent among American motorists. The continent is so large that motorists, noticing a car with a number plate belonging to a distant State, will look upon its driver as a stranger in a strange land and will help him if possible.

Crossing under the Hudson River into New Jersey, we drove through the remarkable Hudson Tunnel, like our Blackwall Tunnel several times magnified. It is well lit and ventilated. Moreover, it is double-barrelled, so that lines of traffic moving in opposite directions are entirely segregated. Notices warn drivers not to get too close to the car in front and not to sound a horn. The reverberation of noise is terrific.

Fast traffic keeps to the left; slow traffic, i.e., trucks, to the right. And there is a toll levied on the tunnel's use. Finally, this staggering urban exit joins up, at its New Jersey end, with what is called the "Sky-way"—an amazing road, engineered right over the top of factories and congested areas, and forbidden to all except fast motor traffic which it was designed to assist in and out of New York. Thereafter, we drove westward on Route 6. The country was dull and flat. Tall factory chimneys rose in the distance on either flank, and a fine drizzle started. Altogether, it was a rather depressing morning.

The places we passed through on this road were typical suburbs; residential sections consisting mostly of neat wooden houses. After the American fashion, these seldom have walls dividing their gardens. At most there is a low hedge, but usually nothing at all. A paved path, ending perhaps in some steps, leads up from the common sidewalk. There is not, in consequence, the air of privacy that we English people like, and, to some extent, the impression of a man's house being his castle is absent. But there is a sylvan air about these little towns and villages which is a great compensation.

One notices at once that the Americans are a nation of tree lovers. Everywhere, there are trees. Old trees have been preserved and young trees planted, so that what would otherwise be a quite ordinary street is nine times out of ten a pretty avenue.

As I came to one after another of these little built-up areas, many of them housing people who work every day in New York, I thought to myself how lovely were the surroundings to which they return every evening, whether the trees are in full foliage or have changed to bare, glittering branches, covered with snow crystals: for on the east coast of America the snow lies thick and crisp in winter.

Once or twice, we took the wrong turning owing to the

". . . once across the Delaware we ran for a time under steep wooded banks beside its beautiful course . . ."

difficulty I had already noticed in picking out signposts from the mass of placards at each cross-roads. If one pulls up only a few seconds before a traffic light changes from red to green, it is really very difficult to read all that is to be read and to decide on one's direction; the right sign is often spotted only after one has started to go the wrong way. Then it is a case of waiting until the light changes again before turning back. Here, the road itself was a concrete pavement, and I noticed with disappointment that it was more slippery in the rain than it should have been. The surface, I decided, was not sufficiently roughened. After a time, we began to get out into real country.

It was the third week in September, and the maples already hung out in welcome their flaming banners. A friend of mine has an idea that the brilliant reds and yellows of the dying leaves in North America is due to the fact that they are thinner than the leaves on our trees at home. This, he says, combined with the added brilliance of the sun, produces an almost blinding effect as one walks through the woods. I resolved to drive up the Hudson upon my return to New York and test this theory for myself.

We passed into Pennsylvania. Once across the Delaware, we ran for a time under steep wooded banks beside its peaceful curves. With the sight of this river, my interest in Amercan history took on an added impetus. The associations connected with any piece of country only achieve reality when one sees the country itself become alive after being merely a map remembered from days at school.

As I drove on through the rolling landscape, books I had read about its past were already flipping their pages in the background of my mind. I felt that soon I should remember more clearly what had been in them and should see it in a truer perspective.

Just short of Tunkhannock, I caught my first glimpse of

the Susquehanna, another river—one with a name to make one think of a lovely dark-skinned woman—which wanders among what the Indians, who named it, call "the endless mountains." Indeed, they do seem endless, these swelling uplands clothed with glorious timber. On one high bluff along this road I stopped the car, and got out to look down upon the river several hundred feet below, and across to a flat piece of land in a broad basin of hills where there was once a settlement of French Royalist refugees. The place is called French Asylum. Beneath us, beside the river, one of the big American trains was making its hoarse way, and looked diminutive as a toy.

We had luncheon in a little restaurant at Towanda— another beautiful name—off sandwiches made of fresh chicken on rye bread with mayonnaise, the best I have ever eaten anywhere. I had two (corresponding for size to four English ones) and three cups of coffee; and the whole meal cost less than two shillings.

A mellow, dignified courthouse stood just across the street, shaded by massive trees rising from plots of carefully-mown lawn. A hundred and fifty yards down the gentle slope behind it, where I wandered smoking a pipe, I found again the Susquehanna.

Within an hour, I had crossed the boundary once more into New York State, and drove now in a more northerly direction towards Elmira. The rain had long since ceased. I was entranced by the warm lights of afternoon upon the great woods and the golden stooks of maize in the cornfields.

Then suddenly, upon pulling up for traffic lights in a town through which we were passing, I twice stalled my engine. Moreover, I had difficulty in getting the car away again because its slow running had gone to pieces. A stop to discover the cause revealed a stream of petrol pouring from the carburettor. But the car was still driveable, and, the

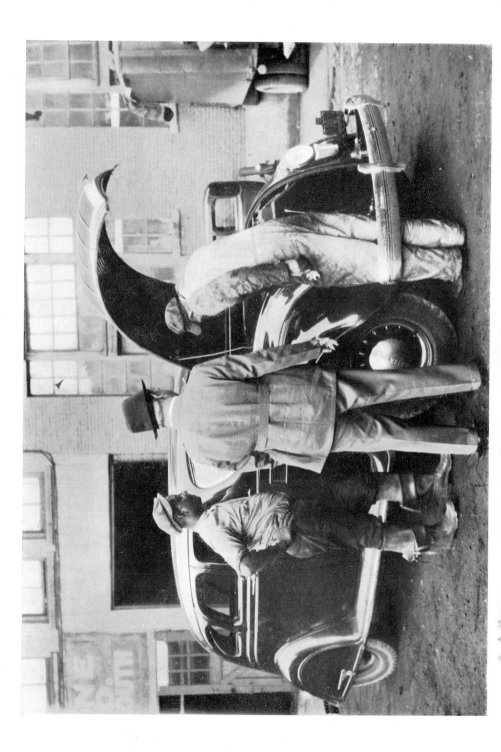

carburettor being unfamiliar and the tools absent-mindedly packed by me under all the luggage (a sorry admission for an old driver!) I lazily decided to push on a mile or two to the next town where there was a Chrysler agent. This I did, and the trouble turned out to be a small fragment of foreign matter that had ensconced itself on the seating of the feed valve; which might easily happen but very seldom does in these days: I hadn't experienced anything like it for years. A quick reassembly was made, and we proceeded. I was quite glad to have had the opportunity of looking over this particular type of carburettor in view of the long drive yet to be done.

But we had not gone far before a detour sign sent us off the main route and away onto country roads running through farming land. Apparently, some bridge or other was still down, a relic of the appalling damage brought about a few months previously by floods of unprecedented weight, which had caused great hardship and loss of life.

The signposting of secondary roads in America frequently seems to have been an afterthought, as it does in many other countries. Too little information is given, and too much local knowledge is expected. At the end of twenty minutes fast twisting and turning up the most likely looking road, which I pursued despite the blandishments of others forking off from it, I stopped in a small hamlet to inquire.

We explained our gyrations to a lantern-jawed old man carrying a pail. He set it down with a clatter and regarded us quizzically out of a pair of small twinkling eyes, deep-set in a face like a russet apple. Shifting his greasy old hat farther towards the back of his head, he rested a horny hand on the nearside front door of the car and patiently listened to us, while rhythmically chewing. At Louis Skinitzero's condemnation of the vague detour sign, a slow smile wrinkled his cheeks.

"So they beat ya out of it down thar," he observed delightedly. "Well, ya should surely have taken the next road back agin."

"But there was no sign," I protested.

"No," he admitted, still smiling, "thar ain't no sign. And now you've gotten so far, I guess you'd best go right ahead." He gave us slow, careful instructions.

Our own temporary ill-humour dissolved before his patent enjoyment of the situation. The fix we were in obviously struck him as highly amusing. We parted the best of friends, ourselves reduced to laughter by his attitude.

Although it transpired that we had to go at least eighty miles out of our way, I was not sorry. The evening peace upon this quiet countryside was compensation enough. I was seeing another aspect of America.

Eventually, we found our way back on the main road to Batavia and drove into Buffalo at about nine o'clock. There we stayed at a large hotel, typical of such manufacturing towns in America. The cooking was rich, the grill room like a political meeting (it was Saturday night), the service brilliantly efficient, yet the whole atmosphere one of great loneliness.

Upstairs by my bedside, and by all the other bedsides in the place, a radio was softly giving forth music interspersed with advertising boloney. The set was neatly accommodated in the top drawer of a small table on which stood the usual reading lamp. Mine did not give forth anything for long. The sense of loneliness would only be increased, I felt, by some unknown person—a lady at that moment—crooning to me while I went to bed. Besides, I was tired and mildly irritable.

I was just going to sleep when the light was switched on and a night watchman politely asked me to lock my door. It is only fair to add, in the interest of respectability, that this

94

precautionary measure was directed against the possible onslaught of hotel thieves rather than a tremendously unlikely visit of the charmer who, from some distant broadcasting station, had recently sought to warm my heart and the hearts of thousands with the assurance, "You are my lucky Star."

CHAPTER II

VIA CANADA TO DETROIT

A BRITISH MOTORIST CROSSING THE BRIDGE INTO CANADA from Buffalo finds more to welcome him than the mere feeling of coming back into his own country, however happy he may be in America (and I was very happy). He finds a complete clarity as regards official road signs; indeed, a much higher degree of efficiency in this respect than obtains in England. So the change is almost heavenly by comparison with the plethora of signs and advertisements customary in many parts of the United States.

I find reference to this fact continually cropping up in my notes, but I am told that in certain American States advertisements in mad profusion are not allowed. Whether this is on grounds of causing danger, or because the placards are held to spoil the amenities of the countryside, I do not know. Both are excellent reasons. At any rate, from my own observation, I feel that all States could do far worse than encourage, in every possible way, widespread organisations comparable with our Roads Beautifying Association. For America is so fantastically rich in scenic beauty that ugly advertisements are perhaps more obtrusive than they would be in many other countries. After driving, as I frequently did later, for a wonderful hour or so across a wild piece of desert ornamented only by the delicate colours of such flowers as will live there, and backed by far-off escarpments of fuchsia-tinted rock left over from a volcanic age, one does not exactly shout for joy when on several successive notice boards of the

The Customs at the Canadian end of the bridge from Buffalo.

Buffalo, from Canada, with Lake Erie in the foreground.

same size and painful gloss one reads an announcement of this sort:

"Morning finds you feeling grim,
Till —— shave puts you in trim."

Or alternatively, on another large board, the overwhelming promise that

"—— soap makes you beautiful all over."

But to return to Canada. A car that is merely going to be driven along the northern shore of Lake Erie and back into America again the same evening at Detroit, slips very easily through the Customs at the Canadian end of the bridge. I suppose in many cases, as in mine, the inspection is reduced simply to a matter of formality, although the polite officials were nevertheless very much on the spot. Revenue officers in every country seem to acquire an instinct for differentiating between the various types of traveller which pass before them all day long. Thus, they themselves have become quite a species recognisable by their stiff air of watchfulness, like warders in a prison, keepers responsible for the larger mammals in a zoo, or police officers in plain clothes as distinct from plain-clothes police.

The first main impression of this part of the province of Ontario is its complete flatness. Hills lie some miles away inland, but along the shore of the lake the ground is like a billiard table, and the road—a concrete one—runs in long straight sections, only occasionally interrupted by wide curves. It is a district of small holdings. One sees these homesteads, consisting of a few acres, scattered all the way alongside. There is an air of considerable freshness and charm about them. Each seems an entirely self-contained little unit; and the

97

sense of great space all round must be very satisfactory, I think, to any one coming from a crowded country to settle there. No doubt, it is bleak in the winter, but not with the bleakness of continual rain and fog. The winters are mostly crisp and clear; it is only the cold, searching winds that have to be tolerated at times. The temperature makes a bold dive below zero, so that snow, of which there is quantities, does at least remain snow—and clean.

I noticed speed limits varying from ten miles an hour at some narrow, blind danger spot to twenty miles in villages and thirty-five upon the open road. The latter, of course, is quite ridiculous. As a stranger, I watched other cars with interest and for some miles I drove with circumspection: I had been warned that the Canadian Police were very hot. But I soon discovered that most of my fellow motorists were cruising at anything from fifty to sixty-five miles an hour, although nearly all of them slowed down to a reasonable pace to pass groups of houses. Consequently, I myself started to shift along and began cruising at seventy to eighty; holding ninety several times for quite long stretches and once reaching ninety-seven despite a slight quartering wind from the north-west which prevented the speedometer showing the level hundred that might otherwise had been possible.

The speedometer was subsequently checked and found to have an excess error of four miles an hour at the top end of its range, so that the true speed attained and held was ninety-three. Under absolutely perfect conditions, I would put the maximum speed of the car I was driving at a true ninety-six or ninety-seven. Other cars of the same make and model might be a mile or two faster or slower, according to their tuning and the way they had been treated when new. The Chrysler was easy and comfortable to drive at its maximum once the general balance of it had been ascertained; for weight distribution and suspension, which largely make or mar

98

road-holding qualities, vary in all makes of car. This chassis rode well. Later, I tested the makers' claim that it is possible for passengers on the back seat to read a book at high speed and found it no exaggeration.

I have quoted actual speeds for a good reason, namely, that they at once conjure up in the minds of all experienced motorists a vivid picture of the type of road over which I was driving; its straightness, its safe surface when dry, and the length of unobstructed view obtainable along it for considerable distances. It was a concrete two-car pavement with the customary soft "shoulders" on either side. In this, it follows American practice. Though the speeds mentioned show how safe these concrete pavements can be on a fine day when one has them to oneself, I cannot but condemn their lack of width, particularly when the surface becomes wet. Cars going in either direction have no option but to drive in one place; and so well drilled are American and Canadian motorists in keeping to their own side of the road that four, faint, slightly different coloured strips about two feet wide are to be seen upon these pavements, and are the marks made by many wheels that have passed over them. These four almost indistinguishable spoors are not to be confused with two darker strips caused by the exhausts of the cars, each of which naturally deposits an infinitesimal amount of oil. But normally, the wheels miss these stains. And even in the rain, when this fine film spreads, it does not so dangerously affect the entire surface as it would in the case of asphalt or macadam.

Even then, I feel that the concrete surface, although superior to normal asphalt or macadam, might well be laid with a rougher finish than it is. This would only add very slightly to the noise made by tyres passing over it and would in no way affect the riding comfort of cars.

For myself, being a European motorist used to driving where I please except when other traffic might be inconveni-

99

enced thereby, I batted straight along the crown of the road. I only left it for the right-hand side on occasional blind bends or when I was meeting another car, or for the left-hand side when I was overtaking. This meeting of other cars on such roads in Canada and America would probably provide most British motorists with their first really uncomfortable sensation. There is enough room, but only enough. Although three cars could doubtless stand abreast, I would describe many of these roads as bare two-car roads. In a case of real emergency, there would not be sufficient margin for the situation to be adequately handled unless the drivers of both cars were expert and cool enough to choose the point at which they would, if necessary, drive boldly off the road and into a field. Hundreds of serious accidents have been caused by just letting a wheel drop off the pavement and not being ready for the resulting gymnastics. Where there are deep ditches on either side, the only line of action is to reduce speed very considerably indeed if the approaching car shows the least sign of being badly driven.

These points are difficult to bring out properly without a certain amount of explanatory detail and reiteration. But all are important points. I have talked with many experienced motorists possessing considerable knowledge of the Canadian and American highway systems, and they have all agreed with me that narrowness is their chief danger. Here the obvious must be stated at once, namely, that the expense of building a four-car road instead of a two-car road would be terrific when the distances involved are taken into consideration. Nevertheless, I think the need for it should be constantly borne in mind, and whenever a section of pavement is to be altered or repaired in any way it should also be made wider. For some years, this would naturally lend a somewhat untidy aspect to the whole road system, both in Canada and the States; but at least the expense would be spread over a lengthy period, and the roads would eventually be brought into line with the rapid development of motor transport taking place throughout the whole continent. I believe that in America thousands of lives would be saved every year if a greater mileage of roads were of adequate width. Moreover, this saving would start to take place proportionately as the widening process was undertaken. One day, the four, six or eight-car *autostrade*, divided down the centre by a shrubbery to obviate headlight dazzle, will be universal.

The "shoulders" to which I have referred are strips of ground on either side of the pavement, and vary from a foot or two to several feet in width. Sometimes, these strips consist of quite a hard foundation overlaid with gravel or overgrown with grass. In some parts of America, they consist only of dirt which may be dry or muddy according to the type of weather, or of sand which also varies and, unlike dirt, is safer when wet than when dry. Where these shoulders are deep, a notice is put up calling attention to that particular section of road. The notice reads something to this effect: "Danger —Soft Shoulders." This, of course, is a help, but as in the case of many other official notices, it is unsafe to rely too much upon the care taken in their positioning. There may be many other sections of road along which the shoulders have become unsafe but where no notice has yet been posted. These shoulders, starting as they do immediately at the sharp edge where the pavement ends, have been responsible for car after car turning over and their occupants being either killed or gravely injured (I am now, of course, referring to America as well as Canada). Their presence demands the closest concentration from any driver who wishes to drive with consistent safety; he has to watch them like a hawk.

On my way from New York to Buffalo, while travelling pretty fast, I had deliberately put the nearside wheels of the Chrysler off the pavement into a fairly soft shoulder some time after crossing the Susquehanna River. The car was then a comparative stranger to me, and I wanted to see how it would behave. In actual fact, I found that it handled very well. But because of its distribution of weight, which in that model placed three per cent more, I think, on the front axle than the back, it was easier to bring it out of the soft shoulder, one road wheel at a time, than to make a bolder steering movement which might have had the effect of swinging the back of the car farther into the shoulder and starting a skid. On several subsequent occasions when I did not like the behaviour of a car coming towards me, I also went into the soft shoulder on my side of the road, but only after subjecting it to a searching scrutiny. As all experienced motorists are aware, it is possible even when moving comparatively fast to see whether the earth visible between tufts of grass is hard or soft; or to pick out the difference, for example, between loose sand and firm dirt. Naturally, I slowed down from any really high speed before driving into a shoulder. But I reduced speed even more when I was not able to edge into one, for I never like to be travelling fast when I meet a car coming in the opposite direction unless there is at least an extra car's width of road at our joint disposal.

So it goes without saying that the cruising speeds quoted which are quite safe with the right tyred car, provided that the road is otherwise empty, have to be used with the greatest circumspection and unremitting care when there are other cars to be met or overtaken.

Now, to return more specifically to Canada: every effort is patently being made to reduce the dangers I have mentioned, for these dangers are as obvious to every one else as they were to a mere visitor like myself. Likewise, the official route numbers and road safety notices are well placed, and confusing advertisements are not for the most part allowed to conflict with them. Huge black and white chequered boards, visible a long way off, call attention to dangerous corners. White posts outline more gradual, banked bends. Every crest without exception is marked: "Do not pass on hill." And such notices are properly placed several yards short of the actual crest. Where a section of pavement is held to be particularly treacherous, there is a notice: "Pavement slippery in rain," or words to that effect. The forethought displayed is most impressive.

In a similar way, villages compete for motorists' custom. "Welcome to So and So," is painted on a placard at the entrance to a number of them, and as a driver leaves the other end of the village he is likely to see, "Will Ye No come Back Again?" on another board, or "Good-bye—Please Return." But remarkably enough, much of this is tastefully done and bears little semblance of vulgarity. I would scarcely have believed it possible. Instead of being annoyed, as by a crude advertisement, quite a friendly feeling is engendered in one's mind.

I pulled up at Blenheim for luncheon, where we had some excellent plain food, well served. I had always wanted to try blueberry pie, and did so. It looks luscious, but is rather disappointing. The young man in charge of the service station where we filled up with gasoline started cleaning my windshield at once without being asked. And his colleague, seeing me take a snapshot of an adjacent road sign, produced a photograph of a smash that had recently taken place at the crossroads and began discussing cars with me. He portrayed a keen interest in general road conditions.

Traffic signals in towns farther on again revealed some variation as to system: in some instances, the red light flickers once or twice before changing to green and in others there is an amber warning light such as we have in England. Why, in this age of universal motoring, some intelligent official cannot be allowed to co-ordinate traffic signals throughout Canada, and another Federal official likewise be permitted to achieve unanimity in the various States of America, is not at once apparent. Although districts or States may be responsible for the upkeep of their local roads, surely the system in general should be looked upon as national rather than parochial, and its appurtenances standardised in the interests of public safety and convenience. This is no more nor less than a case for the exercise of common sense.

As I have stated, most Canadian motorists are good at keeping to the right. Their worst fault is that of turning across the road without any signal at all; one has to be constantly on the look-out for this.

I came up with two motor-cyclists, cruising at about sixty miles an hour. Because of their leather jackets and dark blue caps, I suspected them of being police, but was a little surprised at their speed. I hung back, watching. Then, becoming bored, I chanced it and passed them, although with great decorum—a gentle hoot of warning and a wave of acknowledgment as they drew aside. Observing them in my mirror, I was nervous to see them start to pace me. But after two or three miles at seventy, they thought better of it for their engines' sake. Still a little mistrustful, I kept an eye on the driving mirror, and only when I had drawn half a mile ahead did I gradually accelerate and swing up again into the high eighties.

Arriving in Windsor, which is just across the Detroit River from Detroit itself, we had to drive through a tunnel connecting the two towns. This is like a miniature edition of the tunnel under the Hudson between New Jersey and New York. At the other end of it, I again passed through the Customs back into the United States. The official in charge took a good look at me, and asked me where I was born and other leading questions. Upon learning that I was going West, he became exceedingly friendly and interested. Apparently, San Francisco was his home town. He waxed enthusiastic about it, and was kind enough to advise me to wear a light

" . . . just across the Detroit river. . . . Detroit itself. . . ."

overcoat there in the evenings when the temperature shows a sudden drop.

In Detroit, I learned that the speed limit is strictly enforced. Still, the chief traffic judge possesses a great sense of fairness towards motorists. He holds the sensible view that too much harassing of drivers by the police induces a general state of nerves that is probably responsible for accidents.

The chimes from the Chicago Fair of 1934 were housed in a building close to the Detroit Athletic Club, where I was a grateful guest. I could see the belfry from my bedroom window. It amused me next morning to hear suddenly ringing out, *The Bluebells of Scotland.*

CHAPTER III

A HUSTLE IN THE CAPITAL OF CARS

IT WAS SUNDAY EVENING WHEN I ARRIVED IN DETROIT. TWO coloured bell-boys shouldered my kitbags and conducted me upstairs to a charming corner suite, consisting of bedroom, bathroom and sitting-room—all opening out of a miniature hall, which the renowned hospitality of the Club had caused to be placed at my disposal. Louis Skinitzero, who lived in the city, went home with the car; he was going to have it washed and would pick me up at eight-thirty to go and dine somewhere.

Meanwhile, I had a call to pay. One of my friends in New York, whose judgment I trust and whose wishes a host of admirers make strenuous efforts to obey, had enjoined me not to leave Detroit without paying my respects to a much-loved person living at Grosse Point Farms, a fashionable residential section nearby.

With inward misgivings, because calling on strangers is not my line at all, I duly telephoned. But somehow, the forthcoming ordeal did not seem nearly so bad when I had heard my hostess's reply. Her voice is adored by all who know her. I hung up the receiver much comforted, indeed delighted, and immediately lifted it again to summon a valet. He came—a delightful person, tall and grey-haired.

"Good-evening," said I, rummaging among my luggage, "I'm going out as soon as I can. Will you please press this suit?" I straightened up and threw it across to him.

"Good-evening, sir, certainly, sir," he replied. He appeared somewhat startled but caught the garments full pitch.

I bobbed down again and reappeared with an evening shoe in either hand.

"And these," I suggested, holding them up.

He hastily laid the suit over one arm and adopted a stiff version of the fielding attitude.

"Of course, sir," he murmured, catching first one shoe and then the other. "I'll see the boy shines them at once, sir."

Smiling politely, he departed, possibly as uncertain of my sanity as he was convinced of my nationality. Incidentally, he looked English himself and would certainly have made a good cricketer. Or perhaps it was baseball which had taught him to catch so well. Anyway, I had no time to find out: my immediate objectives were a bath and a highball.

It was now dusk. An hour later, I was on my way to Grosse Point Farms in a Ford taxi. The drive took half an hour, for Detroit and its environs cover a huge area forty miles across at its widest part; or so I understood. Through the open dividing window, I talked to the driver—a nice person. We discussed cars. He liked the Ford because of its short wheelbase and great acceleration, the combination making for unusual handiness. But his heart was with a Plymouth he had driven at one time.

"Always the same," he observed, "day in and day out. YES, SIR! Never gave any trouble and always ready to do anything. Ah, she was a honey."

She sounded to me more like the perfect wife.

Parenthetically, in our interchange of thought on things purely mechanical, he opined that Roosevelt would get in again at the next election because the masses felt they were going to get something, sometime, at the hands of a man who was so well-intentioned towards them (though he himself, a bit of a conservative thinker, viewed the National Debt as a thundercloud), and that Joe Louis, the "brown bomber" from the coloured quarter of Detroit, would be a good bet to win against Max Baer in the heavy-weight contest at New York the night after next.

He stopped his taxi in a quiet road lined with trees. Getting out, I saw the dim outline of a house with a light shining in welcome though the glass door leading into the hall.

"Please wait for me," I said over my shoulder, and made my way up the path.

It was peaceful here by contrast with the commercial centre of the city. Only the crickets chirped unseen all round, and the evening airs sighed through the branches of the dark conifers. Behind me, the engine of the Ford sobbed itself into silence.

I rang. Here, as outside most American houses, a wire, fly-proof door guarded the front door proper, which is left open all through the warm weather.

My hostess, herself, answered the bell. A skirt of plain tweed with a jacket of a check pattern perfectly suited her fair good looks. For a brief matter of seconds, we studied one another, both great friends of the same friend. She held out her hand.

"Do come in," she said, in that quiet, fascinating voice, "I've heard about you and I feel I know you quite well."

This was the high-spot of a prearranged meeting which, apart from the individual charm it held for me, I have described at some length, because in essence it is typical of the behaviour of the "New World," as America, history aside, is not inaccurately called; where a friend of Jack's is a friend of Jill's for Jack's sake and is treated as such, irrespective of personal qualities, until he or she has found a footing and can be reassessed as an individual; and where hospitality, in common with many other terms such as education, amenity, democracy, building, monument, motion picture, airplane, radio, heating, entertainment, automobile, plumbing, etc., nearly always bear a wider interpretation than the one still commonly obtaining

108

in much of Western Europe. If such interpretation can be called an advance (as I think) then to reach those new standards Dame Europe must kilt her draperies and start to " go places."

On my way back to the Detroit Athletic Club, I noticed a vacant building site on a corner. The empty space was utilised as an open garage, and an electric sign blazed bluely above it: " Hudson's Parking Lot. 15 cents. Lock your car." It seems as good a way as any of using ground that otherwise would be more of an eyesore than it is. A number of such spaces exist in most American cities and are badly needed.

That night, I dined with Louis and his wife at a restaurant. The place was of similar stamp to our Trocadero in Shaftesbury Avenue. A vociferous crowd, comprising all sorts, packed it to the doors.

" Lot o' people for Sunday night," I remarked, unthinking.

Mrs. Skinitzero put me right. " No, it's customary," she replied. " Most every one's maid goes out Sunday nights. So they go out, too, and have an extra special meal and maybe meet their friends."

I thought of the thousands of my countrymen and country-women whom usually nothing but battle, murder and sudden death would remove from their homely Sunday supper, maid or no maid, although many of them go afterwards to the pictures. But different days make different ways, and the whole timing of life in Detroit is at variance from, say, life in Birmingham. In the circumstances, the cheery Sunday " night out" seemed to me an excellent plan. Every one appeared to be thoroughly enjoying themselves—a healthily wise antidote to a week of specialised and often monotonous labour. The large majority were patently hard-working, good-natured, responsible and respectable citizens, and doubtless their serious-minded acceptance, in quiet moments, of the natural and economic facts of life would keep them so throughout a troubled existence such as we all have to face. I rejoiced to see

109

that sanctimoniousness, which at one and the same time used to be thought necessary to the conduct of the good while effectually camouflaging for them such trifles as slums, sweated labour and slavery under the guise of necessary punishments for the less good, was as entirely absent here as it is fast becoming in more hide-bound communities where unreal holiness and a hard hat on the seventh day is slowly being recognised, even among the crabbed, as not so effective a passport for eternity as humane living and work well done on each of the previous six.

The Skinitzeros gave me a slap-up dinner, during which we, too, found a lot to laugh at and be vociferous about. Then we drove off to call on Glenn Mooney, the General Sales Manager of the Chrysler Export Corporation, and Mrs. Mooney, with whom I discussed my forthcoming drive to California. Once again, in this pleasant home, where we moderated our amusement so as not to awaken the children upstairs, I was made to feel myself no stranger but some one whose coming had been awaited with genuine pleasure. British visitors to America must often anxiously wonder whether they have succeeded in living up to the standard expected of them. It is as humbling a thought for the individual as it should be a source of pride to the Empire.

Next morning, after writing letters of thanks to a number of kind people in New York, I was driven by Louis to the Chrysler executive offices. These, with the engineering experimental department, are situated beyond a residential district and right away from the respective Chrysler, Plymouth, Dodge and de Soto plants which comprise the Combine.

I was first of all shown the conference room, which happened to be unoccupied at the time. It reminded me of the largest of the old B.B.C. studios at Savoy Hill, where, some years ago, I gave one of a series of broadcasts. Here, as there, the walls were hung with sound-proof draperies (in this instance, the old-fashioned method was obviously used because the whole structure was not permanent). It had no windows and was air-conditioned. A motion picture projector stood at one end, faced by its screen at the other. On a table in a corner was a battery of telephones—special lines to England and to other important centres in the world.

We passed on into a chief executive's office. Its owner, wearing a waistcoat in addition to his coat, looked cool and fit. Yet, the windows were closed and the radiator turned on despite the bright September sunshine outside. Myself, I couldn't have worked in such a temperature for love or money; I would have been a victim to spontaneous combustion.

Then I met and talked with Ledyard Mitchell, Chairman of the Board of the Export Corporation and Vice-President of the parent Combine, and with the President of the Export Corporation. I was to meet Mitchell again in New York, when he returned from England, whither he was going next day, and when I had gone east again from California. After further introductions of an equally pleasant nature, I was invited upstairs to luncheon. To reach the elevators, we had to cross the main office, hundreds of feet long. Here, rows of clerks, now at their midday meal, normally sat at rows of desks equally spaced one from the other, stretching in lines into the distance so that those farthest away appeared quite small. The efficient ordering of this office alone would be no mean feat of internal organisation. Later, I saw it in full blast.

As in many other aspects of American life and its activities, I noticed at once a different *tempo* here, a quicker one, rather tiring to strangers until they learn not to be constantly giving way to it but to keep a reasonable proportion of mental and physical energies in reserve.

There is an obtrusive impression in these places of a system complete in every detail, although constantly under critical observation for purposes of possible revision. Otherwise, of course, it would not be progressive. And progress is the keynote of all large American businesses. An iron routine prevails from which even high executives cannot normally depart. With great appreciation, I discovered that it was being varied in one or two ways for me. For instance, I was shown the first hand-made examples of the 1936 models, most jealously guarded; and my car was specially checked over by the experimental engineering department instead of the service department. This was because I was going to have a talk with the chief experimental engineer about its character, and also because five special tyres were about to be fitted in view of the unusually hard and fast driving that I intended to do during my long zigzag course to the Pacific Coast. Even then, the car seemed to be more or less smuggled into the engineering department in an informal roundabout fashion. Nobody seemed quite to know where it was, so nobody's feelings were hurt. And no one had *definite* knowledge of the routine being interrupted in any way. True, there were one or two smiling faces and a general impression that the experimental department had some excellent reason for being interested in one specific car: but there the matter charmingly ended.

We had luncheon in the chief executive's private dining-room. The chairs were as comfortable to sit upon as those in the most exclusive hotels in the capitals of Europe. In the middle of the room was a long "family" table where Mr. Chrysler, on his visits, sits among the younger men and listens to their gossip and shares their fun. During our meal, I had a long talk with Glenn Mooney, a widely travelled, tolerant and acute observer, about the welfare and particularly the education of those who work in the factories of powerful corporations. I enlarged upon my pet theory that it is impossible to do too much, by means of a bureau, to encourage the operatives to visit a different place every year for their vacation so far as their means will allow; and that it is the best sort of national investment to show them films and lend them books dealing truthfully with the life and habits of other nations—both gestures having the object of broadening their minds as private individuals. For upon the increasing breadth of mind of the bulk of the world's present population and its children and grandchildren, depends the future stability of civilisation; more so, eventually, than civilisation now depends upon the actions of any elected body or bodies, composed only of statesmen and politicians who on a poll-counting basis are not always by any means representative of their country's best thoughts. I met with a considerable measure of agreement upon the principles underlying this idea, which of course is by no means new. At any rate, it served to introduce a prolonged and most interesting discussion.

When we rose from the table, I was not sorry to hear that the Experimental Engineering Department was our next port of call, for to get there meant going out of doors and I was finding the steam heat excessive for my liking. The short walk in the mild sunshine, from one block of offices to another, was a relief. There with the chief experimental engineer, A. B. Couture, known as Toby, I talked technicalities, performance and road-testing: we were at it as hard as we could go for three-quarters of an hour. About the "Airflow" car, I put forward various points noted during my drive from New York. It was interesting to find four of my nine suggestions already incorporated in the new model which I was afterwards taken to see. And of the remaining five, it was agreed that a further four would improve the car from a technical point of view, but could not be incorporated on the ground of keeping the price severely competitive. Only one suggestion was vetoed, and quite rightly, for it was due to a misconception on my part.

This is typical of the way in which honest criticism is welcomed in America. The chief experimental engineer obviously knew more of his special subject than I am ever likely to know. Yet, he was prepared both to listen and explain, and in some instances to agree. He subsequently dashed off to catch the New York plane in order to see the fight between Max Baer and Joe Louis. That rapid American *tempo* again! He never misses a good fight if he can help it, provided it is within easy flying range. But his hobby, he told me, is hunting —we divide it into two sections in the British Isles, calling one shooting, the other stalking—and he is never so happy as when in the woods with a gun in his hand. Incidentally, Toby Couture was the adviser who insisted that I must visit Carlsbad Caverns in New Mexico. I shall always be grateful to him for this. "If you're anywhere within four hundred miles of them, you must surely go," he enthused. Which also serves to show how casually Americans to-day regard distances when motoring.

That night, I dined peacefully off *consommé* and frogs' legs in the club grill-room, while reading the last-day ballyhoo on the forthcoming fight: Max Baer, who later got a hiding, was perhaps unfairly quoted as being loudly and over-whelmingly boastful. Joe Louis, who administered the hiding with imperturbable efficiency an hour or two after being married, and an hour or two later started his honeymoon, was reported to be issuing brief conservative predictions as relentlessly confident as his own body punches proved demoralising.

Next day, the Plymouth Corporation kindly conducted me on a tour of its plant. It is the biggest in the world to be accommodated all on one floor. The maximum output is 2,500 cars a day. No stores are carried in the plant except a reserve of engines and a few bodies. Everything else comes in day by day in exact quantities as it is needed. Because the engines take longest to build and so might hold up the general assembly of complete cars, the engine department works incessantly in three eight-hour shifts; and keeps a surplus of units in hand. The small store of bodies is maintained because on one occasion a truck load of them became held up for some reason on its way to the plant, and a delay of a quarter of an hour took place in the working of the main assembly line. Those fifteen minutes were computed to have cost six hundred dollars.

Automatic machines containing candy and chocolate are situated at intervals throughout the factory. There are also canteens where fresh fruit—oranges, apples, large juicy peaches and pears—can be obtained. Long trains of lunch trucks go through the plant at the appropriate time, so that the men need not move from their positions unless they wish to do so. Needless to say, all these delicacies are sold at prices well within the means of those who work in the plant. The proceeds go to the Corporation's welfare organisation and are distributed among those of its employees who need assistance on account of illness or some other misfortune.

Everywhere, there is the impression of terrific forethought. Every one is striving to improve the general layout in any way in which it is capable of improvement. The general manager, although so close to it all and having watched it grow, is still as excited about it as a schoolboy. In America, indeed, the motor industry has developed to an extent quite unknown anywhere else, yet its continual growth is still capable of arousing enthusiasm in the minds of those associated with it. This in itself, as a feature of what is sometimes thought to be soulless mechanism, constitutes something of a phenomenon, all the more strange when one considers the unromantic attitude of the consumer. Consequently, it is of some value briefly to note the general tendencies combining to produce this result.

The first thing we have to recognise as manufacturers and consumers—and it is important to do so, for the same situation now increasingly obtains in England—is that motoring for motoring's sake is a perquisite of the few and becomes a perquisite of the many only when they take their vacations. Even then, I doubt whether many Americans enjoy driving *qua* driving. True, they go out in their cars in hundreds of thousands at week-ends, but travelling on four wheels is to the vast majority of them merely a means of transportation; there is rarely to be noticed any joy or interest in the actual control of the automobile.

Transportation, in fact, is the term used in the States in preference to motoring. People do not talk about economical motoring, but about cheap transportation. In that fine but definite distinction lies the psychological difference between the ownership of a car in Europe and in America—a difference which is fast disappearing in favour of the American conception.

All this has been said before, but like most generalities it needs some concrete example to bring it home to those who are not able to witness it. Take this one: I was talking a few months ago to the aircraft manufacturer who at that time had more orders on his books than, I believe, any other maker of aeroplanes in the world. They amounted to $9,000,000. Not long before, he had moved from his old factory at Buffalo in New York State to a new one near San Diego in California, and took with him about two hundred and ninety of his most valuable picked operatives and their families. The interesting point is that practically all these men drove their own cars across the continent of America to their new home. They certainly received financial assistance on a scale which my own recent experience of the journey shows was generous; it was a sliding scale—allowing for a single man, a man and his wife, or a man and his family. Nevertheless, a mass migration of this sort over the lengthy highways of the United States is a striking manifestation of the complete establishment of cheap motor transportation and emphasizes the fact that the railways, which have also to face increasing competition by airlines for first-class traffic, must now radically change their own ideas of the function they exist to perform in the economic life of the nation. True, these aeronautical engineering operatives would similarly have received financial assistance had they travelled by train, but it would have cost their employer *more*. I know of many of America's normal working folk who have not been in a train for years!

Our transportation problems in England are obviously somewhat different. Our distances are so short. For instance, I remember leaving London one night about ten minutes past eleven and, after 16 hours and 22 minutes driving, with three hours extra for meals and fill-ups, sitting down washed and changed to a comfortable dinner next day at a house a few miles short of Wick in Caithness. This was roughly a hundred miles short of the length of the whole main island of England and Scotland. The train, with its stops and a change, takes three hours longer, and my fare and payments for meals would have totalled more than my motoring expenses, even including a car depreciation charge. Likewise, I could have flown any decent, really up-to-date plane there in, say, four and a half hours, granted reasonable weather.

By contrast, I drove, across the States, a daily average distance which would have taken me from London well into the highlands of Scotland without seeming to "get any place"—as our American cousins would put it. It is, therefore, because of the very smallness of Great Britain and the fast increasing congestion of its transportation systems, that we should not neglect to take what advantage we can of the trials, errors and successes of a country like America, which has room to experiment and has done so, in order that we may seek evenly to dispose the burdens imposed upon road, rail and air transport while at the same time striving to preserve as far as possible the liberty of the individual to travel or send goods by whatever method he pleases. Naturally, though perhaps unconsciously, we have already faced the inevitable fact that for various modern economic reasons this latter privilege will never be available again in full measure to any of us. But that transportation on a national scale may be so guided as to combine the necessary degree of efficiency with a reasonable freedom of action, is the bounden duty of those who scheme for the future.

The American attitude towards motoring is plainly revealed in various other ways. At all big hotels—and by big, I do not mean necessarily expensive—there are one or more car-park attendants well used to the safe and proper handling of all makes of cars. At such a place, one never thinks of parking one's own car; a door-keeper merely calls by telephone or loud-speaker for one of these attendants to remove it. Many motorists in England take such personal interest in their cars that to allow complete strangers to drive them away and pack them in among a crowd of others would horrify them. Again, an American, parking his own car in a space between two others drawn up nose to tail along the sidewalk, will think nothing of placing one or other of his bumper bars against the corresponding one on the car in front or behind his own and sturdily pushing it a couple of feet in order to make room for himself. And provided it is carefully done, the owners of the other cars do not object. They could not, for they themselves frequently do it.

Another point: while I was walking round this same Plymouth plant—incidentally, it possesses the best laid down engine assembly line which I have ever seen—I learned that the Corporation's advance orders for 1936 models amounted to no less than 55,000. Put another way, this meant that the dealers were assured of 55,000 American motorists coming into their showrooms to conclude the purchase of a car that they had never seen; the latter were content, as we would say, to take a new Plymouth "off the peg." Except superficially, they were not interested, as would be the majority of English motorists, in the particular features of these new cars, preliminary models of which were afterwards kindly shown to me in confidence. They were just buying inexpensive transportation. That they had such confidence in Plymouth products as to do this is, of course, a tribute to the Corporation. But it is really beside the point. What should interest us is the matter-of-fact way in which the bulk of cars are bought in America, for the same thing occurs in the case of other big plants turning out automobiles which are also soundly designed, made and priced.

The preceding examples, chosen at random, serve to emphasize the distinction between motoring and car transportation.

Added, of course, to this nation-wide road transportation consciousness, and partly responsible for it, is the deadly insistence of American motor manufacturers upon supplying a vehicle as entirely suitable as they can make it to the needs of their home *and* export publics. In fact, they go further. Some of them make a definite attempt, easily recognisable as such, to educate the public about the type of vehicle it should drive. I am not now referring to the advertisements of individual companies, but to the general trend of automobile design in America.

Naturally, the manufacturers cannot go too far or too fast in this respect. Limits are set to annual design alike by their clients' psychological reactions and the depth of their pockets. Pockets are the reason why all merchants are critics of economic conditions. They cannot afford to be either idealists nor philanthropists, but are business men out to make money.

Consequently, when all is said and done, their final gesture in respect of the introduction of any new device or series of devices is a bow of acquiescence to public opinion. That they do, nevertheless, mould that opinion, cleverly and almost imperceptibly, is proved by the huge advance orders increasingly obtained by them. During my visit, I only discovered one instance of a retrograde step being taken in design, which was in respect of independent front wheel suspension. This, after being introduced and expensively advertised, was subsequently abandoned by certain makers on the grounds of maintaining a competitive sales price; which is naturally a norm of paramount importance in the composition of any series of mechanical features into one final, appropriate saleable article. I found out that this logical and much needed development in springing was temporarily abandoned by those manufacturers with great regret, for they knew it to be right. They said they thought it would come again, but, so far as the public was concerned, gave it as their opinion that the average motorist might not know, unless he was told, whether his car had independently sprung wheels as such; nor would he care, being solely concerned with the riding effect of them.

Yet, considerable trouble is taken to ascertain mob opinion in a non-technical way. Questionnaires are sent out to hundreds of thousands, and a surprisingly large percentage of them come back. Like all such devices, this is a clever exploitation of the individual's vanity, by flattering it. Still, it serves a quite useful purpose. A particular criticism or piece of praise, or a demand for some specific feature, will often be found to be running through a large proportion of the replies. In a number of instances there are really caustic remarks; not so much professional criticism directed at definite points, as amateur fault-finding related to the everyday behaviour of the car as a whole.

And these are as welcome, possibly more welcome, than any others.

Manufacturers in America recognise that honest straightforward criticism is one of the most valuable aids to the enlargement of their business. Moreover, they pay attention to it—and do so quickly. We, I fear, seldom invite such criticism, and are apt to feel that any is misplaced. Consequently, when we get criticism, we frequently do not believe it; and if we do, act upon it only after repetition. I have always felt this to be a weakness of our own motor industry at home and one of the main reasons holding us back from full enjoyment of our colonial markets. And most of our competitors agree with such a view, although admiring our actual workmanship.

In America, the person most welcomed is the frank but polite critic. It is recognised that he or she may often be wrong, but that among the wrong criticisms there may be one that is right. If there is, it will instantly be seized upon and turned to advantage.

If I were asked to prognosticate the next striking trend in American automobile design, I would plump for independent springing of all four wheels and the engine at the back. No one actually told me this, but it has been obvious for a considerable time to students of automobilism, especially in Germany, where more original work has recently been done than anywhere else in Europe. Also, by talking with a bland expression of innocence to various manufacturers about my experiences with front wheel drive racing cars and independent front wheel springing ten years ago, and leading up to more recent trials of various European chassis including the eight cylinder rear-engined Tatra, I was able to draw my own conclusions. I was met with a display of acute interest, obviously genuine, or with innocence no less phenomenal than my own. Both I took to mean the same thing portrayed in different ways: a game of mental hide and seek, by which we were all amused and none of us deceived. American manufacturers having the estimable habit (only notably shared in this country by one or two firms) of not placing a car on the market until its experimental stage is thoroughly finished, the adoption of these two revolutionary features should be purely a matter of time. And I do not think it will be a long time—two years perhaps, in the case of the suspension, and five in the case of the engine. Only competitive cost may delay the former, and public reaction the latter.

One great problem of distribution, and therefore (working backwards) of production, confronts automobile manufacturers the world over: what to do with "used cars?"

It obviously affects us, too, as individual motorists. But what is more important is the threat of its culminating effect upon any individual Motor Manufacturing Industry, upon the finance of that industry, upon the wages paid by that industry, upon the steady employment provided by that industry, and so upon us as citizens.

In English traders' showrooms there are literally thousands of used cars (in America, thousands upon thousands) absorbing capital on the part exchange basis. A well-known midland dealer states that he usually has 200 such cars in stock and writes them down in value by £1000 a month, i.e. £12,000 a year. A big London dealer may well have up to 700 used cars in stock. They increase his overhead charges by reason of the space for storing them and the staff to handle them, reduce his working capital enormously while they remain unsold and cut his legitimate profit to ribbons when they are sold.

This constriction is like that of a python—a steadily tightening coil of machines taken in part payment and therefore appearing in the accounts as stock standing at a certain figure. It curtails the acceptance of new stock.

It threatens to slow down production in the plants, to stop the drills spinning, the lathes turning, the great presses closing. Here, the problem is not yet quite so grave as in America, but we should take warning from the experience of that huge car-owning community and get quickly off the mark with some well founded scheme of co-operation between manufacturer and retailer before the situation becomes too grave—even more acute than at present.

We must take the broad view, and remember that upon dealers' prosperity depends distribution, upon distribution depends production, upon production depends employment, and upon manufacturers' profits should depend a progressive improvement in the workers' wages and standard of living. This must be our view as citizens, caring for the nation's weal and each other's welfare.

It is estimated that dealers in England have about £20,000,000 worth of used cars on their hands. If that figure is not sufficiently startling, look at the plight of America. There, observers contend that 8,000,000 second-hand cars will probably be handled this year.[1] Watch how devastatingly quickly the evil grows: in 1934 the distribution of 2,292,443 new cars and trucks called for the handling and selling of 3,851,304 used cars; in 1935, it is asserted, the estimated distribution of 3,251,468 new cars and trucks was wrapped up with dealing in approximately 5,362,922 used cars. Is it any wonder that probably not half the dealers made a gross profit and still fewer a net profit?

Waking up late to this crisis, or perhaps being caught unawares by the very speed of its arrival, one or two of the big automobile manufacturing corporations in the States jumped in to help their dealers with an offer of a $20 bonus for every old car definitely destroyed; while dealers themselves, in an endeavour to " move" their used cars, offered purchasers

[1] 1936

of them twelve months' credit, free insurance and a waiving of finance charges. Now the American National Automobile Dealers' Association are seeking to stabilise a gross profit of 20 per cent in their used car markets, and to assess the value of each vehicle at the price allowed for it in part exchange, plus the cost of repairs, plus the cost of handling and selling —these figures to be certified by accountants. To this scheme the Association invites the manufacturers' approval, and hopes that the latter will appoint as official distributors of their products only such dealers as subscribe to it.

The value of the scheme lies not so much in its details, which would be variable according to our local conditions, but in the co-ordination of effort that it portends on behalf of maker and retailer. While manufacturers have reason to rub their hands with satisfaction over enormously increased orders here and elsewhere, that satisfaction is assured of being eventually translated into gloom if the unhappy retailer is not in some way assisted over this formidable stile. For a rich maker of cars to say, even if he could, "Very well, I'll sell my own products," would merely mean the setting up of an appallingly expensive, Empire-wide circle of depots and the transference to himself of this incubus.

No! Co-operation between maker and retailer in the used car market is essential to the further, sound development of what is one of the greatest of our National industries —one that now we are really trying to take to heart certain lessons taught us by those overseas, must inevitably (if we furiously maintain the effort, spurn self-satisfaction and welcome criticism) become an Empire industry. Moreover, a public assured of manufacturer-supported dealers, i.e. those financially able properly to recondition used cars for sale, is a confident public.

After leaving the Plymouth plant, I was most delightfully entertained at tea by Mr. Hughes Hallett, the British Consul, and Mrs. Hughes Hallett, whose hospitable house opens its doors widely to hundreds of American friends as well as to English men and women visiting the city. I greatly admired there a fine collection of rugs, strewn in orderly profusion about the floors of the spacious rooms and glowing richly wherever, through the tall windows, a shaft of late afternoon sunlight warmed them into life. At the far end of a small walled garden at the back, which I would have liked to see in Summer, the previous occupant of the house had built a garage for no less than seven cars, and over it a ballroom. "A truly remarkable combination," remarked Hughes Hallett dryly. But his daughter found the ballroom useful for fencing practice.

Dining that night in a restaurant with the Mooneys, I heard an account of the Baer v. Louis fight coming over the radio, round by round. Except during the intervals, there was silence but for the announcer's dramatic torrent of short sentences: "Louis leads with his left—lands. Baer counters with his right, wildly; he misses. They're in a clinch. Louis is attacking: a rain of short-arm blows to the body. Baer is smiling but Louis has hurt him. They break. Baer leads. Louis blocks it. Now Louis leads—once, twice with his left. Louis is going in. He never smiles; he is quite expressionless. They're in a clinch again. The referee is separating them."

At the conclusion of every round, a buzz of conversation filled the room. Like ourselves, the occupants of each table discussed the respective qualities of the two men, and gave their views or argued with one another. Presently it was given out that Louis had won. The tension relaxed. The scene in the restaurant reverted to normal. We went on more peacefully with our meal, and chatted of other things.

Coloured waiters were serving at our table, men who probably knew Joe Louis, a fighter from their community.

Their self-control won my admiration. At the time, not a flicker of feeling showed in their dark faces, but in the Negro quarter of the city there was naturally tremendous rejoicing. Dancing took place on the sidewalks, and cars with shouting, singing enthusiasts on their roofs blocked the streets until a late hour.   Likewise, the coloured elevator girl at the club, who took me up to my bedroom on the second floor, told me that she was quite tired when the broadcast was over; she felt she had been fighting every round as she heard it. It was an amusing climax to my visit.

Next day I was to take to the road again, driving south-west towards Fort Wayne.

CHAPTER IV

ACROSS INDIANA INTO ILLINOIS

MY DEPARTURE IN THE MORNING FROM THE DETROIT ATHLETIC Club was a little film starish. I had agreed to be photographed for the Chrysler Corporation's house organ or journal, and Louis Skinitzero said the editor himself was coming to see that the operation was as painless as possible. So well did the plan succeed that the first shot, in fact, passed unnoticed. The quarry (myself) was smoking an after breakfast pipe on a seat outside the club when first sighted, a passive, undisturbed figure, thinking no evil. Fire was opened almost immediately from a sheltered position, apparently somewhere on the other side of the porch. True, I had seen two men arrive with a couple of cameras and thought to the English self of my American friends' conception, "Oh, lor', these-er must be the two fellows, what!" and simultaneously to my new-born American self, "Boy, this is the works." But I knew they didn't know me by sight; my clothes at that moment were not such as would betray me; and, banking on the most obvious place affording the best cover, I reckoned I could sit there doggo until Louis turned up with the car.

Not so. A reconnaissance must have been carried out in the hall, information sought and an advance made to a forward observation post whence the animal could be seen, placidly digesting its breakfast and contentedly blowing smoke through its nostrils. Thus the first phase of the attack was concluded, the basic principle of surprise being fully exploited.

Soon things really started to happen. Mrs. Skinitzero

arrived. With pleasure I bade her good-morning, and was promptly photographed. By now, of course, I was alive to my unprotected situation. Louis appeared with the car. Buttoning up my dust-coat, I bade him, also, good-morning, and was promptly photographed again. Thereafter, cameras clicked like gangsters' sub-machine guns. I was shot next to Louis and away from Louis; and entering the car, and by, with and and from the car. The next issue of the *Chrysler Chronicle*, *Plymouth Pictorial*, *Dodge Declaimer* or *De Soto What-ho* was in danger, I imagined, of being stiff with my portraits. Nothing more was needed, I felt, than a bouquet of red, red roses to clasp to my bosom while I told an interested world what brand of tooth-paste was my favourite and scribbled my autograph for the coloured bell-boys on their clean white collars.

This was undoubtedly "the works." No one was more amused than the editor of the Chrysler journal; no one could have been nicer in the circumstances. Being photographed years ago in this or that racing car, at this or that horse-show or wedding in far-away England, was nothing to it. That morning I had got as near as I ever will to being a motion picture hero. At length, Louis looked at his watch and told me where I got off. Then we disappeared into the car—and both got off.

To drive out of Detroit is as tiresome as it is nowadays to emerge by road from any city, particularly large American cities whose outskirts, although more pleasant as a rule than the corresponding fringes of many European towns, are nevertheless subject to traffic regulations evolved for the unthinking and so aggravating to those of us who do think. Incessantly, in these days, there is the boredom of watching for such people driving violently out of side roads, STOP sign or not. On the first bit of new road a close look-out had also to be kept for speed cops. One police car was overtaken at a

128

moderate speed, but otherwise there was no sign of them. After a while the town crush dropped away, leaving only the normal main road traffic which I was told would still be considerable for the next two days; in fact, till we began to cross the great stretches of the middle-west.

I drove through what are known as the Irish hills. These are not really hills at all, but just wooded undulating country such as we have at home. At least, that was the impression I obtained from the road. Coming up behind a long-distance bus, I paced it for half a mile and found it to be doing a steady fifty-five to sixty miles an hour. The passengers, whom I reckoned to be about forty in number, sat happily at ease in their seats. From their expressions, I gathered that they considered this pace to be nothing unusual. It is, of course, against the law in England. But an Englishman to whom I talked not long before I left home told me that he and his wife did quite a considerable tour by bus in America in 1934, and found these vehicles to be very well and safely driven. Although they were both nervous motorists, he admitted that they became quite used to such speeds after the first half hour. These big buses carry two spare wheels clamped side by side on the back—the biggest wheels I have ever seen on any vehicle capable of travelling as fast.

We had luncheon in a little town called Coldwater. Seeing chicken pie on the *menu*, I remembered Towanda and its chicken sandwiches, and hoped that this form of chicken would be as good. Alas, it was not. I ate some of it and some cottage cheese salad, which was new to me. Both were quite good, but nothing out of the ordinary. I have since been told of the probability that many such chickens, when alive, might have borne a close resemblance to calves. The waiting woman, too, was not as comely and genial as the Towanda dame. Here was a thin, painted, contemptuous critter.

Then through a dull, flat piece of country I drove into

129

Indiana. The scenery reminded me much of Norfolk, but it had a wilder look; fewer trimmed hedges, the landscape on a larger scale than our eastern county and tinted with warmer colours. But it was after Fort Wayne that Indiana revealed its true soul. From there on, the land piled itself up in sweeping contours interspersed with vineyards bearing great purple bunches of grapes, and softened by wide fields of maize. The harvest was obviously going to be splendid.

Cosy farms stood about on these gentle rises. Most of the houses were white, and the barns and byres a deep maroon. The crickets chirped. The sun shone. And over all were rich lights never seen in our cold northland. For me, Indiana seemed painted with all the deeper colours on the palette; it looked as its name sounds.

After a hundred and fifty miles it flattened out again as we came towards Illinois, and was uninteresting except for the afternoon radiance upon it. Groups of trees stood in the great distances, like tall ships sailing through choppy seas of corn. In the calmer, open patches of grass, cows lazed and munched. The timber fences, set in a ragged herring-bone pattern, consisted of stakes sticking up and out at all angles—one of the oldest types of American fence. But the ground was mostly divided up by strands of wire and posts. The concrete road went on and on, straight but several feet too narrow; its soft shoulders rendered dangerous what would otherwise be one of the finest highways in the world. My best time that day was a half-hour in which I covered thirty-six miles. Yet I had to be more than usually watchful: I was finding that driving a fast car in America is bad for the nerves, but good for the judgment. To motor safely in the United States depends more upon concentration than in any country I know. Cars doing less than fifty miles an hour on a long highway are exceptions; the majority do sixty, many do more. And one has to pass them close, with an eye always on the road edges

"_The concrete road went on and on . . ._"

so that the ground nearby may be occupied quickly if an oncoming driver appears unsteady.

Motorists travel there in queues, as in other countries, and these are caused as usual by the nervous driver at the head of them. Still, except outside big towns, where they are continuous, the queues are not so long as those in England: the considerable stretches of straight road enable bolder drivers to push past and disperse the queue. American motorists are also much better at sticking to their own side of the road than we are. Yet this virtue is almost certainly induced by the fact that if they don't do so they cannot pass each other at all. And it is no uncommon sight to see a whole family driving west, their car covered with baggage fastened on outside; the final touch is often a baby carriage supported on the front bumper bar.

On this particular day, I saw single yellow traffic lights in some of the towns. These are placed at dangerous corners and continually flicker, which constitutes a good warning. I had meant to reach Springfield, Illinois, for the night; but when darkness came on at seven o'clock there were several hundred miles behind the car, so Louis and I decided to call it a day.

The place where we passed the night I shall call "Nutsburg," which is not its real name. The proprietor, large and breathless, presided in a lobby that we would call a bar. This had a plate-glass window like a shop, which faced the street. Clients to the number of two were sitting there in basket-work chairs as I walked in. Their feet rested on a mercifully cold radiator, and they stared ruminatively in the direction of the dark sidewalk. Our arrival apparently provided a welcome topic of conversation. By passing through two successive glass doors, one could gain access to a gloomy dining-room, also with a window like a shop. Between the two glass doors, wide stairs ran upwards. The dining-room also had a counter at which coffee and soft drinks could be obtained and various groceries purchased. Stuck up among the shelves of groceries were such notices as these: "It's not what you pay, it's what you get for your money." "This business is home-owned. Nobody can please everybody, but we try." "If you don't see what you want, ask for it." Hungry as we were, anything sounded good. "Cream o' tomater" soup arrived—large bowls of it. This was fine; it came out of a tin. We had also ordered steaks. But when these appeared they looked like two halves of a cow covered with bread-crumbs, and were as tough as a pair of boots. I took the least stalwart portions out of mine, a mouthful or two, and fell back on cheese. The beer was all right—light draught stuff. A pint went down like nothing.

The entire place was drab, the smells various, but on the whole it was clean. My room boasted a hard double bed, two small floppy pillows, a stained pine table, no pictures, a horse-hair rocking-chair, and a large Bible advertising some holy society on its cover. It was an insufferably close night, and I foolishly took a bottle of lemonade up to my room to put by my bedside. A light on the landing outside shone in disturbing fashion through a fanlight above the door, so I emerged in my pyjamas and put it out. There was another some yards off, sufficient to illuminate the passage. Then, for what seemed years, I lay drowsing and feverish, half dreaming a silly dream about being caught snow-balling in a pompous *pension* hotel for retired army officers. A ridiculous phantasy! From time to time I drank lemonade, which only increased my thirst.

The railway ran immediately behind the hotel. A train suddenly passing at speed a few feet away seemed literally to be entering the room. Only a belated sense of dignity prevented me from leaving the room at equal speed. The light outside the door came on again. I waited, emerged, and put it out. As I opened the door, a bundle of wire coat-hangers on a hook behind it jangled like a demented banjo.

If anything, the night grew stuffier. I removed my pyjama jacket and lay down once more, to toss miserably on the bed, utterly sleepless and tortured by thirst. At two forty-five the light came on for the third time. Unthinking and furious, I instantly made a sortie, stripped to the waist and looking like an angry boxer, to find myself confronting a mild, grey-haired old lady fully dressed in black silk.

"I beg your pardon," said I and bolted, soon reappearing more suitably clad in a dressing-gown.

"Er . . . must this light be on?" I asked in a wheedling voice.

"Well, you see," she said gently, "if it isn't, folks might fall down the stairs."

"But there is another light," I objected, "isn't that enough?"

In truth there were two more lights, one of them being actually at the foot of the stairs. And anyway I wondered why people should wander about at 2.45 a.m.

"I will put on the other one instead," she conceded doubtfully.

I thanked her. "Could I find some water?" I then inquired, producing my empty lemonade bottle.

"There is some in the lobby," she said. "Come with me."

I noticed that the old lady, herself, was carefully carrying a glass which she kept covered with a piece of tissue paper.

"This is a glass of water," she observed suddenly, holding it up.

"Really," I rejoined, astonished. I wondered why it should be so carefully concealed from view. Still, that was a small point. We descended together in a somewhat guilty fashion, the stairs creaking noisily under our weight.

133

"We must be quiet so as not to wake the folks," my companion entreated.

In the lobby she pointed out a water fountain at the far end. I wished I had known of its existence before. As I approached it, a strangled snort split the uneasy silence, and caused me almost to drop my lemonade bottle. Looking round, I discovered the proprietor, fully dressed, and ensconced in a corral of arm-chairs like a bull buffalo in a patch of thorn scrub. He had apparently been asleep.

"Ugh," said he, "dry?"

"Very," said I shortly.

"Ugh," he repeated, and slept again.

I wondered if he ever undressed and went to bed, or if he sat there nightly throughout the year waiting to see that no one surreptitiously left without paying.

Upstairs again, I drank some of the water. In common with the bath water it stank like an inferno, being impregnated with sulphur. Then I took a sleeping draft and slept the unhealthy sleep of the drugged until seven.

After a morning snack we left, determined to breakfast elsewhere. One or two locals came in for coffee at the counter while I was drinking mine. No one spoke, but the spittoons were much in evidence.

This small hotel belonged to the old type, and was dreadful; yet, as a new experience, I was glad to have been there.

CHAPTER V

OVER THE MISSISSIPPI THROUGH MISSOURI

RAIN, RAIN, RAIN. ALL MORNING I DROVE ACROSS A LEVEL and dull part of the State of Illinois. The surrounding country was mostly under cultivation. Occasional lines of trees did something to relieve the complete monotony of it, but the actual road went grimly ahead with a boring insistence on being straight for too long. In the mood of depression induced by such driving conditions, the endless lines of telegraph poles started to annoy me. For hours there was no sun. We heard only a continual swish: the noise of our own wheels in the wet, swollen from time to time by the like sound of cars we met or overtook.

In Springfield, the capital of Illinois, we stopped at the Leland hotel for some chicken sandwiches and coffee. Both were excellent and badly needed: we had had nothing but coffee, hours ago. I also sent off a letter by plane. Posting by air mail has become a widespread habit in the United States. The charge is only double that for a letter sent in the old way; and a huge number of people, if not yet the majority, think now only in terms of the air where this essential service is concerned.

As I came out of the Leland, I was overjoyed to see the rain had stopped. Driving away from the hotel at noon, I was in Kansas City, a further 332 miles away, at twenty minutes to eight in the evening—not taking into account in this period the gain of an hour by moving from east to west. Still, it was to prove a hard day's driving. After my disturbed night

135

in that unbelievable hotel at "Nutsburg," I certainly did not feel at my best during the morning. But having put some food inside me at the Leland, I got into my stride; and the hours and the miles went happily by.

Springfield, I noticed as I left it, had 71,900 inhabitants. (Information of this kind is put up at the entrance to a great many towns and villages.) This was the biggest place since Detroit. It revealed the usual pleasant residential sections of tasteful wooden houses laid out in rectangular blocks, with the intersecting avenues shaded by trees. Double trolley (tram) tracks ran along the main streets, yet even such streets appeared delightful because of the foliage flanking them. I cannot get over these trees in American towns; they are one of the most delightful features of the whole country.

The road had not yet dried, so my mind returned irritatingly to consideration of the surface. I would have been pleased to think of anything else. Surely, I thought to myself, these roads are built primarily for speedy transportation, or else there is no use for them at all. Why then, in such a progressive country as this, should they not be built or adapted to conform with the conditions most suitable to the efficient and safe use of the modern high-powered motor-car, which, after all is one of the greatest blessings possessed by the citizens of the United States? Whereas the curves on these roads are all well marked and many of them banked, so that there is no excuse for an accident, the long straights, by reason of their narrowness and the hazard of shoulders on either side, seem to me directly to encourage accidents among the thoughtless and headstrong—the types of citizens who can only be to some extent controlled but never, alas, entirely eliminated in any country. Roads, if they are to be truly modern, have to be built with the idea of safeguarding the public from the foolish elements which form part of itself, and will always do so.

136

" And here, a notice board informed me, was the Mississippi—' Ole Man River,' itself."

" Where the houses began . . . a little group of statuary representing Tom Sawyer and Huckleberry Finn."

Studying this road as I drove along it, I felt that that important fact had not yet won, in a practical form, the recognition it deserves.

As far as Jacksonville, and for some way beyond, the country reminded me somewhat of our own Leicestershire; the same grey distances, but none of the neatness of that famous hunting county. Later, there could be noted a gradual but significant alteration in the character of the land; it became more wooded, softer and hilly again. Then, when one had been for some time keyed up to a change of scene, the final revelation came unexpectedly and all in a moment. I pulled up at a toll bridge over which a railway track ran. And here, a notice board informed me, was the Mississippi—"Ole Man River" itself. At this point a bluff covered by a thicket formed the far bank, so that the railway tunnel burrowed into this while the road turned short along its lower face. The yellow water of the river rolls powerfully, ceaselessly, just as the songs about it say it does. There is a sense of quiet might about the Mississippi; and something more, alas, when in flood! Turning left at the end of the bridge, I drove a mile or so down what might have been an English country road. Thus I reached Hannibal, just over the Missouri border, the town immortalised by its association with Mark Twain.

Where the houses began, I stopped after a few yards, for I had caught sight of a little group of statuary representing Tom Sawyer and Huckleberry Finn. This delightful memorial stands at the base of a low hill rising directly from the street. Beside it is a notice board which reads as follows:

"CARDIFF HILL.—This is the foot of Cardiff Hill made famous in Mark Twain's books *Tom Sawyer and Huckleberry Finn*. On the hill, Tom, Huck and their gang played and roamed at will."

There is also a Mark Twain museum in Hannibal, but knowing how many miles I had to cover before night I could not go into it. I didn't mind, for relics have never meant much to me: the general impression of a place is what I have always found essential.

To leave Hannibal, I had to make a short detour because of repairs that were being done to the main road. This sent me climbing out of the town by way of a narrow lane running through lush orchards and quaint little bungalows. But I was soon back on the concrete ribbon and kept to it across some high-lying meadowland for about twenty-five minutes, when fortunately I encountered another section under repair. I say fortunately—because the detour which I had now to make over many miles of rough gravel road, took me through the very heart of the Mark Twain country; in fact through Florida, where he was born. In the middle of this little village, boasting two hundred inhabitants, a bust of the author stands upon a stone plinth. Needless to say, I stopped the car again and got out to look. Whereupon an old man came limping up to me, offering to show the house in which the famous writer (really Sam Clemens by name) was born. But I would not go with him, for I object to seeing things in that way. I would have gone alone, had it been possible, but on no account could I have endured the banalities of a guide. Instead, I just stood there in the street, remembering as much as I could of what I had read as a boy. Then I drove away again.

And now I was glad to be on a lonely side-road with no traffic to absorb my attention. For the whole countryside breathed Mark Twain's name and retold his yarns; the little dales and gentle rises, the tangled undergrowth clothing them, the maize fields, the swamps by the creeks, the cotton-woods. It is a quite unique piece of country, entirely individual in character.

138

In Moberly, the car needed gasoline and oil. The price of gasoline varies considerably as one drives from east to west, and later in this book I will give a table indicating how the price changes. By contrast, oil maintains a pretty constant price level right across America. That day at Moberly, seventeen gallons of petrol cost $2.94, which equals $17\frac{3}{10}$ c. per gallon. It should be remembered that the American gallon consists of four 32-ounce quarts, whereas the Imperial gallon measures four 35-ounce quarts; the difference is one of twelve ounces.

While the tank was being replenished, I went into a neighbouring store to buy a package or two of peppermints, known as "Life Savers," which I like to suck when driving. For a couple of cents I got also a few chocolate peanut clusters to keep me going until dinner.

By now there was the hint again of rain in the sky, yet it never amounted to much. The road West was rather worn macadam incorporating inch stone. Its edges were rough and in some places soft, but there was no drop into sudden shoulders. This, though not appearing so, was a far safer road than any I had driven over that day.

Once more the country was England—the England of Norfolk and Suffolk. Then, by contrast, I came again to woods; the peculiarly soft looking woods that are definitely American. I swung round a curve, found myself facing a long bridge, crossed it, stopped and looked back. This was the Missouri River, broad and peaceful in the dusk. From here onwards the road, which soon became a concrete pavement again, wound through hill and dale country, thickly timbered.

After Lexington it ran for some time beside the Missouri. Night was now falling. The river lay like a smooth belt of silver webbing beneath a lemon sky almost entirely hidden by sombre clouds. A streak like a bloodstain on the western horizon was the only other remaining clue to a sundown which had taken place practically unseen. The first star hung in its place, still, bright, cold looking. A steamer forged steadily upstream; a white, box-like affair, its square windows ablaze with light, its siren hooting. This was the next best thing to "Showboat" come to life for me, and I watched it out of the corner of my eye, fascinated. The skipper seemed to suspect that a girl friend was driving in the car ahead of us, for he kept picking it out with a minia-ture searchlight operated from somewhere for'ard of the steamer's tall smokestack. Every now and then he would sound another cheerful hoot on his siren.

Passing over a succession of little bridges spanning narrow creeks that ran down to the Missouri, I saw the overhead scene mirrored for a moment on their placid surfaces. Miles ahead an aircraft beacon short of Kansas City was flashing its alternate red and white message. Such manifestations continued to show me America, old and young—America as I had often longed to see it. I drank it all in quietly and systematically as the car rolled along. Never shall I forget that particular picture as long as I live. When the road left the river it became just a road again, no longer the fulfilment of a long-cherished dream.

In the dark outskirts of Kansas City I was held up for five minutes at a railway crossing, while a long train of oil tankers moved slowly down the line in the direction of Oklahoma, the beginning of· the oil country. With the train's clanking, I seemed to remember an apparently authori-tative statement to the effect that American petroleum, if exploited at its present rate, will be exhausted in about fifteen years, whereas the British reserves will last for two hundred. And I wondered what truth there was in either estimate, for the problems involved by such a reversal would gravely and in divers ways affect the next generation.

A few minutes later, I was in the middle of the brilliant

lights and high buildings of an up-to-date city, and entered a modern hotel which seemed like Heaven after the one I had slept in the previous night. But the steam heat was fully on, and it was not until I had turned it off and opened every window wide that I started to feel at home. A Bacardi cocktail, the best since New York, completed the process. And just to regain my faith in the possibilities of steak, I decided to dine off one again. I did regain my faith. But, where steaks are concerned, I prefer English cooking—as much as I prefer the American methods of preparing chicken.

CHAPTER VI

FROM KANSAS CITY INTO OKLAHOMA

THE COST OF MY SINGLE ROOM IN THAT GOOD HOTEL IN KANSAS
City was $2.50 for the night, which is not expensive for
such a place. Indeed, I consistently found that rooms in
American hotels are reasonably priced; it is only the meals
that in some instances are charged for at an absurdly high
rate. I refer now to the bigger hotels. In wayside restaurants,
the cost of meals is usually most moderate. And when California is reached, food of all sorts abounds and can be had for
next to nothing; there are no transportation charges over
a distance except in the case of meat. If you buy your own
food and cook it, living becomes very cheap indeed.

The half-lights of morning and evening in modern American towns are nothing if not impressive. Dawn, seen from
my bedroom window in Kansas City, was all I could have
wished. The great buildings, looming opposite like monuments to the industry of man, seemed to stand there in
fearless expectation of the understanding, if not the entire
approbation, of the Godly forces of Nature revealed in the
tender sky. Might not their mute messages be that it is no
good going through this life in more of a funk than one can
help? Which need not be much if the reasoning power we
all have is boldly used, whatever its degree.

I had been called at six-thirty, for we planned a fairly
early start. Having breakfasted, we were actually on the move
by twenty minutes to eight.

The tank was replenished with gasoline and the sump

142

with oil every morning, and the tyre pressures checked. The latter, varied by three or four pounds a day, because of fast driving and the changes in temperature. These chores were done at the first Standard Oil station we came to before leaving the city.

Part of Kansas City is in Missouri and part in the State of Kansas, for the boundary runs through the town. The residential quarter through which I drove on my way out, in a westerly direction, was quite one of the nicest I had yet seen. The lie of the land favoured it, so that dignified and well-built apartment houses, mostly of stone, stood in commanding positions looking down into a shallow valley, the bottom of which was laid out in the form of a public park—a pleasant piece of landscape work. The entire town-planning of this section struck me as excellent.

Once outside the city, I was delighted to find that the road ceased to be a pavement with sharp edges and became again as it had been the previous day, just coarse macadam with gutters that were easy to see. In this respect it was like an English road, and I felt more at home on it; except that it was not as level as the average English road. It had been laid on what looked like a shifting subsoil, with obvious results. In the whole distance that I drove across America —and I didn't by any means travel in a straight line—I found the ideal road, a rough concrete one with low rolling kerbs, only on rare occasions.

I had been warned that the State of Kansas had some of the worst roads in America. After I had been driving for a short time that morning I was prepared to believe it. The particular road that I was on soon deteriorated into a dirt track, along which it was difficult to pick anything like an energetic way. Indeed, in places it was inches deep in mud. Once, striving to avoid what looked like a deep, sticky pool, I ran into another nearly as bad. A shower of muck bespattered the whole car, including the windscreen. I had to stop and clean the latter with a piece of rag soaked in the black water from a puddle. The hand brake, which I had been using alternately with the foot brake in order to save both, was freed only by tugging at it and then accelerating hard in second gear. In this way I burned off the mud, a smelly but efficacious process. Two sparking plugs, thoroughly splashed though they had been with dirty water, soon dried themselves by vaporisation, and the two missing cylinders returned to me. Three inches of rain the previous day accounted for all this mudlarking. I noticed a machine at work scraping off the squelching surface into lines and to some extent rolling-in the remainder of the road again. This, I suppose, is the best that can be done in the circumstances.

I began to look forward to getting back on to one of the big highways. Some of these have attractive names, such as the Lincoln Highway, the Roosevelt Highway, the Santa Fé Trail, and so on; recalling bits of the nation's history which are thus memorised for all time.

The Kansas countryside near Kansas City, itself, is not unlike the agricultural part of Lincolnshire, as distinct from the fens. Farther on, towards Emporia, it achieves a wider aspect still, becoming more like our Salisbury Plain. Where the land is under plough, the soil is seen to be a dark brown colour, fertile but quite different from the rich black of the Mississippi and Missouri valleys.

More and larger woods appeared, as though to deny the simile I was drawing between this district and Salisbury Plain. They proved to be wide and straggling, ending in fringes of short bushy trees scattered like outposts. Between these woods and the downlands which were under cultivation, quantities of mustard grew, rippled by the wind; its yellow bloom looked very beautiful in the bright sunlight. Here, I was well into the south-western corner of the vast drought-stricken area comprising, from north to south, Montana, North Dakota, South Dakota, Minnesota, Wyoming, Nebraska, Kansas and Missouri, from which the good top soil is liable to be blown by the wind for two thousand miles, reaching places as far as Baltimore and Boston. We in England can scarcely grasp what this means. But it is nothing less than stark tragedy. Because in the past too large an area of these high plains was continuously under the plough, even the hillsides as well, and because wind-breaks of trees were cut and natural reservoirs, in the shape of swamps, drained to provide more farming area, Nature has taken charge. The lightly anchored soil is now lifted by the wind in the burning heat of summer, at the rate, some say, of 300 million tons on a certain grim day; and is washed away in the winter floods. Instead of reverting even to the grazing lands they used to be when the Indians ranged them and the pioneers first saw them, such areas are in grave danger of changing to desert. Terracing, damming, gullying, the planting of trees and quickly creeping vegetation, a firm limitation of ploughing, the rotation of crops and the preservation of natural grazing land—these are the desperate measures being taken in the battle of soil conservation, almost the gravest problem now facing a stubbornly courageous people.

At Emporia, a stop was made for coffee and scrambled eggs. Leaving again just after noon, I did a further three hundred miles by nightfall, which included two wayside stops for gasoline and one at Enid for coffee and hamburger sandwiches with melted cheese. The smell of these is with me now; they were mouth-stretchers if ever I saw any; immense, pungent, infinitely satisfying—*mais, comme ils étaient formidable!*

Louis and I did not wish to take by mistake the longer of the two roads on to Amarillo, so we wandered into a local showroom to make inquiries. An old man, rather sardonic

145

but with a twinkle in his eye, sat in his shirt sleeves at a table covered with advertisement folders.

"Am'rilla," he said, "wait, I'll call the bus service. They'll tell ya."

He stretched an arm to the telephone, gave a number and held a clipped conversation.

"Yeah," he said, looking up, "by El Reno, Clinton and Elk City; it's thirty-five miles longer, but it's paved all the way."

He dismissed our thanks with a smile. "Ya welcome," he observed, and picked up the local paper.

So I drove fast to El Reno. And now Kansas really opened out. Any semblance of even the wilder of our English plains disappeared, if indeed one of them can boast an impression of wildness to-day. Here was prairie land. Tall wire cattle fences confined the road, and to right and left the ground ran into clear distances till it became a hard blue smudge miles and miles away. Even then, I knew Texas would show me more on the morrow.

The road was so straight that, although cruising at seventy-five, I had ample opportunity to look about me in the way which seems so dangerous to the uninitiated but is really as safe to drivers well accustomed to fast travelling as though they never lifted their eyes from the monotony of the concrete. Indeed, up to about a hundred miles an hour I find it safer to look about at short intervals; it relieves the strain. Frequent glances, like separate exposures on a cinema film, keep the car where it is wanted, pick out variations in the structure of the shoulders and reveal what room is available—where one can safely go in the event of a tyre blow-out and from what spots on the road to be ready to pull away. This takes long to explain but is, as all experienced drivers know, entirely automatic; it is a matter of practising concentration until it becomes virtually subconscious. When greater numbers of motorists study to acquire this habit of road

146

analysis, and to make use of it at whatever speed they drive, the existing highways of America and other countries will be correspondingly safer—not before.

I gave full attention to the road only when its environs or surface warranted it, or when meeting another car. Meanwhile, I noticed every detail of the loveliest sunset I had seen since leaving the East. Gradually, the bright light of afternoon had given way to the translucence of evening and softened again with the approach of dusk. Along the immense stretch of horizon lay what looked like a horizontal rainbow, fading in such a way that no individual band of colour was sharply defined. Each merged with infinite graduation of tone into the next; from violet through red, pink, yellow to palest green, they ascended in vivid radiance. Below this natural spectroscope ran the solid, blackish blue of distant country seen here in the evening with great clarity. Above it, there still remained for a short space the whiteness of the past day's glare. A long finger or two of cloud stretched like elephant-grey bars across this latest masterpiece of skyscape.

As the radiance sank, appearing to soak into the far off skyline, suddenly a blown slant of cloud to southward was caught and made to flare upward and away at an angle; so that I thought of a prairie fire rising to a giant's touch. An unearthly glory fell upon the scattered trees and the patches of low scrub: where there was naked earth, it now hit the eye as would great smears of brick-coloured paint. After some moments this effect passed also, leaving simply a mauve countryside, its features darker shades of the same tints against an afterglow like ripe cherries. And again, a little later, on this undulating road, I was driving into lilac hollows and up on to opal crests; the road an iridescent ribbon looped low in soft obscurity, or hung over hills still holding the day in talk while patiently waiting the quiet approach of night.

At Clinton it was quite dark, and another forty miles

or so brought us to Elk City, in Oklahoma, where we decided to stay. Here, for the first time, our hotel had a different air about it, a flat-roofed Western, semi-Mexican influence revealed in its architecture; and there were ceiling fans in the rooms with their rough-cast walls. Our baggage was carried up by a merry negro porter in whom the mildest joke produced an uncontrollable cackle of laughter. He almost gave way to hysterics when, freed from so many hours at the steering wheel, I kicked a deplorable hat of Louis Skinit-zero's from one end of the corridor to the other.

"Hee, hee, hee," he exploded. "Landsakes now, dat am fun—dat am. Lawdy me!" And even the sliding door of the elevator did not prove an effective silencer for him. We still heard him cackling in descent.

This matter of Louis' hat was like a recurring decimal. He had protested admiration for a black one which I wore at a gay angle in the evenings at Detroit.

"I once had a hat something like that," he observed. "I bought it in London—you can't get them here, you know."

"So I see," I retorted, staring pointedly and with simulated disapproval at the comfortable old brown Homburg on the back of his own head.

He snatched it off. "You don't like it," he mused, sadly.

Said I, "I think it's a ghastly hat."

"Are you taking your black one out to the coast?" he inquired artlessly.

"I am," I announced. "I intend to take nocturnal Holly-wood by storm in it." (Only when I got there did I realise that practically no one wears a hat in the evening, the air being so warm.)

"And I shall wear this, my oldest one, as we drive across," he said happily, "and on the way, doubtless you will get to like it so much that we will exchange."

148

"My black hat is locked in a hat-box," I retorted rudely, "the key of which is obtainable only over my dead body."

"I have sat on mine several times by mistake," Louis continued, "which accounts for its appearance."

. "Doubtless you will do so again," I threatened. And, indeed, no less than five times during our long trek westward I managed to slip his discarded hat under him just as he was about to take his seat beside me in the car. Once, when he was getting out of the car to inquire our way through some western town or other, I succeeded suddenly in squashing down this remarkable headgear in so sinister a fashion over his eyes, that the person to whom he addressed himself on the sidewalk viewed him with obvious distrust and alarm, thinking no doubt that here was the latest "Public Enemy No. 1," and wondering why the heck the Federal "G" men hadn't heard about the exploits of the gang in the Chrysler by which, alas, he, an innocent citizen, was unexpectedly confronted at close range.

By such innocent devices we contrived to keep ourselves amused when sight-seeing and serious conversation palled, or when a long day of rain, monotonous roads or desert heat left us with a desire to play the fool. Weeks afterwards, in New York, Louis confessed to the purchase of another hat, a debonair hat like mine; he had found a shop, he said, which stocked them for the mad, be-monocled English. But that night in Elk City, it was his unfortunate brown tile over which we packed down in a scrum in the passage.

Being late, we dined up the street, at an all-night *café* recommended by the porter. I ate my first cat-fish and found it like tender chicken. Smoking a last pipe outside the hotel, I watched the arrival of the transcontinental bus. It pulled up sharply with a hiss of Westinghouse brakes. Several passengers emerged, among them a grim, probably falsely holy-looking old man in a wideawake hat, a dark broadcloth

149

coat and brown trousers. He carried a grip and spat freely as he passed into the hotel lobby. Looking round, I found the manager standing beside me. We grinned at one another, and I nodded towards the big grey bus with its comfortable padded seats and head rests.

"Where's she going?" I inquired.

"To the coast," he drawled.

"When do they change drivers?"

"Amarillo; then she goes through with two drivers, one sleeping and one driving. In thirty-nine hours she'll be right in Los Angeles."

As he finished speaking, the bus got under way. She had a surprising pick-up and an exhaust note like a British sporting car. I wouldn't have cared to try to sleep in her, though after a time I suppose one could. Many people do.

"Tom Mix was here last night with his circus," the manager volunteered. "There must have been a hundred people in the lobby asking for autographs. Some of the old timers came in from outlying ranches to see him, and we had a lot of stuff broken up. Maybe you'll overtake him to-morrow; he's giving a show at Shamrock to-night."

He went on to talk about the ex-cowboy film star's caravan, a veritable house on wheels, and said that it must have cost $25,000, with its bedroom, kitchenette, hot and cold showers, stove, fireplace, and so on. Just then a dilapidated car drew up, and some one looking like a sheriff got out and went to fetch the man in the wideawake hat. They emerged together from the hotel, the new arrival carrying the old fellow's grip. The latter spat fiercely and, I hope, finally, before entering the car. I heard him ask some question. The emphatic Americanism, "Yes, sir!" that has scores of contradictory meanings, was the only reply he got. Then the car rattled off.

I arranged to be called at five-thirty, wrote a letter with a very bad pen and went to bed.

CHAPTER VII

ACROSS TEXAS INTO THE SOUTH OF NEW MEXICO

THE TELEPHONE BELL THAT AWOKE ME WAS A CURSE, BUT I had slept well and didn't really mind getting up. Outside, the sky was clear, the early light still delicate, the air decidedly sharp. Breakfast, in the bar of the hotel, consisted of the corn-flakes which are so good in America and a poached egg. We were away at seven-twenty, and in Amarillo, 147 miles distant, in two hours and thirty-two minutes.

Not long after leaving Elk City, we found ourselves driving into Texas; the "Lone Star" State, as it is called. A singularly appropriate boundary stone, possessing the strength of simplicity, was our informant. My eye being caught by the five-pointed star portrayed on its base, I began to think at once of all the favourite yarns by Zane Grey, Alfred Henry Lewis, Ralph Connor and others, which I had read as a boy.

That morning on the Texan ranges was magnificent. Until the sun rose higher, paling everything with its glare, the sky remained intensely blue. The air obviously lay in distinct layers, by temperature; for smoke from a wayside loco-motive shed rose maybe two hundred feet and then drifted away across the prairie at an exact level, as though under an invisible ceiling. It spread across ten or fifteen miles of country at least.

Except for occasional slight curves, the road ran as straight as it had been doing off and on for days. But here its monotony was less marked; the surrounding spaces were sufficiently primitive to maintain our interest and to provide a certain

151

sense of adventure. The railway track ran alongside. Three times in the morning, we saw trains making their long trans-continental trek. Two were passenger trains. These were surprisingly short and were obviously not the famous cracks, such as the "Eagle" or "The Chief," with its proud slogan: "Extra fine—extra fast—extra fare." The third we saw, a freight train, was made up of many khaki-coloured refrigerator trucks carrying fish and fruit eastward from the coast of California. All seemed slow compared with British trains of corresponding types.

In places, the prairie varied a little. Long lifts of higher ground would appear far off and vanish again like faint maroon or lilac shadows on the horizon. One felt not quite sure of having really seen them. Then there would follow a sector of shallow, dry gullies, clothed with a yellowish-green grass. Cattle, unless quite near, appeared like specks on the huge sweeps of surrounding country.

And now the road, from being a concrete two-car pave-ment, became wider and surfaced with gravel, rough and stony in places, soft in others. A long dust cloud rose behind us.

The bigger ranch houses were mostly white wooden buildings with verandahs. Their scattered out-buildings and corrals were of natural-coloured timber, rough hewn. Nearly every ranch had its wind-wheel pump, briskly turning this morning. Then for miles there would be no sign of habitation at all. Above a road junction some twenty or thirty miles short of Amarillo, I saw an eagle soaring.

Soon, far ahead, farther ahead than it is possible to see anywhere than across territory such as this, Amarillo raised its high buildings. First to be seen was a vast grain elevator, aluminium-painted and impressive, short of the town. Then I saw another and yet another; for these were the great corn lands of America.

Forty-three thousand people live in Amarillo, so it is a centre that boasts several big hotels, some excellent modern shops, a number of automobile dealers, and more than just the makings of a pleasant layout.

On Polk Avenue, I bought some kodak films at thirty cents apiece.

"Come back again," said the drug-store keeper, his hand on my shoulder.

The good-fellowship of the West greets visitors like this at every turn.

An automobile dealer with whom I talked, forgot his grievance of being able to sell more cars than the quota allowed him by the manufacturers for whom he was agent, and spoke of shooting ba'ar and lion. By lion, I take it he meant puma. At any rate, he was going to drive five hundred miles the following Friday, and then go on with pack ponies for a further two days until he reached the place where he and his friends went hunting every year.

This car dealer wore a wide Stetson hat, rimless glasses and a diamond ring and tie-pin. He stood six feet three and, except perhaps for the glasses, was an average schoolboy's *beau idéal* of the wealthy, upright rancher whose flaxen-haired daughter doesn't marry "Quick-draw" Ike from Dead-eye Gulch who means to do her wrong (a man with such a moustache must be a wrong 'un), but "One-shot" Sam, the poor, honest cowboy who rescues her (clatter of hooves) and becomes, *ipso facto*, foreman over a limitless number of sharp-shooting heroes. Actually, my tall Texan acquaintance had been in nothing more exciting than the motor trade for twenty-seven years. A most pleasant person.

"When you come through again, look in," he said, and obviously meant it.

That the local car-buying public would absorb more cars than he was then able to handle, was interesting news. Normally, it would have seemed a definite indication of the lightening of the economic depression in America. But here it became a rather more special case. This was an agrarian district, and so susceptible to the President's N.R.A. scheme for assisting farmers. Since then, the Supreme Court has declared the scheme illegal, and I wonder if as many new cars have been sold this year in Amarillo.

Cowboys come to town now in their cars, and have done so these many years. Still, something from the past remains in Amarillo, possibly no more than an impression, but it is there. And I have a happy feeling that it always will be.

Then we hit the modern trail again. The concrete changed to worn macadam and back once more to a dirt road, the latter hugely broad in places—six cars wide at least. And, as it was dry, a reddish dust floated behind us like a plume as the endless prairies started to streak past again on either side. It remained like this almost without variation into New Mexico.

To a lazy driver, or a slow one, these terrific lengths of straight road might be hypnotic in their effect, and tend to induce sleep or absent-mindedness, especially as a mirage taunts one's eyes for miles in certain lights. When driving fast, there is even a definite inclination at times to brake, either hard or gradually, and reduce speed before entering a water splash apparently situated anything from two hundred yards to a half-mile ahead—a water splash which does not really exist.

Where I passed little clusters of houses, I noticed again that each had its wind-wheel water-pump, ugly but grimly necessary in this parched land. At one place, solitary, and miles from anywhere, two service station men in uniform were at work on the car as soon as I pulled up. At a word, as to the brand of gasoline, one immediately started filling the tank; the other, without being told, brushed out the floor of the car, washed the windscreen, checked the oil and water levels

". . . miles from anywhere. . . two service station men in uniform were at work on the car as soon as I pulled up."

and presented a good paper map of the district. This kind of service is not to be found even on the outskirts of London, much less in the "deserts" of our home counties.

Within a mile I met a cow-puncher, loping quietly along the roadside on a wise-looking broncho and leading a second. He gazed at us indifferently from under the brim of his high-crowned hat. To him, we belonged to another world.

Soon we entered the real desert of New Mexico. Sand, sparse dried grass, yucca plants, dwarf cacti; such formed its common clothing, if in this sense it can be said to be clothed at all. Balls of tumbleweed came bowling along the roads before a faint breeze. These tangled collections of dead tendrils are so named because of the way they are blown along, falling over and over. In some places, pretty mauve flowers made a thin carpet, and here and there sudden clumps of black-eyed Susans bloomed in orange patches two or three feet high.

At times, the road ran beside bold escarpments rising a hundred feet and littered with hot stones. To the south-east I saw a line of tall bluffs formed of reddish rock, packed hard by the hands of time. It is such pigmentation that lends to the whole desert a fierce beauty which attracts where one would otherwise expect to be repelled.

Hawks winnowed over this desert, many of them, seeking its small denizens as their prey. Passing a flock of thin, half-starved sheep and goats, I stopped to photograph the little girl minding them; a smiling, sunburned child in boys' overalls and a shady hat. Several of her charges, she told me, had died for want of nourishment. There was a donkey with her, a few months old. It was her pet and followed her step by step. She lived close by, in a tumble-down wooden shack, with her father and mother and three younger children. Some miles farther on, after three long bends, I came unexpectedly upon trees, little paddocks, orchards and a bright neat town: this was Roswell.

As it was Saturday afternoon, the streets were full of parked cars, the shops full of women, and the sidewalks, especially the street corners, packed with men lounging and talking. Many of the men were in their shirt sleeves and some in short multi-coloured blanket jackets or sleeveless jerkins of plain leather; but nearly all wore ten-gallon hats. They had the open faces and calm stare of those used to looking over big distances.

I turned down a side street lined with feathery cypresses of some sort, light green in colour, and with weeping willows. Here, there were one or two Indian stores. Children with straight hair and eyes like sloes scrabbled nearby. Beyond, a one-man garage stood by itself, distinct from the usual swagger gasoline stations in the main street. Its hand-painted notice board proclaimed a standing invitation: "Drive right in. We are friendly."

The use of the royal plural amused me, and I liked the eager look of the proprietor in the doorway, who eyed my big Chrysler hopefully as it rolled soundlessly past with little feathers of dust at its wheels. Unfortunately, I had filled up not long before—at that desert halt—otherwise I would have stopped. His enterprise was reflected in the cleanliness of his little shed, noticeable even at a distance.

The country beyond, surprisingly enough (if one had not long ago given up being surprised) became like Newmarket heath at home: acres of grass bleached by the sun, and lines of tall green trees, stiff and stately. Only that astonishing mauve and pink cliff, keeping level five miles away on the left, and the little bunches of flowering weed in the ditches alongside the road, served to remind one sharply from time to time that this was the far-off cattle-raising country of

156

the west rather than the northern headquarters of the sport of kings.

Another thirty miles changed it all again. Once more, there was the widespread wilderness of New Mexico. Not quite the sort of desert we had recently traversed, but arid plains very similar in character. Yet now, ranges of low, flat-topped hills rose bluely out of the west like a wall mounting in stages, a course or two of bricks at a time. They were impressive, not because of their height, which was only a few hundred feet, but because of their suddenness and the velvety shading of the vertical fissures in their flanks, abandoned one by one by the sinking sun.

I stopped to photograph them (unsuccessfully). Walking some little way off to do so, I rested my elbow on the top strand of a high cattle fence. On the other side of the road, a short distance beyond me, a cowboy in a blue shirt dismounted and got to work, fixing another fence which had a gap in it. His chestnut pony, the reins slipped over its head, remained peacefully watching him. When the man had finished, he stood for a few moments talking to the pony and making much of it.

From Roswell, the road itself had been tiresome. Drainage channels, wide and paved, but steeply graded as to entrance and exit, crossed it at frequent intervals, sometimes not more than a quarter of a mile apart. Although marked at the appropriate distance by big yellow notices, reading, "Dip—three hundred feet," they proved aggravating hazards to encounter at the end of the day, because of the extra fatigue imposed on a tired driver. In some places, too, the warnings had been removed, and the dips loomed up unexpectedly, necessitating a quick braking and holding of the big car. Apart from this, the road was good; tough, rolled stone with some bituminous binding, and firm gravel edges. I made fast time over it.

Yet, as I went, I had ample opportunity to watch the sky-

157

line of low hills on my right grow hard against the amber glow of evening. The Chrysler, speeding in their shadow, must have seemed to a watcher up there like a silent grey beetle slipping swiftly along a road the colour of a black pearl, towards the white houses of Carlsbad showing up ahead.

Reaching the hotel, a gay, thoroughly Mexican building, I asked for a room at the back, facing this rising ground. There, before unpacking, I stood watching for some minutes at the window. By the indescribable glory of the light beyond the ridge, one could think that all the power of God was just the other side.

It was only 6.15 p.m., so I rang for the coloured elevator boy to take me down again, and amused Louis by demanding toast and marmalade. Tea I would not trust here, but the coffee as usual was comforting. Later, we explored the town. Its neat planning, excellent *cafés*, garages, stores, cafeterias and cinema, all outlined with brilliant Neon strip lights and garnished with graceful trees and patches of luxuriant turf by the sidewalks, would have amazed the inhabitants of a corresponding place in Europe, say, on the arid plateaux of Spain. For this was in the middle of hundreds of miles of what is virtually desert, where constant watering is required. Even the night air blew hot on my face.

In an Indian store, I turned over many silver bracelets and rings, and fingered Navajo and Chameo rugs and blankets, before buying two little figures of Indians, most cunningly made, for my children. The half-breed proprietor and his wife were clever salespeople, particularly the woman, though their methods were unorthodox. Two elderly ladies of Bostonian appearance were greeted, on entering, with "Hey, you two girls, I've got just the goods to show ya. These rings now . . ." and so on. She sold them something, too. More than they wanted!

A boy, very Indian in appearance, tried to sell me cigarettes. He was an appealing little chap about three feet high, with a sense of humour and a bright blanket jacket.

"D'ya smoke cigarettes?" he inquired, pulling at my arm. "We sell two packages for a quarter."

I exaggerated cheerfully. "My son," said I, "they make me sick."

He giggled unbelievingly and reverted to roughneck language. "Sick," he retorted, "sez you!"

"That was a good one, wasn't it," I agreed, relenting.

I egged him on to try my companion, but he had no better luck.

This store, I gathered, was once more doing pretty well after a difficult year or two. At any rate, the proprietor had just turned in his old car and got a new one. He held no very definite political views, but was inclined to credit the existing administration with the change for the better. "When times are bad," he explained, "it's the Indians up on the reservations who feel it most in this business, see. We can sell other stuff and get along somehow, see. But they can't—leastwise, nothin' reg'lar. Then's when they pawn their reel old joolery."

He pulled out of a showcase a number of silver rings and bracelets, all of which had been worn for generations and had become smooth with age. It was sad to see them there.

Entering a saloon across the street, Louis and I found we could obtain cocktails; amateurishly mixed but drinkable. Two Stetson-hatted artisans and a service station attendant sat on stools at the bar. Presently, our numbers were increased by the advent of an elderly man in a well-made suit, accompanied by a tall, slinky blonde in a green evening frock, low-backed and skintight as anything out of the Rue de la Paix. She sipped her drink unconcernedly, and no one seemed surprised to see her in such a place. This polite indifference strikes strangers as unusual, but of course it isn't. Nor should it be. It is civilised; that's all. Still, such manifestations of natural good manners—or is it also sophistication by radio, without the baneful influence of eastern gossip writers and photographers which leads to the complete courtesy of the West?—are more common there than in any other country I know. My own distinctly northern appearance caused me more embarrassment, through being stared at, in New York restaurants and hotels, supposedly cosmopolitan, than in any place west of Kansas City.

At dinner, I noticed the hotel was scarcely a quarter full. Late September was, I concluded, its off season. After a dull meal of rock bass (why I chose it, I cannot imagine!) I went to bed with a long drink of iced water.

CHAPTER VIII

THE WORLD'S GREATEST CAVERNS—AND A PRAIRIE DRIVE

I WAS TO RECEIVE MY MORNING CALL ON THE TELEPHONE AT Carlsbad at seven. But fortunately I was awakened by a fresh breeze bustling in at a window and disturbing the single sheet with which I had covered myself; one of those invigorating puffs of wind that so often herald the day. I swayed sleepily across the room and stood heavy-eyed at the window facing the long lift of ground behind the hotel. Dawn must have taken place some forty minutes earlier. It was light enough for the view to wear that newly-washed appearance; yet not too light. The trees were very green, the long slope very dewy looking, the red-tiled roofs of the stable patio a more mellow shade than they would later become. Everything was as soft and sweet and clean as the touch of night could have made it.

Beauty of this kind flows into one subconsciously. At the time, one is only aware of a sense of freshness and a thorough cleansing. I feared lest it rouse me too much, because I needed what sleep was still to be had. So I rolled under the sheet again and snatched an hour more.

After breakfast, I drove the twenty-eight miles across the desert to Carlsbad Caverns. A small tourist camp of cabins, called by the grandiose name of "White City," lies some four or five miles short of the Guadalupe foothills where the caves are situated. Once past these flimsy little shacks, the feeling of being in for something impressive immediately starts to assert itself. The road leaves the desert at that point and enters a ravine with steep sides, full of rocks and cactus plants, through which it sweeps and twists in splendidly graded and banked turns.

The entrance to the ravine is also the entrance to a National Park of ten thousand acres, which now surrounds Carlsbad Caverns. Consequently, it is not surprising to find the road suddenly becoming so good, for where America makes such an enclosure efficiency reigns supreme. Except for the loose surface of the road sides, and the absence of retaining walls on one or two corners where there are considerable drops, I have never driven on a finer mountain road—many Alpine roads included.

It costs $1.50 to go into the caverns, and one writes one's name on a pass. This is neither an expensive nor troublesome ritual to perform in order to undertake the five and a quarter mile walk through the most majestic of Nature's hidden places yet discovered by man. The whole business is admirably organised and arranged. Near the entrance to the caves, solid stone buildings house a souvenir store of Indian-made goods, a refreshment bar, an information bureau, a ticket office and another for the cashier. These buildings possess a plain dignity which conforms well with their surroundings.

The compound, like the park itself, is in charge of rangers in drab whipcord suits, brown riding-boots and wideawake hats. One of them superintends the parking of cars in tidy lanes at an angle of forty-five degrees. The sole jarring note for me was the playing of an excellent victrola in the refreshment room; and I considered myself foolish to allow it to jar at all. But then I am pernickety where Nature's marvels are concerned, and for preference would always like to visit her temples alone in the early morning or late evening—a thoroughly selfish desire to which I cling unashamedly, though quite rightly it is seldom satisfied.

It takes from ten-thirty till four o'clock to go through

162

". . . in charge of rangers. . . . One of them superintends the parking of cars in tidy lines at an angle of forty-five degrees."

Carlsbad caverns. But because I had only a limited time to spend on my way to California, and had to cover at least two hundred miles that same afternoon, Colonel Boles, the park superintendent, most kindly arranged for me to come up in the elevator at half-past twelve, after walking only two and a half miles. Nevertheless, during those two hours, I had descended the full seven hundred and fifty feet and seen the finest caves, if not the largest, which by all accounts is immense. I was told that altogether thirty-two and a half miles have been mapped underground, and that this interesting work is not yet at an end. There is certainly no need to hurry over it. The great expense of lighting the caverns and of building safe trails and stairways in them, is the reason why only a sixth of the full distance is at present open to the public.

These caves were first explored in 1901 by Jim White, a young cowboy from Texas, who was brave enough to lower himself into the yawning opening by means of his lasso. Apparently, the existence of the entrance cave had been known locally for many years. It had been called the "Cave of the Bats," because of the immense number of these little animals which emerge every evening at sundown and fly away to their feeding grounds by the Black River, a few miles south, where they find insects. Every evening between the first of May, or thereabouts, and the middle of October, when they begin to hibernate for the winter, these bats can be seen leaving their particular cave like a long streamer of smoke from the funnel of a steamer. The U.S. Biological Survey estimate that at least three million of them have their habitation there.

No one was known to have entered the caves prior to 1901, if we except the presence of a crumbling skeleton thought to be that of an Indian, which Jim White discovered during one of his early explorations.

These caverns, I learned, have been formed by the seepage

163

of rain water through the limestone of the hills. This water was charged with carbonic acid gas, absorbed no doubt in the first instance from decaying vegetation. Geologists have estimated the age of some of the larger formations down below as being from fifty to sixty million years. Stalactites hang in thousands from the ceilings or jut downwards from slanting walls. Stalagmites have built themselves upwards from the floor or from limestone ledges. In some instances, stalagmites and stalactites have met and joined, while others are approaching each other at the rate of one cubic inch of growth per hundred years.

It is quite impossible to describe such a remarkable place in the few sentences that I can devote to it in a travelogue of this kind. A full-sized book, interesting on every page, could be written about it.

From a purely physical standpoint, I was astounded by the size of the caverns. I did not see the biggest, which is three-quarters of a mile long, as wide in places as six hundred and twenty-five feet, and has a maximum ceiling height of three hundred and forty-eight, except at one point, under a kind of natural dome, where its height is estimated to be more— probably in excess of 500 feet. Nevertheless, in some of the chambers through which I passed, it would have been possible to place Drury Lane Theatre and see it appear almost insignificant. Had a crack motor-cyclist started to ride his racing machine up the zigzag trail of another such sloping cavern, I judged it would have taken him several difficult minutes to reach the top, riding as fast as he could on the short straights between the hairpin corners. This, of course, would not actually be possible, but the vision of it sprang to my mind at the time as providing a good illustration of the remarkable size of these underground rooms. Seen from my position near the tail of the column of visitors, the head of it, passing out at the bottom of a big chamber as we entered at the top, might almost have been composed of termites, making for some secretly burrowed fastness.

The lighting is skilfully arranged throughout. Every care has obviously been taken to show up the lovely natural tints of the various formations. These range from dark grey and drab rock, through deepest amber and all shades of yellow, to pale pink and an opaque white. Where the stone contains a considerable proportion of iron oxide, and an electric light is placed behind a block or column of it, the formation does, in fact, look like a large piece of amber. Sunk in the floor of one of the lowest chambers, I noticed a shallow pool of water, pure emerald in colour.

The long walk down into the caverns was impressive. It also had its amusing moments, because the crowd of sightseers was naturally a mixed one. A young man stood just outside the entrance with a little counting-machine in his hand.

"Any of you folks want lunch?" he asked monotonously, as the people passed him.

When he received an affirmative answer, he clicked his little calculator. I subsequently discovered that one of the huge caverns below was cleverly fitted up as a cafeteria; excellent food could be had if the order was given to this attendant on the way down. But many of the people had bought cardboard luncheon boxes at the refreshment room on the surface, and went down swinging these in their hands. All told, we were a party of about two hundred and fifty.

A young couple in front of me chewed gum steadily and said very little. A boy in riding kit strode ahead of them, probably a visitor from a dude ranch; with him were two girls, one in blue jodhpurs. An old German couple, neither of whom appeared to know a single word of English, tottered along close behind. And there was a party of youths. These obviously came from some college within a motor drive of the place, because many of them sported the small-brimmed black felt hats, tight black trousers, jackets, and so on, all in the Mexican style, which they apparently considered smart. I noticed, also, a trained nurse threading her way in and out of the queue, dressed in the same drab material as the rangers and carrying a small first-aid case.

The expressions on the visitors' faces were various and interesting to watch. Some were laughing and joking, apparently prepared to pay only a modicum of attention to what they saw. Others looked definitely awed, and one or two almost scared.

The party was halted for a few minutes in the first cavern, and we were advised to seat ourselves on the rocks beside the trail. At this point, one of the rangers gave a most interesting talk; the acoustics of the place were so excellent that he had no need to raise his voice above an ordinary conversational tone. After quoting a short history of the cavern, he went on to advise us how to walk on the steeply-descending paths, pointing out that by proceeding absolutely flat-footed it was possible to save a good deal of strain on the muscles of our legs. He appealed to every one not to stray from the trails and not to touch the various formations as they passed them, although these were glistening and attractive, and the temptation to finger them undoubtedly very strong. He told how 600,000 people had already experienced the wonderment of the caverns and had left them unchanged for those who came after them, and he appealed to our party to do likewise—to leave the beauties unspoiled for others.

"Here," he remarked in conclusion, "is the greatest cave in the world; let's go see it."

This little homily, lasting about six or seven minutes, was very well spoken. Just the right note was struck. There was nothing schoolmasterly in his excellently-worded suggestion about the responsibilities and privileges of his audience as American citizens. I was much impressed by the type of men employed in these caverns as rangers. Subsequently, I heard that all rangers now appointed by the Federal Government have to possess a college education. (Again education!)

For the first part of the descent, a smell of damp rock was mildly obtrusive. Then after a time I ceased to notice it, probably because we were allowed to smoke. It was interesting to discover that these caverns possess perfect, natural ventilation, and that the temperature never varies from day to day, either in winter or summer; I believe it always remains at fifty-six degrees.

On one of the steeper sections of the trails, I overheard an elderly lady striving unsuccessfully to draw her companion's attention to a particular feature.

"It's no good, my dear," protested the latter, mundanely practical, "I'm concentrating on my feet."

And again, farther on, the same enthusiastic sightseer, enlarging rapturously upon another beautiful formation which had caught her eye, was sternly cautioned not to bump her head.

Meanwhile, the young couple in front of me chewed gum, held hands and said nothing.

At length, after two and a half miles Colonel Boles kindly met me and accompanied me to the surface in one of the elevators. He told me that it had taken eight months to bore the shaft for them, to bore simultaneously from the surface and from below, and meet in the middle. They had been installed at a cost of $130,000, and make the ascent of seven hundred and fifty feet in one minute. On the way up, he said that the number of sightseers during the current year had already greatly exceeded the number for 1934; one hundred thousand had already been there by September. On one occasion as many as seventeen hundred people were conducted through the caves in one day. Such

167

emergency rushes call for the services of twenty-five guides, and extra men with local knowledge are taken on for the purpose.

Having emerged by the power-house into the sunlight, I stood for a moment looking out over the red and mauve plain of New Mexico, towards the mountains of Mexico proper. The lizards running about on the path were tame enough to be photographed.

Wonderful though the caverns had been, I was glad to be back in more normal surroundings, and to feel the air on my face as I returned fast along the straight desert road to Carlsbad; doing the same twenty-eight miles in twenty-three minutes. There I rejoined Louis, who had been writing letters, and we had luncheon at a restaurant which advertised sea fish to eat. It was a one-room affair, but like many such places it was spotlessly clean and productive of better cooking and service than is obtained in many hotels.

Then we went back to Roswell along the road that we had traversed the previous evening when I had watched the startling shadows creeping up the flat-topped hills. We retraced our tracks, because to go around by the south, through El Paso and Phoenix, would have entailed more than a hundred miles additional driving before reaching Grand Canyon. Also, it probably would have meant staying another night on the way, and we seemed unable to ascertain the best place at which to stop, even if we had had time to do so.

Inquiries for good hotel accommodation bring home to a stranger the great distances between towns of any size in this western land. Villages as such do not exist. There is no question of putting up for the night at a country "pub" as one does in England or in many parts of Europe. Instead, one picks out the name of a town ahead, well marked on the map and about the right distance away, and then asks the manager of the hotel where one is at present, or the attendant in a service station, what sort of a place he considers it to be. It is surprising to discover how few people can supply this information at all accurately—surprising that is, until one pauses to consider that the equivalent in England would be to ask the manager of a hotel in Kent where he would advise one to stay on reaching the borders of Northumberland. Some time, I must work out how many times England could be fitted into states the size of New Mexico, Arizona, Nevada, California, or some of the others. England, Ireland and Scotland together are about equal in area, I believe, to Arizona.

So passing again through Roswell, eighty-one miles back, we continued over a rough and muddy road for a further hundred and twenty-five miles until we came after dark to the little hamlet of Vaughn. We had decided on Vaughn because the big trains stopped there, and in consequence there was a Fred Harvey hotel; of which more later.

This road from Roswell to Vaughn took us across real limitless prairie. I continually saw herds of cattle, so far away that they looked like ants. The mounted figure of a cow-puncher would occasionally show up, outlined on a crest. We met two of them riding beside the road: pleasant, fresh-faced youths. Pulling up, I exchanged a word with them.

Some thirty or forty miles out over these rolling plains from Roswell, I noticed a little group of wooden huts and a neat schoolhouse. It was rather touching to see the usual yellow road sign put close to them: "School Zone—Speed Limit Fifteen Miles." I don't know how many cars would pass that way in one day; it could not be many. I only met two in three hours. And outside the school, the road was so bad that no one but a lunatic would have driven fast anyway. Still, I liked to see this insistence on civilised behaviour so far out in the wilderness, unnecessary though it was.

Right across America, indications of all kinds combine to show that each child is having its chance. Education, good education, is within the reach of all. In its initial stages it is compulsory; and, as one would expect, child welfare societies are to be found everywhere. But somehow, out here, miles from a place of any size, the fact took on a pleasant degree of emphasis.

It induced thoughts most appropriate to my first experience of a prairie sunset. Perhaps some readers will think there is too much in these pages about sunsets. To which I reply that, if they can, and as soon as they can, they should pay a visit to the wide western spaces of America and see for themselves; for the views as the sun goes down are almost unbelievable.

This evening, a range of mountains lay to westward of my persistent car. They were perhaps eighty to a hundred miles away, yet every serration formed by their peaks against the sky was clearly visible. But of detail at such a distance, there naturally was none; no shading could be seen upon their flanks. They rose flat-sided beyond the greying stretches of grass like a jagged silhouette cut from lavendar cardboard.

Both the sunset and its awesome image endured for over half an hour, while gradually the thin crescent of a new moon gathered strength to shine whitely through the gold that now had imperceptibly assumed a uniform green tinge. At length I was left picking a hard way through ruts and occasional pools gleaming with pale loneliness.

The road wandered on, and mile by mile became more difficult to see. American headlights are inadequate anyway, judged by English standards, and quite useless in competition with such a sky. One form of lighting offset the other, and neither was sufficiently bright to drive by, for a new slant of the road brought me facing the direction of the sun's going. Every minute I became more and more blind. A sign, passed ages ago, had stated: "Vaughn 36 miles": and after further ages of lurching about and of straining to see this difficult route, I was beginning to feel pettish. As the car mounted a crest, I peered into the wide-spread gloaming, and hoped to see the distant lights of our destination. But there was nothing.

"Where, oh, where," I complained, "is Vaughn?"

Louis achieved a life-like imitation of a bell-boy.

"Mr. Vaughn," he sang out cheerfully, "paging Mr. Vaughn."

The tension of weariness in me gave way before his good humour.

At last we came to a railway line and found that the road continued close beside it. I took this to be a good sign, and, sure enough, I soon saw lights twinkling on the summit of a long, gradual hill ahead. When we reached them, they did, in fact, prove to be those of Vaughn. Here, I pulled up at the Fred Harvey hotel, a broad, squat building with pillared verandas on two sides of it, situated immediately alongside the station platform. It was good to be there. Apart from the fifty-six miles I had covered to Carlsbad Caverns and back, and my steep walk in the caves, we had come over two hundred since a late luncheon. And the last hundred had been hard and tiring.

Fred Harvey hotels are deservedly famous. They are to be found in many places in the West, including Grand Canyon itself. The management prides itself on providing a twenty-four hour service wherever the hotel may be situated, and there must be hundreds of thousands of satisfied people ready to guarantee that it does so. I must confess that I got quite a kick out of emerging from the wilderness, which reaches to the threshold of Vaughn, to find a charming room, a comfortable bed, constant hot water, good food and a newspaper stall in the lobby where I could buy coloured postcards, depicting a Rodeo, to send to my daughters. This seemed to me to be service *par excellence*.

Between the lobby and the dining-room was a big *café*,

171

opening directly onto the station platform. A continuous counter, rectangular but with rounded ends, occupied most of this room, and swivel chairs with comfortably shaped backs were fixed at intervals in front of it. Here, the most delicious food could be obtained at any moment during the day or night, at a most reasonable price. One might find oneself sitting next to a local truck driver, a railway employee, a cattleman, or some wealthy business executive off a train which had just stopped. The same excellent food was served to all with equal speed and courtesy. And for those who wished a more leisurely meal, there was a dining-room beyond, to seat a hundred people, where they would be looked after by waitresses neatly dressed in black and white.

My companion and I watched one of the transcontinental trains come in. It was called "The Navajo." Besides ourselves, its arrival was watched by several of the local inhabitants, including three or four cowboys. This is apparently a regular amusement.

Interesting cross-sections of the life of any nation can be taken in its saloons or bars. That night, the most unusual person I saw drinking in Vaughn was an ugly white girl in a Chameo blanket coat, who had got off the train. A man, moderately well-to-do in appearance, was with her. She only spoke twice in the quarter of an hour that she was there, and, refusing a glass, drank out of a bottle; and did so capably. I couldn't place her at all. She conformed to no known type. I had the feeling that she could have been more intelligent than she allowed herself to be; that she was posing now and probably did so quite often; and that she was very unhappy. One of the most puzzling persons I ever saw.

CHAPTER IX

BY WAY OF INDIAN COUNTRY I TREK HIGH INTO ARIZONA

AT 5.15 NEXT MORNING I STOOD ON A LOW WALL BESIDE THE hotel, to face the brightening east. The station buildings formed grey silhouettes against the effulgence of the recent dawn which, in a few minutes, became a wide diffusion of pure flame colour.

Figs, bacon and eggs and coffee were as quickly served to us at 5.30 in the Harvey House *café* as if it had been any other time of the day. By 6.10 we were away, all routine jobs on the car done.

As we left Vaughn, we found the road signs confusing for the first time for two days. It was not that anything conflicted with them, but the number plates of routes 54, 60 and 285, which overlapped here, were badly positioned at a fork; so that we took the wrong road, and pursued it for some way before it deteriorated into a rough desert track and finally ceased. True, we might have suspected something of the sort, for shortly before we turned back we had met a grubby Mexican of wild appearance who observed with astonishment the direction of our going. He rode a pony in poor condition. Two others, equally poor and with staring coats, trotted behind him. His savage dog chased the car in silent fury for fully a hundred yards both times we passed him.

Returning to the fork, we took the other road, but only to go wrong again after another couple of miles. Perhaps we were not very bright after our succession of early morning starts and long days in the car. This time, luckily an old cowboy was able to put us right. He was in charge of a small herd that he had brought over from the direction of Albuquerque. Having passed the night some distance up this mistaken road of ours, because there was good feed beside it for his beasts, he was now letting them graze back towards the main route again, while he walked slowly behind, leading his pony.

"Yeah," he said, fingering a grizzled chin, "yonder's your road, it's in fair condition. I came that way yesterday. Lucky you weren't goin' through last week: there was a lot of rain and some snow."

I thanked him and reversed the Chrysler again. To-day was the thirtieth of September.

Now we found ourselves crossing towards the northern end of the range of mountains that we had seen a hundred miles to westward of us the previous afternoon. Then they had been lavender; this morning they were blue. After a further hour and a half's driving, we had gradually closed up on them, so that by Willard, where we turned north, they lay right across in front of us: but the map showed that after thirty miles or so the road would again swing west and we should pass through the foothills that formed their northern extremity. Farther north again, at Santa Fé, the range would once more become higher. Still, we would not see the mountains there, because after Albuquerque our route made almost straight for the distant Pacific.

Among the few scattered buildings comprising Willard, I noticed two, well built of brick, which I took to be respectively the grammar and high schools. Thus, I was again impressed by the facilities for education that are provided even in the most isolated places. These buildings would have done credit to a much larger community.

A few hundred yards beyond, there was a cluster of houses standing by themselves at the junction of a rough side-road

174

" This time, an old cowboy was able to put us right. 'Yeah,' he said . . . 'yonder's your road . . .' "

with ours. As I approached and slowed down, expecting perhaps to see some local vehicle appear and cross our path, a cowboy cantered across instead. To me, this kind of encounter was still so novel that I found myself laughing over it.

On the left here, spreading over the foothills of the mountains, were the first outposts of scrub pine or Juniper, those attractive, bushy, green dwarfs which furnish thousands upon thousands of gently rolling acres in western America. About now, too, the road itself swung west, and soon it rose in long switchbacks through these pines. One noticed how scattered the trees were—yards of grass surrounded each one —although from a distance they had appeared to grow more thickly. Higher up the slopes, they stood closer together, becoming a veritable stunted forest.

The mountains themselves followed, which from a distance had looked so blue to us; but which we found in reality to be cruelly bare and rocky, their flanks covered with fallen heaps of buff-coloured stone, milled small by the action of wind and weather. On part of this heartless ground the Junipers, here quite miniature, had established a precarious roothold. This spattering of dull green only added to the blazing nakedness of the surrounding slopes.

The latter now rose higher on either hand. There was a fierce pallor about bits of this pass to Albuquerque that scorched the senses, yet drew our eyes again and again from the cooler looking surface of the road itself.

Presently, as though through the rugged pillars of a giant gateway, we saw a terrific plain below and ahead of us; its surface like shot silk, purple as to general tone, yet never long the same in any one place, but always resolving into its constituent shades and back again—shades of blue, rose, grey and, in the foreground, of pale green.

Glancing back as we sped swiftly down a straight three-mile drop towards the flat-roofed white and drab buildings of the town, the hard hills, from which we had emerged, seemed to rise vertically like ramparts, their only irregularities being great curves, called wind caves, hollowed out of their faces by fierce currents of air which for thousands of years have buffeted them at certain seasons. Dry grasslands confronted these stark hills, and ran to their very feet without hindrance of any kind.

A need of sandwiches and gasoline accounted for half an hour's pause in Albuquerque, of which my main impression is of dull hot streets, relieved here and there by comparatively young trees and plots of well-watered turf; and of another of those Mexican style hotels, large and cool—probably the biggest and best of its kind that we had been in, although our call was only for food and a wash.

If we English are a nation of shopkeepers, then our Yankee cousins are certainly one of hotel-keepers. The two branches of the family are wise to stick to such profitable plebeian hobbies—so much more satisfactory all round than peddling effete wrong-headed forms of culture, selfishly restricted; which stock, when exhausted, we may cynically note, is invariably replaced by a new line in bloody revolutions—regrettably uneconomic products, involving overhead charges equalled only by the number of producers driven, or laid, underground.

The traffic lights suspended over the main crossings in Albuquerque incorporated the amber warning signal to which we are accustomed in England. The change of signal was also heralded by a bell. Rather to my surprise I noticed that drivers went ahead on the lights and not on the bell, which might have been a temptation to some. Despite it being a little noisy, I was impressed by this system, especially in localities where lights are rendered dim by the sun's glare.

In addition, there were stiff rubber flaps sticking up in

176

the centre of the streets at corners. These have "Stop" written on them and must be obeyed by cross traffic; but if driven over by mistake, they bend flat. They are common in small American towns and certainly constitute a reminder. Still, a fixed sign by the kerb is better.

From Albuquerque, the way to Gallup started out past trees, little dried-up meadows, small houses, frequent service stations and the usual local appurtenances of a small western town. Thus far it curved gently, its surface concrete pavment. The Rio Grande flowed near by. Soon we caught our first glimpse of it as a series of polished silver streaks between shoals of golden sand, fringed here with the light green foliage of cottonwoods, refreshing to the eye. Then the river left us; and once more we entered semi-desert land hotter than any we had hitherto crossed, bare of vegetation except for that ubiquitous yellow weed and scattered tufts of sparse, scorched grass.

The road consisted now of a wavy macadam surface with gravel edges, not bad to drive on in a car as well sprung as this Chrysler. But a mirage danced upon it. Even behind dark glasses, my eyes were screwed against the glare. The sun, striking through the window, found the rolled-back cuff of the thin dust coat which I wore over my shirt sleeves, and bit into my left wrist. By evening, the skin was red and sore. Not long afterwards, I stopped to change a kodak film. As I held my camera inside the door for the benefit of what shadow there might be, the back of my neck was branded instantly— a steady burning, so that I hastened to have done. As I settled myself again at the wheel, the eddies behind a Dodge sedan, passing at about sixty, momentarily made a welcome breeze.

In the last days of September, there could be no certain expectation of such glorious weather, so we were correspondingly grateful, if warm.

To the south, a distant mountain shrouded itself in a

177

glittering haze. Two puffs of cloud stood still above it like prolonged shrapnel bursts. To the north, one of those fantastic stretches of brick-red cliff, with blue shadows, watched us as might some crouching beast. I swung the car over a bridge spanning a dry creek, turned right, continued a mile or two, saw a notice: "Warning—Pavement ends 400 feet" and bumped off on to a harsh gravel highway, loose surfaced, three undulations to the yard, with larger potholes in great variety, crossed periodically by draining culverts and smoking with dust when we overtook an occasional car.

Higher ground now closed in on this old trail; not mountains, but great masses of volcanic rock, often flat-topped, the contrasting strata of them clearly defined in all shades of ochre and green upon their sheer sides. They possessed no appearance of reality, being instead like some macabre form of stage *décor*. Only occasionally was the road chiselled right between two such masses, nevertheless they constantly obtruded because of their weird look of inevitability. One felt very strongly that to them this old trail to Santa Fé was merely a scratch of yesterday's scoring, and the travellers upon it as insects; and that when again there is perhaps no trail, those remarkable rocks would still be there, infinitesimally changed in contour, heedless and unremembering, except in so far as we know that what composes them can just be said to live, although lacking in consciousness as we define it.

After another burning hour, I brought the Chrysler into a twisting defile, mostly arid, but harbouring optimistic vegetation of a sort: some stunted pines, the yellow and mauve and white desert flowers, and a scanty pasture. Indian adobe dwellings made their appearance and also rude shelters of small brush laid upon rugged posts driven into the ground. These last were erected at intervals by the roadside. Indian squaws sat under some of them, and held out samples of pottery and beadwork to tempt us. My boyhood illusions

178

" Indian adobe dwellings made their appearance. . . ."

" Gaily dressed . . . she was walking near the road with her mother. . . ."

withstood with difficulty the fact that these old ladies now sported horn-rimmed glasses.

Camp Laguna came and went. Indians lounging by doorways looked up with a momentary flicker of interest, while papooses in modern clothes grubbed happily in the dust.

Some miles on, one little girl particularly attracted my attention. Gaily dressed, and remarkably clean by contrast with the other children, she was walking near the road with her mother, who carried balanced on her head a basket of newly made pottery. I pulled up and, leaving the car, padded across some half-dried mud to greet them; my rubber-soled driving shoes making it awkward for me to keep my footing. This squaw, a prematurely aged woman, also wore horn-rimmed gig-lamps. With some difficulty, I ascertained that she would not object to being photographed. Her English seemed limited to quoting, in an inappropriate sort of whine, the prices of various pots and vessels. But when she saw that I didn't want these but only sought permission to make her daughter a small gift, she smiled and called to the child to come and be snapped with her; and, speaking her own language, her voice was soft and beautiful.

The child, shy at first, plucked up courage as soon as I laughed with her. I guessed her to be five or six years old. She had a delicious grin and a ready sense of humour; her black eyes were little pools of mischief. She carried another smaller imp on her back, held in the fold of her shawl. For the quarter I gave her, she thanked me in English without a trace of accent, and revealed again a perfect set of teeth. I left her with great regret, feeling that, translated to an eastern cot, such a child might provide infinite joy when the hour came for bedtime stories. Except that a cot would astonish her (though not perhaps so strange an article as in other, less Americanised pueblos) and she is undoubtedly better off

179

where she is, growing up to play a useful if small part in the gradual evolution of her people.

Miles passed. At length we left this shallow, winding valley and emerged again into desert, where scrub pines, scattered as usual on the low ground near the road, thickened into an impenetrable wall a mile away on the slopes to our left. To the right, the plain lay level to the foot of precipitous buttresses some thousand yards distant. These were the most remarkable for colour that I had yet seen. Only the Grand Canyon, yet to come, was to surpass them. The top of each long bluff was flat, as flat as the road ahead, and such was the perspective that some seemed stepped up on one another. Here and there gaps appeared in this stupendous wall, gaps that extended downward almost to the plain; these I took to be the entrances to canyons which I could not see.

The chief tint to-day was fuchsia. French grey was there, likewise mauve and brick red and pale buff. But fuchsia predominated in all shades. I would scarcely have believed these colours, had I not seen them. That they could be so bright and yet harmonise with each other, was remarkable enough; but that, as happened occasionally, a range of ochre from buff through yellow to dark brown, could also merge perfectly with them was nothing short of astounding. I wondered no more that men had sat for weeks watching this overpowering kaleidoscope, and attempting, often no doubt with a sense of frustration, to capture it on canvas in an effort to satisfy their own sense of self-expression as microcosmic units of the Force which made it, no less than commercially for the delectation of their fellows.

Through a choking cloud, I closed up on a Ford *coupé* ahead of several cars whose dust I had eaten. Coming nearer, I observed with amusement that my view through its rear window was confined to hats—three conical, five-gallon hats, on the sleek heads of three Mexican gauchos. As I overtook the Ford, I saw that the man driving also wore an emerald green silk shirt and amber sun glasses. A more amusingly sinister guy I never set eyes on.

Soon I was into Gallup. Dull and dusty itself, the town boasted a most excellent Fred Harvey house, again because the great transcontinental trains stopped there. Luncheon, once more chosen from a *menu* of amazing variety, occupied us for twenty-five minutes in the cafeteria. As at Vaughn, every one sat along a huge counter: workmen, clerks, a cultured half-breed and tourists like ourselves. I like this. Had the governor of the State walked in, or the president of the whole country, I felt that both would have received the same service and no one would have looked more than twice at them. To many in England there is still something strange about democracy on such a vast scale; we go in for it in smaller doses, at prize fights and village cricket matches, round midnight coffee stalls and in the hunting field. *Chacun á son gôut.* No country likes to live except by its own modernisation of its own traditions.

But democratic behaviour in individuals is patently right and proper, apart from being refreshingly friendly, and will one day gain universally by discipline. An arranged marriage between democracy and conservative-socialism in their mature years, the tendency to personal selfishness in the former being counterbalanced by the sturdy community feeling of the latter, is much to be desired by contrast with the senile lust or wild, youthful urge to satiety, now such common features of Governments; the first because over-political republics become incompetent and have to resort to a welter of suggestive speech to regain national energy; the second because inexperience, rightly throwing off the shackles of cruel reaction, makes its usual wrong start by promiscuous whoring after hard-hearted theories, abandons

181

these sirens for the buxom, animal-like mistress of absolutism and, not having wearied yet of her demands, fails to recognise the merits of a good-humoured woman of the world in the shape of stable parliamentary administration, which should be increasingly designed to attract men of all kinds who cherish the tradition of service and subscribe to the doctrine that true aristocracy is of the mind and will.

There was a garage over the way in Gallup. Its front room was given up to a display of Indian workmanship, and the proprietor, with added enterprise, had painted a road map on one wall of the automobile entrance, which depicted the surrounding country for hundreds of miles. I studied this with real interest, because it covered some of the ground over which I was to travel the same afternoon. The juxtaposition of the adjacent Indian reservations was marked, also the Painted Desert, the Petrified Forest and, much farther away, the location of the Grand Canyon.

I drove on. The road, rough during most of the morning, was now fair macadam again and remained so for nearly an hour. The country on either side consisted of hot plains; dreary, as one would think, yet always with a distant view of mountains to relieve the monotony. On account of the proximity of the Zuni, Navajo, and later the Hopi reservations, Indian trading posts became frequent sights by the wayside. These were of little mud huts or more pretentious log cabins. Outside some of them, gaudy rugs and blankets hung enticingly on wooden rails under the eaves of rustic shelters, called ramadas. Quaint painted images were standing beside the doors of others.

Rounding a gradual curve under the immediate shadow of a burning rock face, Louis and I came to the Arizona border. Here, it was necessary to show the car's registration papers to a State Highway Patrol, who took particulars of them. It is not every State that requires a licence to be carried on the windscreen as we carry it in England. And our car from Michigan had no such tax receipt visible.

The patrols had been instructed to make these inquiries in order to stop the bootlegging of cars to California or over the Mexican border. Unauthorised dealers have apparently made a practice of trying to avoid the freight charge on cars being sent by train from, say, Detroit to the Pacific Coast, so as to be able to undercut the prices which honest dealers have to ask. For instance, the average freight from Detroit to California may be said to be $175.00, or $200.00 including handling and insurance charges. By contrast, to drive a car out West costs about $20.00 or $25.00. The bootlegged cars used to travel in convoys of three, one towing two others; and the bootlegger set aside a further $20.00 to put each car in shape again on arrival. Special laws have recently been enforced in Nevada, Arizona and Colorado to the effect that cars may not be towed. The result is that they must all be licensed, and in this way the States are helping the motor manufacturers and traders to combat the bootlegging fraternity.

Of course, the latter still take advantage of the obvious fact that cars may be driven singly across America. No existing law or group of individuals is able to put a stop to this normal procedure. Consequently, it is still possible for them to undercut the authorised west coast dealer, though not to the same extent. There are tourist agencies through which people wishing to go to California can obtain a new car to drive there and deliver. They have only to furnish a driver's licence and one or two references. In some instances, even their meals are paid for by the bootleggers.

The ultimate customer has anything but a square deal in buying a car so delivered. True, it has been titivated upon arrival, and doubtless looks all right, but several different kinds of hell may have been knocked out of it during its long

183

journey from the east in the hands of a non-professional driver.

For a time, in Arizona, we crossed rolling uplands dotted with scrub pine, before dropping again to desert. On the last crest of the uplands, there is a place from which one can see north-west into the Painted Desert. Only a restricted view is to be had, such is the formation of the ground. But the glimpse is sufficient to whet one's appetite for Grand Canyon. At least, that is the way I recollect it now. When I first saw the Painted Desert, I thought it was marvellous. And so it is. But when one has seen Grand Canyon, this curtain-raiser to it—for that is how one may perhaps legitimately describe the Painted Desert—must necessarily suffer by comparison with the greater majesty of the mighty fissure a hundred miles or more to westward.

After staring down awhile over the Painted Desert, I got back into the car and drove on. Within a few minutes, I passed a signpost which indicated that the Petrified Forest lay distant only fifteen miles or so to the south. But Louis and I had set ourselves a definite objective to be reached by nightfall, so I could not turn aside; much to my regret.

Now the miles reeled behind me to some purpose. We were crossing what are called the Arizona "bad lands." Although volcanic hills were visible some way off, there was nothing to look at in the immediate foreground but tufts of coarse grass with sour, reddish earth between them. I gave my full attention to fast driving in an effort to be rid of these depressing surroundings. As evening drew on, we came again to rolling prairie, sweet and fragrant in appearance after what we had just passed through. Then I saw pines again; first the familiar Junipers, and then, to my great joy, full-sized trees. We had been climbing gradually for some miles, so I had frequently used the "over-drive" second gear ratio of the Chrysler, made available by a planetary gear train behind

184

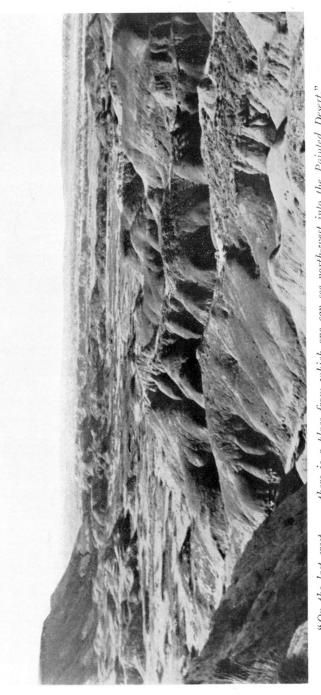

"On the last crest . . . there is a place from which one can see north-west into the Painted Desert."

the main gearbox proper, and engaged (above certain speeds on the normal second or top gear ratios) by centrifugal action upon weights, brought about by a momentary easing of the accelerator pedal—a quiet, pleasant device, yet one which enables the driver to make the wisest use of his engine's power output, especially up long hills or on the flat.

But at this point, by pulling out a plunger locking control, mounted on the instrument panel, I confined the transmission to its usual lower selection of ratios, for the road began curving more sharply and running up through steep, wooded hills. Above and behind these, taller mountains rose into sight, also clothed with pines on their lower slopes but with bare heads and shoulders of rock, magnificently purple in the gloaming now fast coming upon us. I stopped to take a photograph, for this was the sort of light by which I have sometimes obtained attractive results. Leaving the road, I walked some way in among the trees. My feet sank luxuriously into the most verdant grass I had seen for days. Then I stopped to look back; to pick out the particular view I wanted. Except that there was no heather, the scene was in every other way a Scottish scene. And for a moment I had a twinge of homesickness, for although I am an Englishman, there is Scots blood in me, and for years I have looked upon Scotland as my spiritual home.

I trudged back to the firm macadam road, and drove into Flagstaff, where we passed the night. After unpacking, a temporary odour of paraffin drove us out of the hotel dining-room. I was annoyed by this at the time but soon came to regard it as fortunate. Being forced to seek an eating house in the town, we hit upon food as good as any we had had since Kansas City. Our waitress, pert, quick, humorous and with a roguish eye, had her fair hair tightly battened down in curling pins during business hours. She was a dear, and most efficient.

Before we left, an Indian swung in and sat down. I studied him as he strode past our table. He was a beautifully made man, broad shouldered and not too tall. Apart from his bobbed hair and the red silk handkerchief round his head, he was dressed, eastern fashion, in a blue serge suit. He had a strikingly charming face. Two other Indians, a man and a woman, came in later to call for him. But they were untidy; the man in a stained hunting shirt and baggy trousers, supported by a belt, and the woman in a shapeless dress of nondescript colour and material. Their faces, too, entirely lacked the inherent intelligence and charm displayed by their companion.

Had I put a nickel in a little metal slot by our table and turned the handle, I would have been able to start an immense musical box playing at the other end of the room. With some difficulty, Louis restrained me from doing this; but somebody else started it from another table, and the noise was deafening.

On the way out, I was amused by a small wooden cabinet standing on the top of the cash desk. It bore the inscription: "Sanitary toothpicks—We aim to please you."

The door thudded behind us, and we wandered slowly along the sidewalk in the direction of the hotel. Here, in this little highland town in Arizona, I was struck again as on that evening beside the Missouri, by the admixture of old and modern. The railway ran along the other side of the street, and, where motors might cross the lines, there were illuminated red arms continually swinging as a warning: a bell was attached to them, so that they kept up a continuous ding dong, ding dong, all the time. Their rival to-night was the ubiquitous radio, sounds of which emerged from a shop doorway in the form of some crooner's monotonous refrain. Quickly padding Mexican boys passed in couples, murmuring their soft language. An old Indian shuffled along, staring into the shop windows surprisingly outlined with brilliant Neon lights. He wore the usual silk headband round his locks, and his belt was embellished with silver conchos of lovely workmanship. By contrast, his rheumy eyes peered through the apparently inevitable horn-rimmed glasses. Cowboys, lots of them, stood or leaned against the walls, especially outside the saloons. They alternately listened to the radio and spoke to one another in monosyllables. But most of the time they spat methodically and with great accuracy.

High up as we were, the air was keen mountain air—refreshing to any one who, like myself, comes from northern climes. The note of an American locomotive's siren is characteristic of the wild country through which miles of the railroad passes. As I undressed and went to bed, the two engines of a train, about to face a night journey on these steep gradients, let fly a couple of war whoops into the lurking hills behind the town.

CHAPTER X

GRAND CANYON—AND A LONG, HARD JOURNEY ENDING IN A
CROSSING OF THE COLORADO RIVER

AFTER A CUP OF COFFEE AT 6.30 NEXT MORNING, WE DROVE
the eighty-nine miles from Flagstaff to Grand Canyon
before breakfast. For a great part of this distance the road ran
through scenery typical of the wooded straths of Scotland.
The likeness was just as noticeable by daylight as it had been
by dusk the previous evening. The firs and the uninterrupted
grass alone remained different. Even a quick glimpse of the
mountains, seen through the gaps of the trees, did not destroy
the illusion. Never did Beinn More stand more royally than
these, or Beinn Ime, Beinn Arthur and Beinn Vane drape
themselves in cloaks of richer purple, or Morven look bluer or
more eternal against the northern sky.

Only when my gaze lingered, probing, did the fact obtrude
that these Arizona high tops supported no vegetation at
all, not even (so far as I could distinguish) rock plants in
the knife-edged crannies, much less the irregular plots of
coarse mountain turf which, on the hills of Scotland, gleam
suddenly from afar like emerald chips kissed by the sun.

The colours of these harsher hills were simply those induced
by tricks of the brilliant light striking on rocks, themselves
constituted of variously tinted strata; and by the startling
shadows cast by others.

Then for a space these hills withdrew, deploying to either
flank like well-trained troops, while the main body stood in
support behind us. Shallow valleys of pasture land and

scattered fir woods succeeded them. Groups of unbroken horses grazed near the road. Finally, we left such pleasances and again rolled fast over desert-like ground, a stretch some thirty miles wide at that point and made bearable only by the knowledge of hills being within reach, upon the slopes of which green could be picked out—the only contrast to an otherwise uniform drabness of dwarfed, withered bushes, weeds all but dead, and the pitifully brave little flowers, pale yellow and blue and pink, huddled together in scared communities. But in the fulness of time we were among trees again; soon the car rounded long curves edged by firs of medium size, and then passed under a wooden arch which we saw to be the boundary of the National Park that contains Grand Canyon. Here, the song of the Chickadees welcomed us and, occasionally, the harsh screech of the Piñon Jay.

A little way on, the road split left and right where an office stood with a door either side of it, built in log cabin style. We stopped and paid an entrance fee of a dollar. Then we proceeded, once again under the jurisdiction of those courteous, smiling men in the neat grey-green uniform, a garb that I now instinctively associate with people of good education and a substantial knowledge of the subjects most closely pertaining to their job. At the bottom of a slight hill we pulled up again for a few moments, this time at the Information Bureau.

The mundane business of providing information is usually associated in people's minds with bored clerks sitting behind wicket-like windows at a railway station, an airport or an amusement park, and trying to instil polite enthusiasm into responses which they have been making over and over again for days, months or possibly years. Here, by contrast, we found ourselves in a substantial log cabin with a wide stone hearth. A stuffed beaver, beautifully set up in a most life-like attitude in a glass case, faced the door; and the antlers of deer, and meticulously accurate maps of the Canyon Park, hung upon the walls. True, a long desk stood across the front of a recess in this big room, but there any likeness to an information bureau ended.

The ranger in charge had information of all sorts at his fingertips, and was delightfully willing to supply it. We chatted with him about the best road to take on leaving: whether we should go over by Boulder Dam and Las Vegas or directly west by Needles. The latter proved to be a considerably shorter distance, which suited our plans better, because we wanted to stay as long as possible at the Canyon yet not be more than another day in reaching the coast.

This decided, we drove on a few hundred yards to the hotel for breakfast. The car park was literally alongside the Canyon, so I had to walk at once to the brink. Having heard such accounts of Grand Canyon, I had almost persuaded myself that no place could be so stupendously impressive as this was made out to be. But at last I was there, and I could no longer doubt what I had been told.

It was now only just after half-past eight in the morning. Consequently, I knew that the effects I was watching would have changed considerably an hour or two later, tending to become less inspiring as the sun rose higher, though still impressive enough to satisfy any one. For this reason, I would have liked to have been there at dawn. One day, I will be, and will set aside a fortnight to wander in the Canyon and explore its environs. But on this occasion, after six days of such hard driving, averaging nearly four hundred miles a day, it would have detracted from our enjoyment to have risen so early; and I was already short of sleep. I sat up each night to write a short account of the past day's run. These accounts I elaborated on my knee during the first or last hour of the succeeding day's journey, when I always asked Louis to drive, so leaving myself free to work.

" . . . it was now only just after half-past eight in the morning. . . . I would have liked to have been there at dawn."

All the same, I was at the Canyon early enough to see the great capes of the northern rim still standing out prominently in the morning light which slants in lengthwise from the direction of the Painted Desert. And having taken a photograph of them as they were then, I just stood staring, hungry though I was, till Louis reminded me that we should go and eat.

Then I discovered that the ever-enterprising Mr. Fred Harvey was responsible for the organisation of that hotel also. He must be the world's supreme *hôtelier*.

There, at El Tovar, his building was rather special, in the log cabin style, but of a considerable size and particularly well arranged. Heads of bison and moose looked down from the walls in the hall. Passing the hatstand on my way to the dining-room, I saw it to be jointly in charge of a be-ribboned Indian and a Japanese boy in page's grey livery—a catholic partnership.

The waitresses, neatly tricked out in the black dresses and white aprons that we favour in England, were in charge of a dear grey-haired superintendent. Nothing escaped her kindly and watchful eye. I subsequently discovered that she had been for twenty years in the Harvey service. Oddly enough, many flat-out socialists cannot see that traditions which are valuable in mundane occupations like inn-keeping, have their counterparts in the no less mundane business of government. Tradition is not reactionary just because it is tradition; but only when it is dead instead of alive and growing in conformity with the unceasing progress of sound thinking translated into restrained action.

Wide as is the choice of food in the ordinary Harvey House, it was even wider here. There was a quite astonishing variety of fruit and of various cooked dishes. I started with some sliced, fresh peaches and went on to grilled, salted mackerel. It sounds an odd combination, but I seldom remember making a better breakfast.

Afterwards, in the shop off the hall, I bought one or two books on the history of the district. And in the Indian store outside, an exact reproduction of a Hopi pueblo, I picked up a Ute war bonnet of eagles' feathers and a Navajo plaited quirt, both from a well-known collection and undoubtedly genuine. I was particularly pleased with the quirt because those of Indian workmanship are not too common; most old quirts now obtainable are of Mexican origin. This was a lovely piece of leather and had obviously seen much hard service. Nearby, the hogans, or huts, of some Navajos could be seen.

Thus, my appetite for mementoes also satisfied, I was inevitably drawn back to the Canyon. I could now devote myself solely to it; all else being done, including the filling of the car's tank with gasoline. Only in such a frame of mind should one approach the great moments of life, if, as in this instance, the approach is deliberate. Of many situations which subsequently prove to be moving or inspiring in some way, one is not forewarned. The impressions gained are therefore apt to be weakened by current preoccupations from which few of us are ever entirely free. But that morning I had at least some inkling of what I was going to see. And I went to look at it in the way that one sometimes takes a badly-needed drink of water, after deliberately postponing doing so until its refreshing properties can be fully enjoyed.

Grand Canyon is the most remarkable example in the world of natural erosion. Stretching west of its beginning at the mouth of Marble Canyon, fifty-six miles of the Grand Canyon itself is enclosed in a national park. One hundred and five miles of the Colorado River winds through it. From rim to rim, that part of the Canyon which is within the National Park varies in width from four to eighteen miles; and it is a mile deep. Valleys contiguous to it at the bottom are semi-tropical all the year round, though on the rim the climate is that of the Rockies. Its western boundary includes the Havasu Canyon, which is an Indian Reservation and contains lovely waterfalls. At its eastern extremity, the great walls of the Canyon taper off into the Painted Desert. Altogether, the Grand Canyon is 217 miles long. (So much I gratefully gathered from a journal.) Apart from the æons of time during which, submerged for whole epochs, this part of the country was built up by sedimentation to an even greater height than the roughly seven to nine thousand feet at which much of the plateau remains, possibly the Colorado River has taken nine million years to cut down through it to its present bed. The details are fascinating, but a stark fact or two like these suffices here.

In the morning, the northern rim seems to step forward into the light, cape by cape, and gradually rids itself of deep and mysterious shadows. Later, these temples of the dawn, as I have seen them described, change. As they become better illuminated, they lose something of their earlier reserve; the headlands and the gulf are recognisable at one and the same time, while the floor of the Canyon, made up of bewildering shades of green, also grows clear. By noon the whole place appears at its dullest, because the sun is high above it, but even then one can hardly look away even for a second. In the evening, so I am told, the process is more or less reversed: the temples of the south rim loom in magnificent contrast to the plateau at their feet, a plateau which is still twelve hundred feet above the river. Alas, I could not stay to see.

From Yaki Point, farther eastward along the south rim than I had been before breakfast, I stopped and looked about me. I had previously wondered what I would be able to tell my friends about the Canyon. I knew that many writers had tried to describe its physical properties and failed, and I saw no reason to think that where they had failed I would succeed. Nor do I now think that the formations and colour changes in the Canyon can be adequately described in words at all.

Their moods can be captured on canvas by good artists—I have seen several such paintings and wished that I could buy more than one—yet, even then, it is only a single mood that has been reproduced at a time. And out of a dozen such painted reproductions, there will be at the most only one in which something of the spirit of the place gleams through the brushwork.

I cannot describe what Grand Canyon looks like; more especially because I would no sooner have finished one attempt than the light would have changed, and with it the expression that Nature wears there. Instead, I can only indicate my personal conception of the character of Grand Canyon by revealing a picture it painted in my mind as I stood watching its tinted cliffs step forward from the shadows, and seem to advance across the green dancing-floor of age-old memory and peer into the yellow waters of the Colorado River at their feet.

To me, it is the most suitable place for meditation —for worship, if you like—that I have ever seen. In this, from what I have heard, it might be equalled by the Himalayas, except that the Canyon and its contents provide such a comprehensive catalogue of Nature's decrees, whereas those great mountains cannot, I imagine, do this, or in quite the same incisive way. The Divine Intelligence seems very close at Grand Canyon; it surrounds one like a consciously felt blessing.

Phenomena like this, and Carlsbad Caverns, strike a death blow at dogma. Knowing accurately enough how long both took to become as they are, how almost incredibly slowly the wind and sun has changed one and the water the other, it is to me a dreary thought that some men and women can be so gullible as to credit the balderdash with which most organised religions disguise their now shrunken kernels of truth; or if they do not really believe it, yet crave

"... tinted cliffs step forward from the shadows (at Yaki point) ... across the green dancing floor of the age-old memory."

the hypnotic effect of attendant ritual to stifle courageous thought in themselves. Every person of every denomination who flatters himself to be a priest or preacher should be led through Carlsbad Caverns, and be allowed to see Grand Canyon, where the light itself, by which we live, visibly writes such a "Pax vobiscum" on the walls below as should stop even the most bigoted in his tracks and make him ponder.

Here, if we placed our great churches and temples within the Canyon, we would see them become just well-proportioned warts, dully blank except for the colour lent them by their new surroundings. Only the humble care and joy in craftsmanship absorbed by their stones from those who built them, would still remain to hallow them; that, and the aura of such prayers, raised in their vaulted chambers by bygone generations, which had borne the sign and seal of genuineness. For every expression the buildings might represent of material pomp and pride on the part of the dignitaries they housed, as one intolerant sect opposed to another—for these, I reckon, they would take on an added drabness.

One building that here, wherever placed, would still be a jewel, giving back to the Canyon in equal measure what radiance it took, would be the Taj Mahal, built by a man for the overpowering, true and uplifting love of a woman, and showing in every line that human love so enduring has Divine origins, as has this vast cleft of Nature's set since the world was dumb in the place we know now as Arizona.

Leaving Grand Canyon, we drove back over the same road for more than sixty miles and then turned west into Williams, where we stopped to fill a vacuum flask with iced water. While my companion was doing this, I remained in my seat, to smoke a pipe and take stock of the life in this small western hamlet.

An eating house nearby was easily recognisable. It advertised Mexican and Spanish dishes and Budweiser beer on tap.

Through the front window, I caught a glimpse of the proprietor, spraying his bottled goods and melons with what I could only imagine was a disinfectant of some kind or a form of anti-fly mixture. I took this to imply that his food was highly flavoured anyway, and that no one would notice!

Farther along the street, on the other side, a corner site was occupied by one of a chain of " Clean Food" stores. It bore their famous blue and white medallion, embellished with a typical phonetic abbreviation: " Pay'n Takit."

The types of passers-by were many and varied. I saw a Chinese woman, some Indian children, a negro mechanic, a Mexican gaucho, three cowboys, and a college girl in a blue and red jersey—all within ten minutes. This was apart from the more ordinary inhabitants of the place and the occupants of the automobiles passing through. Of the motors themselves, a number were local trucks engaged in haulage or delivery. Others were driven by ranchers presumably belonging to the neighbourhood, and quite a few were higher class machines, such as Packards, Cadillacs and Chryslers, in the hands of well-to-do folk undertaking longer journeys. Altogether, Williams seemed a busy place despite its lack of size.

Proceeding, I drove through miles and miles of the loveliest Arizona country, similar to that lying behind me, between Williams and Flagstaff: blue hills, pine forests, and open stretches of grass rippling in the wind, with horses grazing on them. This was succeeded by a more confined district of green dells filled with shady trees. In one such hollow, I stopped to light a pipe outside a white house of the old Colonial type. Greatly to my surprise, there was a swimming pool becomingly incorporated in the old-fashioned garden. A small sign outside announced that twenty-five cents was charged for a bathe. But goodness only knows who ever stopped at this peaceful, lonely place! For it was miles from anywhere; as it might be in a far away Argyllshire glen.

". . . through miles and miles of the loveliest Arizona country . . ."

"Then by degrees . . . to the stoniest, narrowest, most twisting defile that had yet engulfed us."

Then by degrees we came to the stoniest, narrowest, most twisting defile that had yet engulfed us. Greenery forsook us. The glare striking up from the naked ground was fiendish in its intensity. But so changeable is this attractive country of America, with its alternate stripes of quiet beauty and relentless savagery, that I seemed scarcely to have been tautening my arms for this harder driving or to have wiped the sweat once or twice from my face with a stained driving glove than we were out into as broad a mountain valley as I remember.

It must have been eighteen or twenty miles long, five to ten miles wide in places, and clothed with a dry herbage which for once seemed to gain ascendency over the desert plants. Bending occasionally to a gust swirling out of the defile, this grass ran right to the jagged, multi-coloured mountains that marched in unending procession to left and right. Our road ran up the middle of the valley, and rose imperceptibly all the way. It deviated from the straight by not so much as a fraction. Its surface was loose grit, two inches deep, upon which the car seemed to float, incessantly skidding a little; sometimes four-wheel skids but more often just a tail-wag.

I had confidence in the special tyres which Toby Couture had fitted for me, and in consequence maintained a steady fifty or sixty miles an hour. Yet the valley was so broad and the road through it so straight, that the car seemed to be standing still. Except for its sidewise jauntings and jiggings, there was no impression of movement. I was reminded somewhat of a few motor races in which I drove years ago on the sands of a seashore in England. There, I had found the technique different from the ordinary race-driving which I knew. When the sand became cut up in the neighbourhood of flags round which we had to steer in place of corners, it had produced much the same sensation as this loose grit: a feeling of not being quite on the ground at all. Now, after a few moments, my wrists and shoulders got the rhythmic trick of it again, and I could largely dismiss from my mind the problem of keeping to the road.

For I was dreaming of herding cattle here. No setting could have been more appropriate. To have seen a big bunch of steers kicking up the dust as it came grumbling and bellowing through this place with cowboys on its flanks, would have been an unforgettable sight. As the Chrysler raised the grit in a stinging cloud behind her, so I sat at the wheel in something of a maze; momentarily seeing myself, instead, in a western saddle, my eyes keeping track of stragglers, while the sure-footed cow pony between my knees looked out for gopher holes.

I do not know the name of that place, because foolishly I omitted to ask when we stopped a mile or two farther on at Kingman for luncheon. But to me, it will always be "The Valley of Cattle."

I am afraid Louis was not too happy as we came through it, but I could do nothing to relieve the situation. I protested that, after all, I didn't make the road, that the "Airflow" was taking it well, and that in almost any other car but a Rolls-Royce, Lancia, Mercédés, B.M.W., Packard, Buick, or Tatra, we should have been much more uncomfortable. Moreover, I pointed out that to drive slower would have been worse, as it usually is on a road of that nature. All the same, though unfailingly merry and comic about it, I think he was glad when we got to Kingman. I entirely sympathised with him, for the driver certainly has the best of it in such circumstances, he knows exactly how controllable the car really is.

Feeding at Kingman was a primitive business. By way of experiment, we walked into the first place we saw; a long, narrow eating shop fronting directly on to the glaring main street. We chose a table next to the curtained window and ordered what seemed safest: thin soup and part of a freshly-killed fowl. The bird proved to be without doubt the oldest inhabitant.

There was no place to wash, so I explored the kitchen where the cook, a large man, slow and amiable of speech, filled a tin basin with hot water for me.

We talked while I removed the sticky grime from my hands and face. But little emerged from our conversation except that he was for Roosevelt, like most of the underdogs. They think the "have-nots" are going to get something permanent at the expense of the "haves," regardless of the fact that the latter also include the thrifty and hardworking of all classes, who may not safely or justly be taxed to the point where thrift ceases to be worth while. But of sound national finance, by which alone the standard of living has been raised with a degree of security in any country, they neither know nor care anything. How should they? They are ignorant, through little fault of their own, and their ideas of finance are limited to the apportionment of a small weekly wage.

Only reactionaries ignore the right of these people to better conditions, but, equally, only a government to some extent reactionary fails to insist upon proper explanation in the newspapers of what it is doing to improve matters. Most democratic or republican governments are like this. It is one of their inherent weaknesses. They would abhor, they declare indignantly, a muzzling of the press such as occurs under a dictatorship, whether Fascist or extreme Socialist (i.e., Communist), yet they themselves do not insist on publication of the truth: and a half-truth is often more inflammatory than a downright lie or a rude silence. Vested interests are responsible for this policy of turbulence, but its years are probably numbered. To permit deliberate misrepresentation of facts, especially where the public interest is concerned, is as dangerous as allowing children to play with matches and is respon-

199

sible for much of the bloodshed, unrest, bewilderment and lack of faith current in the world to-day.

We are, I think, gradually approaching the time when some measure of press control will be recognised by all to be essential—not a blanketing of facts, but rather their revelation presented without bias. The great journalists themselves—and some are truly great in mind and heart—are the proper people to devise such a charter and urge its adoption as a law. For a newspaper proprietor should have to be a newspaper proprietor and nothing else; certainly not an active party politician, industrialist or banker at the same time; merely an accurate recorder of facts and the various sensible inferences calmly to be drawn from them. And in respect of political news, its moral presentation should be the measure of his papers' security from interference. Also, truth is now more saleable than lies.

Again, activity in every sphere is now so intense that accurate feature writing is sufficient to retain advertising and secure profits. I am no lover of slogans or catch-phrases, both of which nearly always originate in the low impulse to make capital out of ignorance through the medium of hysteria. But it is not without significance that increasing numbers of people are saying, "Oh, you can't believe what you read in the newspapers." That, indeed, is a fact in some instances. Not until the Italo-Abyssinian War was practically over, for example, did the British public in any quantity learn a little something of what really happened.[1] Still, it goes without saying that only communities with a steadily beating heart and a sense of humour, like the British Commonwealth, the United States, Germany, Italy, Turkey, and one or two of the smaller Northern countries, are as yet capable of successfully operating,

[1] And since then, the public has been partially led to believe, with divers motives, that anarchism ceases to be anarchism when practised in all its beastliness by red Spaniards; and those who fight for such remnants of law and order as that afflicted country has known, are called insurgents.

should there miraculously be a demand for it, any such mutual agreement to speak more of the truth.

After Kingman, we found ourselves at once in the desert again, here even hotter and more barren. As scenery, it was inspiring in the extreme, for mountains stood round us in every direction. The time was now late afternoon, and they were mantling themselves in shades like Indian blankets against the coming of sundown. We reached a formidable pass, like a short Alpine pass; every bit as steep and with as many hair-pin corners as some. Many, corners indeed, were narrower and more dangerous than those usually encountered in Italy, Austria or Switzerland, and lacked a retaining wall on the out-side. In the heat, this meant strenuous driving; my hardest till then. For I wanted—in fact, had been invited by the factory—to test the car thoroughly. Here, then, was the obvious place for indirect gear work and a stern try-out of the braking and cooling systems. Some of the corners were so sudden and steep that in order to make the most of the car's performance I had to use first gear six times; and every one knows what that implies in the case of a powerful American car!

I had cause again to sympathise with my passenger. It was not a pleasant pass over which to drive fast, but I had found no better opportunity for seeing what the car would do under difficulties. Unfortunately, driving west, we had the outside edge of this road on most of the corners, both coming up the pass and going down on the far side; for the road was cut on the northern shoulder of a great mountain. And that day, as things happened, we met a number of other cars on some of the worst corners. With only a foot or two to spare on our side there was a sheer drop of several hundred feet. One or two of these cars (some drivers can't think) were in the middle of the road when they first appeared round the corners. Situations of this kind are always trying for any one except the driver.

I attempted to interest Louis in the view, which was really magnificent; and I think that to some extent I succeeded, because he was by no means frightened, only savage with the other cars—as I was. The descent on the far side was just as steep and strenuous, but I found the worst corners to be guarded by low walls. So I did not have to think up so many quick-fire comments on the scenery, or Louis the equally superfluous replies to them.

Such corners constitute my most serious criticism of American roads. Though I dislike the soft shoulders, and consider many miles of the concrete pavement which crosses the continent as verging on the dangerously narrow, I look upon those unguarded mountain bends on Sitgraves Pass as positively perilous. I feel that if such a nation as Italy, whose cars perforce are built for mountaineering and are more suitable for such work than many an American automobile, can safeguard its worst mountain corners, then America could certainly improve hers. And bringing to the task efficiency such as characterises her National Parks, she could do it extremely well.

More hot, undulating miles of desert with the sun in my eyes, vizor or not, brought us to the Colorado River—a flashing band of mercury spilled between confines of green and set before a background of hills like red rhododendrons. California lay beyond. Driving a little way into that State, I stopped for a last look behind me, and kept turning first one way and then the other: to the flaming evening of California and the reflection of its fire over Arizona.

Then, perspiring and thirsty, I drove the few sultry darkening miles to Needles, the hottest town in America, where once again a Fred Harvey house extended to me its welcome hospitality. Over a highball, which for some time past I had envisaged as being longer and cooler than any I ever drank before, I discussed the question of heat with the manager.

". . . more hot, undulating miles of desert . . . brought us . . ."

". . . to the Colorado river . . . mercury spilled between confines of green . . . against a background of hills like red rhododendrons."

He said cheerfully that the temperature had risen as high as 118 degrees in July and August. I replied that it was hot enough for me as it was.

While we were at dinner, an engine driver, dressed in surprisingly clean overalls, came in and sat down some distance from us. He was an elderly man, and chose his meal with deliberation and restraint. When he had finished, he lit a cigar and walked out to wait for the train which he would take over. I liked to think of a man such as he, an old and valued servant of the railroad, being able to sit down with us all to a comfortable, unhurried meal before starting his next spell of duty—and a very responsible duty at that.

Later, from my bedroom, I watched the moon glinting on the first palm trees I had seen upon my journey. This, then, was really California. There were wire mesh doors to the French windows which opened onto a long balcony; and it was so hot that I kept the electric fan going all night, while I drowsed, lying on my back, tired to the point of restlessness and as bare as at bath-time.

CHAPTER XI

THE MOJAVE DESERT—THEN FINALLY LOS ANGELES

THERE HAD BEEN A MAN ASLEEP ON THE LAWN AT THE BACK of the Harvey House at Needles. I was up soon after five, and standing on the balcony outside my bedroom. I saw him stretched on his face under the palm trees. He looked ragged and down-at-heel. It was impossible to tell whether he belonged to the unfortunate army of American unemployed, now numbering between ten and eleven millions, or whether he was just one of the floating population of hitch-hikers who perennially follow the sun across the States; and flock into Los Angeles every autumn to the number of a quarter of a million or so, many of them unwilling to work in any circumstances and numbering among them petty thieves, confidence tricksters, and every kind of rogue and bum.

All the way from New York, I had passed such men and youths, standing by the roadside and greeting each car with their characteristic, almost professional gesture, which consists in jerking a thumb over the shoulder and smiling ingratiatingly. They call this "thumbing their way across." But all women and most men would be ill-advised to give a lift to some of them. This is particularly the case when the western deserts are reached. On these lonely highways, there might be no one to come to the rescue of a motorist whom they decided to rob after taking a ride off him.

We breakfasted at Needles at six and left at seven, so as to avoid the heat on the first part of the road we had to cover. This was now the safest highway since New York; well graded, evenly laid but not too smooth. Rain was the last

"... the Mojave desert ... hills edged like knives ... a giant bric-a-brac of heated rocks wildly scattered."

"... the railway ... shrunk to the thinness of a spider's strand. ..."

thing expected here for months at a time, but experience told me that this surface would be nearly as easy to drive on when wet as in this morning's sun. We cruised at a steady eighty for mile after glaring mile.

This was the Mojave desert—a preposterous place, stony and bare to the last degree, its sweeping outlines checked, confined and allowed to diverge again by jagged upthrusts of volcanic origin, hills edged like knives; its sole surface variation the giant *bric-à-brac* of heated rocks wildly scattered; the whole, monochrome in colour, pale and fierce, lent character only by light and shade. Had a pterodactyl swept suddenly across the radiator, long-toothed bill snapping, leathery pinions rustling dryly, on its way back to some far-off northern swamp, I suppose I would instinctively have ducked, but I doubt whether I would have been much surprised. I might even have remarked to Louis, as the little boy did to his mother, "Momma, there's a boid;" and being rebuked and told to say bird, have retorted, "But, Momma, it still looks like a boid."

Here, in a wilderness, symbols of the machine age assumed a friendliness which their bitterest opponents would have welcomed: this fine road itself was sure to lead somewhere; sooner or later it would pass an efficient service station, providing food and drink and human companionship as well as gasoline: the railway, as I saw it in one place, shrunk to the thinness of a spider's strand, surely connected two points of civilisation; a man would merely have to walk along it in one direction or the other, and hope the walk was not too far or the trains too few for his endurance. From a scorching rise between two harsh knolls, I attempted to photograph such a train, so far out upon the desert that if the snapshot proved successful, I expected a magnifying glass would be needed to discover the black insect trailing its gossamer pennon of dusky smoke.

Then there were the airway's beacons. These are at once the loneliest and most impressive of the three symbols of man's ascendency; lonely because they have no contact with their traffic; impressive because their very presence proves how now—and more so year by year—man crosses this place hurtling in comfort, reading, scheming still greater schemes for the future, or transacting in flight the larger or smaller business of the world, where his great-grandfather crossed, intent only on his crossing, as temporarily limited therefore in mind as his vision was oftimes blinded by sweat.

These airway beacons consist of orange and white trellis masts, each with its powerful lamp at the head and a small power house of the same colour at the foot. I saw three of them—one on a ridge, one by a bleak pass and one out in the flatness. Doubtless there were more, but my eyes were for other things.

Some miles short of Barstow, by which time the country had become more civilised again, we halted to be checked into California. Presumably, the post is situated here, instead of in the hot desert back on the State boundary, so that living conditions may be easier for the officials. Our car was searched for fruit, cotton, or suchlike stuff. The official performing this duty was polite and informative. He wore neat khaki trousers and shirt, a light solar topee, sun glasses and a plated badge of authority.

He explained the reason for the search, which was the fear of a pest of insects on the crops in the State; and in proof of what might happen, he showed me some English walnuts that he had previously confiscated. These had minute larvæ in their shells, or so he suspected. He had also some cotton pods which a party of motorists had picked by the road and brought with them, probably from Missouri. Under the outer skin of these, grubs might lie before hatching. I admitted to being an Englishman, but not to the present possession of

walnuts. My companion likewise emphatically denied a
passion for cotton. So the inspector genially passed us so far
as *he* was concerned.

Another equally pleasant official, young and dark-haired,
could not admit the legality of our manufacturer's number-
plates for California. He removed these, requiring us to
register the car afresh, and fixed to our windscreen a coloured
receipt for payment. Some discussion taking place on this
point, we encountered the only boor on our journey: a third
man, who was brought into the conversation and whose
opinion apparently carried weight. Whether he was an officer
or not, I could not tell. I hope and believe not, for he retired
into a garage across the road after delivering himself, in an
offensive, take-it-or-leave-it manner, of his reading of the
State's regulations. He had the irritable face of a petty fool,
enjoying his authoritative knowledge of small matters, and
was unlikely to predispose any motorist in favour of California,
before and afterwards found to be such an hospitable and
charming State.

Presently we went on. The countryside continued to show
some signs of a return to grace. A few thirsty-looking trees
and some narrow paddocks lay along the bed of the shallow
valley through which our road ran. Plainly, water was situated
there, though I could catch no sight of it. There were also a
few houses, whose inhabitants were presumably the cultiva-
tors of this strip of oasis.

A service station had to one side of it a row of tourist
cabins—the little auto camps so prevalent now in America.
These looked particularly clean. Their advertised price was
75 c. a night, and included a shower-bath. This would be about
3*s*. 7½*d*. in English money. In addition, an adequate evening
meal could be had for 25 c.; making a dollar all told, or
4*s*. 10*d*. Away beyond these cabins and their thin shelter of
trees, the arid hills rose again, beige and almost shadowless

now that the sun was really up. In this part of the country, too, only the sky immediately overhead had a blue tint to it, and pale at that. The horizon all round shimmered whitely.

We had been using Standard Oil stations practically throughout our trip, for no other reason than that we were conservatively minded. Throughout, they had been beyond reproach; some larger than others, but every one clean and efficient, and their attendants politeness itself. This was not surprising, because the general run of service stations in America strikes a foreigner as being good. They are far better than in Europe. As one approaches the West, they become really remarkable in appearance; their style, and the flowers grown about them, tempt one to stop and stare if not necessarily to buy gas. Some have instituted a *café* service that enables motorists to sit at the wheel and eat: trays of delicacies are clipped onto the door of the car. There are also soda fountains in many of them. Along Broadway, Hollywood, at night, their Neon electric signs are like a static display of fireworks, so bright that the Authorities could easily abolish street lamps and headlights. Somewhere out in the Mojave we also passed a big transformer station. Its tautly impressive power-cables stretched away over north-easterly nothingness to Boulder Dam.

Forty minutes after Barstow, the road turned south. But still we drove through parched lands. Victorville formed only a break in their monotony. Then, heading more directly again for the Pacific Coast, we approached the Cajon Pass that drops down through the Sierra Madre to San Bernardino. It is an impressive pass. The broad road comes to it over hot tablelands bestrewn with Joshua trees, holding up their deformed green arms. The Sierra closes in from the north-west and south-east—a grim line of jagged peaks. That morning, clouds were stretched like a soft bandage across their mighty chests, to leave bare their tall heads to the sky and their great torsos which rested upon the desert: we seemed to be driving over the brink of the world through a gateway forged by Vulcan.

Below us, as we started down in long sweeps, a capacious curving valley opened out, its brim frothy with cloud. Into this we dived, watching for drops on the windscreen for the first time since Illinois. But none came, although I would have welcomed the sight of them. Instead, a dull greyness surrounded us for half a mile—no more; then we emerged again into Californian sunshine and, looking back, could see that the tenuous cloud only existed to veil the plains of orange groves to which we were descending.

Subsequently, we cut round to one side of San Bernardino, avoiding its main thoroughfares, and stopped a few miles on for luncheon at a Wilson wayside restaurant. Here, we spent an amusing hour in a clean, tastefully-furnished room practically on the sidewalk, entirely walled in by glass except for a broad stone hearth across one corner, ornamented by a stag's head on the brickwork over it. We ate wonderful food at a moderate price, served by an extremely handsome waitress, perhaps an ex-Hollywood candidate. The inevitable baseball game was coming over the air on the inevitable radio, eye-witnessed by the inevitable and, to an Englishman, quite incomprehensible announcer. When the quick-fire hubbub died down, I gathered that the "Tigers" had beaten the "Cubs" in the World Series contest at Detroit. This was O.K. by me; there was no reason why I shouldn't be pleased whoever won. Our waitress informed us that the restaurant sweep-stake had been won by the milkman, an Italian, who there-upon promised himself an outsize *ravioli* feed that coming evening. This sounded swell to me.

I returned to my rainbow trout, splendidly cooked, and reflected gloomily that in the few inns in England where trout of any sort can be had, they would not be cooked like this. On the other hand, I would doubtless be spared a radio description of the latest League football match. Life is full of these minor compromises—it is the bigger ones that put us off our feed. I started nervously, and finished ravenously, a salad of cottage cheese and pineapple. I should never have thought, brought up on French dressing, Italian oil and English prodigality where vinegar is concerned, that two such constituents could make a salad at all.

Outside in the garden of this simple yet remarkable eating house, there were orange trees, palms and flower beds prolific with bloom. One side of the building was given up to a soda fountain; its counter occupied by all sorts of people. On the other side, a rustic shelter, many yards square, shaded a lavish display of fruit and great glass jars of what looked like honey or some form of syrup. Such a roadside restaurant properly belongs to Utopia. After early starts on so many previous mornings, I was not quite sure that I was seeing straight.

We drove on. The road was now a comfortable four-car highway. It ran through deep groves of orange and lemon trees, their rich green clumps of foliage alternating with sections of tall eucalyptus. The even darker green of these towered for a score of feet or more, like a glossy wall: it is, indeed, as a windbreak that they are often planted. These were succeeded in turn by a stretch of giant palms, fresh-fronded at their tall crowns, but drooping, brown and bedraggled from thence to their feet; as though they had marched through deep mud to the road's edge and there halted in line.

We began to get into traffic, and so came to Azusa. I am told that this name has its origin in the fact that the city is particular about its inhabitants. It will not allow all and sundry to live there, but insists that from A to Z they shall be U.S.A. But, as a motorist, I remember Azusa because I first saw there a yellow official sign which read: "Stop when

" . . . as though they had marched through deep mud to the road's edge and there halted in line."

pedestrians are in crosswalk"—referring to what we in England call "crossings," ours being marked at present by beacons, which consist of globes like huge oranges on black and white posts.

Near this official sign at Azusa, was another of the same colour, announcing: "Nine trout for a dollar." One was as easy to see as the other, or as difficult—whichever way you think of it. I felt this to be typical of the dangerous conflict prevalent throughout America between road signs and advertisements.

Thereafter, we slipped modestly through Monrovia and Pasadena into Los Angeles. These places, and others farther back, all join onto one another. Steady suburban driving is necessary; it is the only sensible way to drive in such streets. Side roads carry "Stop" signs. Even so, one has to watch everlastingly for fools. At main intersections, where motors on both roads must stop, but where there is no light, the first car to stop is the first to go on. Where trolley cars run on a slightly raised track down the middle of streets, an incessantly swinging disc, aided by a ding-dong bell, guards each crossing. And the trolleys hoot like young trains.

In the quieter streets of the residential section, the houses are low and flat-roofed; some have miniature patios. Many spreading palms rise between them and in front of them. A number of these houses possess lovely gardens; all have green turf, varying from a few feet to many square yards. And most of it is kept surprisingly green, although water here costs more than most things.

Thus we entered the downtown part of Los Angeles, a little disappointing to an Englishman. It is not unlike our midland Birmingham at home except for the glare and a few typically tall American buildings. Here, there is another system of traffic signals, a combination light and arm arrangement. As the light changes, an arm swings out with "Stop" or "Go" written on it. Likewise, a bell rings twice; once as a warning and again when the change takes place. These things are regular boxes of tricks. Most drivers, I noticed, looked at the signal in order to stop, and, having stopped, did not look again; they started automatically on hearing the second bell.

Pedestrians will still step down off the kerb after seeing the "Go" signal swing up, because they know that the traffic must wait for the second bell. But should an accident occur in such circumstances, the law does not protect them—quite rightly. So it is more intelligent to stay on the sidewalk.

We turned, and climbed for nearly three miles along the road to Hollywood and Beverly Hills. The buildings became finer, the boulevards wider, the display of taste more evident. Up there, where many people live who seldom go down town from one year's end to the other, the branch stores were consequently more splendid than their parent buildings at the bottom of the hill. Service stations like little palaces lined Wilshire Boulevard. Before long, their strip lights would be sparkling in competition with the evening glow over the Pacific.

The Chrysler was swung into the forecourt of the Ambassador Hotel, that deservedly famous caravanserai, and became lost among a hundred other cars parked there. The long drive from New York was over. Soon warm darkness succeeded the short Californian twilight. A great moon shone down upon the city; silvering the closely-cut lawns from which palms rose like huge dusky mushrooms. And after a while, there was little sound nearby but the melodious croaking of the frogs in the shadows.

INTERMISSION

INTERMISSION

MOONSHINE IN SUNNY CALIFORNIA

THE CALIFORNIAN NIGHTS DO, IN FACT, PUT A SPELL UPON strangers; more so, than the brilliant days of which an Englishman may tire a little, longing for the softer lights and misty views of home, where from behind a black cloud the sun lays brazen fingers on the purple slopes of Mull, the rounded Border hills rise green and friendly, an unknown something broods behind the dark Welsh Marches, and over the Sussex Downs the Channel breeze ruffles up the fleeces of the sheep.

Having work to do in the way of writing newspaper articles and reading American journals, I generally went out in Los Angeles at night. About five days a week, at my temporary secretary's concise request, my luncheon would come up to my room on a tray.

"A liver sausage sandwich on rye (bread) and an Avocado salad—yes, and iced coffee; at once, please."

Or it might be a chicken sandwich on white with mayonnaise—Mrs. Cotton got to know. She was a first-rate assistant, as understanding as she was efficient. And during the meal we would talk, exchanging views about the morning's output, before resuming work again in the shaded room with its open windows and half-drawn blinds; I pacing up and down in my shirtsleeves, dictating; she taking down, waiting —her pencil poised, then taking down, taking down, taking down; while outside, the bright light beat upon the wide lawns of the great hotel and upon the white and beige buildings of the vastly extensive town. After three hours she would speak again into the telephone, "Tea, please—for two; at once, please."

215

Another tray would come. Then, silly with work, I would suggest a walk; and we would stroll along the boulevards for half an hour, discussing journeys each of us had made or what our respective countries were like to live in—anything to get our minds off work. Then back we went for another hour, this time with the blinds up, for the day's glare was passing.

Thus it was for three weeks with intervals of only a day or two. It had to be. Forty-five thousand words take some producing. And I am normally a slow worker, unused to dictating anything but letters and preferring to write other stuff in long hand.

Most nights I would dine alone, usually in the hotel coffee shop rather than the famous Cocoanut Grove Restaurant, for which the labours of the day only once or twice left me in the proper mood of gaiety. Afterwards I would slowly walk miles in this residential section, up one apparently endless boulevard, across two or three blocks, and home down another. This was the best time of the day. The lines of palms rocketing silently from the sidewalks till they burst out into clusters of fronds, black against the indigo sky, were peaceful companions. The nights were never wholly dark; always there was silver in the sky. When the moon was approaching fulness, its limpid rays poured over house, tree and road like metallic paint. Then the shadows became deeper by contrast, the throbbing song of the frogs sounded even more restful, and only yellow lighted windows indicated the unseen presence of human beings.

Curiously enough, there were no public benches thereabouts. I never saw one in that part of Los Angeles, only down town in the small irregular patch of public garden across the road from the Biltmore Hotel. Consequently, if I wanted to sit out of doors, I had to stay in the grounds of the Ambassador. These were admittedly quiet enough at night and fairly

216

extensive—they even included a very miniature zoo—but I missed being able to wander some distance and then lounge dreaming on a seat, as in other cities up and down the world.

One such night, I summed up serious views that I had heard expressed on my way across the continent and since my arrival. They fell under two main headings: the next Presidential election, and Law and Order. From both I could draw only superficial conclusions, for my survey had been by force of circumstances superficial. Yet, for what they were worth, certain broad indications of the public train of thought seemed plain.

First, there seemed to be no doubt that President Roosevelt would be re-elected. True, I had scarcely been in contact with more than one or two representatives of a vast class of small capitalists (the middle-class, as they are known in England) who must have been hard hit by the Democrats' taxation programme. The fact that those of this class whom I did meet happened to be for Roosevelt, was doubtless a coincidence; and their approval of the President's efforts testified mainly to their own personal humanity and long-range intelligence. They included, for example, the head salesman-pilot of an aircraft manufacturing firm, an experienced minor executive in the automobile industry, and a motion picture employee of round about the $10,000 dollar a year mark. Each of these men sincerely felt that the President (though they considered his advisers not always to have been of the best) is an astute and humane man, who looks far over the heads of the political pack and does his best to plan for the ultimate good of the greatest number; and that he does so, not by wrecking the power-house of capitalism, but by calling upon it for an added share-out of financial current which they held it could well afford. And though they earn reasonable but by no means large salaries according to their class, my informants were quite willing to retrench and do their bit towards bettering conditions for labouring Americans in the future.

Each was a hard-working, competent man, well above the average standard of intelligence and education. As such, they were plainly exceptions. Their class, from which they stood out, might have been bitterly opposed, *en masse*, to the New Deal or any succeeding measures of like sort. But I felt that at least their broad-mindedness augered well for years to come.

Representatives I met of the other two classes—roughly speaking, capitalists on a larger scale or humble artisans or unemployed—were sharply divided; the former, including socialites, bankers, "big business" chiefs, film magnates, certain heads of aircraft corporations, etc., were firmly against President Roosevelt at that time, and the latter, overwhelming in number, as firmly for him. One could not help forming the opinion that even if he made no concessions to industry and the rich—and obviously he would, aiming rightly at greater unity—he would still be re-elected. All foreign observers, German, Dutch, Italian, Swedish, French or whatever they were, seemed agreed upon this. But it was somewhat disheartening to find so many people, whom I knew and liked immensely, opposed to what appeared to be the birth of National Socialism when the alternative, the world over, is a threat of Communist uprisings, against which I repeatedly heard that, in America, the nervous had previously been arming their houses and laying in supplies, particularly at intervals during 1931-33 in the Industrial Middle West.

But even this assessment of surface indications was made then, and is now recorded, with reservations. There was obviously another side to the coin, though a difficulty arose in getting people to describe it in detail. Criticism by the rich was confined mostly to having their incomes reduced: I could obtain few constructive ideas about long-range improvement of working-class conditions which would also benefit their own stock holdings by resulting in a higher standard of living and increased trade, through adjusted production and distribution, rather than partial or seasonal stagnation. Yet this problem stares every one in the face to-day.

The plaint of industry, on the other hand, was the old one of threatened government interference with private enterprise. A harnessing of initiative was prophesied as being an inevitable corollary. Here, naturally, was a real cause for heart searchings if the picture drawn were not exaggerated. Still, there seemed a likelihood of this, and of political capital being made out of it by the Republicans.

To an outside observer there were many signs to indicate the necessity for certain big nation-wide schemes of dovetailing supply with demand, primary costs with distribution charges, retail prices with purchasing power, wages with hours and profits, and hours with unemployment figures. To think that the President would wilfully disregard alike the logical claims of industry and its assistance in such vast reforms would be to rate him less far-seeing than any man capable of reaching his great position could possibly be. It was tantamount to visualising a blunt antagonising of British Industry by the National Government instead of a mutual effort, continuously pursued, to promote National Socialism along lines at once financially stable and ethically sound.

In some instances, well-to-do people seemed to refuse to see the wood for the trees. As with the wealthy classes, was this not, I wondered, also the moment for Industry to take a leaf out of the book of those thoughtful middle class executives and if necessary face a temporary period of reasoned personal sacrifice for the furtherment of national preparedness in all ways; which could inevitably result

219

only in increased welfare all round, for themselves and their businesses no less than for others?

As a matter of fact, the profits of American business increased by forty-five per cent in 1935, so its leaders had no cause to weep on that account. But a number of them had been lamenting to me the absence of business men in politics. Was this, then, not an opportunity such as they might not get again of co-operating with a popular President; of proving, disproving, enlarging or modifying certain of the "New Deal" conceptions (which, after all, the country largely favoured) by an attitude of friendliness rather than by pouring money into political, press and spoof League or Council forms of fostering legislative sabotage and suspicion? Outwardly, at any rate, it appeared that by a sincere attempt along such lines they stood to lose no more than they already feared might happen, and to gain a great deal in the way of harmony, cleaner politics and a richer national spirit.

More healthy was the fact that all with whom I discussed the incident were devoutly thankful for Huey Long's death. No matter whether I questioned the highest ranks of society, the most powerful business interests, the humblest shoeshiner, a coloured housemaid or a barman, I got the same answer. It would be strange if this also were a coincidence. Certainly, I never went to Louisiana, his State. Still, I talked with many diverse people in many States and never met one of his supporters. Mingled with an unwilling admiration for him as a man who had "gotten some place," everybody I encountered variously described him as a mountebank, a chiseller, a dangerous bum or just plain crazy. Some venomously spat out the opinion that the man who shot him should have had a medal. I simply quote them. Without exception, consideration of the man being dead weighed with them not at all. They spoke their minds, and likened him to a mad dog that by some fortunate chance had been run over. And if the harm he did was such as they described to me, their attitude is fully understandable.

None of them were people who would remotely countenance murder; indeed, would normally condemn it with horror. But having seen how helpless were the various laws of their land to deal with what they believed to have been the crass dishonesty, graft and self-interest of a glib upstart masquerading even in Washington as a champion of the people, they openly gave expression to their relief at what had happened, as being to an incalculable degree the lesser of two evils from a national point of view. Yet they had not gone "haywire" on the whole subject of modern leaders of masses. Their judgment of demagogues in general showed a welcome perspicacity compared with the unrealist views I had often heard round dinner tables in Europe. Following on their condemnation of the late Huey Long, I half expected an outright attack on Mussolini and Hitler in response to my guiding of the conversation, but I was soon forced privately (and gladly) to admit the mistake of expecting from sensible Americans the ideas put forward elsewhere by those gulled by an unsound Pacifist or Bolshevist influence.

Most of them were naturally somewhat opposed to the Fascist and Nazi methods alike on Democratic and Republican grounds, but no one insulted the Duce or the Führer by likening either of these sagacious leaders to Huey Long. And those who had studied European conditions quickly revealed their recognition of the difference between building roads in Italy and Germany for the purposes of industry, defence and employment, and the building of them in Louisiana as a sop to public opinion; between imposing discipline on a nation for the nation's regeneration and sloughing of international anarchy, and the ignorant support of a State gained by wild and utterly baseless promises of an imminent financial millennium for all; between the pursuit of personal power to rebuild a nation and the pursuit of power for the person pursuing.

To underestimate the German and Italian elements and ramifications in the United States seemed an obvious mistake. But much more than that, intelligent Americans in general admire efficiency and order, particularly, no doubt, because they see how well it works in their businesses and certain Federal departments, and regret not being able to have nearly enough of it in their State government. I found many looking with keen interest towards Italy and Germany, not in the least desiring the same *régime* in their own country—where, indeed, so different a version would be needed as to be, like an English version, almost unrecognisable—but pleased to see two great peoples putting their houses in order. And downright thinkers said something like this to me: " We can't talk too loud about Italian and German 'purges' as long as we have gunmen, kidnappers, about eleven million unemployed and hell's own political graft system. And will you tell me what prohibition did to our police . . . Oh, boy!"

One omission astonished me: no one in the course of these conversations referred to Portugal, where Dr. Salazar, virtually a dictator, has turned the unbalanced budgets of years into eight successive surpluses, and directs in an unassuming way the lives and welfare of a contentedly cooperative people.

Towards Russia, I gathered, they were turning only the calculating eyes of merchants. The Soviet, for all its astonishing efforts which, in the estimation of the thoughtful, suffer rather than gain by exaggeration, was generally held to be still "in a spot." True, having repudiated all her debts at the time of the revolution, any government that she might throw up could not help but bring about some internal improvement unless it was quite half-witted. After all, most individuals could remain solvent under such circumstances, provided their creditors had no option but to accept the unmoral *fait accompli* of discarded obligations. Still, this, that and the other was needed by Russia, and America was out to supply those needs on a strictly business-like basis. And if the American Ambassador in Moscow chose to encourage polo there, well, it was cuttingly suggested, Abyssinia was not the only country requiring a healthy influence.

Of course, as in England, I met an ignorant idealist or two, so idealistic as to ignore, if not actually to approve, the mass assassination of the Tsar's family and the years of horror that followed; proffering the usual line of talk about the great Russian "experiment," and lacking the imagination to visualise their own womenfolk taken out of trains at wayside stations to be raped by the "investigating" official, their friends shot in batches for being at all cultured, and many persons of upright character and sturdy independence, what-ever their origin, refused supplies of food until they died— purely for these "experimental" purposes. Still, in the main, I had found on this subject the strength of national revulsion that I expected.

What the American Relief Administration had seen and recorded was not apparently forgotten, despite more recent pro-Soviet writing by the foreign correspondents of certain newspapers. If it was not actually remembered that prior to 1922, 1,766,180 people were executed in Russia, of which about 8,800 were doctors of medicine, 6,000 teachers and professors, 54,000 army officers, 105,000 police officials, 355,000 of the upper classes and 855,000 peasants, at least most sensible people I met in America recalled, as do similar balanced folk in England, that something like 20,000,000 Russians died by violence, starvation or disease during the revolution, and that a million or two kulaks have since been "liquidated." Whether convinced or not of the noble aim put forward to justify these events, whether ignorant or cognisant of the fact that millions of peasants used to live in Tsarist Russia in much the same condition as ungroomed beasts in a stall, and now, their conditions still far below those of other working classes, are merely cogs in a soulless machine, the "experiment" remained suspect among the thoughtful Americans to whom I talked. Their verdict was that its actual authors, mistrusted for ever on account of it, and also by reason of the Comintern's unforgivable propaganda in America as elsewhere, should be kept at a businesslike distance till they die, and that only the second and third generations of Communists (if they still remain such) upon whom no original blame can lie, should be differently regarded, always provided they showed signs of evolving in a civilised manner from their bloody beginnings.

As about Huey Long, so about Father Coughlin, the "radio priest," devotees of whose broadcast politics were said to number several millions, I myself discovered little more than a myth. Granted, I came mostly in contact with fairly educated people, but even among the less instructed I encountered no one who paid serious attention to him. This, also, was probably a coincidence, but I would like to believe otherwise. "America's supreme crank of many," was how he was described to me. Yet a wary ear was apparently kept cocked in his direction because of the large number of simple people influenced by him as others were influenced by Long. Dr. Francis Townsend seemed to come in a bad second. He was pledged to the policy of providing £40 in pension every month for everybody over sixty, and forcing them to spend it. But no explanation of his, I gathered, had yet made clear his method to intelligent people.

Of course, there is nothing wrong with the principle of a priest having fans and a fan mail, any more than there is in the case of a film star or a politician. In each case, the extent to which this modern phenomenon occurs every day is a measure of their successful trading of personality for appointed ends. But when a priest, publicised like a film star, yells amateurish politics into a microphone with the spurious authority of his "godly" office, it seems time to an uninitiated stranger that the huge civilised element of a great nation should rise in its wrath to inquire whether it is living in the America of 1936 or an undesirable version of Alice's Wonderland. All question of principle aside, no one with whom I happened to discuss the matter, whether rich or poor, educated or un-educated, admitted to any constructively practical idea emerging from the holy father's "sentimental or subversive boloney"—as I heard his utterances described. I was forced, therefore, to conclude that the bulk of his followers, apart from those with axes to grind, constituted the battalions of cranks by whom I had previously understood the United States, like any other country, to be afflicted.

Contrarily, having been warned that I would dislike the advertising of proprietory commodities with which radio programmes were interspersed, I found myself quickly used to it, as are Americans themselves, and able either to ignore it or extract considerable amusement from its unconscious humour. Besides, probably because of the fees such firms are able to pay artists, the concerts broadcast under their auspices struck me as much superior to the general run of our own. Here, a deficiency of imagination often vies with a similar lack of variety, sanctimoniousness stalks in the guise of chastity, and the best dance bands are apparently taboo. Yet the possibility of an English Coughlin alone is almost justification for the queer control exercised by the British Broadcasting Corporation. Rather than that should happen in these islands, I would personally be content not to have a radio as in past years, to suffer those belonging to my friends with what patience I can muster except for a few unbiased "talks" on interesting subjects, the commentary on the Grand National or a good prize fight, and especially to listen in to theirs, or my cook's, only when the usual left-ish political flavouring is likely to be absent.

Seeing a cross outlined in blue Neon strip-lights revolving on the top of a church as I walked about one night, I was reminded that somewhere in Los Angeles was the Angelus Temple of Mrs. Aimée McPherson, the hot gospeller—whatever a hot gospeller may be! Staring at the church, and thinking how pretty the sign looked against the velvet of the sky and how up-to-date the incumbent was in his advertising methods, I decided against a visit to Mrs. McPherson's *menage*. From what I had heard, I could not see how it would be possible to get out of the place without being reduced to anger or laughter; one being as pointless as the other in the circumstances. Next day I asked a middle-aged friend of mine, a Californian, whether I should go after all.

"As an emotional exhibition—as mass hysteria, you might find it interesting," he observed dryly, "but not otherwise."

So I didn't go. One can always see mass hysteria; it is still regrettably common.

On one of my daylight expeditions near the Ambassador Hotel, I hit upon as good a reason as any for the absence of benches: there are practically no pedestrians up there. Frequently, I would walk a mile or two and pass only two or three. Every one went by car or bus. People like myself, who walked for exercise, were freaks. The majority played some game, tennis or golf, when they were not about their business; and a number rode in the adjacent foothills. Had I lived there, I would have done the same. But being just a short-time visitor, and using my room in the hotel as an office, I looked forward to my exploratory expeditions afoot; for the residential sections of Los Angeles are delightful for walking. Strips of beautifully kept turf lie between the paved side-

walks and the stone curb edging the road. Out of these the palms grow which line nearly every street. Grass banks, mown and rolled, slope down in many places from the houses to the sidewalks. And fine trees ornament these lovely little open gardens: conifers, walnuts, cypresses and many others. Verdant creepers, which need hard cutting, hang like mats on the walls, and fuchsias and lilies grow in profusion beneath the windows. Never have I seen any part of a town so spotlessly clean, so rich in horticultural beauty.

And there is romance of an unusual kind to be encountered there, cheek by jowl with the everyday features of modern life. Alongside busy Wilshire Boulevard, literally just over the railings lining the north sidewalk at that point, are pits of asphaltum from which have been excavated during recent years the fossilised bones of a remarkable number of animals belonging to the Pleistocene era. No more can be seen from the boulevard than what is visible in the photograph on the opposite page: a neatly kept piece of publicly owned garden, with just a glimpse, under the trees, of a small oily looking lake where great bituminous bubbles suddenly break surface in rather sinister fashion. Yet from this lake and other smaller pockets adjacent to it, have been dragged almost yesterday the remains of such creatures as the mastodon, elephant, sabre-toothed cat, "great" lion, ancient bison, large "dire" wolf, camel, antelope, ground sloth, "western" horse, turtle and so on, together with specimens of extinct species of condor, turkey, blackbird and others of their feathered kind mixed up with types similar to birds still existing; also a few invertebrate fossils and some plants. These pits, on territory still pleasingly known as Rancho La Brea, although now enclosed and preserved as Hancock Park, were first noted by Gaspar de Portola, exploring in 1769, but not until 1913 were they properly examined. No contrast is more marked than to stand with one's back to a constant stream of cars hurrying along the fashionable built-up highway between Los Angeles and Hollywood, while trying to picture the cooler, more luxuriantly clothed country where these creatures once roamed and where the treacherously sticky pools engulfed them.

Another day, some one in the film industry discussed with me the second of the two chief social impressions gathered on my drive from East to West: the growing desire for a high standard of law and order. My acquaintance also proved illuminating on the subject of local politics. The discussion started with Mines Field, the Municipal Airport, of which he said the site was chosen for political reasons, in spite of it being the worst from most points of view, including the important aspect of weather. Neither of the two big air transport companies used it. United Airlines fly from the Union Air Terminal and Transcontinental and Western Air Inc. from Glendale.

Astonished, I inquired how such a ludicrously uneconomic situation could arise.

"That's local politics," he retorted. "Why, I despise the system as much as any honest man does, I guess. But it pays to keep friends with those guys; they fix the press, they fix the taxes, they fix the judges, the police, every goddam thing."

"In what way can they fix you?"

"Well, supposing you get into some sort of trouble, they can just arrange delays and paroles and paroles and delays, so's the case is never tried, see?"

I tried to appear dense. "You mean . . . " I suggested.

"Why sure," he went on, "I could get you out of anything here short of murder."

I studied him closely, but he appeared quite serious. "Thanks," said I. "I'll let you know when I feel that way."

Then I drew him on the subject of the British legal system, which he knew all about and respected. It was, he swore, just what was wanted—every decent citizen would vote for it and most political racketeers oppose it—but until America had it, wise guys like himself would keep friendly with the local bosses as a kind of insurance against finding themselves "in a spot." I quote him exactly, and myself take no responsibility for these remarks. But, allowing for a little legitimate exaggeration to impress a stuffed-shirt Englishman, his view fitted in unpleasantly well with what I had heard from responsible sources high up in the business and social worlds. There, too —in fact, in whatever company I raised the question—I obtained the same answer: "Oh, if we only had the British legal system!" Young society folk might joke about graft (feeling there was nothing else to do but make light of it) but those to whom I talked were ashamed that any and every foreigner should know of this canker in their national life. My working-class informants were apathetic about it or openly condemnatory (realising that were they to find themselves "in a spot" they had no influence). The heads of great businesses and financial houses were either passionate or cynical on the subject, according to their kind. But all wanted a change.

"We hate it," one important man said to me. "It's just too bad that we have to use dirty election methods to get clean men into the right jobs. But we know the bad elements will do it, so we have to do it too. That's why our elections are so personal and so bitter: that's why the patronage of a sound official has to be extended to a certain number of more or less undesirable hangers-on—to ensure support on the next occasion. Perhaps those fellows brought in votes here by squaring some vested interest, or votes there by discrediting some important backer of the other side. So they have to be taken care of. We know it's a rotten system, but we just don't seem to have gotten around to cleaning it up."

All the same, I felt that the next decade or two stood a good chance of revealing changes. With so many honest and, in some instances, powerful people scattered through all grades of society, and all wishing for the same thing, a weapon of public opinion was slowly being forged before which the graft system must one day go down. Omens were not wanting. Such a scandal did prohibition become, that it went. So bitterly did the public resent its aftermath of gunmen racketeers that the corps of Federal "G" men was formed. Dignity, except naturally for the praiseworthy bearing of Colonel Lindbergh, sank low enough during the Hauptmann trial for every decent American I met almost to blush when it was mentioned (and since then the attentions of the yellow press have driven the Lindberghs to shelter with us, while the wretched convicted man, a mouse between the paws of the political cat, went at last to his delayed death, the victim mentally of several previous executions and publicised in a manner to make those same decent Americans retch).

Then there was the general feeling, openly admitted, that too little had ever been well with politics in the memory of living man; that in past Administrations ugly rumours had even gathered about the White House; but that now a new idealism, coincident with the Roosevelt *régime*, though not necessarily favouring it or directed against it, was bringing more of the right sort of men and women into the political arena or massing them round its edge as intelligent protagonists of what they felt to be ethically sound for the nation. Of the latter, I met a number of both sexes, youngish but quite beyond the stage of youthful dreaming. These had an objective, a sensible objective, and they were out to attain it. Some held positions of considerable responsibility in business; others were purely socialites, though keen welfare workers; and many belonged to that kind of middle-class which, like other classes, exists in the United States as elsewhere, despite the Constitution's *naïve* defiance of Nature's patent ordination that men and races are unequal.

If it can truthfully be held, as I think, that legal abuses in recent years have started to focus critical attention on the difference between Federal judges—one or two of whom I met and who, as a body, seem to be highly respected—and local elected judges whose interpretation of the laws of the various States is frequently influenced by their desire for re-election, then I believe it equally true to say that President Roosevelt is acknowledged by many, whether upholders of his policy or not, to have awakened the political conscience in no uncertain way. Combining these two still largely unexpressed desires, those for legal rectitude and honesty of political motive, sane opinion seemed to incline towards an adaption of the British legal system as rendering graft more difficult and politics less attractive to freebooters; thereby tending in time to raise the standard of those anxious to serve as Congressmen and Senators.

America is vast, her problems from north to south and east to west as various as her people and her laws. No sweeping change can therefore be a hurried change. As in other countries, indeed, more so because of her size, the cultured await the advance of the uncultured, the honest await a change of heart inspired or enforced in the dishonest: but no one would deny the existence of a widespread and wholly admirable national spirit, proud and upright yet hospitable and kindly. This national spirit is unifying as it gains force, I am convinced. I believe that in our generation there will be a notable placing by the people of the reins of law and politics into hands best fitted to hold them, and I hope to live long enough to rejoice over it with my American friends.

The Sundays that I did not spend away from Los Angeles were occupied in writing and walking. I discovered certain shops to be open and spent quite a long time in the showroom of the Auburn Motor Company; examining their latest models. Neither of the two salesmen, visible in the background, took the least notice of the inquisitive stranger who spent so much time on his hands and knees. Truth to tell, I was starting to feel a little lost without a car. Louis Skinitzero, acting on instructions from Detroit, had sold the Chrysler and departed homeward after my farewell party the night of our arrival, when, garbed in quickly pressed evening clothes, and sporting gardenias hastily requisitioned from the hotel shop, we had sallied forth, tired but once again gentlemen of leisure, to dine by shaded lamplight in Hollywood's Trocadero and watch the personalities of film-world dancing. Then, his employers' generous mission concluded, he had said good-bye a few hours later, and we were not to meet again until weeks afterwards in New York.

I was in two minds about buying a cheap used car and selling it again when I left the coast; for distances there are enormous. It is, for example, fifteen and a half miles from the corner of Broadway and 7th Avenue in downtown Los Angeles to the Santa Monica gate of Fox 20th Century's studios near Beverly Hills; and a further five and a half to the seashore. Similarly, forty minutes from Metro-Goldwyn-Mayer, at Culver City, to Warner Brothers in the Burbank foothills, would be good going if my memory serves me right.

An automobile of sorts is as necessary to a visitor or a business man as a suit of clothes. But people were being as kind as ever on the rare occasions when my work permitted me to go out, and were sending their cars for me or giving me lifts. So, not knowing how long or how short my visit would be, I decided against even a $100 hack and took a taxi or hired a Packard from the hotel when it became necessary. One night the stalwart driver of my taxi told me how he had arrived in Los Angeles with his wife and four children and only $48. We were talking about jobs and places. I asked why he had left Chicago.

232

"I jes' couldn't stand a city like that any more," he said simply.

"You've made out all right here?"

"Yeah." His voice held a thankful note. But he had guts, that man.

Though both hired cars and taxis were expensive, I reckon to have saved money by not buying a hack for the month I stayed on the coast. Still, Los Angeles is not a place to be in without one's own "transportation."

As a stranger, my need of a car became acute whenever I took a bus. On Wilshire Boulevard, where the Ambassador is situated, the latter were not as frequent as I had been led to expect. More than once, after waiting a quarter of an hour, I hurried into a taxi to keep an appointment, only to look out of the rear window and catch sight of my laggard bus arriving. The drivers of these buses drive with one hand and manage the issue of tickets with the other. Tickets come out of a pedestal affair like a ship's compass, with a domed glass over its top like the cover over wax flowers in a cemetery. You put in a dime or a nickel, or a trouser button if you're quick, the driver twiddles a handle or something, a series of metallic noises ensues and a ticket emerges somewhere. I am a little vague about all this because the first time I mounted such a vehicle in mistake for the one I wanted, I was so taken up by trying to get off again, finding it was a "non-stop" to some place unknown to me, that I paid little attention to the finer points of the booking apparatus.

Waiting another day for a more amenable conveyance, I got into conversation with a charming Bavarian girl. She worked quite happily, I gathered, in domestic service; having been deserted by her husband and being faced with the up-bringing of a child, aged three. She had her own apartment and went to work every morning, after leaving the child in a *crèche*. Although obviously of a superior type, or doubtless

233

partly because of it, she was not in the least ashamed of being a servant; her calm self-respect, a Teutonic trait, was admirable.

"What d'you find to do here on your afternoons off?" I inquired.

"I ride—ride in the foothills with a friend of mine who is a student."

This was an eye-opener. A neat household help, speaking German-governess English with occasional lapses into American slang, who was also a mother, lived in her own flat and spent her spare time in the saddle, was some one to whom, so my previous wanderings told me, only America was likely to introduce me. I decided to risk a snub in the good cause of learning something. Explaining that what she had just volunteered would be remarked as unusual anywhere and particularly so in England—or, I added, in her own country—and asking her pardon if I appeared unduly inquisitive, I suggested that, if she agreed, we might meet again and continue our conversation. She looked at me closely for a moment and then laughed.

"Why, certainly," she said, "if you wish. Why not come in one evening? But I warn you it is a very small place."

It was: but I remembered living in much worse quarters during periods of my engineering training as a youth. She had a flat in a kind of communal three-storied building. One went down a long narrow passage out of which doors opened on either side, like a big hotel corridor on a very small scale. Her sanctuary consisted of a bathroom, with a fixed basin and bath, both with running water; a big clothes closet, like a small dressing room; an airy bed-sitting-room of medium size (the bed, she demonstrated proudly, folded easily in and out of one wall) looking out onto some low palms and the next-door garden; and a kitchenette somewhat larger than the closet and boasting a big cupboard, a sink and draining board, a gas stove, a refrigerator and a low window seat.

My hostess welcomed me dressed in a jersey and wide blue sailor-like trousers, most becoming to her slimness. We exchanged modest gifts, as would members of two strange tribes. I offered a few flowers and a dog on wheels for the child, she, the instincts of a proud *haus frau* well to the fore, pressed upon me two expeditiously fried eggs and a glass of milk. Whereafter, we discussed life over her Camel cigarettes and my pipe.

Fully intending to improve her position in the world, she was teaching herself to type in German, Italian and English, and was studying out of exercise books after the boy had been put to bed in the evenings. Her portable typewriter, and a small radio set which kept her in touch with current events, she had purchased on the instalment system. She told me the rent was only eighteen dollars a month (i.e. about £1 a week), which was extraordinarily reasonable for such quiet and entirely adequate accommodation in a country where wages are high for that class of employment. From her, I started to get some idea of the price of food in Los Angeles, which Mrs. Cotton kindly elaborated for me into a fairly comprehensive list, as follows:

STAPLES AND VEGETABLES

Flour	5 cents lb.
Butter	35 cents lb.
Eggs	41 cents doz.
Milk	9 cents quart
Cream	13 cents ½ pt.
Bread (1lb. loaf)	10 cents
Sugar	6 cents lb.
Potatoes (15 lb.)	25 cents
Green Beans	7 cents qt.

Squash—zuccini	5 cents lb.
Squash—summer	5 cents lb.
Green Peas	10 cents lb.
Lettuce (as to size)	3 cents, 5 cents and 7 cents
Grapes	5 cents lb.
Oranges (Graded)	10 cents to 25 cents doz.
Grapefruit	5 cents each
Watermelon	1 cent lb.
Honeydew Melon	10 cents each
Muskmelon	5 cents to 10 cents each
Fresh Figs	5 cents to 10 cents lb.
Avocados	10 cents to 25 cents each
Celery (large bu.)	10 cents

MEAT

Pork chops	45 cents lb.
Lamb	40 cents lb.
Bacon	50 cents lb.
Roast Lamb	25 cents lb.
Roast Beef	35 cents lb.
Pot Roast Beef	25 cents lb.
Chicken (frying)	35 cents lb.

CANNED GOODS

Soups	10 cents can
Salmon	22 cents can
Corn	12 cents can
Tomatoes	12 cents can
Peas	15 cents can

Altogether, I greatly enjoyed my delightfully unexpected glimpse, usually denied to travellers, behind the scenes of a daily life being remarkably well lived: for my chance

acquaintance was undeniably as gallant and wholesome a person as any one could hope to meet in a day's march.

Having arrived with a lot of urgent work on my hands that needed a start made upon it, some days elapsed before I really made the acquaintance of film-land, except for recognising a few well-known personalities like Miss Marion Davies, Mr. Gary Cooper and Mr. Richard Powell at the Trocadero the night I drove into town from the East. Meanwhile, I came to learn how entirely divorced Hollywood and its life is from Los Angeles. Apart from references in the local newspapers, the general attitude seemed to indicate that the presence of an established colony of able, hard-working and sometimes individually eccentric people "up the road" was accepted, but no longer as a matter of particular interest. Each community minded its own business. And judging by what I had heard of local politics, Hollywood was the more capable of the two at the job. But as to this, I have necessarily to go entirely by what I was told, drawing conclusions only upon the balance of opinion. Certainly, as regards its seclusion, one could live for years in Los Angeles, and probably in certain parts of Hollywood, without ever being brought in contact with any manifestation of the motion picture industry. It is all behind doors, and closely guarded doors at that.

Once past the doors, a first glimpse affords the impression of a lethargic Bedlam for the wealthy, where the inmates have built vast tidy sheds like aeroplane hangars, surrounded them with paved roads, ornamental shrubs and flower beds, filled them with a heterogeneous collection of junk, real and imitation, and then decided to sit about in shady offices or stand about in groups in the sunshine, some in fancy dress, others in partial undress, but each and every one determined not to do a thing about it at all. So much for the gargantuan, incomprehensible eyeful which causes a certain type of

237

European visitor in sun glasses to stroll miles beside his guide, emitting such obvious comments as:

"No! not really! Five hundred thousand dollars! God bless my soul! Remarkable! Extraordinary—How many million cubic feet?—No! not really!—So this is her bungalow —HERS. Miss Slap-up's? Looks like a small country house to me.—Your own fire brigade! Really!—and a large one, you say.—Nine mechanics, eh, to keep the studio cars and trucks in repair? Regular bus service, what!—Putting up more what-d'you-call-'ems—er, stages, are you! What's that!— for two million bucks? Oh, no! Good Lord! Ah, yes, of course—dollars, not deer. Stupid of me. That kind of a back-woods crowd scene hasn't been made yet, you say. No, naturally. But you'll make it, of course?—Sure thing!—er— I mean, certainly.—Executive offices, two hundred grand! Yes, I think they're SPLENDID—(Friend's voice: A grand is a thousand bucks, you bonehead)—(Oh, thanks).—Yes, Mr. Nickeldimeus, a grand herd of bucks. So you've got a zoo after all. Well, I never! By the way, is there any stalkin' in those hills over there?—What! no huntin'. No, I didn't think so—not a gallopin' country. Any shootin'?—No, no huntin', you say. Yes, I understood you to say that—(Friend's voice: Hunting is shooting and stalking, you bum)—(Oh, thanks) Well, I'm damned; shoot foxes do they! Amazin' outfit— No, Mr. Nickeldimeus, I didn't say anything.—Of course, I'd like a drink. Thanks. A long drink."

But how efficient these studios really are in their own way! The people standing about in groups were probably at work at eight or nine o'clock in the morning. If a temperamental director is in just the right mood for getting on with the job, they may be there, shooting scenes, till eight or nine at night; perhaps later, perhaps half the night. Taking it by and large, Hollywood is a hard-working community. Sometimes, I fancy, a penal settlement, with its regular hours of sleep and labour, would loom in imagination almost as a rest cure.

Signs of great wealth are everywhere in these studios, but not of obvious waste. The pleasant, shady offices, with their charming secretaries and stenographers and vases of flowers, are plainly part of great, smoothly-functioning machines; unobtrusive only because experience has brought them to a high state of perfection, yet one with which no one is willing to rest content. Money is spent like water on a big picture, but, because this has to be so, the detail planning is correspondingly thorough, not only as regards that one picture but in respect of a sufficiently varied output for the season. No company, however strong financially, could withstand the adverse effect of turning out a series of unpopular pictures. To some extent, it is a case of what they lose on the swings they make on the roundabouts. But, as elsewhere, the object is to lose as little and make as much as possible on both: which in a highly technical profession where good camera men and scenerio writers, of whom the public hears little by comparison with the "stars," earn more than Prime Ministers, implies not only a canny prescience but the closest executive control on the part of the big men at the top.

Presumably, this was not always so. There must have been some foundation for the stories which reached Europe in the past of American producers yelling orders into telephones for the immediate supply of a dozen elephants or two aeroplanes with pilots willing to crash them at half-past ten the following morning. But the incidence of the "sound" technique, upon which the Hollywood Companies are reputed to have spent about sixty or seventy million dollars in equipping the studios for production and their nation-wide chains of theatres for reproduction, wrought a healthy change.

First, the language difficulty soon arose to limit their international market and encourage foreign competitors. In this respect films like *David Copperfield*, *Captain Blood*,

The Tale of Two Cities and *Little Lord Fauntleroy* are their answer to the challenge of *The Private Life of Henry the Eighth*, *The Thirty-nine Steps*, *Sanders of the River*, *The Ghost Goes West* and *Things to Come* so far as the English-speaking world is concerned. Secondly, by being driven, for sound-recording purposes, more frequently into the sanctuary of their hundred and twenty thousand dollar stages than hitherto, sunny California ceased to be as strong an ally for them and misty Britain became less of a handicap to us. These two factors, favourable to their competitors, doubtless caused them to focus keener attention upon their own production costs.

Opinions, I found, were sharply divided on the question of British pictures. Although I, myself, from every other point of view except the technical, had disliked *The Private Life of Henry the Eighth* to the point of publicly protesting against such a travesty of history being distributed in the British Empire, I was delighted to find that as a production it had shaken many of our American friends.

And doubtless Elstree, Iver Heath and Denham have further surprises in store. But having more than once expressed this unfavourable opinion of the treatment and direction of *The Private Life of Henry the Eighth*, though admitting the skill inherent in its production, I feel I should record—and I do so therefore with added pleasure—that Mr. Alexander Korda's *Things to Come*, shown since my return, strikes me as about the most impressive picture, technically and from the standpoint of intelligent entertainment, that I have ever seen. Delighted, I have sat through it several times, on each occasion a prey to absorbing interest in a different phase of its excellent presentation; for not being well versed in sound-motion-picture production, I admit to not assimilating the film's many good points in one visit. The American journal *Time* reviewed it to the extent of a full page. Surely a remarkable and generous tribute!

240

It is entertainment value, of course, that is at once the strength of the motion-picture industry and its Achillean heel. Having started as a novelty, as a new toy, just as automobiles started, cinematography now supplies in a modern world a universal need for mental relief or stimulation which it itself induced; or, rather, of which it made communities aware. People now buy "entertainment" in the form of a radio set or seats at a picture house, just as they buy "transportation" in the form of a car. The idea of novelty has recrudesced a few times in the case of the development of the car, i.e., in four-wheel brakes, fool-proof gear boxes, independent wheel suspension, "floating power," streamlining, "overdrive" and the supercharger, and will probably do so next in the form of engines at the rear. Whereas, also from the public's viewpoint, radio and cinematography have yet only shown two main causes for a transitory quickening of interest: in the first case, the ability to tune-in to foreign stations on an inexpensive set, and now television; in the second, the "talkies" and now colour. In between whiles, they all jog along in the public favour by maintaining a general level of efficiency.

Nevertheless, a motion-picture company stands perhaps to lose most if it is unwary. It supplies the public individually with a great deal for a small outlay, but at vast cost to itself. It gets its money back and makes its profit by presenting pictures good enough to induce vast numbers of people to pay those modest prices. But let it make a few indifferent pictures and it must at once beware. For a seat in a cinema showing a certain company's pictures is not a thing like a privately-owned car or radio, of which the occupant, having purchased it, must make the best; he can, on the contrary, leave his seat and not occupy it again for months, by betaking himself regularly to another picture theatre altogether.

So is it any wonder that in an increasingly competitive market, production programmes are now subjects of confer-

241

ences as thoughtful as those of General Staffs on the Western Front; or that finance, for all the great wealth of the Hollywood Companies and their generous treatment of artists, writers and technicians, is in the final analysis as carefully allocated to the various projects and departments as it is in a big department store, which also cannot afford to make mistakes where the public taste and estimation of value for money is concerned?

The reasons for what is done are sometimes far from obvious to outside observers. But are certain processes exactly plain to uninitiated visitors at an aircraft or motor factory? The analogy is closer than might be supposed. A film, like an aeroplane or an automobile, is the product of a carefully-related series of mechanical operations. The retaking of a scene can be proportionately as expensive as the scrapping of a faulty cylinder block and the recasting of another. Also, like planes and cars, pictures date—and much more quickly. Then, over and above the required mechanical excellence of their photography and sound recording, there is the accuracy of the sets, the exactitude of the dress, the correctness of "atmosphere," the precise sense of drama, and finally the difficult business of the acting itself, as much a prey to human temperament as it is the gift of temperament. And without all this the camera and microphone experts are as useless as skilled machine tool workers devoid of blueprints.

So vast and varied is the accumulation of detail in motion-picture production, of knowledge of a thousand subjects drawn from ten thousand sources and used and paid for accordingly, that after some days of meeting executives in Hollywood and being shown around, I could well believe the story of the great financial expert from the east, who, called provisionally into consultation on a possible scheme of re-organisation, and having come to the coast fully determined to put these "movie birds" on a sound business basis, was soon forced to admit that, though their methods were sometimes unorthodox, he could evolve no more sensible and satisfactory system of handling a trade which was in itself as unorthodox as the Tower of Babel, and forthwith retired once more to New York in a mood of genuine admiration. Moreover, a "movie bird" did not tell me this. Another financial expert told the story.

Still in its early stages, the colour film is now the topic of the moment. It is the latest novelty. As in the case of the sound film, a mint of money is being, and will be, spent upon its development. When real success is achieved, the results are certain to be outstandingly beautiful and will have carried this particular branch of science a notable step further. And in due course stereoscopy will increase the range of effects possible. But most interesting of all will be the inevitable clash some years hence between the motion-picture industry and the television side of radio broadcasting. I have not discussed this with any one, and I am ready to watch a train of factors, at present unknown, intervene to falsify my prediction. But just now nothing seems likely to prevent the final convergence of these two forms of entertainment.

Television programmes have only got to attain a standard of excellence similar to that provided by motion pictures before they start seriously to compete with the latter, at any rate so far as the favour of the occupants of expensive seats are concerned; for they will be the owners of the first high-class receiving-sets. Televison on a full-size cinema screen is now practicable, and the early television make-up —green eyelids, black eyebrows and eyelashes, light yellow cheeks, darker nose, red insides to nostrils, brown lips, is already out of date. Moreover, because the legitimate stage, the opera house and the concert platform still provide a wealth of human talent as good and sometimes superior to that attracted by the film studio, a television producer's task will be little if any more difficult than that of a radio programme organiser to-day. Indeed, it may prove easier, because, if good enough salaries are paid, the film stars themselves might be attracted by short term contracts "on the air." In America, where rich manufacturers use the radio concert medium to advertise their proprietory articles, such a state of affairs is bound to arise. But in England, where radio advertising is forbidden, and the British Broadcasting Corporation's idea of salaries is different, the most talented artists are likely to be seen by the television fan only as an occasional form of advertisement for themselves or for charitable purposes.

For some years yet, there will doubtless be those to whom a theatre or cinema visit is an essential part of an evening out. But probably it will not always be so. And comparatively soon, I suppose, we may expect to see the growth of a class which has an increasing amount of entertainment brought to the comfortable surroundings of its own homes by means of various electrical devices. To such a class will belong the first television sets of real refinement, size and range: for it is plain that the world will eventually be satisfied with nothing less than colour television on a fair-sized screen; and the successive types of apparatus leading up to this, will be proportionately more expensive, just as the big radio plus self-changing gramophones of to-day are the ultra-luxurious expression of the midget wireless and the cheap gramophone.

Then, if not sooner, I can see the need for some kind of *liaison* between the broadcasting authorities and the makers of motion pictures. A film always provides a more complete representation of its subject than can any stage performance. There is room for the correction of errors before the public ever sees it. Once completed, it runs through the projector with the unvarying regularity of a well-made chronometer. No actor, actress or singer can spoil it by being ill or temperamental on any particular afternoon or evening.

The original presentation is available to recur indefinitely in all its excellence.

Consequently, as television develops, I believe a demand is certain to arise, at least on behalf of the aged and those lying convalescent in homes and hospitals, for the broadcasting of films; and there is no adequate reason to suppose that our ingenuity will be baulked by the problem of supplying this demand. Just as the big motion-picture companies now have their chains of cinemas, so I believe they will in future have their own wavelength. Or, if not that, then by agreement with the radio authorities responsible, and between themselves, they will ring the changes on certain popular times of day during which their pictures will be broadcast for reception in the home.

But I also believe, and very much hope, that neither the cinema nor television will ever beleaguer the legitimate stage to the point when survival of the latter becomes an uneconomic proposition. Contrary to the gloomy prognostications of a few years ago, it still shows no signs of such surrender. As many good plays were running recently in London as I ever remember, and I saw some first-rate stage productions in New York. This does not necessarily mean that the same number of theatres remain open, but rather that a well-written play or an intelligently assembled revue is still certain of being patronised. So long as actors and actresses are born to whom a living audience and the hardship, glamour, hopes, fears, successes—the intangible fascination of the stage—mean more, despite smaller salaries, than a microphone, a camera and the heated repetition of the studio, so long will we enjoy the delights of the play, the opera, the revue and the music-hall turn. For to all human beings at moments, in greater or lesser degree, but always because they are human, there comes an impatient desire to see the Muses of drama, comedy, music or the dance, speaking, playing, singing or moving through the living form, the actual presence, of some much-admired or loved personality. And to this fundamental call, the celluloid strip and the thermionic valve provide no answer.

The "lots" of the various motion-picture companies in California are in essence the same, except for size and age and the fact that (or so it appeared) some possessed greater facilities than others for outside shots without sending parties "on location." Fox 20th Century's buildings and lay-out attracted me most. As they are the latest, those responsible for planning them naturally had the advantage of profiting by the experience of all the others. But the properties of Metro-Goldwyn-Mayer, Warner Brothers, Universal and R.K.O. are all more or less equally impressive to a stranger.

I paid three visits to the Fox lot; once to be shown round, another time to meet Mr. Julian Johnson, head of the story department, whom I found ensconced in the writers' building, which is beautifully modelled on the lines of a Norman farm; and on the third occasion to have luncheon with Mr. Joseph Schenk, who drove me across to the Vendôme restaurant on Sunset Boulevard in—welcome sight—an old Rolls-Royce with a *cabriolet de ville* body. It looked a very grand, a condescending old lady among a host of smaller Packards, Chevrolets and V-8 Fords.

Going round a motion-picture lot has been likened to a pocket trip round the world. At Fox 20th Century the process took an hour and a half; driving slowly, stopping, talking and moving on again. There were bits of London; part of 54th Street, New York, complete with trolley cars that really crossed it under their own power; a section of Upper Broadway; jungle groves, actually growing; a Dutch canal on which barges were floating; an English country railway station, rolling stock and all; a corner of Geneva; a Mexican *estancia*; an early Colonial house and garden; an English mansion and garden—I vouch for its genuine similitude; a street in a

246

mid-Western town; a square of houses round a village green, with fully-grown trees, and a church on a hill; part of Grand Canyon; a section of a liner; picturesque corners of old French and Italian towns; a Yangtse River bank with its vegetation and moored sampans; nearly half Trafalgar Square and so on—the list is endless. And it is not as though these scenes are altogether make-believe. They are and they are not. Some sets, for instance, have no backs to them; to save space. Others are complete. But all are well built. One house I saw, erected five years ago as part of a set, now contains the studio cafeteria and can accommodate two hundred people at a time.

The Fox lot at present extends, I believe, over a hundred and nine acres, on an unused part of which there are oil wells in full flow—a profitable sideline. Oil is plentiful near Los Angeles. On the way to San Pedro harbour, one drives through a regular forest of derricks.

Large trees are moved wholesale on Hollywood cinema lots and, because of the climate, they grow. Thus a garden, mature and old-looking, can be made in a few hours. As in many localities which have become virtually desert, only water in sufficient quantity is needed to bring out the astonishing fertility inherent in the soil.

Some indoor sets are ordered to be made in the afternoon and are ready and painted in time for work next morning. Even the big outdoor sets spring up in a day or two. Hundreds of carpenters are turned on to each rush job.

Visiting the huge indoor stages, I paused to watch Warner Baxter and Miss Alice Faye acting in *King of Burlesque*, which reached London the following April. They had to do the same shot seven times. Jack Oakie, who had a part in the same picture, was standing nearby. We talked in the intervals between the shots, and he made himself as funny off the screen as on it. Sidney Langfield, who was directing, bareheaded and gesturing with a thin cane, came across to greet me during

247

a pause in the proceedings. Like every one else with whom I came in contact in Hollywood, he went out of his way to be charming and seemed not a bit disturbed at the interruption of his work by a complete stranger.

A block away, on another stage, I met Victor McLaglen who was being directed by Tay Garnett; the latter dressed in a knickerbocker suit of thick tweed, with a cap to match cocked over one eye. How he stood the heat, I could not imagine! But he, also, made me feel welcome at once. And so did big, genial Maclaglen, who talked football, soldiering and the Abyssinian War, which had just started. I gathered that he had a volunteer squadron of cavalry, raised, I imagine, mainly because he and his friends are great horse lovers and fine riders, and he himself is an old cavalryman. It sounded great fun. I was unfeignedly glad to have come across Maclaglen rather than some of the pretty pretty young men I had seen in the distance since my arrival.

An impression of dire confusion characterises these indoor stages, as is well known. Cables coil everywhere like snakes. Great arc lights flick on and off. Screens are moved in front of them, adjusted, moved again, adjusted again *ad infinitum*. A camera creeps backwards and forwards on a rubber-tyred carriage, either on the ground or high up on a platform, its lens pointing like a gun. Girls sit about making notes for continuity, or apparently absorbed in pages of typescript to the exclusion of all else. Buzzers sound. Whistles are blown. Voices shout for quiet. A short sequence is shot. A voice crys "cut." And a varied collection of people who have temporarily been lounging motionless, as though bored to death with the very business of existing, are galvanised again into life and go easily yet methodically about their individual tasks.

Really, in these recurring situations, a highly-complicated machine is revealing its smooth running, lubricated with plenty of dollars. But most of the human cogs, I imagine, deserve their lubricant. There is no room for inadequacy. Every one is efficient at something. Many possess the highest qualifications in their own special line. To-day, the idea that just anybody can go into motion pictures and make money bears no relation to the truth. It is a busy life. And holidays of any length have a way of being postponed, postponed again and then interrupted.

The Universal lot, lying to northward, over by the San Francisco road, is bigger than Fox. But part of it consists of scrubby hills, and the outdoor sets on it are more scattered. Still, I spent an amusing hour there, driving about through narrow, foreign streets, under arches and past cages of lions. The *façade* of Notre Dame, built many years ago now for the famous picture in which Lon Chaney starred as the hunchback, is still standing, apparently impervious to sun and rain. Every chip on a carved figure of a saint, every indentation in a worn step was faithfully reproduced. In a street of shops, I had to go up to the brickwork and touch it before I could convince myself that it was nothing more than sturdy *papier mâché* on a wooden framework. The eye can tell no difference at a range of an inch or two, either as regards colour or composition. One can strike a match on it to light one's pipe, as one would on brick.

For months, perhaps years, a reproduction street (imitation would be the wrong word, for in a sense they are real) may stand neglected. Then suddenly it will be needed. A host of experts will descend upon it. Curtains will be hung, door-handles polished, sidewalks swept, flowers planted in the window-boxes. By next morning the drug store will display popular remedies of the present day. In the *costumier's* will be seen the latest Paris fashions—genuinely the latest, taken from stock in the studio wardrobe. Cars and taxis of the most recent type will pass one another as on errands bent. A uniformed *commissionaire* will hold open to patrons the door of a smart restaurant flanked by living cypresses in tubs, to which a strolling dog will doubtless indelicately attend. Passers-by will jostle. A cop will saunter slowly through the throng; swinging his truncheon and pausing to stare into the window of a bookshop filled with books that have only been published a week. Hey presto! the illusion is complete.

The sets of a competent motion-picture company in action constitute a supreme essay in exactitude.

Nor, of course, is this large scale accuracy confined to out-door sets. At Warner Brothers' pleasantly planned studios at Burbank, I found an arid part of Arizona brought to life in a building that would almost have housed half the Graf Zeppelin. This was for *The Petrified Forest*, in which Leslie Howard and Bette Davis were to star. The scorched terrain, uncannily familiar to me who had motored across it only a matter of days previously, stretched in all its hummocky unevenness to the surrounding walls, where a marvellously painted backcloth did duty for the distant view of volcanic-looking hills; and did it so well in the carefully-arranged light that the camera's eye, much less human eyes, could distinguish neither its falsity nor that of the foreground with its cacti, yucca and tumble weed.

Instinctively, one felt inclined to shade one's eyes from the glare of a pitiless sun. Nearby, a log shack, a sort of desert saloon and service station, had been erected. Not only was it externally complete as to the obvious characteristics of such a place, but inside one could sit on rough, worn chairs at little tables spread with cheap checked coverings or lounge comfortably against a battered and stained bar, behind which were stacked the bottles of liquor, rows of glasses and coarse, chipped china one would expect to see. Common washing hung on a line outside the crazy porch at the back. And not far away, I saw a trolley supporting the usual aeroplane propeller on silent bearings, which, when electricity caused it to

wi[...]ould set this washing aswing and start the dust
real[...] whispering across the floor of the desert of make-
belie[...]

A[...]oor of the next indoor stage, I met James Cagney
in dr[...]pcord breeches, field boots and with the sleeves of
his kh[...]irt rolled up. As delightful to meet as he is to
watch [...]e screen, and a man, I gathered, whose forthright
charact[...] much respected, he was then starring in *Ceiling
Zero*—n[...]dless to add, a flying picture. This story called for an
exact reproduction of the "weather" room at Newark Airport,
New Jersey, which I discovered on walking into the great
shed. And proceeding out of the "weather" room on the far
side, I found myself on Newark landing field, another
uncanny likeness.

Here was flatness; and again a backcloth took up the illusion and carried it on into imitation space. The lighting at
that moment, whether by accident or design (the former,
I think, for a halt had been called for a conference) simulated
somewhat the soft glow of a Summer's evening. Streaky
clouds floated listlessly on the backcloth above a far-away line
of trees. A two-seater biplane trainer and a monoplane stood
on the sham concrete apron, their shadows long as they would
be at sundown. Apart from the scenery's deception, these
machines looked quite small in the shed's immensity, round
which one could have driven a midget racing car quite fast.
These indoor stages, when arranged, are like toy-shops for
the grown-up; everything is life-like, full-sized and accurate;
one has to pinch oneself to remember it is all, in a sense,
unreal. But for those who possess something of the model
railway mentality, they are places in which to potter happily
for hours, playing with things.

My next call, a few yards away, involved me in the middle
of a pirate fight in the film *Captain Blood*. The "props" were
an apparently genuine frigate, with all sails set but minus

one lot of bulwarks, a variety of cannon and a movable back-cloth which did, in fact, look exactly like the ocean seen from a distance. Errol Flynn, the star, wearing a kind of cavalier's hat and twiddling a sword in his fingers, lounged high up on the poop deck, with the producer. Even higher up, on a large crow's nest affair to one side, the camera rolled slowly back and forth while its operator prepared for the next shot. On the deck below, Blood's pirates stood about in groups or sat swinging their legs. Most of them were stripped to the waist and had their bodies treated to represent sun-tan and sweat. The closest scrutiny revealed no justification for not paying these crowd actors in pieces of eight instead of a weekly cheque convertible into a roll of bills.

On such a scale was the whole scene that its rehearsal, and the actual shooting of it, was ordered by megaphone or loud-speaker—which, I could not distinguish. For myself, I was ensconced with my two guides on a packing-case behind the ship; that is, on the side which had no bulwarks. I could almost have touched the actors, yet was outside the area being photographed. Presently, more staccato orders boomed out. The pirates grouped themselves in readiness. A workman momentarily puzzled me by coming and standing nearby with a fire hose. At a word of command, the sails, pulled by concealed ropes, began to flap; blocks creaked; stays tautened and vibrated; the backcloth rose and sank lazily till one could have sworn the boat was moving; up on the poop deck a man came quickly forward and dropped a smoke pill down the muzzle of a cannon, whence there began to issue rank curls and eddies such as would follow a discharge of black powder; and suddenly I became aware that some concealed apparatus was also filling the whole vast building with smoke, acrid and swirling. But still the men stood fast.

Then, at a signal, pandemonium ensued. Yelling hoarsely, every one surged towards the side of the boat farthest from

252

me. Weapons flashed in the air. Faces became distorted with savagery. One or two men flung themselves at the rigging and climbed it like wildcats. A burning rope fell to the deck in a shower of sparks. Another fragment followed. And another. Then a scattered hail of them.

Astonished, I looked up. Workmen, perched on rafters, were aiming burning wreckage with unerring accuracy between the shouting gesticulating men beneath. One piece fell on a tarpaulin lashed in seamanlike fashion over a hatch, and the whole thing caught and blazed furiously. More than one of the actors threw quick, anxious glances aloft as they rushed from place to place. This was staggeringly like the real thing. The fireman next to me tugged loose an extra yard of hose-pipe from the coil behind him and fingered the nozzle expectantly. It seemed an age but was only a matter of seconds before the loud-speaker boomed "cut," whereupon this fellow was on the deck like a flash, the rubber tube writhing after him, a jet of water spurting from his right hand while with his left he pulled and pushed anxious men from his path. Groups formed here and there, avoiding the blazing patches. From somewhere up by the poop deck, the giant voice besought every one to keep calm. As for my friends and me, we walked towards the door; rubbing our smarting eyes and trying not to choke. We had seen and smelt enough of this game of playing at pirates.

Personally more startling was my experience, a few days later, of watching Clarence Brown directing the boy, Mickey Rooney, on the Metro-Goldwyn-Mayer lot at Culver City. On this occasion, an outdoor set was used. Rooney, dressed as an urchin, was squatting on the grass outside a small house; apparently doing nothing in particular but actually lying in wait for a visitor. As this man left the house and passed through the wicket-gate, Rooney was to toss a squib over his shoulder into a laurel bush just behind the retreating man;

253

the resulting explosion being destined to make the latter jump out of his skin. Synchronisation of the procedure was carefully explained by Brown, seated in a chair near the camera: Mickey would throw the imitation squib, a small quantity of powder would flash off in a laurel bush by means of an electric lead and a switch, and Brown himself would provide the noise by firing a blank revolver cartridge into the ground. Several rehearsals of the actual throwing were done, until the boy judged the correct distance. Then it was done with the man emerging from the house. Then Brown called for a final rehearsal before the actual photographing and the igniting of the powder. But as he unexpectedly added the pistol shot, and as I was standing by him at the time, the only person to jump out of his skin was myself.

A mercifully rapid reaction may enable some of us, without perceptible pause, to continue our outwardly calm and unblushing progress along a street after hearing a car backfire. But we cannot ensure, alas, that our hearts will not as usual hit the top of our heads next time it happens, or disguise from ourselves that momentarily we visualised the astonishing contingency of being shot in the pants. Apart from this temperamental jolt caused to me by his revolver, I had an enjoyable few words with Brown, who is a keen pilot and owns his own aeroplane.

On our way up to that end of the M.G.M. lot, I had also met Jack Conway, who had then practically finished his direction of *A Tale of Two Cities*. At the moment, he was superintending the preparation of that scene in a courtyard when the starving rabble of Paris break through the gates to snatch meat which a nobleman's servants are feeding to his mastiffs. Several artistically dirty *sans-culottes* democratically accompanied by spotless, ringleted young ladies in sweeping, tight-bodiced silks and satins, had been eating clam chowder and smoking Lucky Strikes all round me in the studio canteen, where I had just been given luncheon by Sam Marx, head of the scenario department. And as we had afterwards strolled hither, a sophisticated young lady, hideously disguised as a revolutionary beldame, had spotted us through the overhanging grey wisps of her wig and unaffectedly called across to Marx; asking in orthodox American where the "ladies' room" could be found. Obviously, the poor lamb, one of the crowd actresses, was a stranger to that part of the vast studios and felt she could not take part enthusiastically in a revolution while in a state of anxiety. But I, as a stranger, was by no means sure at any time that I was awake.

Conway, while some underling grovelled in the dust behind him, to measure with a tape the exact distance from the camera to where a tethered hound would shortly be slavering after a bone which he wouldn't get, proved as friendly and informative as every director to whom I had been introduced. Among their many valuable attributes, patience is certainly not the least. And I was glad to have the pleasure of meeting him in particular because, in the same picture, he had recently been directing our talented English actress, Miss Elizabeth Allan, whose professional success and widespread personal popularity with the nice element in Hollywood is a source of such pride and satisfaction to her old friends at home, among whom I am grateful to be numbered. But Conway looked drawn. Only his wish not to keep people hanging about had brought him back to the studio with the effects of a chill yet on him. He said he had been in bed three days, and I felt he ought still to be there.

Ten days before, I had discovered without any sense of disappointment that the coast scenes in the film *Treasure Island* had been shot at Catalina Island, situated a few miles out in the Pacific off San Pedro. Santa Catalina is all an island of "hidden treasure" should be; steep, alluring in sunshine, mysterious under cloud; boasting a dusty cove or two, and, in the middle, a narrow inlet of water from the west that does duty for a lagoon. Sure, a swell place for buccaneers!

I was a guest for the week-end on Donald Wills Douglas's fifty-six ton schooner *Endymion*. My host being, himself, the builder of the famous aeroplanes bearing his name, it was not surprising that the other guests should include General Arnold, of the U.S. Army Air Corps (then commanding at March Field, and Mr. Plesman), moving spirit of K.L.M., the well-known Dutch airline. Mrs. Douglas, Mrs. Arnold and Bill Douglas, a son, completed the party.

We landed at Avalon well after dark on Friday, and went for a walk along the brilliantly-lit foreshore of that little pleasure resort, nestling at the foot of a precipitous cleft in the hills. But it was past eleven o'clock. Apart from ourselves, there was not a living soul to be seen in all the length of path and street and promenade made golden by a regiment of lamps. Eastward, the fretful glow hanging above the huge urban area of Los Angeles and its outskirts was out of sight over the distant line between blue-black sky and blacker sea. In that direction we saw nothing but the pale path of the moon and near at hand the friendly twinkle of the schooner's riding lights. No sound came to us but the sharp echo of our footsteps, the murmur of each other's voices and the lazy sighing of small waves. It was the off season for Avalon. We might have been walking at midnight in a miniature Monte Carlo of the dead.

Like many folk, I am a restless sleeper the first time in a strange bed. I was no sooner half-asleep that night than a mild nightmare jerked me upright like a suddenly released spring, and my head cracked loudly against the upper bunk of the little cabin I was sharing with the general. But Arnold, like a good campaigner, never moved; his even breathing rose and fell without interruption. Ruefully rubbing my skull, I again relaxed. Then suddenly I saw a silly side to it,

Left to right: Mr. Plesman, Mrs. Arnold, General Arnold and Donald Wills Douglas aboard the 'Endymion.'

"Avalon . . . a miniature Monte Carlo. . . ."

and started trying to concoct a limerick which, in fact, did not finally come to me until two days later:

It's odd, you'll admit, that a lord
—though I grant you the case is ephemeral—
Sitting up in a funk
In a somewhat low bunk,
And hitting his head on a board,
Should jar the tailplane of a general.

And so, trying, I fell happily asleep.

Using the auxiliary motor next morning, we started off south-west towards another island, that of San Clemente, a little farther on from Santa Catalina than the latter is from the mainland. But once round the last headland and pointing out again into the ocean, we encountered a big swell, which caused Douglas to put about and decide to cruise back up the lee side of Santa Catalina. As he said with a grin, he didn't want any one to be ill when we were out for the express purpose of enjoying ourselves. Whereupon, I noticed a thankful expression on the face of at least one person who had fallen a little silent during the preceding ten minutes.

A large colony of seals were sunning themselves at the foot of the headland as we returned; and for a time, borrowing a sturdy rod and tackle, I had a line out for a small shark. But my luck was not in. Then, passing Avalon once more, we anchored at Howland's landing, a cove, where we went ashore in the dinghy to visit a camp to which parties of children come in the summer from the mainland.

Douglas knew the caretaker, whom we found gossiping in his quarters with a cowboy down from the hill ranch inland. It was a biggish room in which we found ourselves, with the various implements of a lonely, arcadian existence hung upon the walls or stood in corners. The cow-puncher, one of the handsomest and fittest-looking young men I have ever seen, excused himself soon after our arrival. His bay pony proportionately as young as himself and higher at the withers than other cow-ponies I had seen, started forward as soon as he twitched the reins off the ground and flung them back over its neck. From standing quietly, head down, it suddenly danced light-heartedly as he swung into the saddle, and reared up two or three times. Holding the pony in firmly with one hand, he raised the other to the brim of his black five-gallon hat; doffing it with almost a mediæval flourish. His good-natured eyes smiled at us out of a deeply tanned face, and his courteous farewell, though reminiscent of Miss Mae West, was grave. "If you're this way again," he remarked, "come up and see me."

Then he was gone at a brisk, controlled trot which he soon allowed to develop into a hand canter. And for a minute or two, as we strolled idly on, I watched his slower progress up a thorny hillside no less steep than the roof of a house. Finally, a kink in the trail hid him from view. With his good looks and his all-black outfit, hat, shirt, pants, leather chaps, gauntlets and boots, he was a figure to stir the imagination of any town-bred maiden.

The caretaker, who addressed his various livestock by name, and with the same quizzical eloquence that he bestowed on human beings, proceeded proudly to demonstrate an egg trap of his own making. All his nests, lucky man, were occupied by industrious fowls. But casually removing an indignant speckled hen, obviously nearing the natural climax of her squatting, he picked an egg out of a box nearby and dropped it through a hitherto unnoticed hole in the bottom of the nest, whence it fell gently on a felt-covered slope and did a dignified roll into some suitably padded receptacle farther down.

"Them chickens just caan't figure it out," he explained, grinning. "But it doesn't encourage them to sit too long— No, sir!"

After which, we took a dusty path round and up over the next headland northward; walking slowly in the heat; and, half an hour later, descended again to the shore, this time at Johnson's landing, otherwise known as Emerald Bay.

It was hereabouts, I discovered, that the outdoor scenes for *Treasure Island* were shot. Palms, which are not indigenous to Santa Catalina, were transplanted for the purpose. And near the water an imitation native palisade was still standing, doubtless a relic of some other picture, for the stockade I remembered in *Treasure Island* had been a stouter affair altogether. In this bay, as at Howland's landing, where the *Endymion* awaited us, there were buildings which served as a camp for youngsters in the Summer. Apart from the health-giving properties of these camps, their location must seem like an exciting paradise to those who go there. With some such thoughts as these in my mind, I looked up to see the biggest Eucalyptus tree that I had ever seen anywhere. No self-respecting boy, I swore, would dare catch cold so near as big a tree with such a name!

Picking our way to a small weather-beaten memorial stone standing solitary on a rise some hundred and fifty yards away, Mrs. Arnold and I together made out the worn inscription on it. Apparently, it marked the grave of one, Samuel Prentice, who had entered California in 1824, and died later on Catalina Island in 1852. In those years, the California of to-day was on the point of being born. Leather-clad frontiersmen and prospectors in red flannel shirts, moving, always moving on, were to come from the east to live their tough lives, working, fighting, loving, hating, killing, and die their often sudden deaths under this western sun. For 1849 was the great year of the Gold Rush.

Compared with the natural wealth of the then virgin gold fields farther north, the bygone marts of Tyre and Sidon, Carthage, Babylon and Venice were to be rated but graceful stores for fashioned trinkets, and beside this trail ending in yellow dust and nuggets, the golden road to Samarkand was to become the faintest spoor of long-passed caravans. Wild gambles were about to be won or lost. Great schemes were to be formulated and fail, only to be revived and launched again and again, and finally brought to success when in some instances the idea was second or third hand and its originators squeezed out, broke or shanghaied from 'Frisco.

Later, vines were to grow, flowers to blossom, vegetables to mature, fruit to ripen—all with a freedom, and on a scale, that made it the first great market-garden of the world. Here, there and everywhere, men found oil that no sooner started to gush forth than it turned to dollars in their banks. Great herds of cattle were raised beside the Sierra Nevada. Chicken-farming became a matter of tens of thousands of fowls, of millions of eggs. Strangers talking a new jargon came in search of fine weather; using repeating cameras which they wound with handles; and around them a colony grew up, and then a town financed with nearly as many dollars as the hens laid eggs.

Then, to this little town, the wit and talent of all nations came and grew rich. And some, having grown rich, buried that talent in the tempting ground and soon died, debauched. Here, too, also in search of weather, thoughtful men came, like him whose guest I was, and calculated, planned, assembled, tested, flew and sold aircraft; so that the journey which for flannel-shirted miners had been at best a wagon trek of months, and sometimes the undecided drift of years, became an air-conditioned interval of hours, with drift of another sort neatly set down for pilots in a booklet.

But when this grave was dug the war with Mexico was finished a bare four years. All I have recounted was yet to come. As on that ancient property at Bayside, Long Island, I felt myself thumbing here a page of history.

"Prentice!" said Mrs. Arnold musingly. "I'm sure it's a name well known in Massachusetts. An old family, I think——" She broke off.

Then we wandered on a bit, over the rise to a little inlet, where we searched for coloured stones in the shallow water; and I found one I liked, green and mauve, and brought it away to be mounted as a paper weight.

On our way back to the boat, Douglas and his son and I picked our way along the shore; labouring over the rocks and studying the formation of the cliffs until halted by a sheer face jutting out into the water. Forced to clamber up a steep path past a concealed platform used for cinema cameras, we joined the rest of our party on the track above, winding over the knees of the precipitous ground inland. Finally, we all took a short cut down a fierce slope to Howland's landing; avoiding the prickly cacti as best we could, and negotiating two barbed wire fences which offered less impediment than they might to Mrs. Douglas and Mrs. Arnold, as both were sensibly dressed in wide yachting trousers. Their only difficulty in scrambling through the strands was that of retaining their huge straw sun hats.

As we sat yarning afterwards on the deck, two remarks particularly impressed themselves on my mind. We were talking flying shop. Arnold, one of the first two soldiers in the States to become a pilot, and who still flies regularly despite his senior rank and grey hair, recounted how more than once he had brought his Martin bomber up from behind into the gap between the two lines of a wedge of migrating geese. I forget now how high he put their cruising speed; I know it was considerable; but apparently they still retained a useful margin and were capable of accelerating briskly when frightened by the growing proximity of his plane. And as the conversation took a turn, Douglas, in the course of it, likened orthodox heavier-than-air craft to sea-

261

going vessels likely to sink if their engines stop—and, moreover, carrying no raft.

"Ridiculous, is it not?" he observed.

Coming from him of all people, the remark made me wonder quite what imaginings he harboured.

"We must make what the dollar will buy," he added, somewhat cryptically. "That's how progress is hurried these days."

Still, I fancied his mind was off into the future; questing some distance in advance of his next one or two series of machines, each of which would inevitably represent his economic conception of the logical intermediary steps to take in design. What further vision he had, I do not know. But I have met few men more likely to pass surely from existing successes to greater ones, or to do so with such modesty and quiet humour.

At intervals, Plesman sang unaffectedly in a cheerful bass voice, to our great applause. Sentimental, witty, slightly naughty songs or boisterous drinking lays came as easily to him in French and German as in Dutch. For the time being, the cares of running one of the most up-to-date and efficient airlines in Europe and the East were laid aside; this rubicund, middle-aged man was behaving like a happy college boy. Then he went for a row in the dinghy for the sake of exercise. And later, young Bill Douglas took me in it along the edge of the rocks, where we could peer down through the limpid water and catch glimpses of darting, brightly-coloured fish.

Next morning broke fine; so fine that to me, with a skin easily flayed by it, the power of the sun was obtrusive. I cautiously retained my shirt while discussing child education with Donald Douglas, who revelled in the heat. Plesman, with a slight touch of chill in his back after bathing the previous day, did not appear till we had started down the coast towards the Isthmus, by which time the weather had turned unexpectedly grey and colder.

The Isthmus, as its name implies, turned out to be a strip of low, flattish land connecting the two mountainous halves of the island on its eastern coast, at a point where a deep incursion by the Pacific splits the land from the west. Rowing ashore, we walked across to the head of this natural lagoon, which was a bare half-mile distant. To get there, we had to pass through a broad main street of flimsy, scattered houses, about a dozen of them, each raised above the ground on short piles and possessing verandas, slatted windows and punkas. Towards one end of this dilapidated sandy thorough-fare, into which palms had been introduced, there stood a small white hotel in rococo style. Only from certain angles could one see that it was little more than a sham front. For this reproduction of a street in a small tropical settlement was one of the outdoor sets used, I believe, in the film *Rain*; and, as with other sets portraying a specific "atmosphere," it was truly remarkable that all the houses looked lived-in, and as though they had genuinely been the scenes of much loneliness, dull labour and intermittent, heart-broken drinking by perspiring and fever-stricken exiles.

A few hundred yards brought us to the inland water's edge. Here, it was of the width of a small Scottish loch, and but for their scorched appearance the surrounding hills had contours not unlike many on the Scottish border. We saw on the southern bank a grove of imported palms, obviously placed there by the ubiquitous film producer. Although entirely out of keeping, they were presumably left until such time as it might again be necessary to photograph natives racing in dug-outs towards some shining South Sea strand—without the expense of going there. A worthy economy!

All the same, I felt my first twinge of annoyance. It

263

was more pleasing to watch the skilful flying of three pelicans, diving for fish, and more amusing to observe the antics of two smaller birds, unidentifiable without field-glasses, which splattered with shrill cries towards each successful pelican in turn but invariably arrived too late to share the meal. I felt I would have liked to have had the making of that place into a pleasure resort of the right kind. It could be done without destroying the natural peace. As such, it would be protected from its present untidiness and imitation-Hawaiian blemishes. And what a harbour!

Putting out again from the bay lying eastward of the Isthmus, we left a yacht or two and several small, stumpy craft flying the pennon of the Writers' Yacht Club. I wondered whether any of Conrad's books found a place in each miniature chart-room. In spirit at least he ought to be their Commodore.

For an hour or more we sailed, drawing away very slowly from land. There was but the slightest off-shore breeze which subsequently failed entirely. Thereafter we powered ahead. Plesman, at the wheel, was singing occasional choruses in which the others accompanied him. Mrs. Arnold and I, joined later by Mrs. Douglas and General Arnold, sat cross-legged in the stern; discussing Anglo-American friendship. All were agreed—as were all thinking people I met in America—that this is inevitably the greatest potential power for good in the world. It will reach its culmination, no doubt, after most of us now living are dead, but it will be a power in the literal rather than the purely sentimental meaning of the word.

As the party broke up after dinner and Donald Douglas drove Plesman and me back to the Ambassador hotel, the Pacific Fleet in San Pedro harbour happened to be giving a searchlight display. It accorded strangely with my thoughts. A ceiling of cloud only a few hundred feet high now lay above the seaboard, and upon it the luminous circles cast

". . . imported palms . . . entirely out of keeping. . . . It was more pleasing to watch the skilful flying of three pelicans, diving for fish. . . ."

by great lamps criss-crossing their fingers below made swift and bewildering patterns. It had been an ideal week-end; one for thought and rest and the experience of companionship. The following morning, Douglas would be back at his factory, among the big planes then building, and busy with the detail drawings of those yet to be built. Arnold had already set off to resume his command at March Field. In a few hours, and after a further conference or two, Plesman would fly east; and make his way by stages to Holland to control again an important and growing airline. For myself, the return to earth was signified by a note inviting me to address the Los Angeles Breakfast Club at eight o'clock the following Wednesday morning; which was hospitable but not, I considered, the opportune moment, for me to bore an audience with such ideas as I was formulating. I wrote a note excusing myself on grounds of work and time, and went to bed.

Two week-ends later, I was in San Francisco, where I spent the whole of the first night in and out of a police car. Flying up there after tea, a matter of just over three hundred miles from Los Angeles, I arrived at the St. Francis hotel in comfortable time to have a bath and change for dinner, despite a slightly foggy drive of fourteen miles into the city from Mills Field, the airport. Putting on a dark suit, I wandered round the corner to Solari's restaurant where I had been recommended to dine. Besides, I had a rendezvous there at ten with a plain-clothes inspector from the Police Department.

Solari's, in 'Frisco, is famous from London to Shanghai, from the Klondike to New Zealand. Since I fed there, I have asked a number of far-travelling folk, and all seemed to know it by reputation if not from actual experience. Although its name was Italian, I discovered the present proprietor to be a grave, clean-shaven Swiss, proud of the widespread *clientèle* that comes there for his food. He had been years in the West, but the reserve, dignity and mode of address of a European-trained *maître d'hôtel* remained with him; although he certainly gave an involuntary glance of curiosity when I asked him to arrange for the police inspector to be shown to my table as soon as he arrived. Still, mastering his surprise, he personally gave the doorkeeper instructions and returned to my side.

"You see, milor'," he expounded, gesturing with a long hand, "our decoration : it is simple—in good taste, we 'ope, yes—but simple. And as milor' will observe, we provide no band. We should 'ave to pay a band fifty pounds a week (his tact automatically translated dollars in sterling for my benefit). "Instead, we spend everyt'ing upon food. . . . Our clients, they come 'ere for our cooking," he added with modest zeal, "NOT to 'ear a band."

He picked up a *menu*; proffering it delicately. Whereupon I chose *Bortch*, a Pacific fish done *à la maison*, and a small *tournedos* with cream sauce and mushrooms—a selection that apparently won his approval. The wine list appeared in his hand as if by magic. I glanced through it; finding evidence of an unusually good cellar of the orthodox kind, but with the addition of several Californian vintages.

"Your local Burgundy," I suggested. "What do you recommend? I know none of them."

"Milor' will find them excellent. Not quite the same flavour as the French wines; our soil is different; but very good. If I may——?"

I gave him the book.

"Yes, yes. If I shall venture; a bottle of *numéro* (whatever it was) for milor'."

He hurried away, giving place to an aged waiter, also of European extraction, who studied my expression with fierce intensity from beneath bushy grey eyebrows each time I started a new dish, as though daring me to criticise.

266

And the wine of the San Joaquin valley, when it arrived accompanying my strange fish, was every bit what the *patron* claimed it to be. Though to my by no means expert palate there seemed less body to it than the Burgundies I knew, yet I sensed in its taste a warmer sun; it was smooth and delicious, and I finished it.

With my head in the evening paper, for the Italian colonial expedition into Abyssinia was still hot news, I did not notice the tall, athletic police inspector until he had reached my table. When I had seen him seated, we politely took each other's measure over glasses of liqueur brandy. Outside, his two-year-old Packard saloon stood parked against the kerb. The car had red lamps which could be switched on when its police siren was in full voice, so that there was no question of not seeing as well as hearing it coming. So equipped, it could travel through the densest traffic if need be at a remarkable speed; it could ignore traffic lights and drive on whichever side of the street provided the easiest way through.

In it, we were presently drifting quietly through China-town—the western hemisphere's most famous Chinatown. A voice hailed us from a street corner. "Hallo, there," it drawled.

We reversed a few yards along the edge of the sidewalk, below the gaudy Chinese shop signs and trade-marks which hung down or jutted out everywhere. A short, thickset individual strolled to meet us, and put his head in through the window. He had a rather pale, round face and dreamy eyes which looked as though they saw little but obviously saw much. When he was introduced to me, I gathered that he was another plain-clothes inspector, belonging to the special China-town squad, and on the look-out, among other things, for dope.

A colloquy ensued between the two of them, tall and short. They were obviously friends. Could the short one come with us? He thought he could. What should I be shown first?

267

He suggested a Chinese "family house." And all the time (for this was his particular area) his dreamy eyes glanced aside and across the street at the passers-by. I think he observed every one who passed along either side-walk while he stood there. We left the car, and climbed the marble stairs of what looked like a deserted office building.

No one was about, and the elevator wasn't working. Suddenly, on the fourth floor, we entered another world. The Chinatown inspector opened a door, felt for the electric light switches and successively snapped them down. I walked past him into a big rectangular room, furnished mainly with a few mats, a cabinet or two, and a huge centre table surrounded by high-backed arm-chairs in orderly array, the latter of ebony inlaid with mother-of-pearl. Being told to lift one, I found it needed considerable muscular effort; and I wondered how the table, equally solid, had ever been brought into the building. A faint, foreign aroma hung about. Lovely, delicate Chinese paintings ornamented the walls except for one space, about twelve feet by eight, occupied by a framed piece of embroidery, depicting a lion, essentially Eastern in conception, emerging from a cave on the sea shore and roaring at the rising sun.

"I guess it's kind o' symbolical," explained one of my guides, following the direction of my gaze. "An' it's worth a good many thousand dollars—I forget how many."

Certainly, it was an exquisite piece of needlework, done entirely in coloured silks, and must have involved millions of stitches. My attention was drawn to the ceremonial tea, standing on a small table by the door through which we had entered. The teapot stood in a wicker container, packed round with some material to keep it warm. I lifted the woven cover and found the vessel inside to be piping hot, and was told it would remain so for hours. Night and day, there are always successive pots of tea waiting behind a semi-circle of dainty little cups, thin as egg shells.

A Chinaman appeared through another door; walking quietly in felt-soled slippers. The thick-set inspector nodded and uttered a word of greeting, whereupon the man silently vanished the way he had come. From this and other indications, I gathered that a mutual respect exists between the police and the respectable Chinese, who are mostly as law-abiding as they are hard-working.

Climbing another flight of stairs by the light of an electric torch, we reached a massive pair of wrought metal gates, guarding a farther door which led into the Joss house. Here, an odour of incense became pungent. When the shrine was illuminated, I found myself standing before a narrow table, like a preliminary altar, upon which the inevitable tea was placed and also little ritualistic gifts—of flowers, and food in beautiful china bowls, if I remember rightly—and behind it the Joss itself, gilded and remote, was enthroned upon ornamental tiers backed by intricate screens, in the workmanship of which a veritable maze of colours blended in perfect harmony. Incredible neatness characterised the setting of the whole scene, the position of each gift. Pencils of heady smoke rising from the joss sticks in their holders, twirled tenuously upwards at an angle towards the ceiling, disturbed by the sudden opening of the door. On a balcony leading out of the Joss house onto the roof, we stood in the fresh night air, to look down upon the twinkling lights of this mysterious city where so many races have implanted something of the spirit of their own lands.

"What exactly are these 'family houses'?" I inquired, as we descended again with the aid of the inspector's flash lamp. A voice came back to me out of the darkness below.

"Jes' meeting places for every one belonging to the same
269

crowd, see . . . all the Wongs, or maybe the Wu's. They get together to discuss their own affairs."

"Nothing to do with those secret societies, the Tongs, or whatever they're called?"

"No, these are regular . . . nothin' phoney about 'em."

Our dark police car rolled up a block, across a block, down a block, turned left and stopped outside a theatre.

"Famous old place," commented the tall inspector. "You oughta see it."

We greeted the occupant of the ticket kiosk, who sat in his semi-circular glass affair outside the doors. He said that the last show would not be starting for some time; about midnight, so far as I remember. So we made for a Chinese theatre nearby and spent a few minutes sitting at the back. Here, the performance had already been on for hours. The audience, apparently, wandered in or out as they liked, provided they paid; and they talked, laughed, or sat silent, according to their mood. I have never seen, and probably shall never see again, so many Chinese in billycock hats. By contrast with the impeccable room I had left a short time before, the floor here was filthy, uncarpeted and smothered with litter and cigarette ends. Winning little almond-eyed children, who by our standards should long have been in bed, toddled unconcernedly about or sat sucking their fingers, while their slightly elder brethren played a shrill game of tag near the door. One or two small, solemn maidens stared incomprehendingly at the stage.

I didn't wonder. If, judging by appearances, it was incomprehensible to them, it was doubly so to me. Most of the actors wore long grey beards, presumably false; and whenever any one of them had anything to say, the orchestra, which was on the stage, drowned his words in a flurry of sound, made chiefly by beating one piece of bamboo against another. I was irresistibly reminded of the Macaw house at the zoo, with every parrot simultaneously screeching and trying to get out of its cage. After a short dose of this, I was more than ready to visit the oldest brick-built saloon in town.

Naturally, its interest now was purely subjective. The place had associations, of course, with tougher days, those of the old Barbary coast, a dingy street of gambling dens and shanghai-ing brothels along which we had just driven. But there the shutters were up, and here only stout, prosperous and peaceful looking citizens leaned against the bar. A drink was all that I found objective; and I reached for it gladly, for my palate was still rank with the taste of the Chinese theatre.

One of the corpulent parties turned out to be a friend of the tall inspector's father and by all accounts something of a politician. This prevented me from asking several leading questions, the gist of which, while of an inquiring nature, might have been misunderstood. Instead, I listened but could make little of his reminiscences, couched as they were in terms that still fell strangely on my ears. The second round of drinks was equally welcome; the third and fourth I sipped and elbowed out of sight behind an aspidistra on the counter. My head, though strong enough for most liquor, was not up to too much rye whisky. I preferred to see what was yet to be seen rather than dream it.

After a time, we left the oldest brick-built saloon to its memories of past rough-houses and returned to the first theatre, where we sat at the back to watch a turn or two: some really funny, hard-working comedians, whose splendid clowning made up for the threadbareness of their patter, a chorus whose charms and cheerful faces amply compensated for their fourth-rate antics, and the usual "strip" dance, adequately done by a plump wriggling girl, under not too brazen lighting, to the loudly sensual applause of rows of Filipinos sitting at the front.

Apparently, some of these last constitute a real problem on

the Californian coast. Small, tough, impertinent and apt to go berserk when they fight, which is frequently, they go about usually in couples or small gangs of half a dozen. I seldom saw one alone. By bribes, threats and any method, underhand or otherwise, which appeals to them, they have gradually ousted many of the far more reliable Chinese and Japanese from positions of trust, such as the post of janitor to a block of flats. This often results in serious consequences, for in some cases their respect for other people's property is induced only by fear, and the number of their assaults, attempted assaults or annoyances of women are legion. Not all are like this. Indeed, some make quite excellent servants; and if the attitude of others towards white women is unsatisfactory, the blame may, in part, be attributed to certain of the women themselves who, knowing them to be good lovers, deliberately encourage them. Doubtless victims originally to the influence of low type whites (which no amount of supervision can altogether prevent) nevertheless their general reputation seems to be un-savoury. And most Americans with whom I discussed the subject were contemptuous of the actual Government policy regarding the Philippine Islands. As a friend said to me: "Once having gone there, which is justifiable or not, according to whether you hold, or don't hold, with the civilising mission of definitely superior and more evolved races like ourselves, yourselves, the Germans, Italians and what-have-you's, we should either stay there to put some decency and pride in work into those birds over a long period of time, or else, having chucked our hand in,[1] we should chuck the little toughs them-selves back onto their islands. They're nothing but a plague to us as they are." [Again, I merely quote.]

I said I was all for the civilising mission and the strategic measures necessary to safeguard it against less basically

[1] The U.S. Government is to concede the complete independence of the Philippine Islands before long.

well-intentioned peoples, even if it meant a sharp expedition here or there and periodical disciplinary measures.

"Sure," he said, nodding, "you would be. Your old Empire's been built up that way, which is why half your House of Commons is now afraid of Italy threatening the safety of a piece of it and the other half gives her full marks for stopping the Ethiopians' dirty games, and all those wise guys led by your Lord—Lord——" he hesitated.

"Cecil," I prompted.

My companion grinned. We were motoring at the time on Long Island.

"Yeah," he resumed, "that sounds like him . . . well, he and his pals want all the nations of the League, which entirely failed to call Haile Selassie and Co to order for everlasting depredations on the Italian border, to go to war with Mussolini who's doing a swell job putting down slave-trading."

"Unfortunately," I observed, "you would have to arrange for the ravishing of these warlike pacifists' wives and the mutilation of their sons by Selassie's savages before you could convince them that everything in the Abyssinian garden is not lovely."

"We haven't had exactly a picnic with the Filipinos," he observed dryly, "but a lot of our hill-billies started shooting off their mouths about the rights of such folk to live as they please, so we're pulling out . . . "We'll never join the League as it stands, he concluded feelingly." I hope we never join it anyway."

"I hope you do," said I, "but a very different League—a smaller select League of cultivated and heavily armed peoples allowing themselves to be realistic and protecting properly constituted minorities. Dammit, your fellow, Woodrow Wilson, started this and afterwards you backed out. If you'd stayed, you might have brought a new outlook to it."

"The hell we would," he retorted, "the nation wasn't behind Wilson then and it's still less behind those ideas now. We like you but we're dead against a tie-up with Europe."

Which is a true conversation and representative, I discovered, of a widely held opinion in the States.

But to return to San Francisco. Motioning to me to follow, the police inspectors took me round to the stage door of the old theatre and down some rickety stairs till we found ourselves under the stage itself. This space, low, stuffy and broken up by supporting baulks of timber, formed the only dressing-room. A few screens, plentifully bedizened with mirrors and backed by little tables of cosmetics, afforded what privacy there was. Here, I met the chief comedian, who ran the whole show, and his wife; he in trousers and a singlet, she in a tightly held *négligée*—both very warm under their grease paint, but not a bit put out by the advent of visitors. They made themselves perfectly charming. We talked to the accompaniment of a tap-dance overhead and the giggles of a troupe of girls, vaguely seen as heads and arms and legs bobbing up and poking out from behind various screens. Soon we were flattening ourselves against the wall as they filed past up the stairs to do another turn, as nearly naked as made no matter and delightfully unselfconscious, while the tap-dancer, got up as a coon, hurriedly started undressing as he came down. His coat was off before he reached me and his trousers flapping round his ankles before he reached his screen; his disappearing motion being in the nature of a shuffling hop.

We emerged with moist faces from this brightly lit inferno. Outside, the thin fog characteristic of many San Franciscan nights was starting to glimmer whitely near the street lamps. It is at its thickest in June and July, but this was October the twentieth. I welcomed the cool feel of it, risk of a chill notwithstanding.

"Phew," muttered the tall inspector, "I guess that place

274

would be a death-trap if a fire broke out. But it's an old joint and one of the sights."

Next, we made for the famous Fisherman's Wharf. It was now well after one o'clock in the morning, probably nearer two, but many people were out and about as we drove down towards the waterfront. Turning near the wharf itself, we were spotted by a little Italian who rushed across the road and shoved his face in through the window.

"You ze man I wanta to see," he gabbled excitedly, "you speaka for me, yes?"

"What's the matter, Tony?" grunted the police officer.

"It ees my wife, the——bitch."

"Waal, what about her?"

"She subpoena me on account of ze bambino. It is on Monday zat I appeal. I'ava the work, yes, but not enough money. An' she taka my clothes—see, I 'ava no vest." Dramatically, he pulled open his shirt. "You know me. You coma on Monday an' speek for Tony, eh?" he concluded half-way between his original anger and a wheedling insistence.

The inspector was sympathetic but short.

"I'll say what I know about you, Tony," he promised, "but you've gotta look after that kid o' yours."

"Ah, ze bambino," the little man exploded again. "I notta sure she ees mine at all, but I lova her. But my wife, she ees a——"

My companion cut him short.

"That'll do, Tony," he snapped, "forget it till Monday. I'll see ya then."

We drove on a little way and parked the car. The inspector's thin lips relaxed.

"That poor little wop is surely sore about his home life," he observed patiently.

Then we locked the car and stood for a while on the wharf,

275

to gaze at scores of tidy craft moored gunwale to gunwale below us. In the moonlight, each was the dead spit of its neighbour; they were like phantom cockle-shells, bleached and unreal. Above them, shreds of sea fog were now stealing in from the bay.

We entered a *café* nearby and at once became wedged in the Saturday night crowd at the bar—a crowd such as may be met anywhere, in any city, any country: husbands and wives clearly recognisable as such, drinking quietly and looking about them with an occasional nudge and whispered word if elderly, or talking vivaciously with many laughs and inclined to gulp their liquor if youthful; and a majority of what looked to be business men and tough guys of all ages accompanied by their molls with whom they were bored, amused or openly affectionate. Some were tipsy, some uproarious, some sullen. Guarding our drinks carefully from disaster, the two inspectors and myself formed an inconspicuous island amid this jostling tide that ebbed and flowed in front of the white-jacketed bar tenders.

Before we had been there five minutes, I felt that one or other of my companions had seen everybody in the room. With a jerk of his head and a few clipped words spoken out of the side of his mouth, the taller of the two inspectors indicated to me a few local characters and notabilities. Once or twice the policemen compared notes; apparently checking each other's memories for faces.

Eventually, we moved into the dance-hall and chose a table at the unpopular end of it near the band, and two rows back from the floor. A cabaret show was in progress: a conjuror, a singer, some dancers and an eater of fire. This last is a trick that never fails to enthrall me; I consider none more spectacular. On account of a courteous custom they have in America, one of the dances was announced as dedicated to me —"All the way from England," as the manager put it. The word "England" elicited a spontaneous round of applause which was good to hear. There was more to it than mere politeness, for no one knew which table was ours except the manager, to whom I had just been introduced on the quiet. The crowded room just clapped England for all it was worth. Coming on top of all I had heard and learned on my way across America and during my stay in California, this further sign of friendly feeling between our two nations added to my conviction of the mistake made by those who told me that anti-British feeling in the Middle-West and West of America far outweighed pro-British feeling anywhere else. I, at any rate, did not find it so.

From time to time, we were joined by the hat-check girl, an acquaintance of one of the inspectors. But there was nothing about her of the uniform garb to which we are accustomed in English night-clubs. Of Teutonic origin, and strikingly beautiful in a tall, blonde way, she wore a smart evening frock as it should be worn, walked like a duchess and danced like a professional. She had as a friend a little brunette, lively, equally charming and just as *chic*. They took it in turns to dance with us and mind the hats and coats. And, this being so, it was hardly surprising that we were almost the last to leave.

By now, our wanderings, recorded and unrecorded, had occupied us till about 4.30 a.m. Asked what I would like to do at this stage in the night's proceedings, I sniffed the cool, damp air and said a drive round the city would be swell. The tall inspector agreed it would be nice to get cool again. But the man from the Chinatown squad demurred; he had got some job on about the middle of the morning which called for sleep, and sleep he must have. We slapped him on the back, admired his wisdom and watched his thickset figure set off sturdily through the fine drizzle which had started to fall like spangles past the wan lamps on the sidewalk. Then

277

we two survivors made for our car; shivering and turning up our collars.

We drove, I suppose, for forty minutes; and I shall never forget the mysterious charm of it. Following upon the hours of sightseeing and night life in one haunt after another, the fog—now quite thick on the waterfront—the cool damp, the silence, the dark shadows and air of desertion alike were welcome. Occasionally, we saw a furtive figure slouching, or maybe two that would stand stationary, moving only their heads to watch the car approach, draw level and disappear. This was in streets a little way up one of the many slopes which drop to the harbour. And once, rolling down a long straight canyon of buildings abutting on the waterfront itself, we saw a knot of lurching figures drunkenly arguing directly in our track.

At such an hour, unless warranted by emergency, it would have been a shame to use the police siren at full blast for fear of waking people. But the merest touch of it, resulting in something like the mew of a big cat, and a fierce wink—on-and-off—of our red lamps, were sufficient to wipe the street clean of any living soul. The distant group silhouetted a moment before like gesticulating marionettes against the blank screen of the harbour fog, seemed to have dissolved into nothing.

"Guilty consciences even when lit up, I guess," remarked the inspector succinctly.

To him, this was merely an early morning potter round a town he knew well, after a night spent in parts of it that were admittedly curious yet equally familiar. But to me, it was my first acquaintance with the nocturnal moods of a seaport famous up and down the world—with San Francisco, where men and women of nearly every nation have long fore-gathered, a city with as tough and romantic a history as any. Sitting back, I let my thoughts browse on what I knew or had

278

read about it, while the ill seen masts of ships reeled slowly past like ghosts in the mist and were succeeded again, as we soared inland up one of those terrific hills, by clearer streets of barred and bolted shops, mutely announcing their names in every language. Thus a few minutes after five in the morning I finished up, sober and of my own volition, at police headquarters.

In a booth opening off a bare charge room, I looked through the call book for the night. There had been, I seem to remember, a hundred and thirty-six transmitted since 10.30 p.m.: accidents, stolen cars, suspected persons—the usual story. Still, it had started by being Saturday night, which covers (or doesn't) a multitude of sins the world over. Then a demonstration message was sent out for my benefit. The inspector snapped down a switch and spoke into a microphone. His voice took on the easily distinguishable monotone well known to gangster film fans.

"Calling all cars," he droned, "Calling all cars."

Standing beside him, I experienced a similar sensation to that which has more than once assailed me when broadcasting from a B.B.C. studio; the feeling of being instantaneously in touch, whether I liked it or not, with fellow human beings who were complete strangers. But this was no restful room where, unseen, one strove hard for composure and modulated diction, while at the other end, if I may so describe it, were indifferent, bored or interested listeners in arm-chairs. Here was a bald apology for an office, a stained table, a thumbed note-book, and at the other end keen ears and— action.

I found the criminal record department housed in a big chamber two or three floors above the street. The custodian on duty kindly showed me some of the earliest photographs kept there, dating back to 1861. This was history with a vengeance, the seamy side of a great and lovely city's life. I wished some one could write it, but of course the idea is impossible. Even after this lapse of time, there must be relations living whose feelings would be wounded. Perhaps in another hundred years? What stories, too, could be told about the old-time underworlds of great European towns!

In an album for 1930, I found the photographs of a man and a woman on the same page. There were many pages like it. But, in this instance, the respective characters portrayed appeared strikingly different: the man looked what he was— a crook, whereas the woman had the world's innocence in her face, and so obviously that it worried me. Amused but ready to oblige, the officer in charge turned up their records for me in the card index. He found them in a matter of seconds and handed them over. The man was a professional car thief, the woman merely with him on one occasion when he was caught; no charge was preferred against her.

There is no point to this story. And it fulfils no useful purpose, for appearances are notoriously deceptive. Still, I am glad she got off and pleased to have been right about her.

After humorously taking my own fingerprints but politely giving the record to me instead of filing it, the kindly Police Department, which had been my host for the night, bid me good-bye. Dawn had broken when I lay down in my hotel at six o'clock to snatch a short sleep, and eight-thirty was upon me almost before I knew I slept. Nevertheless, I was up and at the window, then into a bath at once, for at ten-thirty my tour of San Francisco by daylight was to begin. Alas, that my stay in that fascinating city was to be so short.

This morning, my host was a friend of a friend whom, with his wife, I had originally met through my oldest friend in America: which is the chain-invitation way of American people, whose kindness to strangers is legendary and not in the least exaggerated. And my oldest friend in America I had met nearly thirteen years before in the hot wayside railway station below Assisi on its hill above the Umbrian plain, midway between Perugia and Foligno: which is the way of Providence, outwardly casual with its blows or, as in this instance, with its favours. Now the chain had brought me to a famous city called by the name of the gentle being of Assisi, to a massive up-to-date hotel also dubbed the St. Francis, and to a Lincoln car standing in the sunlight outside, in which was the friend of a friend of a friend, accompanied by his second daughter and her schoolgirl companion, the last two home for a week-end at half-term.

My friend's friend drove me round and about. The terrific hills of San Francisco, which the night before I had noted just as rows of street lamps and shop fronts unusually tilted against the darkness, were now visible in all their genuine steepness. Except in some small Tyrolean hamlet, I had never seen streets so standing on end. Yet the trolley cars made light of these gradients, and rumbled up and down the fiercest with a load of unconcerned passengers. But when an accident does occur, it is likely to be a bad one. I was shown where a trolley car had got out of control a year or two before, and had gone down the hill like a roller coaster until it left the tracks with a grim loss of life. No one but a fool would park his motor against the kerb at anything less than a forty-five degree angle on these hazardous pitches. But, of course, a good many do.

Practically on the summit of such a hill, we stopped at the corner house once occupied by Robert Louis Stevenson. Three of the four roads which meet there slope away like ladders, so that his view from the windows must have been glorious. In two directions he looked straight over the great bay below; bluer this morning than the sky above it and backed by ochre mountains. From here, I thought, when tired of the labour of writing, Stevenson must often have watched the spreading of the fog that had rolled through the Golden Gate of an evening and listened to the mournful hoots of the ferry steamers. One of these, dwarfed by distance to the size of a water beetle, cut across my line of vision at that moment. Black smoke from a tall funnel blew ahead of it like a thin feeler, and its stumpy hull pencilled a wake of diverging lines across the unruffled surface of the bay. It passed between the shore and an arid-looking island, seemingly overwhelmed by sprawling grey buildings.

"What is that place?" I inquired, pointing at it.

"It's the penitentiary on Alcatraz," my host replied. "Al Capone is in there."

The place and the name jarred.

Turning east, I studied the skeleton of the new bridge in process of erection between San Francisco and Oakland Bay. The effect from so far above was that of two threads hanging in loops over a line of black pins. Actually, the bridge is eight and a quarter miles long. When completed,[1] it will support three lanes of trucks and two electric railway lines on the lower level, and six lanes of automobile traffic on the upper level. Ships passing below will have two hundred and eighteen feet of clearance at low water. Constructed at a cost of nearly $77,000,000, and due to be opened in November, 1936, it represents one of the greatest bridge-building feats in the world; and looks it. By such means as this, and the Hudson tunnel, and the New Jersey elevated road and so on, American cities are dealing with their traffic problems of entrance and exit.

On our way to this eminence, from which it was so difficult to tear oneself away, we had driven past Fisherman's Wharf—one of the scenes of my all-night wanderings. To-day the little craft, in their special harbour, as closely packed there as sardines, revealed themselves literally in their true colours as the sun blazed down upon them at their moorings. The effect was that of an immense bath filled by children with impeccably neat boats of every hue in the rainbow.

[1] It is now complete.

"Practically on the summit of such a hill . . . the house once occupied by Robert Louis Stevenson."

"'What is that place?' . . . pointing at it down the vista of the road. 'It's the penitentiary on Alcatraz.' . . ."

At length, we dropped cautiously downhill from Stevenson's house towards the west; alternately down a steep declivity, then level for a few yards over a cross street terraced out of the hillside, and then down again; repeating this switchback form of travel until we reached flatter ground, where we drove leisurely through the big permanent military camp and passed on through pine woods towards the Golden Gate. There again we paused, this time to look across the famous harbour entrance which shares with that of Rio the reputation of being the most impressive in the world.

The hour was barely past noon, but already a haze was forming to seaward and lying threateningly above the wooded bluffs opposite. Or perhaps the sun had not succeeded in dispelling the previous night's mists. At any rate, the Golden Gate was living up to its reputation, for the ocean outside seemed mysteriously to gloom although the bay within lay glittering. I wished I could have stood there as night fell, to watch for the advance guard of the fog, and see it march in ponderous ranks below, where now a liner, no bigger than a clockwork model, made its smooth way beneath the cables of another budding bridge and set a course for far Japan. And had I been there a few days later, I would have seen the spirit of these bridges exemplified in terms as modern as they are themselves; for well above the Golden Gate, and at a great pace, the big *China Clipper* passed upon her inaugural flight, her first stop Honolulu.

We got back into the car, descended a mildly serpentine road to the lower level of the coast outside the harbour's mouth, and drove the length of a flat straight promenade, built on what was once sand dunes, until we reached an open-air swimming pool surrounded by a high, fenced plantation. Privately, I wondered why my host was so keen for me to see a mere swimming pool. "It's good of its kind," was all he volunteered about it.

When we stopped at the entrance, he sent the two school-girls in with me, and said he would stay by the car to mind our coats. Upon our return in five minutes' time, we found him grinning like a schoolboy himself, his hands full of hot-dogs in paper bags, of which he had bought four (one each) at a stall across the road. As for the pool, it was undoubtedly very fine; fully three hundred yards long, I should judge, and set in the centre of a pleasant, shady garden; an enchanting place to spend a hot afternoon.

Some distance back along the rather dull shore promenade, we turned off into a park of pine trees and sandy roads—a striking and beautiful contrast. We were now, so to speak, starting to cut round behind San Francisco to the south. Soon we reached the famous Japanese garden, a picture of great peace and charm, full of bamboo groves, dwarf pines and small lily pools spanned by semi-circular bridges, made in traditional fashion at the expense of a former Emperor of Japan and presented by him to the city.

Moving on again, we began to drive up an old mission trail over by the bleached eastward flank under the Twin Peaks and obtained a magnificent view of San Francisco and its bay, there spread below us. In long sweeps, we dropped down the far side into woods once more, to Burlingame Country Club—not unlike our Hurlingham, but on a smaller scale. And thence, after a welcome cocktail, we proceeded a short distance to the home, at San Mateo, of my host and hostess; who at once made me feel that not only was their charming, liveable country house entirely at my disposal, but that I myself was as one of their own family, home after a long absence.

At luncheon, I found myself talking happily of travel to my hostess and of flying to a flaxen-haired girl on my right, herself keenly improving her recent ability to fly and already possesssing a number of hours' experience. In the afternoon, they took me to an amateur baseball match nearby, at which my host acted as umpire and convulsed the spectators by his astonishing methods of signalling the score and giving decisions. The game was played with a soft ball and turned out to be one of the funniest semi-serious, semi-comic exhibitions I have ever seen.

We, in England, are too apt to condemn the Americans' individual specialisation in certain games, and to complain, when they beat us, of their deadly earnestness. Myself, I was able to rejoice again and again in their tremendous gift of humour. With such facility, indeed, did they play the fool that at times I could hardly believe I wasn't at home. Perhaps we are the folk who do not show our silly side often enough to them? Certainly, two nations with such an apparently inherent sense of the ridiculous can never seriously quarrel, and are bound to turn the world into a saner place as centuries roll by; a process likely to be accelerated by a stronger dash of humour in our respective public, as distinct from private lives. Is it not true that more than one labour deadlock in the past started to loosen from the moment a jest was exchanged, paving the way for friendlier negotiations? Likewise, against the timely ribaldry of the downright, were it given rein more frequently, corrupt political thinking would give way as quickly as hypocrisy. And there is too much of both on either side of the Atlantic. I have seen somewhere the quip: "Most of our industrial troubles are caused by workers who do not think and thinkers who do not work." True enough. The thoughtless and the ineffective we have always with us. But even their masses are not potentially so dangerous as diplomats and statesmen who are afraid to interpret openly the humour of the countries they represent.

From the baseball circus, I was taken on to tea with some neighbours. Having lived for a time in Sussex, they had built into their stone Californian house something of the influence laid upon them by our county of hazel copses, deeply small meadows and rolling downs, picketed with beeches. A stone-flagged square of rose beds led into a walled enclosure of shaded lawn, like dozens I know nestling inland as one flies from Brighton to Chichester, within sight of Ashdown Forest and the sea. Below, in terraces, they had made a typical English garden; here fruit trees, there a path meandering through flowering shrubs, with a wide border beyond. Only the brown hills were different, betokening a strength of sun unknown to England. It was in this house that I first saw a Japanese parlourmaid dressed in our orthodox black and white. And neat and nice she looked; not a bit out of place in garb or gesture.

Here, too, I gleaned something of a serious problem: the over-production of graduates on the part of the Universities. More men and girls, I heard it said, receive a cap and hood than can afterwards be accommodated in jobs suited to their specific qualifications. "Many are called," it appears, "but few are chosen." And I was told that not infrequently they cannot summon the will power to alter themselves to suit other jobs. This is understandable. For to drive a taxi or sew dresses after living for the day when one will graduate as a Bachelor of Science or a Master of Arts, is to drink the gall in life's cup at a pathetically early age. Not, plainly, that either driving taxis or dressmaking are professions of which to be ashamed (both are useful, necessary and honourable; and I well know the former, at least, to have its interesting and often amusing side), but because it usually takes a philosophical, worldly-wise man or woman, rather than a boy or girl barely out of their teens, to face with success, if not with equanimity, an unattractive reassessment of values, and virtually to start again from small beginnings. This plethora of trained theorists, many with little or no practical experience, forms a steady stream of hurt youngsters, at best disappointed, at worst embittered. And from the latter can only too easily be recruited agitators, suicides, non-triers and even criminals.

It is out of place for discussion in this book, but we ourselves are not strangers to the phenomenon. We remember, for instance, that the ranks of the Civil Disobedience Movement in India, to which no particle of good feeling or constructive suggestion is readily traceable, were swollen by considerable numbers of University graduates —parrot scholars, unfitted to a large extent by their education, but still more by their own hot-house outlook, to take any useful part in the life of the community whither they returned with false ideas of Westernism.

Of course, the average School or University curriculum, and the present examination system, are responsible. One emphasises the humanities at the expense of humanisation, the other frequently "fails" budding genius, probably for some psychological reason, while it "passes" a stream of mediocrity. The result, in a competitive, industrial world largely at the economic mercy of international financiers, is bound to be somewhat chaotic. Only when courses in science or arts, etc., are made chronologically subservient to a broad grounding in International as well as National history, to a fixed minimum understanding of geology, biology, physiology, ethnics—of evolution in general, and a decent acquaintanceship with ethics (an understanding of the basic need for self-discipline by the individual and mass-discipline by sane law) will undergraduates be more confident of their initial choice of a profession and emerge into the workaday world with a better chance of combating its vicissitudes or of bowing gracefully to the inevitable; losing neither heart nor goodwill towards men. Under the present system, a newly-fledged Doctor of Philosophy is often less usefully (and, in the other sense, also less philosophically) equipped than an artisan who, by a courageous swallowing of experience, has not only made good at his first trade, however humble, but in course of time has left his name high on his country's roster.

That night after dinner, my host and I got deep into sporting experiences, with duck-shooting predominating. And later, when we joined the ladies, the talk turned yet again to State politics, to the realisation definitely dawning among the young that the "right" people should be in politics, to clean them up, rather than dusting their hands disdainfully outside. I did nothing to guide the conversation; it took its own trend according to the individuals present. But once more I was hearing evidence of widespread desire for a stricter, more upright, political system.

Of course, San Francisco and its neighbourhood is a nerve centre. One would expect to encounter broadminded views in a community constantly in business contact with the world at large and containing many men and women who travel. Still, I thought I saw now, and had certainly seen at luncheon, the influence of aviation: its provision of easy, frequent contacts at distances and the co-operation it calls for between nationals of different countries. More, it is itself starting to have a long-range effect on politics—and for the better. Success in commercial aviation demands an unusual standard of education and intelligence. Consistently safe flying is not an easy task for any individual, though many think it is; and its organisation on a company basis presents a whole succession of intricate problems only to be solved by personnel of a high standard subscribing to a stiff code of personal behaviour and commercial integrity.

From whatever class they may have been attracted, probably more of the "right" people of every country are in aviation than in any other pursuit. And because that pursuit takes them repeatedly, rapidly, and in increasing numbers from one country to another, and all over those countries, it may not inaccurately be dubbed the founder of a true League of Nations; with possibilities still unfathomed but upon which a mounting hope of peace is placed, safe as its devotees should remain, intellectually and spiritually, from the unmoral depredations of the more misguided types of governments. Many who constantly fly on week-end visits from their own countries to friends in Germany, Italy, France, Austria, Poland, etc., would now take up arms only with a bitter reluctance.

In a comparatively few years' time, the day of the doctrinaire, a damnable danger in public affairs, will be over—thanks to the free and continuous interchange between nations of the "right" type among their young men and women. And the right type is classless; it is recruited from the aristocracy of mind. Any one can qualify for it. Only hard work, the burning of midnight oil, and the exercise of moral courage is needed. Lindbergh, as one would expect of a man commercially and scientifically qualified as well as by courageous achievement, states very soundly the point of view of the responsible aviator. Speaking in Berlin on the 24th July, 1936, he said:

"During my journey in Europe I have been more deeply impressed than ever with the gravity of the situation with which we are faced. When I perceive that in one or two days a degree of devastation can be effected which no lapse of time could ever make good, again I realise that we must make provision for a form of security which is dynamic and not static, and which rests on reason and not on force. But in the fact that aviation is dependent on reason, I see a new hope. More intelligence is required to pilot an aeroplane than to dig a trench or fire a rifle.

"The training which is required in aviation must also teach the value of the achievements of civilisation. The responsibility

289

which we incur by creating a powerful destructive force is lightened by the knowledge that this force is being controlled by reason and experience, and that we have separated such a force from ignorance. I find hope in the belief that power which goes hand in hand with knowledge will not be a menace to civilisation. The combination of force and reason—that is the mark and the responsibility of the airman."

But in North America, still isolated from Europe (though not for much longer) by the absence of trans-Atlantic airlines, other than an occasional Zeppelin visit, aviation is so far confined to exercising the more unforeseen of its influences: that on politics. Never have I heard such biting scorn expressed on the subject of jiggery-pokery as that emanating from the American airlines and the aircraft industry. The picking of Mines Field, Los Angeles; the cursedly awkward Municipal Airport, Washington; the arrogant ignorance responsible for taking the air-mails out of the hands of companies organised to fly them in most weathers and handing them over to the Army, whose pilots, new to such specialised routine, killed themselves one after the other till the experiment ceased; the terminating of the late General William Mitchell's career for telling and demonstrating the truth about the degree of vulnerability of capital ships to air bombardment; these and other examples, when brought up, are sufficient to turn the air blue wherever knowledgeable flying men and women are gathered together.

Wilbur Wright did more for his country than he thought when he made an aeroplane fly. He sowed the seed of a legion of clear-eyed, straight-thinking Americans which, thirty years later, was to begin writing a warning on the wall for political careerists. True, the process has barely begun and is still to a great extent shackled. But I do not fear for its ultimate effect. The personnel is growing rapidly and constitutes the best there is.

I slept in the room belonging to the eldest daughter of the house, who was away on the east coast. Her mantelpiece was loaded with silver cups that she had won riding, and her father proudly showed me the inside of her clothes closet door, on which she had pinned all the first, second and third prize rosettes handed to her at horse-shows. Photographs of her performances in the ring and a few treasured books and ornaments completed the personal furnishings of this pleasant bedroom, with a look-out in two directions—onto the drive and into a grass patch surrounded by slender trees, where the sunlight next morning made the sort of patterns seldom captured on canvas.

Just after 9 a.m. my hostess, herself, most kindly drove me to Mills Field, a bare ten minutes away. And within another five, my plane had taken off and was climbing steeply before turning over the southward end of the bay, and I was looking back towards the timbered slopes of San Mateo, conscious once more of deep gratitude for the good-fellowship extended to guests in America and genuinely regretful to be gone so soon upon my way. In Los Angeles again, over three hundred miles away, and dictating to Mrs. Cotton before midday, my San Francisco week-end perforce faded to a mere kaleidoscope of rapid impressions. But in retrospect they have now regained their clarity, aided by my diary.

One is struck, I think, as much as anything by the ease of entertaining in the environs of Los Angeles and the efficient charm with which one is oneself entertained. Domestic servants, often Chinese, Japanese, or coloured men of various races, receive substantially more wages than we are used to paying in England. But they do far more work.

For instance, Hugh Walpole was good enough to give a dinner party for me one night at his house in Benedict Canyon, Beverly Hills. We were nine or ten; R. C. Sheriff, his mother, Edmund Gwenn, John Collier, Jean Hersholt, myself, and one or two others—all occupied or interested in the film world. Yet one coloured man proved sufficient to wait on us, and performed his duties with zeal and care; grinning all over his good-natured face whenever the conversation amused him. Judging by what I had already learnt of household management on the coast, I imagined there was probably but one other domestic on the premises, out of sight in the kitchen; doubtless coloured also, and possibly, though not necessarily, provided with extra help for the evening. Nevertheless, an excellent five-course dinner was the result, with a beautifully-cooked turkey as the *pièce de résistance*, which I had to carve because Walpole had a damaged hand.

A few nights earlier, I had dined with two more friends—another author and his wife, herself a famous scenario writer. They kindly sent a car to fetch me to Hollywood from the Ambassador. A Chinaman in neat livery was at the wheel, who drove me with admirable restraint to their house in Milner Road. As I entered, he vanished, only to reappear again a few minutes later, garbed in a spotless white tunic and bearing a tray of first-rate cocktails. At dinner, I was fortunate enough to find myself between my hostess and Mrs. Edward Robinson, the wife of the star of *Little Cæsar* and many other capably done pictures, under whose happy influence I tumbled into one of those splendid conversations when every other word produces gusts of laughter until the entire table joins in. But out of the corner of my eye I watched the deft Chinaman, waiting with all the skill and twice the speed of an old family butler.

And the meal itself, especially a pudding of brains and spinach which accompanied some tender veal, was so exquisite that I felt bound to compliment the lady of the house upon it. Whereupon, she confided that it was all done by two Chinese, one of whom was the chauffeur-butler, and the other the cook. What others there were on duty during the day were at any rate taking no part in the evening's proceedings. Yet I have never had a meal better chosen, cooked or served in my life. Douglas Byng's songs on the gramophone eventually ended an evening during which I had laughed more than I had for a long time.

Then a week later, in a lovely house, high above Pasadena, where guests descend several steps from the hall of a courtyard into a fine rugged room full of books, with a grand piano at each end of it, and an immense open fireplace, I experienced the smooth, watchful attentions of other coloured servants who, needless to say, made no mistakes: where, after another admirable dinner in an adjoining room, this time in company given over mostly to the theory and practice of aviation, we continued talking or sang songs round one of the pianos or stood outside on a broad terrace, itself boasting the usual feature of a great hearth in the wall of the house, and from there looked down between conical shrubs like dark sentries over the carpet of twinkling lights spreading to meet the distant velvet of the sky, powdered with brilliant stars.

I had done, I remember, a terrific day's work, and the peace of that place was as welcome as a drink at a hill stream after a hot climb. And, as we leaned there, my hostess was speaking quietly of her rides in the foothills back of us; of how she had collected a complete old outfit, silver-mounted Western saddle, bridle, and so on, which she always used; and of how she and her husband would be glad if I would join one of their parties one day.

It seemed almost too good to be true, so good that I could not then bring myself to decline, although I knew I had too much work to do. I had to refresh myself with the idea, at least for an evening. I thanked her; said I would love to go; would try to go—and did subsequently try. But with Mrs. Cotton's arrival next morning, my pile of unsorted notes

293

forcibly recaptured an erring allegiance; and the next morning and the next—until, despite my efforts, it was too late to go riding.

Beyond all doubt, visitors with work to do in Los Angeles must turn themselves into hermits to succeed. If one were living there, things would be normal. But as it was, I had deliberately to forgo following up a generous stream of verbal invitations, and explain instead that my time was short and engagements pressing. I hope I was believed. Only in the last few days, with the end of my work in sight, did I dare to break out regularly for luncheon and in the evenings; knowing that even an entire surrender to the temptation of loafing and having a good time could not now matter seriously.

Alfred Cohn, the U.S. Collector of Customs for Los Angeles and a most successful writer, gave me luncheon one day at the Vendôme, to meet that renowned author, Rupert Hughes. Their combined wit and wisdom caused the hour or two to pass all too quickly. Hughes' gently satirical account of the film world, in which he has many firm friendships, cried out to be recorded for a gramophone record. No subsequent audience would have enjoyed it more than the film world itself. He also introduced me for the first time to fried soft-shelled crabs, blissfully good eating; and Mrs. Hughes, as red-headed as myself, quickly and charmingly convinced me that I knew nothing about melon by telling me to squeeze the juice of a fresh lime over it. To me, used to quantities of sugar, the result was nothing short of a heavenly revelation.

Here, too, at the Vendôme, Elizabeth Allan came to luncheon with me, and administered a good-natured wigging because I hadn't previously declared my presence in Hollywood: dear "Liz," as popular there as here, and a splendid unofficial ambassadress for the British stage, just by being her radiantly cheerful and sensible self. We had at least four years' gossip to exchange, and probably spoke with our mouths full. One sitting was obviously inadequate, so we had to go to the Trocadero a few nights later to continue talking, and to dance and sup in between whiles. And still another night, a friend of hers gave us two tickets for one of the weekly boxing shows, where we saw the tough Filipinos taking fantastic punishment with a fixed grin, and spent the rest of our time passing bottles of Coco-Cola along the row to thirsty spectators situated farther away than ourselves from the gabbling vendor parading the aisle. Across the ring from us, and at its side, I saw Miss Mae West, watching every fight closely. Somebody told me that she is a very keen fight fan, and goes every week when she is there.

Thus a month's stay on the coast, interesting and varied if somewhat laborious, drew to a close in a last whirl of happy friendships, old and new. October the twenty-sixth came —a day of tidying up, packing, paying accounts, writing letters of farewell and correcting a last newspaper article to send home to David Grant. For the evening, I had planned in gratitude to give a modest dinner.

The imitation palms in the far-famed Cocoanut Grove at the Ambassador bent in farewell above the table. The music throbbed, rising and falling. We danced and talked, sat down, then danced again; planning the parties we would have when my guests next came to England. The Duncan Sisters appeared singing their songs as cleverly as ever. Two professional dancers followed them, their dancing putting all of us to shame. One by one the people at other tables left. Then we left. Finally, at nine-thirty next morning, my eastbound plane left. A first stay on the golden coast of California was finished.

The major part of such aeronautical experience as it was possible to acquire during my visit, is isolated for purposes of clarity and continuity in the following section of this book; together with similar experiences on the Atlantic coast.

PART II

PART II

CHAPTER I

A COUNTRY THAT LIVES AVIATION

AMERICA IS MAKING THE MOST OF HER UNRIVALLED OPPORtunities for developing fast, long distance flying. Hers are unrivalled opportunities because they occur within the confines of her own private piece of continent and adjacent to her aircraft factories. At their backdoors, so to speak, she has every type of terrain; high mountain, forest, swamp and desert; and every sort of temperature and weather from snow at many degrees below zero to fog, tropical squalls and blinding heat. Besides, she has followed what I believe to be the far-sighted initial policy of heavily subsidising more than one airline for the carrying of mails.[1] Thus the companies themselves have been free to expend these resources on technical development, which has reached a very high standard indeed.

True, we have the same weather conditions available to us in the British Empire, and in even more staggering proportions. But to encounter some of them we have to go far afield, passing over other people's bits of continent (not always a popular proceeding); and when we reach them, we are out of easy touch with our factories and experimental departments. Consequently, we have tended to develop our airlines by comparatively short sections; using on each the type of aeroplane that we have considered most suitable; instead of having been able in one fell swoop to evolve a general purpose machine capable of covering all sections efficiently. The truth

[1] £35,000,000 in twelve years, whereas just one British Company, Imperial Airways has been assisted—and only to the tune of about £3,500,000.

299

of this was never more strikingly demonstrated than in the England-Australia air race, when a standard Douglas D.C.2 transport ship, carrying passengers, flying farther, and making frequent scheduled landings, finished second to our own specialised racing plane, built solely on account of the contest in question.

We won all right. And world-wide credit was given to us in all informed circles for having done what we had set out to do in a specific manner. Yet there were many people who rightly gave as much credit to the Douglas, as being the immensely worthy representative of a more practical type of aeroplane.

Unfortunately, Douglas protagonists in our own country, well meaning though they were, seemed to give insufficient weight to the considerations set out above, with the result that the inevitable reaction set in and even Government spokesmen thought it necessary to bolster up the performance of our De Havilland Comet—a performance that needed no such delay-action support and would have stood for ever on its own merits as one of the world's greatest flights; two magnificent pilots in a startling machine. But we still lacked then the up-to-date transport aeroplane, which is one reason why Australia has been ordering machines from America as well as from us.

In such a maelstrom of nationalist good intentions and pernickety arguments, it is hardly surprising that many uninformed leaders of public opinion nearly stultified for us the value of the Douglas lesson. As so often happens, nationalism was confused by the thoughtless with patriotism, and common sense nearly went by the board; as though it is not obvious that true patriotism leans more to balanced self-assessment, moderation and sanity. If a plump Jingoism ever gains as much influence in our Government as it possesses in some of our industries, we shall lose our goodwill among other nations just as surely as we have lost valuable markets to our American cousins and to the Japanese.

Fortunately, Lord Beaverbrook saw fit to charter a Douglas and be flown about Europe in it. This was wise. He is one of the few men who could do it, and he did not keep his impressions to himself. Fortunately, Lord Rothermere assisted the building of a fast transport plane by the Bristol Aircraft Company; which was a considerable start in the right direction.

I say a start, because nobody with any knowledge of aeroplane manufacture, least of all an experienced body of men like the Bristol designers, would have supposed it possible overwhelmingly to surpass at the initial attempt the Douglas, which is undoubtedly the world's finest all-round passenger aeroplane; any more than sensible people would imagine that Donald Douglas, most charming of men, is sitting still with his engineering staff of two hundred and twenty-nine, resting on his laurels and paying no attention to the future. Nevertheless, the Bristol, although carrying a smaller load, gives relatively a 50% higher performance for its horse-power than does the Douglas D.C.2. Our current Armstrong Whitworth monoplane is also in the same class. But we must remember that the Douglas D.C.2 is not now a new type.

To-day we have to reckon with the D.C.3, already well in production; a bigger, faster edition of D.C.2, carrying twenty-four people by day and sixteen in number at night. Then D.C.4 is due soon; to carry forty passengers by day or twenty at night, with a range (according to load) of 900 to 2000 miles, a top speed of 230 m.p.h., a cruising speed of 193 m.p.h. to 210 m.p.h., between 60 per cent. and 75 per cent. power, and four 1000 h.p. engines—any two of which will take it up to 9000 feet. Here again, we must look to four-engined machines now under construction by Armstrong-Whitworth and De Havilland to keep our end up.

301

Never having seen American civil aviation described in a way that presented me with what I felt to be a complete picture, I determined to go and see for myself. And not solely for myself, because it is important that we should all know what is being done. For not only does our trade demand that, in the friendliest way, we should give our American cousins a run for their money in European aeroplane markets, but it is increasingly vital that a close and understanding relationship should be maintained between the flying communities of the two great English-speaking nations. And by flying communities I mean all who commonly fly or are flown, and those about to fly themselves or now laggardly reaching the stage of thinking it is time they started to use airlines. It is not too much to say that upon the mutual interest of those who will shortly visit each other's countries by air, depends to a considerable extent the combination of aim which, if anything, will make the world more peaceful for our children's children.

In America during the autumn of 1935, I was flown on airlines on the Pacific and Atlantic seaboards, and from coast to coast across the continent. Several people also kindly allowed me to fly their own planes; and, in addition, I met and talked with more than half the aircraft manufacturers in the United States, and one or two representatives of the Army Air Corps. It is a summary of what I learnt that I have recorded here, as far as the dictates of courtesy towards my infinitely hospitable hosts will allow.

On the second evening following my arrival in Los Angeles by car, I gladly accepted a joint invitation from Major Lester D. Gardner and Professor Clark B. Millikan to a dinner of the Pacific Coast section of the Institute of the Aeronautical Sciences. Lester Gardner, whom I had met in New York, is the Secretary of the Institute, and a mine of information on aeronautical history. Moderately senior though he is in years, it would never occur to him to board a train if he could climb into an aeroplane. He called for me in a V-8 Ford *coupé* lent him by Donald Douglas. Complaining that he did not know Los Angeles well and had never driven a V-8 before, he nevertheless drove me like a safely-aimed projectile to the Chamber of Commerce Building, where the dinner was held; making only one mistake on the way.

Clark Millikan, who was in the chair, is a professor working in the Guggenheim Aeronautical Laboratories of the Californian Institute of Technology. Unlike most people's idea of a professor, he is still in his thirties and flies himself. I mention these facts as indicative of the viewpoint on living which is common to most of the charming people in America who are interested in aviation. Their interest is nothing if not lively, up to date and practical.

At dinner, I sat between Donald Douglas and Glenn Martin, who is the third oldest aircraft manufacturer in the United States, known now particularly as the builder of the Martin bombers and the new Clippers. Sitting opposite were Robert Gross, from whose plant emanates the Lockheed " Orion" and "Electra," and Gerard Vultee, responsible for the speedy planes that bear his name. Beyond Martin was Anthony Fokker, over on a visit. Northrop, another famous manufacturer, was also in the room, and so was A. V. Wilgoos, chief engineer to Pratt and Whitney. Reuben Fleet, President of the Consolidated Aircraft Corporation, came in after dinner; he had at that time nine million dollars worth of orders on his books. Altogether, the men sitting round the table were responsible for more than half the aircraft built in America.

The talk turned naturally enough to commerce. Uninformed government interference with those who understood the job of making aeroplanes was condemned there as it is here; but who said what, and why, is nobody's business. From commerce, the conversation swung naturally enough to war. It was held by some that there will always be wars intermittently until sufficient world-wide understanding exists for tariffs to be abolished.

And so the shuttle went back and forth between us.

After dinner, Donald Douglas, as President of the Institute, went to the microphone and said a few words to the assembled members numbering between one and two hundred, mostly young engineers. Then three papers were read: *High Altitude Air Transport Operations* by W. C. Rockefeller, *Problems of the Pressure Cabin Airplane* by Professor A. T. Klein and J. E. Lipp, and *The Performance of Rocket Planes* by William Bollay.

The latter, although one of the best delivered, and one in which none of the professors present were able to pick a hole when they tackled the speaker, is nevertheless of no immediate interest to us. Of the former I can truthfully say that though much of the matter they contained was above my head, I realised that I was listening to the results of what is perhaps the most advanced thought extant in practical stratosphere flying. Manners forbade too close an inquiry into the current experiments being made; but I left with the definite impression that a further five years might well see the advantages of this great leap in speed made available in a safe form to the public. Of that five years, doubtless three would be occupied by the development of a reliable system of carrying internal pressure in the cabin, of evolving and regulating a source of air and doubly safeguarding its maintenance, and a further two years would elapse while the system is regularly operated by mail planes, with the object of eliminating anything unforeseen before members of the public are borne to and fro at such considerable heights.

This is obvious if it is considered that even partial failure to maintain correct supercharging of the cabin would result in great discomfort for the passengers in a sleeper plane, when owing to unconsciousness of what is going on, they would neglect to swallow during a descent, thus not equalising the pressure in their ears. Indeed, it applies to-day in unsuper-charged cabins, and from such modest heights as 10,000 feet. A more serious breakdown might, of course, result in death.

Of many facts brought to light at that meeting, one is particularly important to all who are interested in this next stage of high-speed flying: namely, that the aeroplane must be completely variable. It is useless to have a machine designed to operate at one specified height because of the very strong winds which, it is suspected, may sometimes be encountered at great heights, despite the fact that the latest stratosphere balloon to go up only travelled across country at about thirty m.p.h. Moreover, the wind increases its westerly component up to the level of the stratosphere. Above that, it decreases it; or increases its easterly component. Consequently, a machine made to fly economically and efficiently at a certain given height might only be able to do so in one direction, which would be patently useless.

Normally, forty thousand feet appears to be the most desirable operational height for stages of one thousand miles. To climb to that height for a hop of five hundred miles would not be worth while; more time being occupied in doing so, and in descending again, than would be taken by the orthodox fast plane of the present day flying at a normal height.

Much more will be heard of stratosphere flying in America before long. We ourselves are by no means ignoring the question. General Vallé, the Italian Under-Secretary for Air, is credited with saying that the future of flying lies in the stratosphere and that Italy may shortly make experimental flights. And we can be sure that the Germans, with their usual solid efficiency, have the matter well in hand. And, doubtless, Russia too.

After the meeting at the Los Angeles Chamber of Commerce building, some of us adjourned to the lounge of the

Biltmore Hotel for a nightcap. Donald Douglas, Glenn Martin, Robert Gross and Gerard Vultee had to slip away, but among those who came were Lester Gardner, Anthony Fokker, Clark Millikan, Reuben Fleet, and several others. We made a circle of arm-chairs. Soon there was the pleasant sound of ice clinking in tall glasses, and the air became blue with smoke.

Coming out of the Chamber of Commerce building, Fokker had wandered along beside me, giving life-like vocal imitations of an aircraft engine warming up and alternately of an American police syren. He and Fleet were in great form and chipped each other unmercifully about the respective aircraft they built. Fleet was winning by the sheer incessance of his drollery when Fokker took the wind out of his sails by remarking whimsically that he, himself, was all right now that he was a salesman for Douglas—a joking reference to his building under licence of Donald's famous planes in addition to those of his own design.

Yet the remark was sufficient to start me thinking again that possibly no greater tribute could be paid to the Douglas machines than that so many European countries should need them and that the famous Dutchman, who was responsible for the "Fokker scourge" during the war, should be assembling them in Holland.

Well, we have let it happen once. We must not let it go on happening: we must try to ensure that the next big transport plane in popular demand, or the next but one, will be British —in addition to our smaller machines which are already so sought after by reason of their fine performance for a low horse-power. Aviation is at least a study that by reason of its own character encourages wide thinking. And there is a greater proportion of younger, keener, more broadminded men in leading positions in it than in the motor trade. In aviation within the Empire, we have already shown that we

306

do not run quite the same risk of being so mesmerised by our home markets that we can scarcely focus those more distant, which, in consequence, where cars have been concerned, have lain largely at the swift mercy of American enterprise with its concentration on detail planning for every climate and the needs of each locality. We have now partially awakened to the latter. As regards the former, we have not yet been to sleep—only a little heavy-eyed. Aviation, marvellous as are the strides it has made in the last five years, is still quite an infant compared with what it will be.

One of the party at the Biltmore delivered himself of some views on the British Air Ministry's regulations.

"Yards of red tape," he observed. "Ideas framed originally by old men."

The method recommended for arousing the old men in question sounded violent but efficacious. In the *rôle* of interested listener, I sat for the most part in silence, but I remarked that there were signs of a distinct change of heart. The speaker struggled with the name of our new Air Minister.

"Cunliffe-Lister," I volunteered. (Since created Viscount Swinton).

He nodded. "That's the man," he said. "I sat next to him once. He has got it here," tapping his head, "he is all right: he sees it."

The talk drifted again to war. I brought it back.

"What about our new——?" said I.

A speaker was at me like a terrier. "A high performance," he said. "Probably very good indeed. But the point is that with that sort of machine you are only now where Douglas was two years ago."

I quote these views exactly as given.

After more chaff, Fokker rose to go, declaring that he was becoming frightened of building aeroplanes at all now—with their flaps, brakes, retractable under-carts, lounge seats, head-rests, reading-lamps, lavatories and everything else. As for the stratosphere problems which we had heard discussed that night, he thought it would be easier to redesign the passengers, and put a valve somewhere in the blood system. To the accompaniment of other Parthian shots, more personal in character, he said good-bye all round and disappeared.

Millikan and Fleet started arguing about the merits of low-wing monoplanes as trainers. When they were allowed to nose over, said Fleet, the pilot was nearly always seriously hurt: a biplane saved the man if his belt was tight. He was now putting metal tripods on some fast monoplanes for the U.S. Government for that very reason. Besides, if the engine coughed out, he disliked the steeper gliding angle of the low-wing as against a biplane. Millikan challenged this and politely appealed to me, both of us being pilots. But I disclaimed the right to express an opinion in more experienced company, although I mentioned that I felt it would be hard to find any high performance monoplane with a flatter gliding angle (de-flapped, and if one needed to stretch one's glide) than a Miles "Hawk."

A fortnight later, on Donald Douglas's schooner, off Catalina Island, another party of us discussed aerial attack on towns. It was brilliantly sunny, and I had been fishing for shark, but without success. Douglas, stripped to the waist and as brown as a berry, was lounging against the wheel. He is rated the best skipper along that piece of coast, and at one time or another has won every race for which his boat is eligible. The night we crossed from San Pedro to Avalon had been bright, and the *Edymion* had lain over until her port gunwale was almost awash in the silver path of the moon. We had to wedge ourselves on the sloping deck, for there was a bit of a sea running, and with a stiff breeze the yacht was making eleven and a half knots. Suddenly, to our great delight, Douglas, reserved and usually rather silent, had started quoting Masefield's immortal lines, beginning, "I will go down to the sea again." I had known them for years. I suppose we all had. But so well spoken, and in such a setting, they were arresting in the extreme. I remember that none of us spoke for a minute when he had finished and stood there silent again, peering ahead, with the schooner's wheel kicking in his hands. To me it was obvious that although his name is a household word in aviation, and he is at the top of that particular tree, it is to the sea that he goes for rest and relaxation; and much of his heart is given to ships.

But it was of other, rather fearsome things that we talked in the following day's sunshine; of fast, high-flying bomber squadrons, of ground defence against aircraft, and of interceptor planes. We were four, and we all knew something of the air; some a great deal, I least of all. What we said and who said it, doesn't matter. But later again, back on the east coast, talking to Cy Caldwell, the star writer of *Aero Digest*, and to others, I formed the opinion that it was as widely recognised in informed circles in America as it is here that interceptor planes are no adequate defence against modern bombers. Most nations have tested them out.

We all know the facts. Let us face them. Modern bombers travel so fast, are so easily manœuvred, carry first-class gunners who have nothing to do when attacked but shoot, and whose field of fire now includes even the old blind spot under the tail, that interceptor planes lucky enough to establish contact with the raiders are virtually taking on a series of forts little slower than themselves and much less assailable or vulnerable.

Even under peace conditions, when for the purposes of experiment definite information about the approach of bombers is given to interceptor squadrons, a huge percentage of the raiders still penetrate the defended area. Interceptor planes have to some extent become propaganda equipment. They look efficient. They sound magnificent. Their performance is impressive on paper and in fact. But it is not practically so impressive, and the public ought to know this. It is only fair that it should. Other methods of defence, if any, must be found and built up to augment the comparatively little assistance that can be offered by these highly-developed but over-handicapped interceptors. That a raid against a watchful country may doubtless be carried out only at sacrificial cost in men and machines, is no compensation to the public attacked. The raid will take place just the same. And who can judge the possible effects of a first blow of that kind?

Among many other kindnesses shown me, I had permission from the Adjutant-General of the U.S. Army to fly at Langley Field. But, alas, I could not fit it in. Still, I saw much else and talked to many people. I came home with the definite impression that, military machines and personnel being pretty well equal, our Air Force is as far ahead of the U.S. Army Air Corps in organisation as our civil aviation is behind America's civil aviation in speed, frequency, bad weather equipment and layout of aerodromes. The progressive officers in that fine corps will, I know, find nothing to cavil at in such a statement. Some may welcome it, impatient for their cherished and most sturdy child to be weaned.

Nor should it be a matter of any congratulation for ourselves, because if ever there may be need of two sane nations to stand together, or two great Air Forces to be ready to uphold peace—if necessary by the threat of mercifully applied but always damnable force, then America and England, speaking almost a common language and springing mainly from common stock, will be those two. For to-morrow, figuratively speaking, our distance apart will become of little account.

By the courtesy of Gerard Vultee, I was able to go up in

his latest transport plane and handle it. Vultee aeroplanes are built at Glendale, California, by the Airplane Development Corporation, a division of the Cord Corporation. The model I tried was the V-1A, with accommodation for two pilots and eight passengers. It is an all-metal, single engine, low-wing cantilever monoplane with split, trailing edge type, wing flaps; an extremely efficient aeroplane of its kind. Powered with a Wright "Cyclone" model F2 engine, which develops 735 h.p., it has a maximum speed of 225 m.p.h., but can land, by reason of its flaps, at 63 m.p.h. Its range is 1000 miles.

While in the air, I purposely spent a few minutes in the passengers' cabin. The fuselage, being of true monocoque type and modified elliptical cross-section, provides plenty of space for given outside dimensions. The arm-chairs are unusually comfortable; in fact, the most comfortable aeroplane seats that I sat in. And my impression was that there is less noise in the cabin than in the average railway carriage, although I had no accurate information upon which to base my opinion in respect of the train. The noise level of the Vultee cabin is sixty-eight decibels.

In addition to the usual lavatory accommodation, and a ventilator, heater, reading-light, ash-tray and foot-rest for each individual passenger, there is also running ice water, a pilot-controlled temperature indicator and an air exhaust. Other American transport planes have similar devices, but this happened to be the most luxurious equipment that I inspected.

Naturally, the V-1A has retractable landing gear. This is of the type that enables the wheels to fold up inwards instead of backwards, which is the more common method. Moreover, when folded, they are quite flush with the leading edge of the wing's bottom surface. This method certainly makes for a cleaner line, with its attendant advantages of reducing

311

wind resistance; but, unlike the Douglas and Boeing, it leaves no portion of the wheel visible, or in a position to rotate, should an emergency force the machine to land with its under-cart still retracted.

The gear comes down in sixteen and a half seconds by electro-motor propulsion. The pilot has merely to snap over a switch. Still, he has an emergency manual gear and three warning devices: a gauge on his instrument board, showing the position of the wheels, coloured lights that glow with the same object, and a motor horn that sounds in the cockpit if the throttle is closed while the wheels are still up. That last, about which I had been warned before leaving the ground, and subsequently forgot, nearly caused me to go through the roof with fright when it came into operation.

Maintenance has been carefully considered in the design of the V-1A. The nose sections of the wings are removable for inspection purposes; a damaged fuselage panel may be removed merely by drilling out the rivets and can then be used as a template; the entire power plant assembly is interchangeable with that of any other V-1A model; and so on. These are all points that the builder of modern aeroplanes needs to study with increasing care.

When the machine was handed over to me, I found myself cruising at 204 m.p.h. on about three-quarter throttle. Nevertheless, the cockpit was so well ventilated by means of adjustable ducts that we could smoke cigarettes with normal comfort, yet the enclosed space never became in the slightest degree stuffy. Perfect normal turns could be accomplished with both feet off the rudder, there being no sideslip until the turn was purposely made abnormally steep. I found the machine a little difficult to trim at first, but then I was not used to the type. The V-1A being so fast, it was possible to gain height at a staggering rate unless one kept one eye on the altimeter. But when I had sorted this, I found the plane

312

"... 204 m.p.h. on about three-quarter throttle ... we could smoke cigarettes with normal comfort."

"... these huge rock faces ... swiftly change from neighbourly shapes into forbidding ramparts. ..."

delightful to fly. It accelerated in the air like a good "sporting" car on the road.

Levelling off at 7,500 feet, I flew out towards the island of Santa Catalina, but turned over San Pedro Harbour, diving to look at the fleet lying at anchor there. Afterwards I headed across to Pasadena and circled for a while, to pick out Clark and Helen Millikan's house on a hilltop. A dust storm was blowing out of the mountains to southward; I went in to look at that too: an impressive spectacle but a bad thing in which to get involved. Then I flew straight at the mountains themselves until, noticing my companion's sidelong glances, I turned the machine away. It is fascinating to approach these huge rock faces at two hundred miles an hour, and watch them swiftly change from neighbourly shapes into forbidding ramparts looming fiercely above the aeroplane; knowing that a slight, co-ordinated movement of hand and foot, made with ample time to spare, will send one racing along beside them, a safe distance away, seeing their grandeur as one could never see it in a whole week's climbing on foot.

Altogether the V-1A is a splendid aeroplane; pilots of really great experience agree on this. Single-motor equipment is no longer considered suitable for a public transport plane. But for a wealthy private owner, or the executive staff of a big business house with offices in distant places, the machine is ideal; and no one could doubt the capabilities of the military version of it—a sinister and heavily-armed light bomber. Moreover, the way it is built should be a lesson to many. At the same time, our recently produced Fairey "Battle" has it beaten by a large margin as a military machine.

Another day, Robert Gross kindly showed me over the Lockheed plant at Burbank. He had several "Electras" going through the shops, but unfortunately they were not ready to fly, so I could not try one. They were destined for Poland; and while I was glad he had got such an order, I remember hoping that we, who are geographically so much closer, were supplying our share of Poland's purchases or would perhaps be in a position to scoop the next lot.

The "Electra," too, is an all-metal monoplane, but with twin motor equipment. It is one of the most graceful twin-motor planes extant. Conforming to sound, accepted practice, it is well known as a high-class transport ship with an excellent performance; although now outclassed by our corresponding new Bristol and Armstrong Whitworth models. It is smaller than either the current Boeing or the current Douglas, but I was much impressed by the roominess of the pilot's cockpit. In this respect, it is better than most enclosed planes; I could move my head quite a distance to one side and look downwards at a very steep angle before bumping against the sliding glass window.

The "Electra" has the most quickly operated retractable landing gear in America and probably in the world. The wheels are raised in $7\frac{1}{2}$ seconds and are fully dropped in 6 seconds. This is remarkable, and Mr. Gross may well be proud of it. Incidentally, he knows what every part in his factory costs to make, which is a good effort—and unusual in chief executives.

One of the machines in the shop was being fitted with over-size supercharged motors, with a view to meeting a specification (from United Air Lines, I think) for planes for certain of their feeder services. The desired qualification which caused this increase in power was the not inconsiderable one of being able to do a one-engine take-off from Mexico City, which is over seven thousand feet above sea-level. True, the motor would be giving nearly its maximum power output at about that height, but this shows the sort of standard that our American cousins are setting. We had better pay close attention.

The Boeing, Douglas, Lockheed "Electra" and the Vultee,

of those I saw in the multi-seat class, were (and some are still) superior to our corresponding types in "passenger appeal," i.e. fully adequate comfort allied to reliability and high speed, if not achieving our standard of lower operational cost. In the latter field it must be remembered that not all those American machines are new types; their successors, which will be due before the successors of our new types, will be more formidable. This makes it necessary for us to take an extra big jump with our next batch—a thing we are thoroughly capable of doing. No one can better rise to an occasion once the need for it is recognised. The more I travel the more I am convinced that the worst fear of our enemies in war and our competitors in peace, is that something will quicken our national reaction. For when we are thoroughly roused, history proves for the most part that other people have often taken a back seat both as regards fighting and commerce. Unfortunately, the few rather than the many now seem to recognise genuine patriotism as the constant facing of facts in relation to the country they live in.

The pleasure of visiting American manufacturers is hard to exaggerate; they are so ready and willing to make sure that one sees and understands everything which they are at liberty to show. I hope I shall soon be able to visit some of them again.

As Robert Gross drove me back to my hotel that morning, we talked about travel. He said he had crossed the Atlantic thirty-six times. Yet, like myself, he is still the right side of middle-age. Then our conversation turned to horses and the cost of keeping a pack of hounds. His family are keen riders. Altogether it was a very pleasant morning.

CHAPTER II

TO FLY 300 MILES IS JUST LIKE COMMUTING

UNITED AIR LINES CAN TAKE ONE FROM NEW YORK OR Philadephia via Cleveland, Chicago, Omaha and Cheyenne to Salt Lake City. There the line splits: one can go on to Sacramento and San Francisco, or North-west to Portland or Spokane. Their west coast service will transport one as far north as Vancouver and as far south as Agua Caliente; landing at various cities en route. By taking advantage of their efficiency and courteous service, I was flown up from Los Angeles to San Francisco, and back, for a week-end that I spent with some friends.

The cost to the public of this round trip is $34.11, or roughly £6 16s. in our money. For this modest sum apiece the passengers are transported for 693 miles in very fair comfort at about 170 miles an hour, being offered at no extra charge a meal appropriate to the time of day. I actually took the 5.30 p.m. plane north on Saturday, flying non-stop and direct, a distance of 330 miles. It landed at 7.24 p.m., so we had averaged 173 m.p.h. Returning on Monday I caught the 9.20 a.m. service south, being put down at the Union Air Terminal near Los Angeles at 11.30 a.m. But on this latter trip we took a longer route down the San Joaquin valley, so as to land passengers at Fresno. We might have had to land again at Bakersfield, but did not. The extra distance was 33 miles. We were five minutes at Fresno from touching down to taking off, and lost perhaps another ten minutes coming in there and climbing out again to our required ceiling.

The ship was a twin-motor, low-wing, all-metal Boeing. These monoplanes are powered with super-charged 550 h.p. Wasp engines by Pratt and Whitney. They carry ten passengers, a crew of two pilots and a stewardess, and a cargo of mail, express and baggage at a cruising speed of 171 m.p.h., and can attain a top speed of over three miles a minute. These speeds are naturally subject to the vagaries of wind, as were the actual times I have given above. Such a plane weighs $6\frac{1}{2}$ tons fully loaded, has a wing span of 74 feet, is 50 feet 4 inches in length and 14 feet high (including the radio mast). The landing speed is 58 m.p.h.; take-off run 770 feet; rate of climb (from sea level) 1130 feet per minute; climb in ten minutes 8,000 feet; service ceiling 18,400 feet; absolute ceiling 20,500 feet.

Needless to say, the machine has retractable landing wheels. These could withstand an emergency impact of $32\frac{1}{4}$ tons. When they are drawn up into the wings, twenty miles an hour is added to the speed of the plane. While I was out West, the Line was testing constant speed airscrews; of which more anon. They are not the same as those simply of variable pitch design. Or, rather, they are themselves a variation of it and an improvement.

Even at the end of 1934 the daily arrivals and departures of airliners on the Union Air Terminal were as follows:

DAILY ARRIVALS AT UNION AIR TERMINAL

Arrival Time	Via	From
5.50 a.m.	United Air Lines	Vancouver B.C., Seattle, Portland, Medford, Oakland, San Francisco, Fresno, Bakersfield.

Arrival Time	Via	From
6.15 a.m.	General Air Lines	New York, Cleveland, Chicago, Omaha, Denver, Cheyenne, Salt Lake, Las Vegas.
8.35 a.m.	United Air Lines	San Diego.
10.00 a.m.	United Air Lines	Oakland, San Francisco, Fresno, Bakersfield.
10.30 a.m.	Palm Springs Line	Palm Springs.
12.07 p.m.	United Air Lines	Oakland, San Francisco.
2.27 p.m.	United Air Lines	Seattle, Tacoma, Portland, Medford, Sacramento, Oakland, San Francisco.
3.22 p.m.	United Air Lines	Oakland, San Francisco.
6.07 p.m.	United Air Lines	Oakland, San Francisco.
6.40 p.m.	Varney Speed Lines	Mexico City, Gaudalajara, Mazatlan, Los Mochis, Obregon, Nogales, Mexicali.
8.15 p.m.	General Air Lines	San Diego.
8.30 p.m.	United Air Lines	Oakland, San Francisco, Fresno, Bakersfield.
11.27 p.m.	United Air Lines	San Diego.

DAILY DEPARTURES FROM UNION AIR TERMINAL

Departure Time	Via	To
2.00 a.m.	Varney Speed Lines	Mexicali, Nogales, Obregon, Los Mochis, Mazatlan, Guadalajara, Mexico City.
6.05 a.m.	United Air Lines	San Diego.

Departure Time	Via	To
8.30 a.m.	General Air Lines	San Diego.
8.50 a.m.	United Air Lines	Oakland, San Francisco, Sacramento, Medford, Portland, Tacoma, Seattle.
10.00 a.m.	United Air Lines	Oakland, San Francisco,
12.30 p.m.	United Air Lines	Bakersfield, Fresno, San Francisco, Oakland.
2.42 p.m.	United Air Lines	Oakland, San Francisco.
4.30 p.m.	Palm Springs Line	Palm Springs.
4.40 p.m.	United Air Lines	Bakersfield, Fresno, San Francisco, Oakland.
8.00 p.m.	United Air Lines	San Francisco, Oakland.
11.00 p.m.	General Air Lines	Las Vegas, Salt Lake, Cheyenne, Chicago, New York.
11.45 p.m.	United Air Lines	Bakersfield, Fresno, Oakland, San Francisco, Medford, Portland, Tacoma, Seattle, Vancouver B.C.

Probably there are a number more now: I hadn't the time to assimilate everything. But the airport hums with activity.

I was shown over it before I started. It is a splendid field of 234 acres, having three paved runways of $3650' \times 300'$, $3550' \times 300'$ and $3500' \times 300'$ respectively. These intersect, making a five-finger system that is found fully adequate for such alteration of wind direction as takes place in California —usually the loveliest and most reliable of climates. I know nothing like these runways in England.

The rest of the airport is laid down to alfalfa, irrigated and cut, so that there is no dust. Of course the airport is completely equipped for night flying, and the lighting system is in operation from sundown to sunrise.

I inspected the hangers, steel and concrete, providing a total floor space of 159,052 square feet. The thick glass doors of these are in sections and hinged at the top, so each section shuts down or rises independently. Each hinge is, in effect, an electric motor. It is started in one direction by pushing one button and in the other by pushing a second button. A third red button stops it in whatever position the door may be. These were the best hangar doors I had ever seen. I seem to remember that they closed in 56 seconds.

The Spanish looking main building has the usual booking hall, waiting rooms, balcony, lavatories, etc., in addition to the administrative offices. It also has a restaurant and a barber's shop, and a covered gangway to the planes that ends only at the wing-tip of the waiting machines; this despite the one comparatively short rainy season in Los Angeles. Our Croydon is a better building, but I never think that the most is made of it. Why, in the damp, bitter weather that is our lot, we should have to walk some distance to our planes, or splash across to the adjacent hotel for a cup of tea, is a mystery. All the same, there are some snags to American airports too. I shall mention them later. The Union at Los Angeles happens to be a specially good field, which is why I devote space to these details. The best in the world is probably the Tempelhof field near Berlin, or it will be when the new canopy is built under which machines will load and unload. Nevertheless, we have built a splendid place at Gatwick and will doubtless build more airports on much the same lines.

I inspected the "weather" room. Here weather maps were being drawn, and next door a row of teletype machines spouted information in the shape of paper ribbons. Others, silent at that moment, were ready to transmit the local information elsewhere for general co-ordination. I also listened to the operator sending out his regular radio-telephone reports to pilots. He began speaking exactly on time. The pilots of a score of machines at different distances and heights approaching or racing away, would shortly before have slipped on their earphones to wait for this very rigmarole of symbols now being read in a practised, repetitive monotone from the slip of paper that I was studying over the man's shoulder.

I had tea with one of the executives of the line; and we were joined by Mr. Putnam, Miss Amelia Earheart's husband, in search of a lemon squash. Then I boarded the plane, of which eight seats out of ten were occupied, and it taxied away at precisely 5.30 p.m.

I had watched two planes leave previous to ours. Each, I noticed, had been throttled quickly back as soon as it had gathered sufficient rolling impetus to turn away from the gangway. Consequently, the spectators and other waiting passengers were not inconvenienced by the slipstream from the propellers. This was a small point, but indicative of the constant thought exercised for the public's benefit. The same procedure was followed in the plane I was in.

Then it was taxied comfortably but briskly to the extreme end of the appropriate runway, where, after being turned into the wind, each of its motors was "run-up" against the wheel brakes before the actual take-off.

There was no question of the machine being pulled off the ground; it was allowed to fly itself off, smoothly and almost imperceptibly. Then we made a wide, easy turn and headed for the Sierra Madre; gaining height steadily. In the dusk, the home beacon flicked a repeated good-bye.

As we climbed, so the Pacific came into view, pearly and remote. But we lost sight of it as we approached the mountains, the peaks of which, like old dark teak, protruded from a layer of evening mist the colour of elephant hide. Beyond their western extremity, where lay the coast, the sun was sinking in a welter of red and yellow—real flame colours.

The usual evening sky of California stretched above, shading upwards through pale green to a zone almost of whiteness; although immediately overhead the velvety skull cap of night was snuffing out the glow minute by minute with gentle deliberation. Looking down, I saw the main road southward outlined, as it neared Los Angeles, by the regular pinpricks of the street lamps. Northward, into the sombreness of the pass, its direction was revealed only by the headlights of cars, like glow-worms in procession.

Soon we were over the mountains. The skyline of them was blackly silhouetted against what faint crimson tinge remained in the west. Thus a tree-crowned hill appeared to have its crest manned by troops. Air currents caused by the steep declivities beneath caused us a few minutes unsteadiness. For this reason the illuminated sign at the front end of the cabin had not been switched off; it still adjured us to keep our belts fastened and not to smoke. But knowing that the smoking part of it referred only to landing and taking off, I lit a cigarette: for cigarettes are permitted in American transport planes.

When we started, the men had made a great show of reading their evening newspapers, but with the first signs of bumpiness they switched out their reading lamps, asked the stewardess for pillows and settled down to sleep. Once high enough above the mountains, the plane's flight became smooth again, and some of them really slept, their chairs tipped back to a restful angle by means of a lever. Outside, the starlight gained in brilliance.

The stewardess had been round, checking our tickets by her list. Being an old traveller by air, I had taken one of the two rearmost seats. The other was reserved for her. When she sat down, we were not far apart and could talk, although with some difficulty. She was a cheerful little soul, and her neat uniform suited her. United Air Lines have carried stewardesses since 1930; they were the first to do so; but this girl had only had the job since July. To get it, she had to be (like the others) a graduate nurse of three years' training. But she smilingly confessed that she, herself, had been taken off the Cheyenne section of the line because she had been airsick and could not get used to it. The early morning planes often had rough trips over that high, hilly piece of country, so the company had kindly transferred her to the west coast service; and now she was all right. She told me that each of the girls work a round trip a day, six days a week. Then every month they have an extra day off, although during the second day they have to regard themselves as being in reserve. Their duties are to seat the passengers properly, check tickets, provide newspapers and magazines, point out interesting parts of the route, and look after any one who may feel unwell. She appeared thoroughly to enjoy her occupation and had obviously come to look upon spending her days in the air as something quite commonplace. The attitude of these young women should shame some of the tough middle-aged business men who can face a falling market but still seem mortally afraid to contemplate travel in an aeroplane.

I asked for my supper. Not that I wanted it at that hour, or indeed at all, for I meant to dine in San Francisco. But I had promised to try it. There was a good assortment of cold meats in separate cellophane envelopes. Rolls and biscuits and cheese were similarly wrapped. There was even salt in a little wooden castor. Grapefruit salad could be had out of a carton, and excellent hot coffee out of a thermos. Everything was fresh, good and daintily served. But the meals on this line, or any other American line, are not in the same category as those served in our big Imperial Airways ships, where I have had hot five course meals served to me on a table—and better than in many London restaurants I could name.

The current types of Boeing and Douglas have no pantry accommodation, only cupboards; and a small lavatory for the passengers. The centre gangway in the Boeing is narrower than that in the Douglas, which itself provides only just enough room. The seats in both are most comfortable—as comfortable as in our ships—though, like everything else, they will be improved as time goes on. But the pace at which these planes get along more than makes up for cold meals and a certain lack of room. In them, one is certainly "going places." They are nearly twice as fast as our big machines of established types and little greater age; and to say of them that too much comfort has been sacrificed to speed is grossly untrue.

Attention is undoubtedly being paid to the increase of comfort, but so it is also to a further increase in speed. If we want fully to compete in foreign markets, we must not think that our standard of comfort is sufficient, and that all we have to do is fly faster. We need to plan and scheme as never before if our machines of two years hence are going to be better than what I imagine America is going to produce. Incidentally, I thought the Boeing noisier than the Douglas, and there was more vibration. But then it is an older type. Compared with our London-Paris ships, I would judge the Boeing to be noisier and the Douglas quieter. The Douglas is my first choice. But I would sooner travel in either of the latter modern aeroplanes than in our types in corresponding service. This, of course, is a quite natural preference: for unless I am mistaken, several of our machines must be nearly due for replacement after giving yeoman service and carrying the bulk of cross-channel traffic for years.

We were now nearly at our destination. I could see a series of twinkling expanses far ahead, and we would not take long to reach them: that farthest away betokened San Francisco. I returned to my seat and switched out my lamp. Unfortunately,

324

there was no moon. I imagined I could just distinguish the ocean some distance away to port, but the starlight was not really bright enough for me to be sure. When we left Los Angeles, I knew there had been 18 to 20 m.p.h. head winds reported. Still, I reckoned these might die with sundown. Apparently I was right, for we were well on time.

The warning notice flashed on again at the front of the cabin, and the stewardess went round helping sleepy passengers to fasten their safety belts. Four minutes later we touched down at Mills Field. The pilot made an excellent wheel-landing, as they always do with these transport ships, for it is more comfortable for the passengers if the tail is kept off the ground until the machine is rolling comparatively slowly.

Then through the typical, thin evening fog of the Fall season in San Francisco, I drove into the city. This, like the drive from London to Croydon, or Paris to Le Bourget, or Rotterdam to Waalhaven, or almost any city to its aerodrome, is a distinct nuisance. It took over a half an hour. We shall all have to run electric trains to these places before long. Future air traffic will warrant it.

Leaving San Francisco again on Monday morning, my plane took off exactly on its scheduled time: 9.20 a.m. After gaining adequate height to do so, we turned out over the bay and headed south, still climbing steadily to our predetermined level.

Westward, I could look across to the wooded hills round San Mateo. Immediately below, the water appeared putty-coloured and carried a slow ripple. Farther back, where the sun caught it, it was the blue of willow pattern china. San Francisco itself, jutting out into its landlocked bay, became visible over my left shoulder: a fascinating collection of buildings, some modern and placed with precision like vast stalagmites of a new fashion, other older ones, more squat,

325

spilt higgledy-piggledy in the hollows and round the fringes of the steep rises over which the city spreads.

At the seaward extremity of the city, I could just distinguish the twin towers of the new bridge which now spans the Golden Gate. Brown, arid mountains framed the bay as I looked north.

There were mountains ahead of our plane, too, as we flew south-south-east. Passing over a few patchwork fields on a flat shelf of shore, we came to them. Mountains are so perfectly seen from above in this clear atmosphere that every fold in their flanks is noticed for the first time. One realises how numerous they are, each like the creases in a felt hat. Many are pine clad, but more are naked.

Looking down, the terrific upthrust of the earth's surface when still malleable is plainly recognisable although from the ground any idea of it seems remote.

After twenty-five minutes, we left the mountains behind and came out over a great plain; this was really the vast San Joaquin valley. If it were greener, it would be similar in appearance to the plains of northern France, and the very fact would obviate the need for the many watercourses seen below. For irrigation is the making of this burnt-up western coast-land.

The Pacific itself had long been out of sight behind the Diablo range of hills to starboard, because we were taking the longer, inland route via Fresno.

Ground visibility ahead looked to be about twenty miles. Then there was a surrounding belt of heat haze and what I took to be dust, although I was a stranger there and could not be certain. Inland, above this belt, the high-flung line of the Sierra seemed to float, snow-capped and unchanging.

We made a drawn-out descent on Fresno. As we came down, so the haze belt appeared to rise until it engulfed the great peaks—perhaps eighty miles away or more. Soon they were gone, and we were flying for the moment at the sort of cruising height customary over much of western Europe. Below, all was flat and much of it under cultivation. We crossed the San Joaquin river, twisting and edged here with trees. Neat little farms flashed by beneath, each with a wind-guard of tall eucalyptus. There was now far more green about the landscape to break up the brown monotony. Really, the illusion of flying over northern France in June was almost complete, except that here were vineyards.

The chief pilot throttled back. Down went our flaps. Down went our wheels. Then the approach was made with a bit of engine. I liked this; it is always conservative flying. He made the usual wheel-landing, and a very good one; only just felt. The tail touched an appreciable number of seconds afterwards. The time was now 10.19 a.m.

Another plane stood ahead of us at the airport gangway, so we waited some yards in rear, our motors ticking over. A rustic trellis screen stretched in front of the main building; and I had time to admire the Virginia creeper on it, the leaves richly tinted.

We took our place at the gangway at 10.21. The other plane had just taxied away and was now turning into the wind. Her pilot "gave her the gun," and she roared away, rising quickly and apparently lightly loaded. We, ourselves, dropped several passengers but only took on one for the remainder of the short trip; this made us four in a ten-seater. At 10.24, we taxied off once more, having been there five minutes.

And now we headed again across the flatness. Here, it was browner. Tilled patches were interspersed with great ir-regular areas of unclaimed desert, lonely by contrast. But how lovely this country must appear in Spring, ablaze with poppies, Lupines and Thistle Sage, the more delicate shades of the Desert Aster and vivid patches of Indian Paint Brush!

327

The Sierra again rose into view, this time to port, for we had altered course and were flying south with a bit of west in it —making down the valley towards Bakersfield.

In this clearer light, the sun being more directly overhead, I was not so sure that there was snow on the high tops after all. Perhaps it was the utter bareness of them, and their pale colour, which from a distance shone so whitely. Yet Mount Whitney's 14,496 foot peak, the highest in America, was somewhere over there, and other giants besides. Despite the blazing Californian Summer, such as they retain their frozen night-caps.

A red-haired stewardess brought me an excellent cup of steaming hot chocolate and some biscuits. I grinned at her, for among the copper-topped there is a fellowship unknown to less iridescent mortals. She showed me my photograph in a San Francisco morning paper. This was not so pleasing, but I had been unable to avoid it. All the same, looking back on a three months' visit, I can legitimately congratulate myself, having only twice been caught by a camera.

I had an invitation to go into the "office," or pilot's cabin, and at this stage I took advantage of it. The view that met me was remarkable. Ten or twelve miles ahead, the haze, now become white and thin, spread like a calm sea; and out of it rose the pale blue mountains over which we must pass to reach Los Angeles. Unlike any normal cloud effect, it was one of the most eerie sights I have seen in my sixteen years off and on of flying.

Having no occasion to stop at Bakersfield, we were going straight ahead, so I slipped on a pair of earphones and listened to the Los Angeles beam signal and such information as came through. The signal came to me as a steady intermittent note. Had we veered off our course to one side, it would have changed to "dot-dash, dot-dash," or, had we wandered the other way, to "dash-dot, dash-dot."

I removed the ear-phones and talked to the chief pilot.

The plane was one of those fitted with constant speed air-screws, which automatically vary their own angle of pitch according to the density of the air. Once the take-off is completed, the engines, subsequently feeding on cruising mixture, can be set at a required rate of revolutions per minute, and the airscrews will keep them at it whatever the change in height. Consequently, the pressure in each intake manifold will remain constant, so the pilot is largely relieved of anxiety about taking too much power out of his motors. He can give his time to navigation or to the control of the plane itself, instead of also having to fiddle about with throttle levers. This is a boon, especially in bad weather.

At the end of the San Joaquin valley there was a large group of oil derricks, stark and ugly, although to us miniature in appearance. We came over the mountains at 7,500 feet, and, at 11.16 a.m., started our gradual descent above a precipitous valley. Dry brush and scrub pine covered the lower hills, and fire paths had been cut along many of their highest ridges. The air was a bit bumpy for some minutes, but not seriously so. Then the mountains gave place to foothills with Hollywood and Santa Monica ahead, Los Angeles beyond, and the Union Air Terminal in the foreground.

I was impressed by the quiet efficiency of the chief pilot's approach with the Boeing. His hands, in their hogskin gloves, held the wheel with nonchalant familiarity. The column moved apparently with his thought. He judged his distance calmly through the big sun glasses that he wore, and leisurely chewed gum. He put the flaps down and took us in at eighty, landing at sixty—another first-rate wheel-landing. This was at 11.30 a.m. to the minute. Half an hour later, I was dictating letters in my room at the Ambassador Hotel, having comfortably travelled nearly four hundred miles between an unhurried breakfast and noon. And forty minutes of that time had been occupied by slow driving in a car.

CHAPTER III

Speed, Weather and Wireless

I HAVE OFTEN HEARD PEOPLE SAY IN ENGLAND THAT THE average speed of American transport planes is exaggerated. So I propose to give the exact speeds over various sections of a flight from Los Angeles to New York which I took as a passenger on the Transcontinental and Western Air Line.

The machine was a Douglas D.C.2; and when I have said that, I have doubtless said enough for most people. This machine is so well known in Europe that I need only go into the barest details of its construction and performance. Like the corresponding Boeing, it is an all-metal, low-wing, twin-motor monoplane. But it is a later type, and by reason of its design is faster, quieter, more commodious and more comfortable. It seats fourteen passengers as against the Boeing's ten; or now that a uniformed stewardess is carried, one less. When I travelled on the line, the company had not yet started a service of hostesses (in plain English, stewardesses). This personnel was only then undergoing training. Passengers were attended to by the second pilot, which I did not think was a satisfactory arrangement. United Air Lines was better in this respect than T.W.A., but now this service is the same on both lines.

The Douglas D.C.2 cruises at 200 m.p.h. on 75% power at 14,000 feet. At 2,500 feet, its cruising speed is 168 m.p.h. at 28·5 manifold pressure. The makers of the engines limit the cruising manifold pressure to 28·5, the power to 75% for all normal purposes, and the revolutions per minute to 1,850, or a little in excess. And as the average passenger is usually experiencing a certain amount of discomfort at 14,000 feet, that height is not now reached except in an emergency caused by really bad weather below. About 12,000 feet, or lower, is the normal operational height.

Consequently, one sees readily that, subject to wind variation, the average speed of Douglas machines in still air on the T.W.A. line is likely to be in the neighbourhood of 180 m.p.h. The line itself states its block to block speed[1] as 161·61 (Block to block speed includes climbing and taxi-ing i.e. wheel-stop to wheel-stop). And the figure of 161·61 m.p.h. is taken from eighteen scheduled, daily flights, and includes the slow service such as the New York-Los Angeles westbound "Comet," which makes many stops and averages 139·68 m.p.h. (against prevailing winds) as well as the eastbound Chicago-New York express, which averages 188·30 m.p.h.

The block to block time of the "Sky Chief," Flight No. 8 from Los Angeles to New York, is 183.94 m.p.h., or 14 hours 12 minutes for 2,612 miles. But I did not take this plane because I wanted to experience more of both day and night flying on my way to New York. So, instead, I took the "Sky Queen," Flight No. 2, which dawdles across America, so to speak, between 9.30 a.m. (Western time) and 6 a.m. (Eastern time), stopping at eight places.

The lady was dismally slow, poor sweet, from Glendale, Los Angeles, to Albuquerque. She had north-east and north-north-east winds against her; varying between 18 and 25 m.p.h. With the necessary corrections for drift, her average loss of ground speed was 10 m.p.h. So for 711 miles at a height of 12,000 feet, she merely ambled along at an average of 177 m.p.h.! Mr. Rice was chief pilot during that period.

[1] At that time. It may have increased with the D.C.3.

After Albuquerque, the Sky Queen's majesty was threatened by more westerly winds. These blowing from the north-north-west and backing to south-west, varied from 30 to 10 m.p.h. and averaged about 10 m.p.h. in her favour after due corrections for drift had been made on each of the next three blocks or sections of the line. With this kick in the pants or, rather, pat on the petticoats, the Queen scooted the 285 miles to Amarillo at a ground speed of 193 m.p.h., the 295 miles from there to Wichita at 192 m.p.h. (while it got dark and the outside temperature dropped to 30°), and the 178 miles to Kansas City (skirting a thunderstorm and seeing some grand lightning effects) at 189 m.p.h. Mr. Brill was then in charge of her.

But apparently she was not any too satisfied with that; or the wind wasn't. Mr. Smiley took her over. Whereupon, favourable south-west and south-south-westerly winds averaging between 19 m.p.h. as far as Indianapolis and 17 m.p.h. thereafter, gave her such a crack on the crupper that she beat it for 459 miles to Indianapolis at 204 m.p.h. (through snow at 10,000 feet for 75 miles and torrential rain at 6,000 feet, and missing out St. Louis because nobody wanted to have anything to do with her at that place) and went on 341 miles to Pittsburg at 202 m.p.h. There, owing to fog and ice-forming conditions, and not because she was tired, she sat us on the ground from 2.29 a.m. to 7.19 a.m., which, after all, is better and wiser—and as the authors of *1066 and All That* would say, a GOOD THING—compared with the practical certainty of being forced down and having our remains scattered for the kindly people of America to retrieve.

Here, it is apposite to remark that the T.W.A. Meteorological department has been maintaining a 98% standard of accuracy in its weather forecasts. But as the department consists wholly of men trained in the practical application of the

332

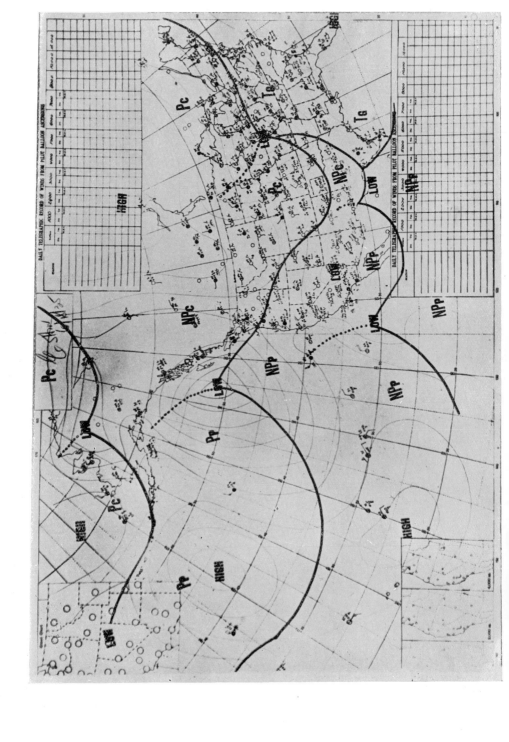

Norwegian Air Mass Analysis, and there are more of them in it than in any similar bureau in the United States, this high degree of exactitude is not altogether surprising.

At six hour intervals, incessantly, the three T.W.A. weather offices situated on the coast to coast route at Newark (Eastern terminus), Kansas City (main operating base) and Los Angeles (Western terminus) receive reports from the U.S. weather bureau at Chicago. These come over teletype machines. An hour and a half later, the Company's meteorologists have completed their maps, made their analysis and issued their forecasts. The maps are then available to be studied by pilots and by the dispatchers of the planes. The latter, termed flight control officers, are themselves pilots, some of whom have had as much as twenty years' flying experience. They have to approve the conditions of each flight before it is started, having thoroughly acquainted themselves with the weather *en route* and at the next regular stop. No plane can leave without the O.K. of one of these officials. In addition to the four daily reports from the U.S. Weather Bureau, the T.W.A. offices have regular *liaison* with the airway sequences organised by the Department of Commerce. This means that in every hour about 110 stations send observations to the Kansas City office; 100 to Newark; and 80 to Los Angeles.

The system is therefore as complete as the ingenuity of man can render it at the present. Not only does it make for safety, as I myself have seen, but it caters for the comfort of passengers, because areas of really turbulent weather are so accurately determined that it is now possible to avoid them by flying round them. Moreover, it ensures the maximum possible degree of regularity of operation. From October, 1934, to March, 1935, T.W.A. flew on an average 89·66% of their advertised schedules. During the Winter (1935-36) the line hoped to raise the average to 95%, over 750,000 miles a month. But it proved to be an unusually severe Winter, and whether they achieved this I do not know.

As a result of the high-speed flying of its Douglas machines, T.W.A. also met, and was able largely to overcome, a rather interesting problem in radio reception. Static interference was found to increase with the pace at which the aeroplanes moved through charged particles such as dust, rain and snow. It was already known that turbulent air increased static interference, an antenna placed in the propeller wash being more affected than one located in non-turbulent air, say, under the nose of the machine; because in the former instance the particles which touched the aeroplane were mixed with others not touching it. Thus the two sorts of particles were non-uniformally charged and set up an alternating current which made reception difficult. As a result of the effects of these two factors, speed and turbulence, becoming well recognised, and their combined effect on radio reception noted, T.W.A. evolved the now well-known loop antenna, eighteen inches in diameter, which is mounted on the top of the fuselage six feet or so from the tail. It is claimed to be more than twice as efficient as the commonly used beacon antenna, and largely to have overcome the hindrance caused by static to the use of all the well-known radio aids to flying.

The Flight Plan

PRIOR TO A FLIGHT OVER ANY GIVEN SECTION OF THEIR AIR lines, Transcontinental and Western Air Incorporated require the crew of the aeroplane, i.e. the chief pilot and co-pilot, to be at the airport an hour in advance of the stated time for departure. During this period they consult with their flight control officer and with the meteorologists, and plan their flight. They inspect the air mass analysis map in

334

" Upon this information the pilots settle their flight path. . . ."
[Photo by courtesy of T.W.A. Inc.

*" . . . calculating the height at which they will fly and their arrival time at
the next intermediate station."*
[Photo by courtesy of T.W.A. Inc.

detail and the written forecast, so that they know the velocity and direction of the winds, the position of the weather "fronts" (cold or warm—according to the Norwegian system), the probable change of conditions and temperatures during the next six hours along the route in question, and the particular characteristics of the air masses involved.

Upon this information, the pilots settle their flight path; calculating the height at which they will fly and their arrival time at the next intermediate station. To appreciate the amount of care expended, one must realise that the pilots are faced with the problem of maintaining a fast scheduled service in any conditions in which flying is considered safe, and yet with the maximum degree of operational economy.

In an aeroplane, the engine induction manifold pressure curtails the performance at low levels. The manufacturers of the engines installed in the Douglas D.C.2 limit this pressure to 28·5, and it is only above 8,500 feet that the maximum allowable percentage of power for cruising, namely, 75 per cent., can be used without putting up the manifold pressure. So although the cruising speed of the Douglas at a given percentage output of power increases with height, as does that of any aircraft, it is only when 8,500 feet is reached that full advantage may be taken of it. (T.W.A., for economy's sake, try not to take out more than 65 per cent. power). Apart, therefore, from other weather considerations, favourable winds at low levels may not so much influence a pilot's flight plan as consideration for his motors. Against which, of course, he has also to bear in mind the time lost by over-much climbing—time which may not be made up by his increased cruising speed after levelling off. Moreover, his rates of ascent and descent are definitely limited by consideration for the passengers' comfort. So for short flights of about 250 miles, it would be normal to find the aircraft flying at a moderate height, say, roughly between 4,000 and 8,000 feet, unless the winds higher up were specially helpful or the pilot thought it advisable to climb above an area of bad weather.

While the machine is climbing at a given speed and in a straight line, it will obviously cover a certain distance in a certain time. To this time is added the total taxi-ing time, which T.W.A. assess as an average of seven minutes. From this, it is easy to determine the distance still to be covered, the time it should occupy being already known; for the latter is according to schedule. Consequently, a simple divisional sum results in the cruising ground speed which must be maintained.

And as the machines are operated at 65 per cent. power, and the temperature and wind velocities are predetermined, the flight path becomes a matter of pretty exact planning. Should later contingencies cause an alteration of plan, it is left to the pilot to use his own good judgment; and, of course, he reports to the ground organisation what he is doing. Whatever happens, all aircraft flying east travel at an even number of thousand feet and those flying west at an odd number. Thus the chance of a head-on collision is obviated even when the pilots are flying blind.

When the pilots leave the meteorologists' room to take their places at the controls of the plane, they each carry with them a satchel which opens by means of a zip-fastener. This, like the doctor's little black bag famed in music-hall ditties, contains everything likely to be needed in any eventuality. To those simple souls who still go about thinking that an airline pilot is a brave but begrimed individual with a mental outlook only slightly superior to that of a junior machine-shop operative, one of these satchels, when opened, would prove to be a startling revelation.

Instead of harbouring, as their own mental outlook would lead them to suppose, a clean shirt, a copy of *The Filmgoer*

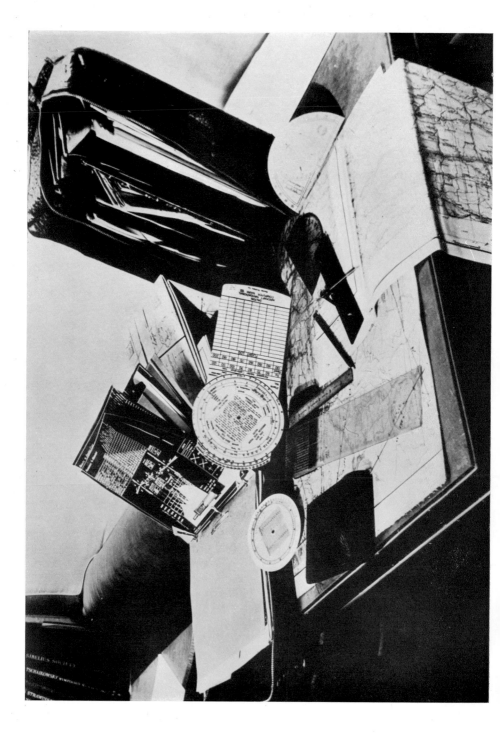

and a box of cigars, it holds the following: a profile map showing the elevation of all points on the line in addition to the radio beam stations and courses; a computer (performing the same function as a slide rule) for calculating ground speed, wind drift and velocity, and petrol consumption; a protractor, used to determine the true course as laid out in advance; a radio range map showing all radio ranges in the Eastern and Western regions, both on and off the T.W.A. courses; the Dalton Wind Drift table; a chart showing cruising speeds necessary to conform with schedule on all flights; Department of Commerce bulletins, company orders and other papers in connection with the flight; pencils, dividers, a ruler, duplicate Flight Plan forms and so on. It is the equipment of a first-rate skilled navigator. When the case is opened, the loose-leaf file portion of it, thickly packed with reference graphs and tables, forms a comfortable writing-pad.

The uninstructed would no doubt be surprised to hear that the pilot of an airliner has time to write while flying, that he is not all the time engaged in juggling with hand and foot controls of a rather unreliable nature, while he finds his way across country (with a good deal of luck) by means of a compass, a series of quick sidelong glances at the ground, and the aid of a small-scale National Survey Map. The thought is surprising, but in all countries one can still meet thousands of people who do not know how scientific the piloting of transport aeroplanes has now become. Airline Companies, here and elsewhere, are themselves responsible for not conducting an advertising campaign suitably framed to overcome this lack of knowledge and so increase the volume of their own air-borne traffic.

Actually, on a flight half-way across the American continent, which now needs less than eight hours flying time, the pilot does not devote even one hour to manual control. He takes the machine off, lands it and takes it off again for the one stop *en route*, and lands it once more at the end of his particular beat. For the rest of the time, the Sperry Gyro Pilot is in action, automatically flying the plane on its given course and at the determined height; and flying it more smoothly than any human being could fly it, because possessed of quicker, more uniform, and more delicately-graded reactions.

Meanwhile, the chief pilot is constantly keeping track of his progress to see how close to schedule he is travelling, is reporting his position at regular intervals to the appropriate ground station, is himself receiving reports from there and also listening to the observations of pilots in other planes, and at length is to be heard specifying in advance his actual minute of arrival. His satchel, at any rate for part of the trip, lies open on his knees, while he fills up forms, makes calculations and speaks into his microphone with the calm deliberation of a senior business executive.

The co-pilot assists him with the routine radio reports and other navigational duties. From time to time, the eyes of both of them stray thoughtfully up and down the rows of gauges and tachometers opposite to them on the instrument panel, and subconsciously their ears are attuned to the regular beat of the big radial motors on either side of them.

I have watched this whole procedure for hour after hour; frequently slipping on the co-pilot's earphones myself and listening to the ground stations. It is all fascinatingly unhurried and precise. As in our country, only a fine type of man is employed to fly these transport planes; the standard demanded is high, mentally and physically. They are splendid pilots, to whom a machine responds as does a well-schooled horse to a first-rate rider, and, Gyro control aside, they are required to do enough practice piloting to keep thoroughly

338

TRANSCONTINENTAL & WESTERN AIR, INC.
FLIGHT PLAN

FLIGHT 2   DATE 10-27-35   FILING TIME 8:40 a.m.   STATION Glendale

CLEARED TO: Albuquerque   SCHEDULE ELAPSED TIME 4 H. 15 M.   H. M.   H. M.

TOTAL DISTANCE 711   SCHEDULED DEPARTURE ✓ LATE DEPARTURE   H. M.

LEG	FROM	TO	MC	ALTITUDE	TEMP.	WIND	DRIFT CORR.	GAIN OR LOSS	CRUISING GROUND SPEED	NECESSARY T. A. S
1	LA	BC	34	12000	32	NE 20	0	-20	177.5	197.5
2	BC	GC	72½	"	33	NNE 18	-5	-7	177.5	184.5
3	GC	AB	87	.	34	NNE 25	-8	-2	177.5	179.5

AVERAGES: 12000 33   -10   187.5

FROM LA TO AB. FROM TO FROM TO

% POWER TO MAKE SCHEDULE	65			
% POWER TO BE USED	65 % RPM 1775	% RPM	% RPM	
CORRESPONDING T. A. S.	187			
GAIN (+) LOSS (—)	-10			
AVERAGE CRUISING GR. SP.	177 C.D. 648	C.D.	C.D.	

FUEL ON BOARD	TOTAL	USABLE	TOTAL	USABLE	TOTAL	USABLE
USABLE SUPPLY IS TOTAL LESS 65 GALS.	500	435				

	ESTIMATED	ACTUAL	ESTIMATED	ACTUAL	ESTIMATED	ACTUAL
*FUEL CONSUMPTION	92	80				

	HR.	MIN.	HR.	MIN.	HR.	MIN.	HR.	MIN.	HR.	MIN.	HR.	MIN.
FUEL RANGE (USABLE)	4	45										
CLIMBING TIME		36										
CRUISING TIME	3	40										
ELAPSED TIME	4	16										
REMG. FUEL GALS. (USABLE)	41											
REMAINING RANGE @ 65 % MILES IN STILL AIR @ 187 MPH	88.5											

ALTERNATE AIRPORTS   Prescott   Otto   Tucumcari

1500 FT. OR BETTER (RADIO RANGE)

REMAINING USABLE FUEL	HRS.	MIN.	HRS.	MIN.	HRS.	MIN.
☐ 1500 FT. OR BETTER ☐ BROKEN & UNL.						
REMAINING USABLE FUEL	HRS.	MIN.	HRS.	MIN.	HRS.	MIN.

STATE DESTINATION IN CASE OF TOTAL RADIO FAILURE _____

REMARKS: _____

I HAVE THIS DAY FAMILIARIZED MYSELF WITH ALL RECENT CHANGES IN AIRWAY AIDS, EQUIPMENT AND FACILITIES.

PERSON CONSULTED _____   SIGNED _____   PILOT _____

ESTIMATED TIME TO POINT NO. 1	BC	1:37	11:07	11:01.5	-5.5		EST. GR. SP. LEG NO. 1	167	MPH
" " "	GC	:50.5	12:5½	12:5½	+7		" " "	180	MPH
" " "	Gallup	1:02	1:56	1:52	-4		" " " 2	185	MPH
" " "	AB	31.5	2:30.5						
" " DESTINATION			+3						

*BASE OR 52 GPH. ☐ 65% POWER

Glendale to Albuquerque—711 miles at 177.5 m.p.h.
[Photo by courtesy of T.W.A. Inc.

in form. But for most of the time on regular scheduled flights, they sit at ease in their cabin, in much the same way as the master of an ocean liner leisurely paces his chart-room, stares occasionally out of the portholes, receives wireless messages and gives his mind to navigation when it becomes necessary.

Without going into too much technical detail, some further reference to the actual "Flight Plans" of my own trip across the States may be of interest. Certain data, as I have explained, is obtained from the meteorologists. This relates to winds, temperatures, the character of air masses and the changes likely to be encountered. From this, the best path is plotted. The journey of my plane from Los Angeles to Albuquerque was completed non-stop, but for purposes of plotting it was divided into three legs: Los Angeles to Boulder City, Boulder City to Grand Canyon, Grand Canyon to Albuquerque. 12,000 feet was the height chosen throughout.

On leg I. a temperature of 32 prevailed and a north-east wind of 20. Drift correction to maintain a true course was nil. Gain or loss resulted in –20. The cruising ground speed came out at 177·5 m.p.h. and the necessary true air speed at 197·5.

Leg II. was productive of the following figures: temperature 33, wind north-north-east 18, drift correction –5, gain or loss –7, cruising ground speed 177·5 m.p.h., necessary true air speed 184·5.

Leg III. differed again: temperature 34, wind north-north-east 25, drift correction –8, gain or loss –2, cruising ground speed 177·5 m.p.h., necessary true air speed 179·5.

The averages for the three legs were: height 12,000, temperature 33, gain or loss –10, necessary true air speed 187·5. The power to make schedule was curiously enough the

339

percentage not usually exceeded by T.W.A.; namely, 65. The power to be used was naturally 65 per cent. and the revolutions per minute 1,775 for a corresponding true air speed of 187. This, less the average loss due to adverse winds, resulted in the 177 m.p.h. average recorded above. As a matter of interest, the estimated ground speed on leg I. was 167, on leg II. 180, on leg III. 185. On estimated time to Boulder City, we were 5·5 minutes; late to Grand Canyon, 2 minutes early; over the intermediate town of Gallup, 4 minutes late; and one minute late at our first stop, Albuquerque. This is accurate flying with a vengeance.

Our fuel on board was 500 gallons, of which 435 was usable; 65 gallons are always in reserve and not even included in the calculations. Our estimated consumption, based on 85 gallons per hour at 60 per cent. power, was 92 per cent.; our actual consumption 80 per cent. The fuel range (usable) gave 4 hours 45 minutes. Our climbing time was 36 minutes, cruising time 3 hours 40 minutes, distance covered 711 miles, elapsed time 4 hours 16 minutes, and remaining gallons of fuel (usable) 41. This surplus would have given us a further range of 88·5 miles in still air at 60 per cent. power and 183 m.p.h. without encroaching on the final 65 gallons emergency reserve. In addition to the normal airports, we had three alternate fields *en route* at which to land in case of need.

The two "Flight Plans" for the remainder of the journey —to Amarillo, Wichita, Kansas City and thence to Indianapolis, Pittsburgh and Newark—are equally interesting. I have chosen to comment on the first as being productive of the most simple figures, and in doing so have further simplified the pertinent information. The forms themselves, for all their numerous columns, headings and abbreviations, are not really complicated when they lie before one. But of necessity they lose something of their clarity when described

340

FORM 6061-REV. 9-80

TRANSCONTINENTAL & WESTERN AIR, INC.
FLIGHT PLAN

FLIGHT **2**   DATE **10-27**   FILING TIME **2-45 M**   STATION **AB**

CLEARED TO **AM**   **WI**   **KC**   SCHEDULE ELAPSED TIME **1 H 42 M,**   **1 H 48 M,**   **1 H 12 M.**

TOTAL DISTANCE **285**   **295**   **178** SCHEDULED DEPARTURE   LATE DEPARTURE   H   M

LEG	FROM	TO	MC	ALTITUDE	TEMP.	WIND	DRIFT CORR.	GAIN OR LOSS	CRUISING GROUND SPEED	NECESSARY T.A.S
1	AB	AM	74	11000	40	NNW-30	10-	8+	187	179
2	AM	WI	45½	″	40	WNW-22	7-	10+	182	172
3	WI	KC	✓	6000	55	SW10	0	10+	176	166

AVERAGES:

	FROM AB TO AM		FROM AM TO WI		FROM WI TO KC	
% POWER TO MAKE SCHEDULE	60		62		53	
% POWER TO BE USED	65 % RPM 1750		66 % RPM 1765		65 % RPM 1700	
CORRESPONDING T. A. S.	185		182		179	
GAIN (+) LOSS (—)	+ 8		+10		10	
AVERAGE CRUISING GR. SP.	193	C.D.255	192	C.D.261	189	C.D.161
FUEL ON BOARD	TOTAL	USABLE	TOTAL	USABLE	TOTAL	USABLE
USABLE SUPPLY IS TOTAL LESS 65 GALS.	500	435	500	435	500	435
	ESTIMATED	ACTUAL	ESTIMATED	ACTUAL	ESTIMATED	ACTUAL
*FUEL CONSUMPTION	92		93		92	
	HR.	MIN.	HR.	MIN.	HR.	MIN.	HR.	MIN.	HR.	MIN.	HR.	MIN.
FUEL RANGE (USABLE)	4	45	4	45	4	40	4	40	4	45		
CLIMBING TIME		20		19		22		20		17		16
CRUISING TIME	1	20	1	22	1	22	1	25		54	1	00
ELAPSED TIME	1	40	1	41	1	44	1	45	1	11	1	16
REMG. FUEL GALS. (USABLE)	282G	289G.	296GA		320GA						
REMAINING RANGE @_____% MILES IN STILL AIR @_____MPH						

ALTERNATE AIRPORTS

1500 FT. OR BETTER (RADIO RANGE)	Wichita		KANSAS CITY		WICHITA	
REMAINING USABLE FUEL	HRS.	MIN.	HRS.	MIN.	HRS.	MIN.
☐ 1500 FT. OR BETTER ☐ BROKEN & UNL.						
REMAINING USABLE FUEL	HRS.	MIN.	HRS.	MIN.	HRS.	MIN.

STATE DESTINATION IN CASE OF TOTAL RADIO FAILURE **Proceed to CLR TWP Station**

REMARKS:

I HAVE THIS DAY FAMILIARIZED MYSELF WITH ALL RECENT CHANGES IN AIRWAY AIDS, EQUIPMENT AND FACILITIES

PERSON CONSULTED **Dept. Weather Reports**   SIGNED **George W Bull** PILOT

ESTIMATED TIME TO POINT NO. 1 _____ H ____ M   EST. GR. SP. LEG NO. 1 ____ MPH
   "   "   " 2 _____ H ____ M   "   "   NO. 2 ____ MPH
   "   "   " 3 _____ H ____ M   "   "   NO. 3 ____ MPH
   "   "   " 4 _____ H ____ M
   "   DESTINATION _____ H ____ M

*BASE ON 63 GPH. @ 60% POWER

Albuquerque to Amarillo—285 miles at 193 m.p.h. Amarillo to Wichita—295 miles at 192 m.p.h. Wichita to Kansas City—178 miles at 189 m.p.h.

TRANSCONTINENTAL & WESTERN AIR, INC.
FLIGHT PLAN

FLIGHT 2 DATE 10-27-35 FILING TIME 8:45 PMC STATION KC

CLEARED TO: 10-PG SCHEDULE ELAPSED TIME 2 H 51 M 1 H 58 M

TOTAL DISTANCE 459 341 SCHEDULED DEPARTURE 9:23 LATE DEPARTURE

LEG	FROM	TO	MC	ALTITUDE	TEMP.	WIND	DRIFT CORR.	GAIN OR LOSS	CRUISING GROUND SPEED	NECESSARY T. A. S
1	KC	SN	8½	10,000	40	SW30	+7	+18	176	158
2	SN	ID	71	10,000	40	SSW35	+8½	+20	176	156
3	ID	CO	84½	10,000	45	SW25	+5	+18	198	180
4	CO	PG	83½	10,000	45	SW20	+4	+16	198	182
AVERAGES:	142 / 88½			10,000 / 10,000	40 / 45			+19 / +17		137 / 137

	FROM KC TO ID		FROM ID TO PG		FROM TO	
% POWER TO MAKE SCHEDULE	-50		61			
% POWER TO BE USED	65 % RPM 1750		65 % RPM 1750		% RPM	
CORRESPONDING T. A. S.	185		188			
GAIN (+) LOSS (—)	+19		+17			
AVERAGE CRUISING GR. SP.	204	C. D. 448	202	C. D. 277		C. D.
FUEL ON BOARD	TOTAL	USABLE	TOTAL	USABLE	TOTAL	USABLE
USABLE SUPPLY IS TOTAL LESS 65 GALS.	500	435	500	435		
	ESTIMATED	ACTUAL	ESTIMATED	ACTUAL	ESTIMATED	ACTUAL
FUEL CONSUMPTION	92		92			
	HR.	MIN.	HR.	GAL.	HR.	MIN.	HR.	GAL.	HR.	MIN.	HR.	MIN.
FUEL RANGE (USABLE)	4	43	4	43		
CLIMBING TIME		28		28		
CRUISING TIME	2	02	1	28		
ELAPSED TIME	2	30	1	56		
REMG. FUEL GALS. (USABLE)	205		260			
REMAINING RANGE @ 65 %	2:04		3:04			
MILES IN STILL AIR @ 75 MPH	412		525			
ALTERNATE AIRPORTS	CO, CV, CC		CO & CV			
1500 FT. OR BETTER (RADIO RANGE)	CO		CO			
REMAINING USABLE FUEL	1 HRS. 13 MIN		1 HRS. 51 MIN		HRS. MIN	
☐ 1500 FT. OR BETTER ☐ BROKEN & UNL.	CV		CV			
REMAINING USABLE FUEL	34 MIN		1 HRS. 12 MIN		HRS. MIN	

STATE DESTINATION IN CASE OF TOTAL RADIO FAILURE *Next TWA field open.*

REMARKS: *Flite 2 passing up SN, account weather.*

I HAVE THIS DAY FAMILIARIZED MYSELF WITH ALL RECENT CHANGES IN AIRWAY AIDS, EQUIPMENT AND FACILITIES.

PERSON CONSULTED *Dungan* SIGNED PILOT

ESTIMATED TIME TO POINT NO. 1 ____ EST. GR. SP. LEG NO. 1 ____ MPH

NO. 2 ____ MPH

NO. 3 ____ MPH

DESTINATION ____

Kansas City to Indianapolis—459 miles at 204 m.p.h. Indianapolis (missing St. Louis) to Pittsburg—341 miles at 202 m.p.h.

There, held by fog. Author has no detailed record of subsequent flight to New York.

in print. Still, with the help of photographs of the actual Flight Plans mentioned, I hope I have succeeded in giving an accurate, if necessarily limited, account of how efficiently our American friends operate their fast transport machines between coast and coast in any weather considered flyable. What one actually experiences as one traverses the continent needs a chapter to itself.

CHAPTER IV

THE TRANS-CONTINENTAL TRIP ITSELF

IT WAS A MORNING LATE IN OCTOBER WHEN I BOARDED THE "Sky Queen" at Glendale, the Los Angeles airport used by Transcontinental and Western Air Inc. While waiting for my luggage to be weighed, I wandered round the booking hall to admire the stalls of apples, oranges, grapes and flowers, arranged along one side of it. Almost anywhere else but in California, one would have been surprised to find a workaday aerodrome so garnished. But there it seemed natural; the shortest stay in Los Angeles quickly accustoms visitors to a profusion of fruit and blossom.

Seeing a negro porter disappear through some glass doors with my kitbags, I followed him, and set my watch by the aerodrome clock. Presently, an unseen official, his voice magnified by a loud-speaker, announced from somewhere above my head that Flight No. 2, for Albuquerque, Amarillo, Kansas City and all points East, was now loading; and would passengers kindly take their seats. I knocked out my pipe against the railings and mounted the three steps that led up into the shapely silver-coloured fuselage of the Douglas. My name was ticked off on a list by Mr. Kingman, the co-pilot, as I entered. Normally, I prefer one of the rearmost seats in a low or middle wing monoplane, mainly because the view from there is better, but I found that the one immediately facing the door leading into the pilot's cabin had been allotted to me—a kindly piece of forethought, because I was to spend much of my time with the chief pilot, and only

342

return to the main cabin for a meal. A glance at my watch when the machine started to taxi showed me that we were 30 secs. late; the time was 9.30½ a.m. We actually took off at 9.32.

Glendale airport might be better situated. As its name implies, it lies between two long upthrusts of hill, that to the north-east being the higher. To experienced pilots it presents no difficulties, but I can well imagine novices getting a powerful lot of practice in gliding S-turns, or, in their next stage, thinking it necessary to side-slip off a fairish amount of height so as not to over-shoot the field when approaching from certain directions. As we climbed out at a comfortable angle, I could soon see the sea glittering to my right beyond Los Angeles, and on its horizon the dark blue smudge that was Santa Catalina Island; where three weeks before I had stood with Donald Douglas, the builder of these very planes, watching pelicans diving for fish, and noting the way they did a half-spin in their dives, so as to keep their quarry in view, and only fully closed their wings in the instant before submersion. To my left lay khaki hills, with other higher mountains behind, lavender-coloured in the morning light. A tenuous streak of transparent mist still floated above the next valley.

In a car, the stretch of houses below seemed interminable, as I had discovered more than once. But from the three or four thousand feet that I judged we had already gained, their miniature rectangular blocks and the shrunken boulevards dividing them were seen to have an end, although that end only came at the foot of the rising ground, except where at intervals buffer states of orange groves, darkly green, had staked out their claims upon the plain. A watercourse caught my eye, and I traced it right back into its valley. Its bed was mostly dry, for the rains had not yet come. But here and there were pools, opaque and of a light jade colour—a

343

daylight water tint unknown to me elsewhere, being found as a rule only in caverns. Along many of the wriggling ridges of the foothills ran the usual sandy fire-paths, dividing the combustible scrub pines. The fierce rocky peaks high above and beyond do not need them.

Looking back with something of regret, for I had made a number of fine new American friends in Western aviation circles and among that brilliant, much maligned community in Hollywood, I watched the glowing terrain of the Pacific coast, in which there is always pink, fade softly, from being hard, into a white shining horizon that met the sky.

By now, we were over the top of the Sierra Madre; flying above a rugged pass and being tossed about a bit. For some few minutes, our approach had been across a district of closely-wooded foothills, among which lay an irregular shaped piece of water that I took to be Lake Arrowhead, a famous mountain resort of the wealthy from Los Angeles and Hollywood. The sun turned it a brilliant turquoise as we sped past. Far beyond it, a forest fire was burning.

Ahead of the Sierra, my eyes encountered a drop to complete flatness; to absolute desert. Appearing sandy enough in colour if not in substance immediately beneath the plane, such ground then assumed the inevitable blue tinge of distance the farther off one looked. Behind us, to the west, this effect naturally deepened by reason of the light and time of day; and as we drew away, so the brows of the mountains came together in a violet frown.

It was only a month since I had driven across this same Mojave desert, sun-baked and blindingly hot, on my way west. Then my surroundings, although fascinating because of their weirdness, had seemed as monotonous in appearance as the impression they created was primitive and unfriendly. At a steady 80 m.p.h., I had made for where I knew there would be the welcome green of trees beyond the mountains, where the heat would no longer be sufficient to cause a mist on my dark sun-glasses, and my thin dust coat would no longer be dank with sweat. Now, looking down upon the same scene at my ease, the relief-map effect familiar to those who fly showed me the other aspect which I expected.

The desert below might have been modelled in plasticine, its general tone drab, its sole variations the tortured volcanic outcroppings cooled into stark groups and caterpillar-like ridges, and the giant incisions with which these alternated. As the sun rose higher, shining down more directly upon this waste, this complete no-man's land, what basic colours there were, crude and inevitably associated in one's mind with things prehistoric, strengthened and became glaringly visible from above although to my knowledge remaining some-times indistinguishable to labouring travellers in the glare below. So, too, the shadows shortened and grew blacker in the depths of steep ravines, seen vertically.

For some time past, I had been up in the cockpit compart-ment with Mr. Rice, the chief pilot, while the co-pilot was aft attending to the wants of passengers; regulated the heat of the main cabin, gave information about the landscape in view, and generally tried to ensure that the flight was as pleasant as possible for all concerned. In the intervals of watching Mr. Rice make out for me a duplicate "Flight Plan" (previously described: see pages 334 to 341) and listening to his painstaking explanation of it, I strove to take in the details of an unfamiliar instrument board; which I could do only when he paused to compute the result of a series of figures by means of the scale lying on the top of his open satchel, full of maps and graphs.

After a while, I had familiarised myself with the position of the main instruments, such as the manifold pressure gauge and revolution indicator for each engine, the air speed indicator, the turn and bank indicator, the altimeter, the climb indicator, the automatic pilot control, the artificial horizon, the directional gyro, the bank and climb gyro, the compass, etc. The petrol and oil gauges, the thermometers, and the air temperature gauge—with the grim warning it could give about the danger of ice, were, I saw, situated opposite the co-pilot's seat. The radio panel was centrally placed above the V-shaped front window, within stretch of an arm; and the fuel cocks, together with the elevator, rudder and aileron adjusting gear were on a box-mounting midway between the two main control columns (with their comfortably shaped hand wheels) and short of the actual instrument board itself. On the top of this box-mounting were also located the twin throttle levers in their quadrants; they and practically every other control being equally easily reached by either pilot, as is the common practice in modern air liners.

We were flying at 12,000 feet, and had been there for over an hour. But such a height is not unpleasant when no exertion is demanded, and except for a certain dryness in the mouth, which a cigarette disguises for a time without, of course, overcoming it, no untoward effect is noticed by the average person in a chair. Just then, Mr. Kingman put his head round the door, and I inquired how the other passengers were enjoying flying so high. He said that most of them were reading their newspapers or looking out of the windows. He withdrew again, leaving me to continue my instruction in navigation "to schedule" at the capable hands of his chief.

There was another point: my own propulsive plant sometimes needing fuel of a high octane rating (for, alas, we cannot redesign ourselves as Anthony Fokker yearns to do) it is my harmless fad to carry round the equivalent of a small chemist's shop; but the bottles in my dressing-case, even the hair lotion, also withstood the difference between the ground pressure inside them and the reduced exterior pressure at

346

Instrument board of the Douglas D.C.2.

12,000 feet. Not a single cork popped. So that at the least I was saved the discovery of a dire mess upon opening the case in New York, and at the worst a revolting smell. Other people have not always been so fortunate.

The needle of the air speed indicator remained steady at 187 m.p.h. Our actual ground speed was a little less, owing to a quartering wind. Allowing for drift, Mr. Rice computed this loss to be 10 m.p.h. Presently, we saw Boulder City, at which point we were a trifle over five minutes late, and nearby I was able to pick out Boulder Dam, the building of which, at a cost of £80,000,000, has been one of the greatest engineering feats in the world. Behind its tall, curved rampart is harnessed some ten billion gallons of water which come from the Colorado and Virgin rivers, and the great artificial lake, 115 miles long, in which these two meet. Here is a huge and endless source of electrical energy. Here is the means, now at length made available, of irrigating a portion of the hitherto unclaimed desert so that it may, indeed, "blossom as a rose." Here will certainly spring up in the future a pleasure resort destined to be second to none in popularity, situated as it will be in one of the most romantic spots on earth.

But seeing the dam to-day through a pilot's cockpit window at 12,000 feet, its seven hundred and twenty-seven feet of wall was simply a small curved piece of man-made fabric, aloof from its setting by pale symmetry alone; a tiny structure placed by human beavers to block a thread-like stream; beyond it a jagged patch of water mirroring the heavens, and around it the harsh browns and reds of desert rocks, still to be there when what we build has gone and earth no longer supports the mortal genus.

And so across more waste-land and naked mountains we flew towards Grand Canyon; watching for its monstrous edges to become recognisable among the gaudy jumble of savage country ahead.

The path of our Douglas through the air more or less followed the southern rim of the gorge. I sought for, and traced, the road by which I had approached its brink a month before and stared into its mile of depth. But from the air, the highway now looked like a thin, yellow ribbon laid straight and flat as a ruler upon the face of the desert to southward. Nearer the canyon itself, it wound in and out of the neighbouring pines with the ordered inconsequence of a coloured streak in a carpet's pattern, and led my eyes to the points at which I had stood and surveyed the overpowering majesty of the chasm's contents; those many-hued mountains which, stripped to their hard nakedness by Nature's plan, man it as rugged soldiers man a trench, while on their bare backs and flanks the changing light of day strikes shadows, and glows with such varying tints that all beholding them must stand entranced. As a geologist has written: "If any one of these stupendous creations had been planted upon the plains of Central Europe, it would have influenced modern art as profoundly as Fujiyama has influenced the decorative art of Japan. Yet here are hundreds of them swallowed up in the confusion of multitude."

At 12.10 p.m. we had passed the canyon, and the co-pilot came forward to say my luncheon was ready in the cabin. I went aft with him. He fitted a light metal tray across the front of my passenger chair; it had two prongs that entered sockets recessed into the front ends of the latter's two arms— a neat and rigid arrangement. Then he brought me a tidily packed cardboard box, containing the same sort of meal as that served to me in the United Air Lines' Boeing plane, flying up to San Francisco a fortnight earlier: a variety of cold, sliced meats in cellophane envelopes, olives and gherkins, rolls, biscuits, cheese, fruit salad in a carton and a raw apple. He offered me cold tomato juice out of a vacuum flask and hot coffee out of another—all to my ill-concealed embarrassment. For to me, an amateur pilot myself, it seemed incongruous that a trained pilot on a great Air Line should be doing a steward's job. I felt bound to apologise for being such a nuisance to him. Of course, he replied with some smiling disclaimer. Still, the system was obviously wrong.

Put another way, an airsick man would almost certainly not object to being comforted in a practical sympathetic manner by a stewardess whom he knew to be a trained nurse. A woman would certainly be glad of it. Whereas, in like circumstances, the ministrations of a young man would be almost unwelcome to another man and doubtless definitely distasteful to a woman, it being known that the co-pilot was not in the ordinary sense of the word a doctor. Such psychology is elementary. I wonder how even the fact that a seat occupied by a stewardess entails a financial sacrifice on the part of the operating company has weighed against it for so long in the case of many airlines both in Europe and America. So far as T.W.A. is concerned, a change of policy has already come about, and the planes now carry a "hostess"; which shows that the company, though leading its competitors in certain ways, is not too proud to own to having been behind them in others.

This change is typical of American business methods and is at once a tribute to the frankness and acumen which usually characterise them. I often wish these methods were more widely adopted in England. The tacit admission of a competitor's superiority in design or salesmanship that is implied by taking a leaf out of his book, is sensible rather than undignified. Moreover, if accompanied by a strenuous effort to render the copy or adaption better than the original, and then to be the one to set the next fashion, it will attract far-sighted customers rather than lose them. Active deprecation of his own goods is the sign of an unwise merchant, but the blind upholding of them against articles obviously more suited to

349

public demand is just plain foolishness. We are too addicted to it: and that is why the dozen or so manufacturers in our combined aircraft and automobile industries who do not suffer from this false type of patriotism, particularly in the latter trade, stand out from the ruck like hills from the plains of Mexico. On them (our wise merchants, not the hills!) we may safely pin our hopes for the Empire's future trade.

I had eaten only a few mouthfuls when Mr. Rice left his seat to fetch me back, saying he had something to show me. I hastily unshipped my tray and placed it on the floor, afterwards joining him again in the pilot's cabin where the automatic gyro pilot was in charge, keeping the big transport on its course with unerring delicacy and skill. We were crossing the Little Colorado River, a sun-flecked streak so deeply confined to its serpentine course that black shadows hid it at every eastward-facing curve, making one think of it at those points as almost subterranean.

But Rice was pointing ahead to Indian villages, those of the Navajo and Hopi tribes, over whose Reservations we were now flying. After noticing with interest their self-protective sites, chosen mostly on the crests of precipitous slopes, I returned to my luncheon and finished it quickly; not liking to discard it after all the trouble Kingham had taken with it. Then I went forward once more into the cockpit, and closed the door behind me. I knew that I would be free to stay there until we reached Albuquerque.

The chief pilot was sitting with his file open upon his knees. He read one or two figures off his "Flight Plan," did a quick calculation on his ivorine computer, and neatly wrote down the answer with a sharp pencil. Glancing at the clock, he reached down his earphones from their hook; at the same time motioning to me to don the co-pilot's set. After a few seconds, I heard the operations office at Albuquerque talking. Then the Westbound "Sky Master," Flight No. 3, reported its position, height, speed and the conditions it was encountering; concluding with a notification of its prospective time of landing. It was outward bound overnight from New York and, having left Wichita a few minutes after we left Los Angeles, would reach Albuquerque about an hour ahead of us. Then Rice gave out our position, height, speed and so on; receiving an O.K. in reply. We both hung up our earphones again. The machine droned on.

We flew past the Painted Desert, across which, from a vantage point on the road to Holbrook, I had peered through the haze one afternoon as I drove from Vaughn to Flagstaff. All over its scorched surface lie grotesque rocky shapes of every tint, like prehistoric monsters asleep. As at Grand Canyon, one's eyes traverse the scene in wonderment. One knows that impressions formed here at noon would be changed by three o'clock, and that by evening nothing familiar would remain. Even the rocks would have gained or lost in conformation as the light flowed across them. What, at early morning, were half-seen mysteries slinking in grey obscurity among their fellows, and by midday had become huge crouching reptiles, crimson of hide and glowering of mien, would alter chameleon-like as dusk approached, and fade to mauve or else a scaly green, then loom larger than life as night drew on, and finally drowse in black and silent herds watched by the lazy moon.

Still farther south there was the Petrified Forest, where parts of trees, which must at one time have been of stupendous size, are scattered upon the ground, preserved as solids by action of the elements—one of those giant museums founded by Nature's whim.

An hour passed, and we listened-in again. We heard of the arrival of the other plane at Albuquerque. I looked at the clock. The "Sky Master" had apparently been landed there to the very tick of its pilot's estimated time. We, ourselves, were then above the wide, blistering valley whose fuchsia cliffs had marched beside my westward road for many miles. Gallup fled past below—the dusty town into which three Mexicans in flaring shirts, five-gallon hats and a Ford *coupé* had raced me before I called a halt for luncheon. South of Gallup would be Zuni, village headquarters of the Zuni Indians whose tales yet refer to the encroachment of Coronado in 1540, as well as to the past glories of their own tribal customs.

Now, twenty miles ahead, the Continental Divide confronted us; a range of mountains stretching interminably North and South, like the teeth of a saw on edge against the sky. We would be over them in less than seven minutes. Somewhere near them in a line with Zuni, a glimpse might be caught of Inscription Rock, the natural Monolith on which, in 1605, the Spanish Conquistadores, laying aside the heavy mail they wore even when exploring across these burning wastes, had carved in their hours of ease some history of their passage.

We were momentarily leaving behind the dusty puckered folds of the desert, upon which the rare signs of husbandry by Indian or Paleface stood out like small patches of moss in a disused quarry. The ground became fairer, less tortured in appearance. Juniper trees lent it a certain grace. As we swept down across the mountains—for we had just started our gradual descent from 12,000 feet—the pines reached up as though to wave at this great silver bird. Among them in sheltered hollows the snow was lying, and all around was sunshine and the calm of hills.

From being, for a minute or two, and after so long, within close view of normal ground, it was fascinating to watch its complete falling away again as we left the mountains and shot out over another stretch of wasteland. Only travel by air can provide such striking contrasts. At one moment I

352

was peering down eagerly among the adjacent trees, in a search for signs of whatever wild life exists there; at the next, the moulded slopes took a sharp tilt desertwards, and I was again blinking at sandy soil far below, lapping about their weather-beaten shins.

To fly across America is overwhelmingly to realise the importance of this means of transport to business men and women, and also where the carriage of mail and express freight are concerned. Although, in our present conception, huge goods trains remain unsurpassable for their purpose, and, comfortable air-conditioned passenger trains make the coast to coast trip in little more than half a week—a period regarded by some people almost as a short holiday, to be occupied in rest and reading—still the long-distance plane has already skimmed the cream of executives hard pressed for time, of the film colony on vacation bent, and of the modern pleasure seekers, part of whose pleasure lies in a constant haste to search for more. Already this constitutes a large *clientèle*. With the passing of remnants of a generation mostly unused to flying, it will become very much larger, encouraged by further progress in the already remarkable amenities and degree of safety provided by the aeroplane.

There remains the automobile. This, like the train, will never be outdone. Both these older forms of transport will get from the newcomer an enforced re-orientation of their respective lines of development. Indeed, they are already experiencing it. But all three modes of transport will grow together, each one the complement of the other two. To see a country properly, we must fly over it. To pass comfortably through it, we can take a train. But to know it in passing, we need a car. And really to live in it, we still ride horses or walk, according to our fancy.

Southward I soon saw the Enchanted Mesa, upon which, like an eagle's eyrie, is set the Indian village of Acoma,

353

continuously inhabited for longer than any other in America. The site of this sky city, as it is called, was chosen for reasons of defence, like those of the villages I had seen upon lesser eminences farther west. Here, where sheer drops guarded the Mesa from a surprise attack, the red men had made their adobe houses reasonably secure against marauding bands from other tribes and the frightening arrival of invading Spaniards. Nearer, by the familiar road, I could distinguish Cubero and Laguna, where as I drove between them I had stopped to chat with an old squaw and her children.

Soon the air speed indicator showed close on two hundred miles an hour. Albuquerque, seen as a miniature cluster of buildings, was now in view ahead. Still at our same modest angle of descent, almost imperceptible to passengers, we whistled earthwards towards the basking town sprawled on the desert's floor. The latter, as it stretched towards us, toppled sharply into a valley, thus seeming to east-bound air-borne folk to offer up Albuquerque as a set piece on an imitation plateau. Hills of bleached ochre hotly shimmered in the background. Before the town, the stainless sky's reflection made blue the sand-barred reaches of the Rio Grande.

I picked out the aerodrome with its hangars and main offices. It was situated some little distance our side of Albuquerque. Kingman, the co-pilot, came forward, and I made way for him. He slipped into his seat on Rice's right, while I remained standing in the space between and slightly in rear of them. Rice had throttled back and levelled out, so that we were flying at less than a hundred miles an hour a few hundred feet up. He had been talking to the ground station and had received the O.K. to go in. A red light glowed in a panel on the right of the instrument board, mute warning that our wheels were still in their retracted positions.

The chief pilot issued a terse command to Kingman.

"Flaps," he ordered.

354

Kingman operated the appropriate control. The long adjustable sections underneath the trailing-edge of each wing were wound down.

"Flaps," he echoed.

Our speed dropped to about seventy. Sighing quietly, the big Douglas seemed just to paddle through the air and would have appeared deceptively near stalling point to any pilot unused to the more deliberate approach permitted by the use of flaps, now a commonplace.

"Wheels down," remarked Rice.

Kingman busied himself again. "Wheels down," he said, a few seconds later.

But in direct contradiction of his words, the red bulb continued to glow malevolently.

Rice twisted his head, looking out and back at the port landing wheel, visible through his window. I looked too. It was down.

"Is your wheel down?" he asked Kingman calmly.

"Yes," said the co-pilot.

"Well, pump a bit."

Kingman obediently grasped the handle of the manual hydraulic pump and made several sharp strokes with it. Still the red light would not change to green. The implication was that the undercarriage, although down, was not fully locked.

When this uncertainty first arose, Rice had headed slightly away from the aerodrome to the south; making a wider turn to gain time while investigating the cause.

"What pressure is there?" he now asked.

Kingman told him. I cannot recall what it was.

"Well, bring it up to five hundred," he replied.

Then, turning to me, he explained that some part of the shock absorbers (which part, of course, I could not know) sometimes did not quite move the last fractional distance

355

into place upon extraction of the wheels, so that the electrical circuit which would normally cause the indicator bulbs to change from red to green was not closed.

"But as long as there's five hundred pounds pressure per square inch showing on the gauge," he added, "it's O.K. to land. Still, I'll touch the wheels pretty hard first before putting her down—just to make sure."

His hand reached out to the throttle levers, and the soft muttering of the engines died away to a whisper. The nose of the Douglas sank, stopped turning and pointed dead over the nearest extremity of the aerodrome.

For myself, nothing could have pleased me more than this minor *contretemps*. It is always satisfying to see a real expert at work. To a greatly experienced pilot, constantly flying these fast transports, there is nothing very much in having to touch his wheels and then stay safely in the air for a further number of seconds before making a proper, smooth landing. But I knew that I, myself, would not have made a particularly tidy job of it. So I welcomed the chance of seeing a neat exhibition and being able to learn from it. With either hand I took a firm grip of the backs of the two pilot's seats and studied the roof with some interest; deciding where not to bump my head if bumped it might turn out to be. Then I crouched a little, flexing at the knees, and waited on events.

Rice brought her in beautifully, like the artist he is. Flattening out very low when once we were inside the aerodrome boundary, he sent her along with a bit of engine to steady her, and, with his right hand on both throttles, ready to open out and take her off on another circuit, he deliberately flew her onto the ground. I held on tight while she bounced hard and ballooned back several feet into the air, where Rice held her level with the apparently casual touch that betokens the veteran pilot. He looked down quickly at the nearside wheel, revolving rapidly as a result of its sudden contact

356

with the runway. It had stayed in the normal "down" position. His head jerked round to look straight ahead again. He questioned Kingman over his shoulder.

"Is your wheel O.K.?" he asked.

"Yep."

"Certain?"

"Yep, it's O.K."

Rice instantly pulled back both throttle levers the last three-quarters of an inch in their quadrants. The machine sank, whispering again. He eased the control column back a trifle—the machine still sank; back a fraction more—she touched; she was rolling normally along after a perfect wheel landing. All was well. He let the tail touch and she slowed. Whereupon he braked, turned her almost on her axis, and taxied up to the depot.

No passenger apart from myself realised that the slightest thing was amiss. If they noticed anything at all, they probably only thought that the pilot had not landed quite as smoothly as is customary on the T.W.A. line. Actually, he had done a splendidly efficient piece of mild emergency flying without taking any risks. And it is only fair to add that if by some hundred to one chance the wheels had not remained locked in their fully extracted position, the machine could later have done a belly landing on them in their retracted position; although probably at the cost of straining things a bit, wrecking both propellers by fouling the ground with them, and startling the passengers. But that would doubtless have been all.

Rice and I were the last to get out. I heard him quietly tell a foreman mechanic to check up on the landing gear and tell-tale lights. Then we went together into the reception lounge of the main building, where he kindly introduced me to Mr. Brill, our chief pilot for the next stage; and also told him what had happened. According to my watch, we had

357

arrived at 1.40 p.m., a minute later than Rice had announced by radio telephone an hour before. One way and another, we must have occupied the odd sixty seconds in that slow approach of ours, and sorting the matter of the wheels. Anyway, we were due at 2.45 p.m., having lost according to Albuquerque (mountain) time, an hour on our way from west to east. But we had covered 711 miles at 177 m.p.h.

The hall of the reception building struck me as rather cramped. A *café* bar which might well have been situated elsewhere, occupied a lot of the available room, and left little for two loads of passengers and the company's officials and porters to move about in. In other ways it was attractive, with articles of Indian workmanship hung upon the walls; tacit reminders that the trail we followed was the one originally made by moccasined feet, long before the days of prairie schooners, the first panting locomotives and now the progressive monoplanes.

A quarter of an hour passed while I smoked half a pipeful and stood talking to Rice and Brill. Then I said good-bye to Rice, pocketed the duplicate "Flight Plan" that he had made out for me, and followed Brill back into the machine. We took off at 1.59 p.m. by my watch, or 2.58 p.m. by Mountain Time. On this occasion, I determined to stay in my comfortable seat in the main cabin, to read and write. I had spent nearly as long a period in the cockpit during the morning as the airline pilots themselves are called upon to do, but with the additionally tiring effort of trying to assimilate a new technique.

We cleared the aerodrome boundary with plenty of height in hand and then made a long, wide turn eastwards; still climbing hard. For in that direction, behind Albuquerque, there stood the background of mountains over which we had now to fly. Here, I looked down with added interest, because we exactly traced for some miles the road down which I had

358

hummed in the Chrysler, then temporarily glad to be exchanging the white glare of the stony slopes for the sense of shot-silk distance on the plain.

We flew directly above the same fierce pass. I recognised corner after corner in it. But instead of holding a big, fast car to its proper course round each of them, my left hand dropping to make gear changes, my right foot alternating between throttle pedal and brake, my eyes watching every yard of each curve for loose stones off the hillside or a fool driver in his wrong place, I looked down idly to-day from my arm-chair in an air-conditioned cabin at several thousand feet and felt more than a little sleepy.

We swept out over the far end of the valley where there were pines with expanses of soil between them, cultivated in patches. On some, I could see stooks of maize. These patches grew in size as the ground levelled; becoming huge squares, rectangles and triangles in various shades of brown. For a few minutes (we were doing over a hundred and eighty) the pines still stretched out to southward. Then they fell back. The mountains likewise withdrew, and I was to see no more of their kind. Thirty miles to starboard I picked out two lakes that I had photographed on my drive up from Vaughn. Finally, even the signs of cultivation came to an end. Nothing but prairie lay ahead.

In those parts, it is often possible to see great distances. Granted perfect visibility, the horizon distinguished by air passengers at 8,000 feet is 118 miles away. A glance from side to side embraces 236 miles of country. If the visibility remained as good throughout the 2,567 miles of a quick flight from coast to coast, it should be possible to have looked over 605,812 square miles of scenery, or twenty per cent. of the entire United States. Only by the otherwise boring use of figures, is it possible adequately to convey a sense of the distance seen and felt on a flight across America.

But at this point it became dull. The ground was a uniform buff. A few kopjes stuck up away on the starboard side like anthills. At intervals, a water hole gleamed with the dull look of pewter. Studying a map, I judged that in another hour and a half we would be over the Texas Border.

At length, my private prophecy was fulfilled. Then we came to wheat farms, thousands upon thousands of acres of them, their ordered plough contrasting strangely with a sudden sheer canyon, jagged-edged, like a giant crack in the level ground. Now there were not even blue smudges on the horizon that I could take for distant mountains—just nothing but space, space, space. By my watch it was 3.25 p.m., but by the time here about two hours later: for the soft glow of late afternoon was already spreading with infinite charm over these wide American corn lands.

We were descending. In a few minutes, I saw the tall aluminium coloured granaries on the outskirts of Amarillo. Then the town itself reeled past below our port wing. Mr. Brill made the usual conservative and unhurried approach to the aerodrome beyond, and I yawned and stretched and thought with some pleasure that a cup of coffee was just what I wanted. By which time, he had made the best landing of all the good ones that I was given in America, and had brought our plane to a standstill. We had done the 285 miles from Albuquerque at 193 m.p.h.

By contrast with those at Albuquerque, which, for all their Indian decorations, I had thought scarcely adequate, these aerodrome offices struck me as definitely poor. And I wondered at it, being already aware of the efficiency which was characteristic of T.W.A. Efficiency is perhaps the wrong word to use, because the airports provide most of what is strictly necessary. Rather, I should say that the passengers' comfort and pleasure on the ground appears not to be as carefully studied as it is in the air; probably on account of expense. The reception rooms present for the most part the dull, cheerless appearance of charitable institutions. Although there seemed to be enough lavatories, and nicely arranged (in America they are often deliciously described as rest-rooms), I noticed more than once an insufficiency of comfortable sofa or arm-chair accommodation for passengers waiting to board the aeroplanes, and a total absence—so far as I could discover—of any provision for sleeping, should a plane be held on the ground at night owing to the prevalence of non-flyable weather.

I soon realised that I had been spoilt by my experience of the United Air Lines terminal at Los Angeles. Yet, indeed, that line, when I came to consider it, did not provide as good an airport building as I expected at Mills Field, San Francisco. As regards T.W.A., I look back now to its Albuquerque field as being the most homely and cheerful place for passengers to congregate, despite the slightly cramped quarters to be found there. Not till later did I discover that all the air terminals are not only municipally owned but municipally controlled. Consequently, the airlines have no say in what facilities are provided except in so far as they can persuade the politicians to make improvements. Politics again!

I do not seem to remember paved runways at Amarillo. Or, if there were, I do not now recollect that we used one when landing or taking off; which adds to the excellence of Mr. Brill's handling of the Douglas. I think it must be the bumping we received when taxi-ing away to take off again that has impressed this on my mind. For somewhere on the transcontinental flight I had a definite impression, although to a lesser degree, of the pitching and tossing to which we are subjected at Croydon—an aerodrome that, for other reasons as well, would probably not be licensed by the American Department of Commerce. If I am wrong about Amarillo

Field, I apologise to all concerned; but not on account of its depressing building.

We were due away at 5.50 p.m., but actually left at 5.48 p.m. according to my watch which I had now re-set; by what clock, I am not now certain. Over mile after mile of the same flat plough we again made our swift, regulated way up to a ceiling of 10,000 feet, where Brill levelled off and flew us along the beacon line towards Wichita.

Real evening had come upon the earth. Only for a few minutes longer would we, at our great height, retain some semblance of day which was already denied to folk in the widely-spaced ranch houses below; lighting lamps in their living-rooms that to us were merely pin-points. A dark purple shadow, like the bloom on a ripe plum, encircled the horizon. The now almost indistinguishable chocolate of the great fields merged into it. Above, harmonising perfectly, a ring of misty pink was superimposed, which in turn faded into lemon with the faintest suggestion of green, and at our level into a blue remnant of day rapidly becoming night. Beneath the centre of this inverted bowl of transient loveliness, flashed out the first airway beacon on our course: a brilliant pencil of light describing the full three hundred and sixty degrees like clockwork, the red back of its lamp alternately swinging into view with so sharp a flick that one felt it should be audible.

Boqua started to come round with the dinner trays. While I was untying the square, white cardboard box containing edibles, he kindly poured out some tomato juice for me. In the box, I discovered two each of three sorts of sandwiches, a cold stuffed egg, some fruit salad and a slice of chocolate cake. I hankered a little for something hot, as one does when one has been eating nothing but cold food at successive meals. But what I had was really excellent and gave no cause for complaint. Later, Boqua brought me some good

362

black coffee. I lit a cigarette and came to the conclusion that I had had a much better dinner than was warranted by my lack of exercise since the morning.

I had been dining by the light of a reading lamp, built into the sound-deadening panels beside my chair. Now, for a time, I returned to my book and another cigarette or two. Then I switched out the lamp and watched the beacons below. By daylight, so I had been told, it is still possible to see near them the remains of the deeply-rutted trails made a hundred years ago by the prairie schooners, dragged by their sweating teams of horses—the only means of communication between the frontier outposts of St. Joseph and Kansas City and the sparsely-settled country farther west, over which I had been flown that day, and where the American pioneers had established themselves in the face of constant attacks by hordes of Indians.

Scenes of the sort had been often in my mind during the hours of daylight. I felt I had only to close my eyes to picture them. But here, in the presence of the airway beacons, essentially emblems of the modern age, such dreams became so remote as to defy recapture. From our height, the circumference traced by the bright ray of one beacon appeared just to overlap that of the next. The regular sweep of them, and the friendly flickering of their red backs, must have made night flying a matter of little account to thousands of passengers who might otherwise have felt it a little strange at first. To a pilot, they are a joy. Had I been flying myself over the line, I would have welcomed them almost with affection. But as an idle, slightly *blazé* passenger, I found the effect of watching them mildly hypnotic. If we had not then run into an area of cloud, I should undoubtedly have gone to sleep.

We hurtled close over the first wisps of some strato-cirrus, impressively lonely-looking pennons of dusky grey, tattered and holed, intermittently masking clusters of minute lights

363

below, which, like yellow diamonds on black velvet, indicated a rare farm or small town. Then we flew fair and square into a patch of it. The plane, as planes do when they encounter cloud at high speed, lifted sharply, dropped and fled on. This one also yawed a bit from side to side. I glanced curiously at my ten fellow passengers (we had four empty seats). They looked up, shaken out of their lethargy for a moment, but soon returned to reading their magazines or to their tentative efforts to doze. None of them, I think, noticed the yawing motion. I guessed they were business folk. An aeroplane to them was just a means of rapid transport; unless the weather became really bad, they would not notice how it responded.

It was now 7.10 p.m. Boqua emerged from the pilot's cockpit. He bent his head to mine.

"The outside temperature is down to thirty degrees," he remarked. "Would you like a rug?"

"No, thanks," said I. "I'm very comfortable."

In truth, I am a warm person anyway; and the cabin struck me as being at just the right temperature, besides being excellently ventilated. I was wearing a flannel suit without a waistcoat, and had so directed the individual air duct above my chair that it blew softly down about a foot in front of my face. Passing along the central gangway, Boqua asked the same question of each passenger in turn. I noticed that one or two of them accepted his offer, whereupon he wrapped them up as tenderly as a nurse. Why they wanted rugs, I cannot imagine.

I felt suddenly that we had started to descend. The hands of my watch pointed to 7.15 p.m. It was the airport of Wichita that was beckoning, or beaconing, us down out of the moonless sky. And we were there at 7.33—five minutes in advance of our scheduled time.

I can remember practically nothing about our halt in the

364

darkness at Wichita. On any long journey, one will be bored or sleepy or lazy somewhere, and the camera of the mind will stick, only one or two exposures being made in jerks instead of the usual number on a smoothly running spool.

I know that Brill pulled another beautiful landing out of his bag, and I recollect leaning on the railings of the covered gangway and talking to him about the future of express sleeper planes. But that is all. I did not go into the reception hall of the airport.

We took off at 7.50 p.m., which was probably dead on the scheduled time of 7.48 p.m., for two minutes at least would have been occupied by a short taxi into position and the subsequent running-up of each motor. And later, I was to learn from a duplicate "Flight Plan" that we had averaged 192 m.p.h. for the 295 miles from Amarillo. But, as I say, these are only rough prints of the few mental snapshots taken between the time I saw the lighted field coming up and the time when it dropped away again.

Similarly, the next short stage of 178 miles to Kansas City was notable only for some fine effects caused by distant lightning. We were skirting a storm which fortunately was moving along some way off, so that we did not have to alter course or height for it. Here, I distinctly remember thinking what an original picture, and how representative of modern times, could subsequently be painted by an artist who took the trouble to make sketches and colour notes in a passenger plane lit up by lightning. The elliptical interior with a long narrow gangway between the metal chairs, the dark figures slumped in attitudes of sleep, the yellow glow of an occasional reading lamp illuminating an interested or anxious face peering out at the suddenly apparent cloud shapes, the brilliant magnesium-like light outlined in the rounded windows and striking sharp black shadows on either side of its paths athwart the cabin; these would combine to make a vivid work

365

of art such as I do not think the school of aeronautical painting has yet produced.

I enjoyed our approach to Kansas City. Here were the first American buildings of any height that I had seen from the air after dark. The city, itself, formed a bright parade of electricity visible for miles. And as the plane, with flaps in action, came muttering slowly down towards the aerodrome, several tall cubes and squares detached themselves from the ruck of houses and rose to their feet like challenging pickets clad in closely spaced checks of twinkling windows; all these being symmetrical but having no apparent connection with their invisible support or with each other. We landed exactly on time at 9 p.m., having come from Wichita at 189 m.p.h.

Here, on the concrete, I said good-bye to Brill and Boqua. This was the end of their beat. The plane would now be taken over by Mr. Smiley, who had Mr. Ross with him as co-pilot; they would fly us on through the night to Newark, the New Jersey airport outside New York. So for a moment I was alone and could prop myself comfortably with a shoulder against an angle of the main building near the entrance, while I sucked a pipe (most welcome after being restricted to cigarettes in the machine) and kept a somewhat somnolent eye upon events.

A small crowd of interested spectators stood a few yards away, grouped behind the railings. They were thickly clad in heavy overcoats and scarves, and had presumably been there some time. I had noticed a smaller number when we left Amarillo just over three hours ago in the gloaming. In such towns as had an airport, it was apparently the custom to drive out there in the evenings, or after supper, and spend an hour watching the arrival and departure of the big ships; in just the same way that I had seen cowboys in lonely parts of the West stroll across from the local saloon to the railway station

366

to stare at the train. But by force of circumstances these were more sophisticated folk. They would never think of standing on the platform at Kansas City to watch trains. It was aeroplanes that interested them. And in a few years, it would be for the most part only their children who would want to watch even these. Among grown-ups, the airline ships would then be providing amusement for marooned cattlemen.

I heard an announcement that Flight No. 12, for Chicago, was then loading; and would passengers kindly take their seats. At once, an orderly hustle ensued. What looked like a complete plane-load of people walked briskly forward and up the four steps into the fuselage of another Douglas, standing ahead of ours. The door was shut behind them.

This machine, the 9 p.m. plane from Kansas City to Chicago, took off in the beam of a miniature searchlight. I stood watching the onlookers return to normal. The tense, eager expression worn by most of them would suddenly relax. Singly, or in twos and threes, they would lower their heads again until, in place of the rows of upward gazing faces, pale in the bright glare from the arc lamps, one saw only noses and chins below the black shadows cast by their owners' hats. Cigars, cigarettes, or gum popped back into some of the rows of variously shaped mouths between the noses and chins. With the slick promptitude of automatic machines, various remarks popped out.

"Waal, they're sure on time—these ships."

"You've said it."

This from two unidentified voices.

A girl on my right chimed in meditatively: "Swell, I guess," she remarked.

"I'll say they are," replied her escort.

Then a woman turned to leave, but her companion stopped her: "Here, waita minute, wai-t a minute," he said, "this other ship's gotta go yet."

"O.K. then."

"I'd sure like to be goin' in her."

"I know it."

"Jake, I'm cold."

"Aw, nuts, honey; it's not cold."

"But I AM cold."

"Then will ya have a cup o' cawfee?"

He kept looking apprehensively over his shoulder as they made for the airport building.

Among the group, I had noticed a boy who ought to have been in bed. Now he piped up, tugging at his father's sleeve.

"Say, dad, what kind of a ship is that old biplane outside the hangar over there?"

"I guess it's a private ship, son."

"What's it doing here, da-ad?"

"Search me. But it looks like two cents alongside these Douglasses."

"Yeah," the little fellow agreed, "it's lousy."

One of my fellow passengers came up to me. He was a business executive of sorts, a charming, well-educated person. We had started together right from the door of the Ambassador Hotel, Los Angeles, that morning.

"Guess I'll have to say good-bye," he remarked.

"Oh, really," said I. "I'm sorry. I understood you were going as far as St. Louis."

He grinned ruefully. "I was," he replied, "but they tell me they're not landing there to-night on account o' fog, so I reckon I'll stop off here."

"You mean for the night?" I inquired.

"Well," he observed, "I just can't seem to figure that out: I promised to see my old mother, who lives in St. Louis, and if I take a train I'll be there in the morning anyway; but I kind of thought I'd have a proper night in bed at an hotel here and catch a plane bright and early."

368

"It's up to you," said I, "but at this time of the year fog hangs about a bit. You may be out bright and early, but the field at St. Louis may still be shut in; in which case the answer's a lemon."

"That's so," he agreed. "I guess I'll take the train. Anyway, it's been a wonderful trip as far as here, and I'm real pleased to have met you."

He held out his hand.

"Good-bye," I said. "I've much enjoyed meeting you, too."

Which, indeed, I had.

He made a smiling gesture of farewell, pushed his way through the swinging glass doors into the reception hall, and was gone. He belonged to a nice type in a country generous of nice types, and I was sorry to see the last of him. More especially because in the conversations that I had held with him at odd moments during the day, he had betrayed a real interest in aviation and its future, and had asked me a lot of questions that I strove to answer to the best of my ability.

He, himself, afforded an excellent example of the help that air transport is to busy men.

While hurriedly eating my luncheon in the morning, during an interval out of the pilot's cockpit, he had told me, I remembered, that he was just completing a round of important conferences which would have taken him at least a week longer, had he travelled by any other method.

He had flown west by United Air Lines overnight to San Francisco, washed, changed and started his first conference at eleven in the morning. In the afternoon, he had attended a second, and followed it by a good night in bed. United's first plane next morning had enabled him to meet his colleagues in Los Angeles at ten. He had then gone on to San Diego, dined with other associates and conferred all the third day with them before returning by the evening plane to Los

Angeles. On the fourth morning, he had left with me for St. Louis, where he would only be a matter of a few hours late by reason of the fog—itself quite unavoidable. I could well believe him when he talked of having saved a week; it might well have been eight or nine days. Moreover, taking into account the cost of all the meals for which he would have had to pay on the trains day by day, and his tips for the same period, the airlines fares would add up to very little more in the long run. And by saving a week of his time at head-quarters, he would probably more than make up for the total travelling expenditure.

Seeing Mr. Smiley go past to take his place at the wheel of our Douglas, I strolled after him. And by the time our remaining passengers—eight, I think, or nine—were shepherded in, I had parked myself comfortably; this time with my chair well tilted back by means of the lever-operated locking apparatus that held it at any desired angle. By missing out St. Louis, our next stop would be Indianapolis, the best part of five hundred miles away, and I intended to sleep if I could. Finding a rug placed ready in the rack above my head, I now succumbed to its allure, for no other reason than the psychological one that I find it easier to sleep covered up than uncovered. I was certainly not uncomfortably cold or hot at any time throughout the whole flight, though the conditions outside varied from warm Californian sunshine to the ice-forming murk of a late October night in the east.

I observed that there was a general desire for sleep. Most people were tucking themselves up and adopting comfortable postures. It was here, too, that I noticed the advent of a sour-faced female of uncertain age, who was being settled in with admirable solicitude by Mr. Ross. Nothing seemed quite right to her, and I did not envy him his job. Like myself, I think he would definitely have preferred to put a real sweetie to bye-bye. Catching each other's eye, we exchanged quick

370

smiles. I thought then that a co-pilot's job with T. W. A. must have its lighter side when, as frequently happens, a glamorous star of Hollywood's motion-picture colony is journeying to or from another triumph. But with the engagement of stewardesses by the Line, that particular glory has since departed from Israel; and now co-pilots mostly sit where they ought to sit, at their set of dual controls, with their radio earphones on a nearby hook—a distinctly modern improvement, after all, upon the old time lot of exiles, sojourning by the waters of affliction, with their musical instruments hung on adjacent trees.

I had with me an eye covering, like a mask without holes, but having shaped padding along its lower edge except where it actually rested on the bridge of the nose. Fastened behind by a piece of elastic, one of these sleeping masks can be raised or lowered like a mask worn at a fancy dress ball; and its soft padding entirely excludes any light without the necessity for a tight fit. Such devices are in fairly common usage in the States, but I know of very few people in England who have them. In fact, I cannot recall ever having seen one for sale there, although, doubtless, they are to be had if one knows where to look for them. Mine was of American origin, but I had had it some time. It proved to be of the greatest use on this particular trip.

We took off at 9.34 p.m. unless my watch was lying. We had actually been due away at 9.24, and I imagined we had overstayed our time because we were not going to stop at St. Louis. A glance at the schedule by the light of my reading lamp confirmed this: normally, we would have arrived at St. Louis at 10.49 p.m. and left at 10.59. Switching out the lamp, I watched the orderly glitter of Kansas City disappear behind us. I had been moved across to the front seat on the right hand side of the cabin, so as to rest undisturbed by the periodic opening and shutting of the door into the pilot's

371

cockpit. My last impression on looking out was of the exhaust manifold of the starboard motor glowing redly in the gap between the motor's cowling and its streamlined fairing. Then I donned my sleeping mask and lay back.

Still, sleep was not to come my way for a while. Soon I heard an unmistakable hissing all round the machine—the impact of snowflakes encountered at speed. It was a sound known to me since 1920 when, in my early days of flying in a dual control Avro, my unauthorised instructor had force-landed me near Bristol in a blizzard. I had last heard it with disgust in a land-plane over the middle of the North Sea in 1934. But to-night I didn't care a damn. In a warm, up-to-date airliner, flying over country studded with flashing beacons and emergency landing fields, and beautifully piloted by first-class men with a radio signal sounding in their ears, or a calm informative voice telling them what changes, if any, to expect in the weather, there was nothing except the immutable risks of mortal life to care a damn about. And reason demands a complete disregard of the latter, as being the line of least resistance where all resistance is useless.

So I sat up to peer out, interested for a moment. Then inwardly smiling with satisfaction at the comfort of present day aeroplanes and in anticipation of still more comfortable journeys in future years, I readjusted my mask and reclined again; twisting entirely sideways in my chair. And this time I slept like a child, not waking until a change of engine-note penetrated to my inner consciousness, and I drowsily rose up to see the lighted aerodrome of Indianapolis.

Smiley or Ross, I forget which, told me on landing that we had got into the snow at 10,000 feet and that it had lasted for seventy-five miles. It was very dense and caused so much static interference that they could scarcely hear the radio beacon. Coming down to 6,000 feet to get out of it, we had encountered heavy rain for quite a time. I had been asleep by then and did not hear it. But what with snow, rain and ground fog at St. Louis, it seemed to have the makings of a dirty night.

Despite it all, we had come the 459 miles from Kansas City at 204 m.p.h. We were therefore a quarter of an hour early and had that extra amount of time to wait, making twenty-five minutes in all. But fortunately it was now fine. I was able to stroll up and down smoking my pipe, without getting either cold or wet. A cup of coffee would have been very welcome, but would later have made me sleepless. So, knowing that I would probably be tempted to have one if I went into the brightly lit *café*, I stayed outside.

Even at that late hour—it was ten minutes after midnight —I counted half a dozen spectators. They had seen us arrive, and while I stood there they were rewarded by the sight of another plane leaving: a Boeing belonging to another airline. As at Kansas City, a searchlight kept the departing machine in sight until it was well clear. I, too, was greatly impressed. To see these American airports in action all through the night is tangible evidence of the huge strides made in recent years by civil aviation. Jules Verne, had he been there, would have gone home to bed a happy man. Later, these six muffled watchers would see us take off again. After which, for their own sakes, I hoped they also would betake themselves homeward; to sleep if not to concoct a yarn, called, "A thousand leagues up in the stratosphere."

Only two of my fellow passengers had emerged with me to sample the midnight air. And they also repaired again to the dark-looking doorway in the ship's shining belly as soon as they saw preparations being made for getting under way once more.

We left at 12.34 a.m., a minute early. On this occasion, I felt like taking precious little interest in the backward sliding view of any aerodrome or town, however prettily

373

lighted. Instead, I masked myself forthwith like the burglar of tradition, and slumbered without interruption until the plane, after missing out Columbus, slowed up to land at Pittsburg. We touched down there at 2.29 a.m. by my watch, or about an hour later according to the difference between Mountain Time and Central Time, for which I had to make a correction. Our hop had been 341 miles and our average speed 202 m.p.h.

For the sixth time, I descended from the Douglas, but now to find the atmosphere chill and slightly misty. There was something forsaken, too, about the appearance of the aerodrome offices. Through the glass double doors I saw lights gleaming in the hall, and also from the windows of a *café* on the right. But nobody met us, those of us who got out of the plane; we just trooped into the place behind Ross, the co-pilot. And needless to say, there were no spectators at this early hour on such a morning. I shivered, and was glad when the doors swung shut behind me.

Immediately upon landing, Ross had warned us that we would be held there (at Pittsburg) for some time on account of the prevalence of ice-forming conditions. Apparently, the fog had become deeper and more widespread the farther east we had flown. And it was bitterly cold, the temperature having dropped to a dangerous degree. We were told that the delay would be at least two hours. But later, it became a question of remaining indefinitely; in fact, until the weather experts could satisfy the dispatcher that it was safe for us to proceed.

When the statement was first issued the dissatisfied woman in our midst had straightway shown signs of running true to type.

"I reckon it's disgraceful," I overheard her saying to Ross.

Her expression led me to suspect that she gave highballs a miss in favour of vinegar and soda. She sat muttering and

374

shrugging disapprovingly in her chair like an angry-looking image on a spring.

Said I in disgust to Ross when we had got out, "There is only one cure. T.W.A. should keep old two-seaters for you, with open cockpits. Then you could take such idiots for a ride; promising for the reputation of the Line to try and get them through to their destinations at all costs in a special machine. Five minutes' hedge-hopping in a freezing mist would be enough for the likes of her. You could say it was too bad after all, and put in two crazy circuits before landing; yelling at her down the speaking tube, 'Hang on, madam, it's all right. I think we'll get down safely. Hang on, I say—in case we hit something.' Then you could land like a scared kangaroo, and her husband, if she has one, would bless your name because she mightn't utter for weeks."

Ross chuckled. "Something like that would fix her," he agreed.

Then we went together into the *café*, where we found Smiley, the chief pilot, and another of the passengers perched on stools in front of the counter. The latter, by his talk, was a more than commonly useful golfer: names of partners or opponents like Hagen fell from his lips like peas from a pod. On the subject of that game I kept mine shut, being in the main as uncertain of the destination of a ball as I am painstaking in my various methods of addressing it with the different clubs I have, which all look so nice. But he was a pleasant person; very cheery in spite of the hour, the place and the fog; and I was glad to listen to him.

Meanwhile, I ordered a fried egg sandwich on rye bread and some coffee. To me, this was a new and happy experience in sandwiches. The young man behind the counter suggested it. He wore a flat, round white cap like an American sailor's, and was remarkably quick at cooking and adding up figures in his head. Only four of us had found our way indoors;

375

making six with the two pilots. The place, itself, was the most cheerful in the whole building, being bright and clean. The hiss of the cooking, too, was comforting. But even there, a sense of desertion persisted, caused by the little wilderness of empty tables to be circumnavigated before reaching the counter, and by the steam on the windows which, if anything, accentuated the feeling of cold dreariness outside.

After eating, I visited the men's rest room (grand name!). It was underground, if I remember rightly. One went there down some gloomy stone stairs. I found it depressingly untidy, and the water was cold; altogether not what passengers using Pittsburg airport in the small hours of an October morning would either appreciate or expect. With some idea of fetching my overcoat out of the Douglas, I wandered upstairs again. Ross met me in the hall, and asked whether I would like to sleep in the plane—the other passengers were doing so—or first see the operations room. I chose the latter.

There, I talked to him and a be-spectacled radio operator for half an hour or so. There was very little going on in the narrow room, with its switchboard behind a desk-like barrier at one end. The operator told me that all the liners in the fog-affected area had been put down safely and were being held at various fields pending better reports. I heard him transmit a couple of times to other bureaux. The time was now about 4.45 a.m. Ross kindly went through with me the contents of a T.W.A. pilot's satchel. Then together we made out a duplicate "Flight Plan" for the two blocks we had flown since Kansas City. Afterwards, I sat reading a bundle of reports until a protracted fit of yawning sent me slouching sleepily across to the Douglas for forty winks.

The three other restless passengers had retired some time before and were now presumably asleep, like those who had remained from the first in their sloping chairs. I opened the door as quietly as I could and stepped into a frowst that nearly knocked me down. There were at least eight or ten heavily swathed and heavily breathing human beings in the cabin. The result can be imagined! Coming from outside, I found the air sour and vitiated. The windows were blurred over by films of condensation through which the glow from the aerodrome buildings, a few yards away, penetrated in the form of a cold twilight. An intermittent rattling snore emanated from the front of the cabin. I traced it to a blue-jowled individual, much burdened with adipose tissue, who occupied the chair across the gangway from mine.

"Gosh!" I thought, "he trumpets like an elephant." And my hopes of sleep received a momentary setback.

But the immediate task was to close the door. This I found difficult, being unfamiliar with the latch, or perhaps because the frame may have been a little strained. In any event, situated as it was in an unlighted alcove at the rear of the cabin, I could not see what I was doing and had to investigate solely by touch. If I tried to shut that infernal door once, I tried twenty times. At first, I was patient and persuasive. Gradually, I became critical and applied silent force. Finally, I attempted a little slam, a less modest slam, a definitely immodest slam and a grand slam. But still the door swung open, admitting volumes of cold air such as I knew the sleepers would not welcome, however good it might be for their respiratory organs.

I had an uneasy feeling that the cantankerous female would wake up and make remarks.

"If she says a word to me," I breathed silently, "there will be the devil's own row."

For, because I am one of those individuals who revolts from a scene more than from anything in the world, I have got quickly and bitingly angry when, on one or two rare occasions, I have been dragged into one.

377

"She will say this," I thought, "and I will say that. And the fat man will wake up and take her part, and I shall hit him—undoubtedly I shall hit him."

I even pondered over where to administer a knock-out so that he could not hit his head in falling; there were obvious difficulties connected with a free fight in an aeroplane. Still fumbling in the darkness, I was almost guilty of blaming my generous friend Donald Douglas.

"I will send him a wire to-morrow," I planned, "to say that his rotten doors won't shut."

Then the still, small voice of reason awoke within me. "Light a match, you clown," it said.

I did so, and shut the door at once.

Mercifully, the terrible old woman slumbered throughout like the mother of all pigs. I tiptoed past her; averting my eyes after one horrified glance at her bad-tempered face with its slack mouth wide open. Curiously enough, she was silent. Compared with the other stertorous inmates, she might have been dead, so still was she in the arms of Morpheus. Poor Morpheus! And if she passed away—well, it was entirely a private matter for her. By contrast, the fat man was now plunging gaily up and down the scale in imitation of a deep-toned saxaphone. But of the two, I preferred his appearance. And not even his nasal efforts could keep me awake when once I had ensconced myself under my rug. Masked and swaddled, I added my own quota of heavy breathing to the general chorus, and knew no more till Ross awoke us at a quarter to six. He announced that we would leave soon after seven and that the Line wished us to be its guests at breakfast.

"Thanks," said I, and made a bolt for the wide open spaces.

For the interior of the cabin now reminded me of a closely shuttered barrack room, if any colonel would permit such a thing; and there was a sweet, unhealthy taste in my mouth that only coffee could eradicate. I was the first into the *café*

378

for breakfast and the last to board the plane; having made merry with great quantities of ham and eggs.

This matter of having to sleep in an unventilated aeroplane really focused my criticisms of existing American airports. It is undeniably proper to keep a ship on the ground while weather such as we experienced persists. There is nothing else to do until the problem of de-icing is satisfactorily solved and machines can be landed on fog-ridden aerodromes by what amounts to automatic means. On the other hand, if the hold-up happens at night, provision ought to be made for the passengers to sleep in comfort. The unavoidable delay is inconvenient enough; there is no reason to add to it.

Without exception, I found American transport planes well ventilated while actually flying. Fresh air is forced through the various ducts by the movement of the machine itself, and the thermostatically controlled steam heating apparatus takes care of the temperature. But when the machine is stationary on the ground, these advantages no longer apply.

I have referred more than once to the lack of restful accommodation in the buildings themselves. That night at Pittsburg I looked into every room I could find open or lit. The only sofa which I discovered stood in a cold lobby. One person could have slept on it (presumably the cross-grained dame); and that left no chance of any one else sleeping anywhere else but in the parked Douglas. I felt that at those airports where it was not unknown for one or two plane-loads of passengers to be held for some hours by bad weather, there should at least have been two sitting-rooms, furnished with a number of settees or comfortable chairs, in which men and women could be segregated and allowed a chance of healthy sleep. And if these rooms were ground floor rooms, convenient of access, they would doubtless gratefully be used during the day by passengers with moments to spare in which

379

to glance at an illustrated magazine, or by their friends waiting to meet them.

A better plan, of course, would be the erection of rows of small cubicles; each with a narrow bed or couch, a basin with hot and cold water laid on, a wall mirror and some form of heating. Food apart, these are the bare necessities that our general way of living has taught us to expect, particularly in the United States. In my opinion, it is a mistake not to supply them even in an inexpensive form. Admittedly, the sitting-room idea is cheaper, because the rooms can be used in other ways during the day. But my complaint—no, I was so courteously treated that I should not complain at all—my suggestion, rather, is that I was unlucky in not finding such a sitting-room; although in every other conceivable way my wants were kindly provided for by the officials of the Line, and I thoroughly enjoyed my trip from start to finish.

Lester Gardner[1] favours the introduction of a truck carrying an air conditioning plant which can be connected up to the aeroplanes on the ground. This would mean that passengers in day-flying machines would find it cooler to stay in their seats than to get out during a twenty-minutes pause at an aerodrome in a hot climate, and those who found themselves sleeping in a plane at night could do so in pleasant conditions. Obviously, the truck would not be brought so close that the humming of the plant could keep any one awake.

Major Gardner goes even further and suggests the building of air-conditioned hangars where silence would prevail. His idea is that machines delayed at night should be taken straight into these quiet sidings, so to speak, and that passengers should have the alternative of staying in the cabin or of using portable dressing-rooms such as one sees placed near a set for the convenience of the more important film stars.

[1] Secretary of the Institute of the Aeronautical Sciences in America.

Such an arrangement strikes me as ideal, especially when combined with the use of proper sleeper planes fitted with upper and lower berths. Incidentally, American Air Lines have had such machines in commission for several months. These are Curtiss "Condors," and they have proved very popular. Also, Douglas's D.C.3. sleepers have now been out some time; and doubtless the other important manufacturers, such as Boeing, Lockheed, etc., are at work on the production of excellent machines with sleeping accommodation. So the task is being tackled with true American thoroughness. 1 expect to see evidence of a great advance in this connection when next I am flown between the Atlantic and Pacific seaboards.

We took off from Pittsburg at 7.19 a.m., an hour and nineteen minutes after we were due at Newark airport, New York. No one but the irritable madam was annoyed, however much they may have been inconvenienced. Within the limits of its existing resources, the Line had done its best to study our comfort. And our safety had certainly been assured; it would have been madness to have flown on through the early hours of that morning.

As we now rose from the aerodrome by daylight, I realised that at one end it was somewhat of a plateau. There the level ground suddenly ceased, a shallow valley taking its place, so that in the machine one had the impression of added height instantaneously gained. To a lesser extent, the same feeling is experienced when taking off in (I think) a north-easterly direction from Le Bourget, outside Paris. As we shot out across this sharp drop, an extraordinary sight met our eyes. Scores of little wooded knolls lay below, with a manufacturing area built over and round them. Their crests, the last refuges of trees against a creeping tide of brick, rose wanly above the mist until the whole country looked like a rolling sea of dark-capped waves. Factory chimneys, belching smoke in the valleys below the mist level, enhanced the effect. But they themselves were scarcely discernible, only the smoke traceable to them—other shadows, as it might be, in the troughs of the sea.

At about 5,000 feet, we topped the upper haze, and half an hour passed before we could again clearly see the ground.

When we did, it was to see a succession of ridges, clad sombrely with trees. But not with the junipers or scrub pines of New Mexico, Arizona or California; these were the forest trees of the east, maple, oak, ash and beech, which had shed their summer foliage and stood brown and hardy, braving the onslaught of winter.

One after another these ridges passed below, almost parallel in their ranks, each couple sheltering between them a chequered verdant hollow. Looking back as the Douglas flew over the last, I got the effect of the sun directly on them: they turned the true nut brown that timber country does in winter, a colour associated with the smell of wood smoke. Then line by line, they faded out of sight.

For a while, the land flattened and became dull—just the criss-cross pattern resulting from many agricultural activities on a small scale. Haze still hung about, so that in places the sun penetrated half-heartedly; but the cattle, black and dun specks in the meadows, were wandering forth to graze. Many miles ahead, the flatness was again interrupted by what I took to be the Alleghany Mountains, through which I had driven in September. Beyond them, low-lying fog, cloaking the far horizon, glittered like a mirage of the Atlantic Ocean which in reality would be about forty minutes farther on. By 8.24 a.m., we were above these rounded hills and crossing the Susquehanna, curving southward to its pow-wow with Chesapeake Bay.

But the fog spread everywhere in front. For twenty-one minutes, we descended gradually until we were rushing along

382

in a frustrated manner only a few hundred feet above a blanket of cotton wool. We wanted to get down at Camden, the aerodrome for Philadelphia, which was our next port of call. But the chances seemed irritatingly remote. Here and there, a clear patch had formed, yet almost as one watched the vapour would close in again. If there happened to be an opening when we arrived over the airport, we could get in; otherwise not. I have seldom seen conditions more aggravating to pilots and a ground office staff.

Where the fog was down, it was pretty close down and made no bones about it. The top few feet of factory chimneys actually stuck up above it. There, the ceiling could not have been more than 150 feet and the visibility below it three or four hundred yards at best. Then an open area would follow, as clear as could be, with the drops of moisture that coated everything sparkling in the sun. A maddening business! Through one such gap, I saw we were coming to another river, obviously the Delaware. But the derricks lining its farther bank at that point gave the impression of floating on the top of the fog. So things continued.

And so we continued; our flaps in action, our engines muttering on a reduced throttle opening. We were literally feeling our way along, directed from the ground. At 8.48, I saw our landing wheels extracted. It was then clear below, and I judged our height to be about 600 feet.

"We're going to make it," I thought.

But no, we again found ourselves over more fog. Then a clear lane showed itself to port, while to starboard all remained blank. Then the lane vanished, and once more there was nothing but fog. We accelerated for some seconds and slowed down again. I saw the ground through a wide hole some four hundred yards square and judged we were lower, possibly 400 feet. But the clear area was no use to us; it was in the wrong place, and was succeeded by as impenetrable a blanket as that obtaining farther back. At 8.55, Smiley must have been told to go on, for I noticed our wheels being retracted. We climbed away, accelerating rapidly.

The enthusiastic golfer was looking out behind me.

"Damn," he ejaculated with humorous resignation, "I wanted to get off there. And now, to make matters worse, we're flying right over my house."

"These things happen," I murmured sympathetically.

"I guess so," he grinned, and sank back in his chair.

Meanwhile, at about 3,000 feet, we were heading nor'-nor'-east across New Jersey, towards New York. Although Newark, its airport, was only a few minutes away at our pace, I knew the weather there must be clear enough for us to land or we would have been taken somewhere else. But at the moment, the same conditions persisted. Abandoning Philadelphia, there had been a remarkable moment as we passed over a scattered regiment of tall smokestacks, their tips just visible, sending up dusky spirals above the shining surface of the fog—one of those sudden sights that compensate a little for thoroughly unpleasant weather near the ground.

By 9.5, it was clear below. By looking back, the murk behind us could be seen for what it was: a layer of varying thickness, hanging above the trees and houses and rendering every feature beneath it cold and gloomy where it did not actually engulf them. Thus a bright, unhidden area of ground, with its green fields divided up by roads and fences, appeared by contrast to be bravely facing the encroachment of a broad glacier, destined as of old to hide the earth with many feet of ice. So realistic, and at the same time so fantastic, was the impression of this formation, that I never looked ahead again till I heard our motors throttled down. This was at 9.14.

At 9.15, our wheels were extracted once more. It was misty here, misty enough to prevent me seeing the high buildings of New York, now only just beyond Jersey City and over the Hudson River. But at least this was mist, not fog. We were at about 500 feet, and I began looking out this way and that for the airport. Then, noticing our descent steadily maintained, I realised we must be making a head-on approach and that there was no reason to circle; so I would not see the field until we were almost landing. We came whispering along through the thin vapour, across a piece of marshy ground, and were now not more than fifty feet up. Smiley gave the plane a short burst of engine. She accelerated and then started to sink again. Finally, I saw the aerodrome boundary sliding towards us. We touched, never bounced an inch, and rolled ahead on our wheels—so long impatient to make contact. The time was 9.20 a.m.

Thirty-five minutes later a comfortable T.W.A. car, having dropped every one else *en route*, deposited me at the Weylin Hotel on East 45th Street and Madison Avenue, New York. Unshaven and unwashed, I stood at the desk inquiring for my mail. The manager welcomed me back.

"You're a little late, are you not?" he inquired.

"A little," I replied. "In any event, I took the slow plane, and we were held up at Pittsburg early this morning with fog. But this time yesterday, I had only just started from California."

"It's a marvellous service, isn't it?" he observed.

"Yeah," said I, in my best American, "it's swell."

Then I stepped into an elevator and was whisked up to my room and a bath. And as I went, I blessed the speed and efficiency of public airlines in America.

CHAPTER V

THE PERSONAL EQUATION IN WORLD FLYING

AVIATION, NOW AN INTEGRAL PART OF WORLD TRANS-portation systems, whether organised for peace or war, remains the one whose ultimate destiny still defies accurate prophecy. It will not always do so, but up to date uncertainty about it persists.

The difference between it and the older forms of mechanical transport—railways, steamships and automobiles—is that of being ex-terrestial (in a conservative sense) although international good manners forbid its exponents to claim ex-territoriality either in flight or at rest. Where the other three are subject to set limits, terrestial or aquatic, and to local variations of those limits, this new form of transport is governed only by weather and the ingenuity of man: and as the latter continues its rapid growth, so the sometimes constrictive grasp of the former will be weakened until it no longer exercises any power over the free movement of air traffic. This state of affairs is much nearer than most people think.

The modern steam locomotive, if we consider its development period of more than a hundred years, is not radically different to Stevenson's "Rocket," which did 30 m.p.h. in 1829 and was by no means the first engine built by that remarkable man. Traction power and reliability naturally increased progressively, and so to a lesser extent did speed. But the block-to-block speed and comfort of trains only started to show a steep upward trend when the competition offered

" Aviation, now an integral part of world transportation systems. . . ."

[Photo by courtesy of T.W.A. Inc.

by road transport became threatening. And even now in some countries, including England, there are still too many wooden carriages in use, which results in the effects of an accident being rendered infinitely more terrible than would be the case if steel rolling stock was compulsory.

Generally speaking, the fastest trains in the world are not propelled by steam at all,[1] but by internal combustion motors, either Diesel or poppet-valve; and many derive their propulsive energy from electricity. Yet the steam locomotive remains in the van (i.e. the lead, not the guard's van) when one considers longevity and the ability to haul heavy loads over great distances at an adequate pace. But compared to big airlines, all railways are patently limited in scope by the extent of each country itself and by the character of their thousands of miles of permanent way, upon the condition of which their speed depends. More and more, as the lives of my own generation draw on, we shall see public demand (which influences economic conditions) confining the railways to comparatively short-haul work for passengers and long-haul work for heavy goods.

Similarly, the steamship companies stand to lose a certain proportion of passengers to airlines. Already they have lost many hundreds. The Croydon-Capetown (and Nigeria), Croydon-Karachi (and Antipodes and shortly Hong Kong), Croydon-Berlin (thence northward, eastward and southward), and the Croydon-Scandinavia and Croydon-Spain, the Paris-Saigon, Paris-Madagascar, Paris-Natal (in Brazil), the Amsterdam-Batavia, the Berlin-Buenos Aires and New York-Miami, San Francisco-Manilla (and shortly New Zealand) and

[1] The train with the fastest block-to-block speed is the Super-Chief on the Santa Fé railroad; it averages 83·7 m.p.h., hauled by a 3,600 h.p. Diesel locomotive. Nevertheless, there are isolated instances of steam locomotives attaining very high speeds (as high as 124·89 m.p.h. over a short distance); drawing a train with 100 passengers. This advance is mainly due to efficient stream-lining, and may lead to valuable developments. For the steam locomotive has still much to commend it.

the projected Southampton-New York; these and other air services are examples tending to sharp realisation of how the web's strands are being woven.

The world's air services flew 103,432,000 miles in 1934 alone. What they flew in 1935 has yet to be computed. True, the thousands of passengers now intermittently lost to the railways, and the lesser number lost to the steamship companies, constitute at present only a small proportion. But it is not going to remain small. Indeed, it is rapidly becoming larger. With the comparatively imminent conquest of weather conditions by meteorologists, wireless engineers, and specialists in aero-dynamics, it is going to become very great indeed in our lifetime.

Whereas trains are now only delayed rather than endangered by fog, and are stopped by nothing short of a landslide or a collapsed bridge; and aeroplanes are rapidly overcoming their one remaining obstacle, which is safely staying up or getting down in a certain kind of weather; ships are still held up by fog and seriously inconvenienced by storms, apart from being limited in range by conditions aquatic as trains and automobiles are limited by conditions terrestial.

Besides, they are slow. Thus consideration of these two handicaps, a proportional loss of passengers to aircraft and a definite limitation of range if not yet of speed, gives us some indication of the future trend of shipping.

For some years, and probably always, ships will continue to carry passengers who like the seclusion and sea air obtainable by no other means, those not in a hurry and those who wish to cruise for pleasure. They will also accommodate the small proportion who will never care to fly, in the same way that the airlines may attract, after an initial experience, those who now refuse to travel by sea.

They will still carry raw material, finished goods, coal, cattle and foodstuffs. They will still carry troops in the trooping seasons of peace, if not later in the frantic hustle of war; which God's inspiration forbid!

But they will lose, and lose soon, even more of the *de luxe* travellers who hurry, and then start to lose ordinary travellers; as airlines, becoming more widely established, reduce their fares below the *de luxe* rate for long overseas flights and institute a second class, now being considered, or even a "steerage."

Steamships, like locomotives, have progressed steadily rather than in a spectacular manner; a process traceable to some extent to their huge initial cost which can only be written off over a number of years of service. From the simultaneous invention of the screw propeller in 1836 by Francis Pettit Smith, an Englishman, and John Ericsson, a Swede, and of the compounding of steam in 1824 by James P. Allaire, an American, subsequently perfected on Clydeside by John Elder and incorporated for the first time in the *Brandon*, it is a far cry to the great *Bremen*, the smaller, no less excellent *Washington*, and the vast *Queen Mary* of the present day.

When we think that the power-weight ratio of early steamships was in excess of a ton per horse power, and is now a matter of pounds, we realise how far shipbuilding has advanced. But again it has been gradual—a matter of well over a hundred years. As in the case of trains, we have had to wait too long for safety devices to be adopted, such as twin, triple and quadruple screws, watertight bulkheads, adequate life-saving equipment, fire-proof fittings and paint, fire alarms, and so on.

Where automobiles are concerned, we have not had to wait so long for safety developments, although it has been long enough. Automobile accidents to-day are caused in nine hundred and ninety-nine instances out of a thousand by the human element, not the cars themselves. In England, there is no control of pedestrians and little of cyclists, who

389

are primarily responsible for a large number of accidents, though there are many careless drivers here as elsewhere; and in America, where pedestrians are more disciplined and the number of cyclists is negligible, a visitor like myself, having carefully observed a cross-section of the continent, may perhaps be pardoned for thinking that more recklessness and drunkenness persists among motorists, though the general standard of driving appears to be higher.

But many of the machines themselves—all-steel bodies, safety glass, good braking systems, blow-out proof tyres, etc., apart—are basically the same as in 1900. The engine is still in front—although originally underneath or behind—there is a roughly rectangular frame, a central gear-box, a long propeller shaft, front and rear axles—still too generally sprung by longitudinal leaf springs, and seats for two, four or seven passengers, some of which are in the most uncomfortable positions on the whole chassis.

With the exception of four-wheel brakes, adopted in a laggardly way some time after the war as a direct product of road-racing—the incubator for automobile improvements—and the now thirteen-year-old patenting of his type of independent front wheel springing by the Italian, Lancia, there have been until recently no radical changes in design. Improvements, yes; but changes, no.

Only during the last year or two, have we seen tubular backbones for chassis, or, more commonly, really stiff versions of the old frame; only then the forward mounting of engines by such firms as Chrysler and Ford, giving seating for all within the wheelbase; only then independent front wheel springing by Rolls-Royce, Packard, and others; only then roomy, vibration-free bodies with an aero-dynamic tendency —also by Chrysler; only then fool-proof gear-shifts in one form or another by most manufacturers, and so on. Only now, shown by Burney and led by Mercédes and Tatra, are

390

we thinking seriously of engines in the rear (the ultimate place for them; avoiding weight and frictional loss, and enabling a body to be designed primarily for passengers' comfort instead of as a mere adjunct to a chassis), or of independent suspension all round (essential in the full interests alike of safety, comfort and the most efficient transmission of power to the road wheels), or of the now reliable, quiet supercharger (not necessarily as an aid to speed, but to flexibility, acceleration and economy—the three essentials demanded of an engine to-day). And recently, the Auto-Union racing car has shown us that, even in a desperately light form, a combination of these virtues is safe on the road at 200 m.p.h. in the hands of the right men.

Yet, motoring has been quickest to develop except aviation. This is not surprising, because mechanical development is directly related to human ingenuity; and who would deny the remarkable growth of man's knowledge and ability since the start of the twentieth century? But what is motoring going to lose to aviation? Little, in my opinion. The passenger who goes by air will reach the aerodrome by bus (preferably by train to the field's private station) and will use an automobile at the other end of his flight. The rich man will drive to the air terminus and send his chauffeur back with the car; another will meet him when he lands.

Until there are many more aerodromes and air services, incidentally necessitating so strict a code of Air Ministry or Department of Commerce rules that what we have now will be child's play to them, the long distance bus will remain (and doubtless will always continue to accommodate the non-drivers who like motoring) and the local bus certainly will. The owner-pilot will have a car wherever he has a house (one has only to look at cheap road "transportation" now, and think!) and wherever else he is, he will hire or borrow one. No, motoring will not lose as much, if anything, to aviation

391

as will shipping companies and railroads. How much it ought to give back to the railroads in the form of heavy goods traffic, is another matter.

Aviation, then, is what we see to have been already the most prolific bearer of good things. The character of what it has yet to give us is still somewhat a matter for speculation. Having made more progress in fewer years than all the other means of transport put together, it is still in its infancy as regards development if adolescent in respect of reliability.

An infant prodigy! Its scope is so vast that the most experienced designers, realising that their scientific colleagues have many more surprises to spring on them—pieces of new knowledge to be dovetailed in with the results of their own researches—hesitate to set limits of usefulness or horror to what is already unsusceptible to terrestial boundaries. All they know is that they and their *confrères* are actively improving year by year the speediest forms of transport machinery ever known, and incidentally the first complete units of merchandise capable of being fetched or delivered in a more or less straight line from the factory door to the consumers' premises in any part of the World, without transportation charges other than their own fuel and (if delivered) ferry pilots' expenses.

This, in itself, is a telling thought apart from its commercial aspect. A nation at war, if one or more of its own aircraft factories had unluckily been bombed with some accuracy, could partially re-equip itself within a matter of hours, certainly of a few days, with aircraft built by a friendly neutral not subscribing to the League of Nations. A bomb-wrecked Britain could be succoured in this way by American ferry pilots safely using the North Atlantic route to bring Douglasses, Boeings, Martins and Curtisses. An anxious America repelling attack on her Pacific Coast by a nonmember of the League, I trust might equally hope for the arrival of Avros, Armstrongs and Bristols. And the point is that this could be done *now*.

Until we pause to consider these possibilities, some of us are apt not fully to realise the strides made in aviation. The British Empire and America, two vast communities controlled by those with a similar will for good and a common language, might do worse than store up such thoughts against a worse day which both pray to prevent.

With all due respect to that incredibly versatile and accomplished person, Leonardo da Vinci, whose treatise, the *Flight of Birds*, dates back to 1505, and who would almost certainly have got some apparatus into the air if he had had an engine, practical flying began in 1903 with the Wrights, Wilbur and Orville, two courageous, skilful and painstaking Americans. In 1908, Henri Farman and Louis Blériot made the first journeys of any length by air, the former covering seventeen miles, the latter some miles farther; and Graf von Zeppelin drove a dirigible for nearly four hundred miles.

Next year, Blériot flew the Channel, and my much-to-be-admired friend, John Moore-Brabazon, flew a circular mile on an all-British machine to win £1,000 and the honour of being the first Englishman to fly in England.

From 1903 to 1936 is not a far cry; thirty-one years; a bare generation. But it is a far cry from the Wright Brothers, to Jack Alcock and Whitten Brown, the Englishmen who first flew the Atlantic non-stop, to Lindbergh and Wiley Post, pilots with staggering records of courage and accomplishment, to Webster, Waghorn, and Boothman, successive and joint winners outright of the Schneider Trophy for England, to Agello, the brilliant Italian, present holder of the World's Air Speed Record at 440·67 m.p.h.; and it is a farther cry from the first touring aeroplane of Blériot's to the Douglasses, Bristols, Blochs, Heinkel 111's, Junkerses and Savoias of to-day, and to the flying-boats of Short Bros., Martin and Sikorsky.

This is where the great difference exists between aviation and other forms of transport. For, unlike them, modern aircraft bear little resemblance to their prototypes. Except conformably to the demands of the elementary dynamics of flight, the latest passenger planes of to-day bear no more resemblance to the Wright's machines of 1903 than do many animals to the lower types of life from which, through thousands upon thousands of years, they have evolved. And considering how recent is the boom in Civil Aviation, we have not had to wait so long for safety devices, for which the search is unceasing, although the standard already attained is high.

What has brought about this amazing advance? Why should aviation have so far outstripped its rivals in speed of development? One reason is obvious; that automobile engine development was in the early days the handmaid of aircraft engine development. Although the ways of the two types of motors have diverged, while still remaining in sight, aviation owed a big debt to the early petrol engines, originally designed for cars.

Another reason for the aeroplane's rapid advance is plainly that of romance—of adventure, which possesses an age-old appeal for man, especially if there is the likelihood of a pot of gold to be found where the rainbow ends. Engineers with skill and vision saw big profits to be made one day out of the latest mode of getting about. Men with courage and vision flew those weird contraptions. Women with more courage and, in those days, less widely admitted vision, went with them.

Such were the two mainsprings of aviation: available power units almost from the first, and foresight governed by commercial shrewdness.

The War of 1914–18 proved a brake. Manufacturers were forced to build at maximum output pressure the best of a few hurriedly-tried types; they could not give their minds to over-much experiment, so intense were the routine demands of keeping up supplies. Then came the false security of a muddled peace, followed by descents by nation after nation into the muddled depths of economic depression—the tragedies preceding bewildered attempts at readjustment.

But somehow, a few aircraft manufacturers held on, precariously sustained by vastly reduced Government orders. Some, to their everlasting credit, modified old war designs and tried to get Civil Aviation started, while patiently setting to work on a small scale at new designs. With the gradual return of part of the World to sense, the slow approach to some doubtful promise of a measure of prosperity, these firms were the first to raise their heads and straighten tired shoulders.

As the promise assumed a likelihood of fulfilment, other and newer firms joined them; making modest beginnings. And now that in recent years prosperity, although of a new order, lower scaled but more fairly apportioned as between man and man, has shown signs of being sustained and even of being increased, aviation has leapt forward like one of its own catapulted products. And none but the foolish attempt as yet to dogmatise upon the ultimate extent of its potentialities for good.

What is the reaction of people to aviation? This is the first part of a question of paramount importance to all who study World affairs with an eye not to dominance, but to wise domestic government and sane, cultured international recipro-city in the interests of civilising humanity at large.

In the long run, nothing in aviation is more interesting than the human aspect. And plainly aviation is not unique in this particular; for the general effect of any development, whatever the field under review, can be finally assessed only in terms of the benefits or otherwise which it affords mankind.

These, in common with advantages or disadvantages attendant upon the growth of knowledge and practice in other sciences which result in widespread customs, may only be stated in general terms during the course of a chapter. To examine them at the length they deserve calls obviously for a book, and an erudite one at that. Nevertheless, the broad tendencies are visible to all who have eyes to see, and so can be noted.

For instance, it is all very well to prate of the new outlook, the tolerance and broadmindedness brought about in thousands of minds by modern amenities of travel in cars and aeroplanes (I like the theory myself; there is a great deal in it; and I bore a lot of people with it), but many of us tend to disregard the physiological effects of this new rate of living, of assimilating ideas and surroundings, and of the constant strain of safely controlling fast-moving machines or merely being in them, upon what is after all only the second generation of those who have done so.

Yet, it is important to remember this side of motoring and flying, to keep track of it and obviate any ill-effects which can definitely be charged against it, because the psychology of a nation is directly affected by the physiological state of its people, quite apart from the inherent traits of their race.

In this connection, we may contemplate the fact that before the War, in the chief countries, most of the exciting, still somewhat new, pursuit called motoring was indulged in by the class from which leaders are usually drawn; and that Europe went up in flames. And also that most of the thrilling, still somewhat new, pursuit of flying is now done by the same classes in the same nations; and that Europe is once again uneasy.

From these phenomena, we may draw any conclusion we

like, or no conclusion at all, dismissing them, if we wish, as forming merely a far-fetched coincidence. And, in any event, I am not—as it might now appear—arguing against the petrol age, of which the beneficial fertility has far exceeded the ill-effects of its own growing pains and the labour of its birth.

All I suggest is that we should bear these quaint ideas in mind as being at least analogous to the fact that dogs, who have added five or six generations to their general evolution since cars appeared, now usually cross the road wisely, after looking, and for the most part accomplish it in safety, while human beings with barely two generations of motoring experience at their beck and call, are killed in thousands through their own crass stupidity and lack of adaptability.

Of the two most potent evils of our time, lack of clear thinking and an almost universal mistrust of frankness in official circles throughout the World, the first at least may in part be charged against increased speed in its general application, i.e. speed of communication, operation and transport. There is still a too general lag, not in physical ability to keep pace, but in mental organisation of our increasingly crowded days.

As for the second, it does not concern us for the purpose of this discussion, and we may dismiss it, probably not too inaccurately, with the thought that a generation of pre-War Pharisee politicians, who for far too long have stood in our temple and the temples of several of our neighbours, thanking God at each election that the electors are foolish enough to think of them as not as other men, have got to die before certain modern truths are openly admitted.

Returning to the former general epidemic of muddle-headedness due to the acceleration alike of movement and the presentation of new knowledge, I hope we are justified in optimistically assuming that it is, like most outbreaks of

397

disease, only transitory. What speed has induced, speed will eventually reduce. Or so I think.

So far as sheer bulk of plane usage is concerned a reply is found in the following figures (again, for conformity's sake, I must use those relating to 1934, although those for 1935 are now available):

Country	Passengers Carried
U.S.A.	561,370
Germany	165,846
France	50,019
Canada	103,531
Great Britain	135,100
Italy	40,930
Netherlands	57,339

In proportion to the total population of each country, its number of air passengers may not be considered high—if we except Canada, whose circumstances are peculiarly favourable to aviation owing to the difficulty of opening up distant parts of that Dominion by any other means. But remembering that this phase of transport in a public form is new, and that mass psychology among the middle-aged and elderly is its worst commercial enemy, the figures at once become remarkable and significant.

How proportionately greater they would have been but for the War, is an idle speculation. Probably their increase would have been huge. That they are now going to soar steadily is a prophecy which even a half-wit can safely make. For this growth, it is the function of Air Ministers, Departments of Commerce and the Airlines' propaganda bureaux to prepare.

The matter of mass psychology where flying is concerned needs analysis. From an economic standpoint it militates against airlines, as weather still does to some extent from an operating standpoint. Only propaganda will overcome it!

If Air Ministries and Departments of Commerce rightly insist upon certain rules making for the safe public use of aeroplanes as a method of transport, and if the airlines conforming to these rules, successfully achieve (as they do) a tremendously high percentage of scheduled flights safely and practically made, then surely the latter should take more trouble to let the public know it. I have constantly been struck by the general absence of good airline propaganda both in Europe and America.

Perhaps propaganda is the wrong word. One of the most enterprising and successful firms of advertising agents in London recently issued a *questionnaire* to its friends and clients, begging for their comments on the word "propaganda." Why it wanted the information I don't know; it was no business of mine to ask. But one of the directors told me that such terms as "lies," "lying" and "deliberate inaccuracies" characterised a large number of the replies.

This I regard as a hopeful sign of grace. People have not forgotten the deplorable flood of untruths in which the World War was waged; to the mental and moral bankruptcy of thousands who stayed at home and reading it daily or listened on Sundays to many of the "men of God!" ranting or intoning according to the occasion and the strength of their vocal chords, and invoking His wrath upon thousands of German, Austrian, Hungarian and Turkish men and women who were no more responsible for the war than I was.

In my ignorance, I used then to attend a smart London church, presided over by a "popular" preacher with the Union Jack hung up behind his pulpit. I was a boy and a patriot. Now I am a man and a father, and no less patriotic. But as long as I live I shall remember that church, that man and that smug congregation with a feeling of spiritual nausea.

And if people had forgotten the ghastly misrepresentation of 1914–18, they have been reminded by the spate of lying,[1] so obvious as to be farcical, that issued from Addis Ababa, the core of the plague-spot of Abyssinia, where some of the customs of the inhabitants are so disgusting as to leave no well-balanced person in doubt that if Italy had not succeeded in bringing there such civilised ways of living as most of us now share, then some other nation would eventually have had to do so—possibly, alas, ourselves.

We can regret, and regret sincerely, the methods Italy found it necessary to use, but in fairness we must remember that the dilatory and inept procedure of the League of Nations was, in the first instance, equally responsible for those forcible measures against a barbarous people.

Besides, we can condemn them only when we ourselves are prepared to remove our bomber squadrons from the North-West Frontier of India. And we are not prepared to do so. By a humane use of them, for restrained threats and the destruction of villages after repeated warnings to their guilty inmates, we do in fact preserve there a certain state of civilisation not otherwise possible at present. But we are not, as the Italians were, at war. Our bombing is "peace" bombing. What would we do against a general uprising?

Much as the apparent impracticability of a campaign of peaceful penetration on her part may be regretted, no one but

[1] By contrast, it is interesting to read the testimony of Dr. M. M. Moran, F.R.C.S., Eng., an Australian surgeon, who spent two months on the Italian Northern Front, and remained until after the battle of Lake Ashangi:

"Up till that time (April 1st) neither I nor any of the foreign journalists (English, American, French, German or Polish) had seen any evidence of the use of gas. We had seen prisoners, but none with signs of gas upon them; Abyssinian dead, but none with marks of gas burns. The use of gas, then, must have been extremely restricted. In any case, there seems no foundation whatever for the statement that thousands of women and children have been blinded by the use of this arm."

a fool wished to see a sanction-crushed and embittered Italy upsetting the balance of agreement and commerce in Europe; none but an idiot fails to recognise that what territory she has taken from the Abyssinians will be (indeed, it is already, as an unbiased American observer on the spot can testify) a better and happier place for the natives under her administration than under the recent primitive rule, or lack of it, during which slavery flourished, trade in infant eunuchs was a recognised profession, and the support of the "men of God!" was retained simply on account of a lip service to Christianity, induced originally by superstition and doubtless founded subsequently by Haile Selassie, upon politic regard for the hypocritical susceptibilities of the supporters of the League of Nations.

No, propaganda is the wrong word to use. I hope it goes out of fashion or assumes a cleaner meaning.

Let us talk of publicity. (And by publicity, I don't mean the understandable, open-window side of a film star's life (however nicely or indiscreetly the window is opened); nor do I mean the dying duck photographs and undignified terminological inexactitudes with which some English gentlewomen, through the advertising columns of the daily papers, advertise beauty parlour products to housemaids; nor do I mean the murder, sex and human-wreckage stories sniffed out for the American tabloid sheets, those venal outlaws of the world's press. I mean plain, honest publicity—the wide dissemination of *facts*. The airlines should concentrate on this.

Every one knows that even the reputable press will give more space to an aircraft accident than to a whole series of regular flights safely accomplished. This is natural. The accident is *news*—the case of the man biting the dog rather than the unexciting business of the dog biting the man.

But airlines must see to it that the magnificent record

401

possessed by most of them is better known to the public. Occasional, dignified editorial mention is not enough. If they cannot get more of it, written with greater enthusiasm, they must advertise like the railways and bus companies. They must circularise their public by means of leaflets. In the United States, they can use the radio. Do they? I hope so. I didn't happen to hear them. For Civil Aviation to be able to show such splendid statistics of millions of miles flown and thousands of passengers carried for each of their rare accidents, and *not* show them, is a great mistake.

How great a mistake it is, I discovered by chance; although I had always looked upon it as at least an error of judgment.

Shortly after my flight back from Los Angeles to New York in one of their Douglasses, Transcontinental and Western Air Inc. most kindly put a similar ship and two pilots at my disposal to take a party of my friends for a flight over New York from Newark. Thus I learned what types of people would fly, what types wouldn't; and why.

A number of my American friends do not live in New York at all; they are scattered up, down and across the continent. Of those who do live there, some couldn't and some wouldn't come. So the list of invitations had quickly to be extended to include my friends' friends as well. For fourteen seats, a preliminary list of thirty people was made. I do not remember all of them, nor what their respective professions were; but an example or two will suffice.

A wealthy man in his thirties, engaged in what is known as "big" business, would not come because his wife was afraid and he—although he had previously been up—had promised her not to fly again for a further period of four years, until flying was *safe*. French trains, and American steamers such as the *Morro Castle* were apparently all right—and, of course, no one is ever killed in an automobile!

A well-known banker and his wife refused; he because,

although the plane was to be flown by regular T.W.A. pilots, his insurance policy covered him only for definite scheduled flights along the proper airlines; she because he wasn't coming. There was no question of fear.

A motion-picture magnate and his wife also thought better of it. He, not having flown before, said frankly that he would sooner experience it for the first time alone, or almost alone, than with a big party—a sound reason readily understandable to all except the unimaginative clodhoppers of this life, who are often so wrongly described as brave. His wife, also without previous experience of flying, would have come with him but not without him.

There were a number of others who admittedly funked it, or made transparent excuses.

Not until one gets down to brass tacks with individuals on the personal question "to fly, or not to fly", is one sharply reminded that airlines in all countries are still confronted with immense buffers of prejudice; simply the result of ignorance and the garbled, bloodthirsty press accounts of creditably rare airline accidents. At present, America is probably the most air-minded of the nations where public transport is concerned.[1]

Spend much of your days with flying folk, or stay near an American air-route, and you will think Aviation has taken such a hold of the nation that it may be looked upon as a commonplace. True, you will see it still arousing interest, yet it is obviously the interest allied to enthusiasm rather than that aroused by something novel. But get among the millions, who, at the best of times, will only come to look on it as transportation, and you will soon discover that they are far from being convinced of its safety.

This ignorance is what the airlines must fight with sane,

[1] In America, 15,204 commercial and private pilots were under licence on July 1st, 1936. In Great Britain on May 31st, 1936, there were 4,559.

truthful publicity. In each country, there are certain newspapers upon whose editorial co-operation they can rely. Such stand out head and shoulders above their contemporaries and, on most topics, can be trusted to treat both sides of the case with fairness and restraint. Where Aviation is concerned, subject only to their praiseworthy desire to safeguard the public's safety, they do not as a rule condemn a crash before its causes are apparent or over-praise a useless if spectacular flight.

But in the common herd of newspapers, airline operators will be wise to buy their space and quote their own noteworthy facts. They know as well as I do that in no other way will they "put over" the truth. The temptation to make a "story" is too much for most feature-writers on the yellow papers, who are trained in the purveying of garbage in order to retain their jobs, poor devils.

I often think that when the newspaper files of this era are studied two hundred years hence by our successors—fortunately wood pulp products will probably not last as long— the general verdict will be that eighty per cent. of the World press in the post-European-war years did little but preserve old false doctrines, spread dangerous new half-truths, encourage vice and lying, foster cheap sensationalism, teach a low standard of morals and politics, and, in general, debauch the public mind. And when I gratefully remember how many able journalists I know, whose personal integrity is unquestionable, I am sorrier than ever that their combined influence is apparently not yet powerful enough to bring about neccessary reforms in the great profession to which they are proudly in thrall.

My final party in the Douglas consisted of twelve—seven women, including two middle-aged wives of business men, three younger New York society women, one unmarried and all workers, a Scottish *débutante* and an Indian princess;

404

and five men, including one elderly international banker, two stockbrokers, both past middle-age, a Canadian who had been a flying instructor in our Flying Corps during the war, and myself.

It was a tea-time party in November, so the visibility was not all that it might have been. But we had a smokily attractive view of New York which, for myself, was just the contrast I wanted; because my only other sight of it by air had been on a showery September morning when I had seen the city's famous skyline of giant buildings impressively clear and classically graceful against a sunny, rain-washed sky. Now I was pleased to see the skyscapers in their workaday garb, still graceful if a little dishevelled.

Several of the party had not previously been in an aeroplane. My friends and I had particularly wanted to take this chance of providing as many novices as possible with their first experience, for no passenger machine that I know is quieter or inspires more confidence than a Douglas. I put myself within talking distance of two of these initiates: a man and a woman.

It is admittedly hard for people, who have flown a lot, to shed the years and imagine themselves in the places of those who have never experienced it; especially when a big all-metal cabin monoplane is the medium provided, as opposed to the smaller, open cockpit conglomerations of wood and fabric, stayed with quantities of struts and wires, in which thousands of us were given flights or handled a joystick for the first time, while the whole outfit twanged and lumbered through the air propelled by a roaring, spluttering, oil-slinging rotary motor of somewhat uncertain habits. I recall, for instance, over sixteen years ago, a certain sparking plug that lazily struck work, parted company with its base, was flung through the engine cowling like a bullet and sang smack into a starboard strut, where it left a deep impression

405

of its fingerprints before descending earthwards towards an unsuspecting herd of cows. I was just seventeen, and it gave me the jitters.

But I know it is a help to talk to people. Politeness compels them to think up answers. And this takes their minds partially off the idea of leaving the ground far below, which, modern plane or not, is undoubtedly a trial of nerve.

In a very few minutes, our five novices had become sufficiently acclimatised to leave their seats and wander up and down the gangway like the rest of us, congregating in groups of two or three to discuss the marvellous overcast view of the harbour and downtown New York visible from the windows. All of them enjoyed their flight; only one showed a trace of nervousness when landing, not by her expression, which was admirably calm, but by the whiteness of her knuckles as her hands gripped the arms of her chair—a thing that those adjacent to her successfully affected not to notice.

This kind of scene is typical of novices quickly taking to the air as passengers. I have witnessed it in a number of countries and in respect of members of most European races and some Asiatic. Knowing, as I suppose I do, more of the few remaining dangers of well-conducted flying than, at any rate, many air travellers, I have no hesitation in saying that I would far sooner fly with a qualified airline pilot in an up-to-date machine in bad weather than go by train or pilot myself, and I would regard it as very much safer to do so than go by car unless I myself, or one of a few trusted cronies, was driving.

Mention of bad weather brings us to the question of how best to reassure air passengers as ships' officers humour those voyaging by sea. This, in my opinion, is important to the progress of Civil Aviation and should not be neglected. I can think at once of four instances during my journeys by

American airlines, in three of which some reassurance could with advantage have been given to passengers.

First: while flashes of distant lightning were illuminating the night sky between Wichita and Kansas City, I noticed a certain tenseness in the interest taken by those passengers who were awake.

Second: the hissing onset of snow in the darkness between Kansas City and Indianapolis—here I was the only one awake, and I knew what it was, but other passengers probably would not have known and might have been anxious.

Third: our fog-impeded attempt to land in the morning at Camden.

And fourth: a dirty approach to Newark at the conclusion of a flight from Washington, also by daylight.

The last instance is perhaps the most striking, not only because it was physically more uncomfortable for the passengers, but also because the swift change of surroundings was obviously not without its psychological effect upon them.

Eastern Airlines were bringing me up to New York in the latest of their three morning planes; the one leaving Washington at 10.30. Incidentally, there is a bad aerodrome, if you like. Beautifully situated in a living page of history beside the Potomac, with impressive glimpses of the Lincoln Memorial, the Washington Monument, the distant pearly dome of the Capitol, and, on a hill near by, of the Unknown Soldier's tomb and General Grant's tree-girt house, it is nevertheless as awkward a place for an airport as I have seen for some time. I cannot help thinking that its manifold disadvantages will not long be tolerated by such a nation of airmen, and that another site will be found or made.

We actually took off at 10.36 a.m., six minutes late—a matter of no consequence, for we would have a tail wind. The take-off was a grim business to me; and I do not suppose for a moment that the airline pilots appreciate having to do it there, or to land. That morning, the direction of the wind caused us to taxi back beside the river before turning for our run. We bumped over a road which crosses that end of the field, and proceeded as far as possible before turning into the wind. Greatly surprised, I tightened my belt and prepared for the father and mother of all bounces. But the chief pilot, poor fellow, to save his machine and passengers from such ghastly treatment, just managed to lug the big monoplane off the ground before reaching the road. How he must have loathed committing such a *bêtise*!—although he did it safely, which seems a contradictory statement to make.

The ship left the ground with what I can only describe as a sickening lurch, slow, heavy and unwilling. True, he had her nose level again as quick as a knife, and she remained air-borne, gathering speed before he put her into a normal climb. But I, like our Queen Victoria of glorious memory, was "not amused."

The less said about Washington airport the better. Washington itself, outlined by the limpid curves of the Potomac, did a lot to help me regain the composure, in fact the phlegm, which reasonably polite Britishers try like anything to assume in order not to disappoint some of their American friends, who expect it, and which I for one nearly always forget. The new buildings, clean white with red tiles, were standing up out of acres of older, dark brick, ranged beside a central crest of grey blocks and squares, the latter mellowed without by weather and within by the councils of famous men. In every street could be observed the softening effect of trees. Also, clouds dappled the city with their shadows.

It was a pretty morning. Near the ground, conditions were a trifle rough. But in twenty minutes, we had climbed above an intermittent layer of cumulus piled in Junoesque shapes: and above these siren phantasies, in brilliant sunshine, we rode smoothly and fast, towards the North,

"Washington itself . . . the new buildings . . . standing up out of acres of older dark brick . . . in every street . . . the softening effect of trees."

[Photo by courtesy of Eastern Air Lines

with streaks of cirrus stretching overhead to point our way like arrows.

Later, the cloud below changed in character. It became unbroken and sinister, a deep stratum extending downward for thousands of feet and terminating in grey tatters only a few hundred above a drearily damp and gloomy countryside; as a stained, sagging plaster ceiling, in imminent danger of entire collapse, drips relentlessly through bulging orifices upon the wet boards of a shuttered room. Through these millions of cubic yards of murk, we had to make our way down to Newark.

That we would get there was a foregone conclusion, for the pilots had the radio beam to guide them. They had only to follow the regular pinging of its oral instructions in the earphones. Even without the beam, I would have trusted men of their experience and high standard of training to bring us out pretty close to our destination.

But that, to me, was not the point: I was wondering how many of my fellow passengers knew enough about flying to harbour the comforting realisation that the risk of collision was remote. Did they understand that no other transport ship would be allowed to impinge on our course, plotted laterally and vertically? Again, in these days when so much exaggerated nonsense is talked about any one being able to learn "blind" flying, did they appreciate that only a double-dyed fool of a private owner would be up and charging about on a day like this; and that double-dyed fools don't last long in aeroplanes anyway?

I felt that they didn't know these things; that is, if I could judge by the expressions of anxiety displayed all round me when the illuminated notice flashed on, warning us to fasten our safety belts, and the plane shot down into swirling grey obscurity where it pitched and yawed in a manner gravely disconcerting to the ignorant. Men with hunched shoulders moved restlessly in their seats, looked out first one side and then the other, glanced across the cabin and then glued their noses again to the window next to them. They made praiseworthy efforts to appear unconcerned, to read their newspapers. But no sooner did they pick them up, their nervous hands rustling the sheets, than they let them fall again on to their knees and resumed their endless watching. Others openly clung to the arms of their chairs and put the best face on it that they could.

As on the T.W.A. airline at that time, no "hostess" or stewardess was carried. The Eastern Airlines' co-pilot, presumably busy assisting his chief, was too occupied to leave his seat and come back into the main cabin with a cheery word of assurance, that the prevailing conditions would not last long, and a reminder that the plane was in touch with Newark, where an adequate ceiling prevailed for landing. I did what I could without being obtrusive, being able to say something appropriate (I forget what) to the passengers immediately in front and behind, and, across the gangway, to the one opposite.

We emerged all right over New Jersey, and within sight of Newark, where we were beautifully landed, thanks to the same skill which had kept us out of trouble leaving Washington. Had this not been the case, I might not be writing this book. But it should not, I felt, have been necessary for me, an Englishman, to attempt to reassure Americans travelling in their own country. Perhaps, after all, it wasn't.

Still, I could not help feeling that on this, as on two of the three previous occasions I have quoted, means should have been devised—in fact, should have been already in existence—to ease the minds of passengers, to keep them reminded of the actual measures taken for their safety, and to inform them, within reason, of the actual state of the weather ahead and the estimated duration of the discomfort they were undergoing.

Now, no doubt, a stewardess does it. But I am not sure that even thus the psychological need is adequately supplied. To see a junior servant of the line summoned to the cockpit whence she soon returns as the bearer of comforting tidings, may satisfy some passengers without satisfying all. There will frequently be those whose imagination will lead them to "smell a rat," to suspect a deeper significance of underlying what is obviously collaboration.

Myself, I would prefer to see the installation of a microphone in the cockpit, connected with suitably-mounted loud-speakers in the cabin, through which at such times (and only at such times, for general comments would be a nuisance to all concerned) the chief pilot, so announcing himself, could issue such reassurance and information, as, in his judgment, seemed fit.

Some arrangement of this nature appears to me to be a paramount need in the proper conduct of public air services. Such services, subsidised or not, draw revenue from the public. They will draw increased revenue, and so develop more quickly, if they pay closer attention to the physical comfort of passengers on the ground and their psychological well-being in the air. It is of great importance to the peace of the World that airlines should develop rapidly, and one of their chief means for doing so is an intensification of sane, truthful publicity at all times, even in the air.

These ideas mainly concern the passenger members of the public. Now, to attempt to answer the second part of our question, "What is the reaction of people to aviation?" we must briefly consider the pilot members of the public, i.e. those who actually fly themselves but for the purposes of this discussion are not professional airline pilots.

Severe is the strain of initiation which falls, mostly, on the

411

present generation. For a young man or woman to put down the early morning teacup in London, reach for the telephone, order the plane to be checked over, drive ten or twenty miles in thirty minutes to the aerodrome after breakfast, have an early luncheon at Lyon and a not too late dinner in Rome, is outwardly nothing unusual to-day. But inwardly, in the mind of that boy or girl, almost a revolution took place the first time he, or she, did it. And on each succeeding flight of the same sort, a minor upheaval resulted.

This they would hotly deny; having probably felt nothing but physical fatigue. Yet, older people, not by reason of any superior intelligence, but purely because of experience which provides a more accurate assessment of knowledge, would know that it was true.

Think what such a flight means: arrangements, purchases, customs formalities in two languages apart from their own, or at any rate in the difficult broken English version of those languages; assimilation of weather reports and their implication; map-reading and the nuisances attached to it; navigation of quite a respectable degree of efficiency if the weather is tricky; an eye for country; a sense for the vagaries of the air; and several hours of incessant noise, still abnormal compared with those associated with life on the ground and intensified in effect by the subconscious waiting for a change in it portending mechanical failure.

All this almost indefinable strain of pilotage is augmented by a host of impressions of different places, peoples, scenic effects and the thoughts occasioned by them, crowded into one day instead of their father's two days and a night of eating, drinking, sleeping, and browsing in a George Eliot novel while in the train, or their grandfather's three weeks in a two-horse barouche reading Tacitus on his knee, with her ladyship beside him sniffing smelling salts, and the children sitting meekly on travelling hassocks at his feet.

412

This is a great change, and it has taken place very quickly. Young people who travel like this to-day get valuable impressions at first hand, I grant you, and more of them. But instead of analysing them at the end of the flight, they dine and dance at a night club, sleep late next morning and then equally hurriedly conduct their business or take their pleasure—all except a few. Speed of travel is just at that awkward stage when places that young people want to visit can be reached in a day. But it is still a hard day; and it leaves no time for the reading of history or the close study that their ancestors gave to current World affairs. And this is a pity, for it has been said truthfully by one Patrick Henry, "I know of no way of judging of the future, but by the past."

Such a statement is horribly accurate where mass psychology is concerned. So is it any wonder that the younger generation in Europe do not seem to be approaching mutual appreciation rapidly enough, or that they misunderstand, or are in turn misunderstood by, an older generation which, though a small proportion of it may use the air, does so as leisurely passengers, content to browse now among the pages of Hardy or Galsworthy, and oblivious to the crowded, tense minds of the younger folk in whose piloting it places a trust that it refuses to bestow in everyday affairs?

Some of us will live to see speed of travel advance to the stage where places can be reached in a day to which there is little point in going, except purely for pleasure, because the men living in those places are, by reason of their familiarity with them, more capable of dealing with local problems of statesmanship and business than any hasty visitor. Those same men will come to headquarters for a leisurely conference and then return to put through the policy agreed upon, thus relieving the strain upon their superiors with whom the ultimate decision rests.

By then the hearts of countries nearer to us, places like

Rome, Berlin, Warsaw, Lisbon, will be a matter of an hour or two away instead of several hours. Even Washington will be a matter of a day. And, eventually, there will be no need for faster work or travel, and people will have time in which to think and read and get to know those they meet.

In England, we are just starting to visualise this so far as Paris and Berlin are concerned. Flights by really fast machines to those places are now reckoned, for all intents and purposes, in minutes. No air-minded person thinks of allotting a day to reaching them. Such trips are merely incidents before or after a summer day's work, like catching an electric train to Brighton; and soon a winter's day, even in our hemisphere, will be furnished with similar abilities—bad weather or not.

And so it looks like going on: an increasingly rapid development of speed that will eventually obviate the need (a kind of lust) for crowding three days' journey into one. Speed, itself, implanted this urge in our consciousness when first we began to travel really fast. The convenience of more than one mode of modern transport is due to it, so that we cannot condemn it out of hand as do people with a solely pedestrian outlook. Yet, for some time to come we must not neglect to include its effect on modern minds when we consider the future of private pilots.

Now, who are the private pilots? To my way of thinking, the class subdivides itself into three categories: the paid pilot, the owner pilot and the hiring pilot. And I place them in what is likely to be their general order of skill.

The first class is barely in existence yet, only a very few examples being known, although there are probably more in America. Nevertheless, it is a class which is bound to grow; and the rate of its growth will be contingent upon the passing away of a generation of rich men and women who do not care for flying, and their succession by middle-aged sons and daughters who do.

414

"Speed, itself, implanted this urge in our consciousness when first we began to travel really fast."
[*Photo by courtesy of Eastern Air Lines*]

These may themselves be pilots but have tired of it, or do not wish to take over control except occasionally on a fine day. Or they may not be able to fly at all: the point is immaterial. But what they will bring into fashion is the air-yacht, although that is possibly a wrong term to use, because aeroplanes of the size which they will keep for such a purpose cost a fraction of what a yacht providing similar travelling comfort would involve. At any rate, call the machines what you will, it is the captains of these aeroplanes, large or small, fast or comparatively slow, who will form the paid pilot class to which I refer.

Only the narrowest line can be drawn at present between these and professional pilots of the big transcontinental airlines used by the public. The same qualifications which govern selection of the latter should, and probably do, although unofficially, influence the engagement of the former. Both types must be "B" licence pilots with sound records, possessors of a ground engineer's certificate, up to a certain standard as wireless operators, and preferably holders of a second-class navigator's ticket—here, obviously, I write of qualifications obtaining in the British Empire.

Such men are worth, at a minimum, several hundred pounds a year in salary—and deservedly worth it. Senior pilots on the European services get more.[1] And why not? Their training has been long, arduous and expensive. It is the exception to find a pilot of real repute who has not the backing of a sound secondary school education; which I contend he needs. And apart from the qualifications listed above, this effectually disposes of the parallel that I have heard thoughtless people draw between the paid pilot of the future and the chauffeur of to-day.

General education is making at least some headway. And

---

[1] U.S. Transport pilots get from $2,500 to $9,000, i.e. from approximate, £500 to £1,850. British pilots get much the same.

we can be grateful, mainly because upon education and not upon brittle pacts rests the future security of civilisation as we must try to guide it. Consequently, the chauffeur's son of to-day may well be the paid pilot of to-morrow—an advance in the standard of work and living that all would welcome who have the interests of humanity at heart.

Moreover, by then, public service aircraft will be more truly the liners to which they are now prematurely likened, so that the commanding and flying of them will call for more division of responsibility and perhaps even higher individual qualifications among their officers than is the case to-day; and the gap between professional pilots and paid pilots—if such a distinction can still be made—will have widened to that which now divides the skipper of a steam yacht and the captain of a vessel like the *Normandie*.

The future for this new class of paid pilots is crammed with possibilities. Men are needed for it who, in addition to their qualifications as airmen, have the character to become *persona grata* with the officials of foreign aerodromes throughout the world and the *savoir faire* to deal successfully with an air-sick employer, his nervous wife, two overjoyed children, an hysterical lady's maid and the family Pekinese; in fact, to be a first-class *courier*, and a guide, counsellor and friend to those who will be willing to pay him for his valuable services a monthly cheque just ten times bigger than his father's ever was.

Were I a successful chauffeur or a clerk in small circumstances, I would do all in my power to encourage air-mindedness in a son and get him employed at an aerodrome, in however humble a capacity, just as soon as he completed his time at a secondary school. With the help of night-classes, the goodwill that is proverbial among flying folk, and his own keenness and wits (if any), he would stand in these days an increasingly sporting chance of becoming eventually a paid pilot. For quite a heavy demand for such men will be, I believe, a feature of aeronautical development during the next ten or fifteen years.

The owner pilot and the hiring pilot are types more familiar to us at present. Because the aspirations of these two classes are probably similar, differing only in degree, they can usefully be considered simultaneously. If anything, it is logical to suppose that owner pilots are likely to be more practised performers; they can fly when they like and are presumably better able to finance greater activity. But there are naturally exceptions: men who have flown a lot at one time and find themselves no longer able to afford their own plane—these, at any rate for a time, will remain more skilful than many owner pilots. So it is hard at present to consider owner pilots and hiring pilots as separate classes.

There are no really large numbers of people flying themselves. And even when that time arrives, the distinction may not be possible, depending directly, as it does, upon the development of the easy-to-fly machine, which we will touch upon in a moment. If I venture a personal opinion at all upon this point, it is that the distinction will be drawn, as it is now, between owner-drivers and those who hire a car at week-ends during the summer months.

The latter are certainly not as practised as their fellow motorists who drive regularly throughout the year. And in flying, as we still know it, practice means a lot, because mistakes of judgment which lead to a mild collision in a car still have a habit of turning into something grimly serious in an aeroplane, although this tendency will without doubt be greatly reduced. Thus the only distinctions we are justified in making now must apply both to owner and hiring pilots, and are the customary ones made between experience and inexperience, sense and the lack of it.

People who know nothing about flying are frequently

heard to say that it is easy. They quote as their authority somebody who has probably forgotten his novitiate as a pilot and is thinking merely of his later experience, which may genuinely have been without untoward incident. And so the statement gathers impetus; serving no doubt quite a useful purpose in getting a few hesitant people into the air, where their pride rightly urges them to persevere against the trials soon experienced: by which their characters and therefore the general tone of the country undoubtedly benefits. For this reason, it would be folly to condemn the "flying is easy" slogan altogether. Besides, it cannot be said to be untrue. Ease is a matter of degree, and it is upon this that individual opinions are at variance.

We know that a properly designed aeroplane, once in the air, is not difficult to keep straight or level or to fly in a series of gentle turns. But is landing so easy for all? Are there not many owner pilots who "pump-handle" their planes on to the ground—more of an arrival than landing?

And are there not several courageous, experienced and deservedly famous private pilots whose landings cannot be relied upon always to be good? To some, that particular form of three-dimensional judgment is easy; others never acquire it—to the same degree.

Why, if not because of this and many other reasons, should staid instructors, well versed in human nature, remind the cock-a-whoop pupil who has recently got an "A" licence that he, or she, is now just about ready to learn real flying and that only continued concentration and unremitting care will make him, or her, into a good pilot?

Frankly, we know it is because there are still difficulties to be overcome in learning to fly well as there are in learning to drive well; but with this difference—that the dangers attendant upon carelessness in the air are at present usually more grave than those resulting from foolishness on the road.

All this naturally points, as do most considerations affecting modern travel, to the importance of encouraging advance in design; which in turn opens up a huge subject, the ramifications of which spread far beyond the limit set to these remarks. All we can say now is that the safe flying of the light aeroplanes we know to-day calls for too much training, and too high a standard of serious-mindedness, for them ever to be used in huge numbers by the masses as distinct from those who have time to give to being properly taught. This is the only retarding influence that we can welcome in aviation. In fact, it is a blessing; for the domestic arrangements of the World are not suited yet to private ownership of aeroplanes on a scale analogous to that of automobiles.

Setting aside the expense, it is too much to expect that the average man and woman with a hard week's work behind them will devote the week-end to a pursuit involving definite difficulties at the outset and a certain intangible strain always, when the day and a half's rest they have earned can be given up to a more simple form of pleasure. Much water must flow under the bridges before they do.

There will probably always be an owner class and a hiring class of pilots. There will probably always be, as among motorists, the serious, far-travelling folk and the local potterers. Only the pottering area for us may one day come to include a lot of North-Western Europe, and for America the bulk of her Continent!

The serious aviators will probably not overlook the advisability of at least biennial refresher courses at Hamble (the English University of Aviation by the Solent) or some similar place. For the growth of aids to navigation, such as beam wireless, the knowledge that meteorology is giving us of how clouds form and how the air itself moves because of temperatures and the contours of the earth, and the facilities for flying blind through weather that hitherto has resulted in "pilots' days," is becoming so rapid now as almost to bewilder those who may have many other things to do as well as fly.

If, later, abridged refresher courses can also be put within the financial reach of potterers at their local aerodromes, much benefit will result; especially from the inclusion of lectures touching upon the recent history and current developments of countries that are signatories to the Air Convention. It is not really enough for a pilot to be able to reach a foreign aerodrome without losing himself or breaking a regulation. He is a better neighbour to the country he is visiting and a better citizen of his own, if he knows how to conduct himself while abroad and how to analyse impressions to give his family and friends upon his return.

That Civil Aviation ought to lead to a sounder understanding of each nation by the others has been said with some truth. And there can be few people so insular as not to hope that in a generation or two this may indeed prove to be the case.

Such a hope is founded largely on a trust in the intelligence, broadmindedness and integrity of the future pilots of the world and of inveterate air passengers. Where the telephone brought a voice instead of a letter, the aeroplane now brings a complete personality instead of a voice. Surely, it is one of the missions of our generation to ensure as far as we can that the effect of such rapid transport on the minds of those personalities, is an increasingly fruitful one rather than the merely barren stimulation resulting from general excitement.

That there will always be a purely sporting side to aviation, is beyond doubt. And it is welcome because of the good qualities of character that it encourages in addition to skilled flying. But we must not miss seeing the wood for the trees.

Fundamentally, modern Aviation is only the start of a revolutionary transport system which will put every country on the front lawn of every other. And that this may prove—as it should prove—eventually to be of immense benefit to mankind, bringing to the peoples of the world peace, neighbourly interest and increased leisure and happiness, is ultimately the chief responsibility of all who fly.

Finally, we must think of the future of transport in general; of how aviation, the newcomer, now extending its sphere of operations, can be fitted into the existing network of public services. Except where the airlines of one or more nations combine to provide long-distance services, and tend through this new form of commerce towards that reciprocity which is so essential to peace, each country has naturally to think for itself. And it is only on behalf of my own country, rather than America or any other, that I may venture to put forward a general suggestion.

I hope, for instance, that our Ministry of Transport is keeping an eye cocked heavenwards (delightful thought!); likewise that the Department of Shipping sometimes gives Davy Jones' locker a miss in its thoughts. Both these two steady-going institutions should not be so like little Johnny Head-in-Air, except where their own immediate provinces are concerned, that they may in fact—although head-in-air—miss what is going on in the sky; because the paths of hasty passengers and express freight already lie there, and will carry a quickly increasing volume in the future.

In the same way, I trust that the Civil Aviation authorities will not so clearly remember the Air Force motto *Per ardua ad astra* that they will forget to contemplate lowly happenings upon the earth.

Friendly and thoughtful *liaison* between shipping, railways, road transport companies and airlines (to place them in order of age) is essential on a broad scale if there is not to be overlapping and price-cutting—two elements that often combine to produce poorer service for the public on account of fine margins in everything, including safety, although they are generally supposed to result in a competitive standard of efficiency; which I think is something of a fallacy, depending, of course, upon one's idea of efficiency.

To perform this intermediary function, such government bodies are ideal; provided they select their best up-to-date minds for the job, and not too many of them. Nothing is more futile than a big committee of amateurs dealing with specialised subjects, or a small committee of specialists in their own subjects dealing with a general policy embracing others. The one-track mind is as dangerous as the no-track mind. We need a dozen men who know their own subject backwards, and have put in six months' intelligent work on acquiring an adequate mastery of the other three.

Nobody can do this thing better than the impartial British Government servant. Our Civil Service is a case in point. True, there exists to-day a real danger of it becoming so influential by reason of the manifold complications of modern government that we may well shout a warning and start the hare of "bureaucratic rule." But its influence is not malevolent, nor is it to any extent personal: Parliament, sensitive to reaction, ponderous in thought and prevaricating in execution, could solve the problem as and when it willed by giving its mind to it.

What matters for the purposes of this discussion, is that the standard of the individual in our Civil Service is high; I should say the highest in the world; and that in company with other government services its motto might well be that of a Prince of Wales: *Ich Dien*—I serve.

Who then, could better advise how to dispose of anachronistic incongruities in the public transport services, or more fairly hold the scales of justice between one service and another? The companies themselves cannot be expected to do it.

Not unnaturally, they are biased. The business instinct is strong in all enterprising merchants. Besides, commerce is a hard master and shareholders temperamental mistresses. No, the various government departments concerned with all forms of transport are the people who should plan the trend of events they cannot foresee, and if necessary seek to alter those apparent to them.

In the interests of the country, and of the Empire as a whole, their function should be to help old-established companies up the hill of protecting their investors' capital and at the same time give new companies a loose rein. They should arrange as far as possible that old and new are driven singly or in double harness by their boards of directors, but do not cut across one another to cause a financial accident.

Forethought of this kind is of paramount importance to us all as citizens, which is the first consideration. Quantities of our savings are bound up in transport, in the form of investments in railroads, steamship companies, automobile and aircraft plants, and in the ancillary manufactures that serve them. The collective efficiency of the Empire's trade routes in peace or war is also directly affected by these considerations of transport.

Finally, descending to our purely domestic viewpoint of them as motorists, which is of importance although to a minor degree as compared with the others, we do not want to be dangerously crowded on the roads by passengers or goods properly belonging to the railways or the airlines.

To distinguish between the various classes of traffic may be thought difficult. I do not minimise those difficulties. But that to overcome them is thought necessary and that the task is recognised as not insuperable, is instanced by the comparatively recent appointment of Traffic Commissioners. This is a start in the right direction, if only a start.

The theory of "planning," as such, is often lightly condemned. The failure, or partial failure, of some (not all) of the boosted Russian and American large-scale plans is responsible for this. Besides, we cannot forget our own initial encounters with "marketing" boards. Going farther back, the Versailles treaty stands (or rather falls) as a monument to the unjust interpretation of an international kind of plan. And the dangerous pass to which a well-intentioned, not always ineffective but generally unpractically constituted, League of Nations has since brought us, serves to remind us, so far as world planning is concerned, that the march of true civilisation, in which we once played the wisest part—and will again—is better served by forthright statesmen, common-sense civil servants, and blunt soldier-administrators than by a host of clerkly sentimentalists presided over by unrealist or merely unmoral doctrinaires.

And yet, so interdependent are nations, trades and even individuals in this highly involved world of ours, that the need for limited planning becomes more clearly defined every year. Not one of us can afford to ignore it.

I often think of these particular problems of transport as I drive along the roads. One has only to see a train in the distance upon a viaduct, or an aeroplane cutting across above the horizon seen through the windscreen, to be reminded of them. Then, perhaps, one starts to count motor trucks and long-distance buses, and to wonder how much of that traffic could equitably, and in the interests of national efficiency, be returned to the railroads, and how much is going to become, and should become, air-borne in our generation.

The same problem exists in the United States, as indeed it does throughout the world. But the American version of it is different. Theirs is more analogous to the Russian, Chinese and South American versions, or to those which Canada, Australia, India and South Africa are facing as Dominions. Excluding their share of international airlines, Americans' great distances are within their own country. Our greatest are within a scattered Empire. Thus the need for developing airlines that are both fast and reliable has been brought home to them earlier than to us, because it is more of a domestic problem which they are meeting. Their aircraft are general purpose aircraft, for their weather conditions are as varied as those obtaining in our Empire. Likewise, I have the impression (possibly wrongly) that because their secondary roads are not as good as ours, because the area to be served is so vast, heavy goods remain to a proportionately greater extent on the railways.

The nerve centre of their territorial possession is not a little overcrowded island like ours, where road and rail are almost on top of each other and a big percentage of the winter weather is bad flying weather, thus rendering more difficult the economic development of internal airlines already handicapped by the short distances to be covered.

No! Ours is a hard problem in Great Britain. To overcome it, we must plan for it. We must view all forms of transport with a sympathetic, a truly patriotic eye; just as we recognise that we are all pedestrians as well as motorists, and that some of us are cyclists. And to a greater or lesser extent, the same applies to all nations. Planning was needed to produce aviation. Aviation on a large scale has arrived. Details apart, the need to plan its general use remains.

EPILOGUE

EPILOGUE

A Pause and a Departure

NEW YORK LAY SULTRY UNDER A HIGH CEILING OF DULL CLOUD when I returned from the West. Stepping out of the plane at its eastern terminus, I had hoped for crisp, bright Autumn weather when once the morning fog had dispersed —something that would be a bracing contrast to the rich languor of the Californian sun, something with a kick in it like a good cocktail. But it was not to be, either that day or for several days afterwards. I found my friends in New York sweltering; the men still in their Summer suits, the women, faithful fatalists of fashion, grinning and bearing the latest Autumn modes, but all surprised and victims of lassitude.

"For goodness' sake!" they'd say, "there hasn't been a Fall like this in years. The weather's gotten all wrong."

Then they would proceed to tell me how New York usually was around then; how the sun shone and there was a hint of Winter in the air, making every one feel grand after the torrid Summer months, and that it was lovely to take sharp walks in Central Park. And I would agree that it must be nice and would mop my brow with my third handkerchief for the day and surreptitiously edge nearer to the window, open upon an overcast street where the temperature was over eighty, and accept yet another highball, clinking with ice, which later would make me perspire even more than I was doing at the moment. But it was fun to point out that in England we would all be rushing about red-faced and hearty, in our overcoats, and billycock hats, and the girls peeping entrancingly

429

over their furs or high stylish collars; until some one would retaliate by innocently asking how one could tell an entrancing girl from a red-faced man in a chronic fog, and cap it with some disgraceful exaggeration about leaving a hotel in Piccadilly one evening to buy a box of candy and not being able to find the way back.

"Go on," I jeered, "say our policemen are just too cute and one of them brought home Momma's little angel."

Whereupon, there was nearly a free-for-all fight.

Still, it was a rum time for the best part of a week. I never thought to be writing in my shirt sleeves by an open window in New York in November, and sleeping under nothing more than a sheet, and with the central heating turned off.

I had once more ensconced myself in the same unpretentiously comfortable bedroom at the Weylin, which is immediately flanked only by low buildings to the north, so that my view was unimpaired and I got what benefit there was to be had from any movement of the air. A new night club was in process of decoration down below on the other side of the street, but it was not open until a few nights before I left in December. And even then, the additional late night traffic proved no obstacle to sleep; largely because I, myself, was often in some other night club, and, when I wasn't, was sleeping the sleep of one who has visited several and means in the next few nights to visit several more—in open acknowledgment of the platitude that one of the joys of work is the subsequent joy of relaxation.

Except that relaxation is the wrong word! Any spasmodic whirl of gaiety may be a change, a welcome change, but in New York of all places it results rather in violent stimulation. Many visitors comment on the astonishing regenerative powers of the place, which I was inclined at first to underestimate. Still, it is undeniable that one can do more there, and get away with it, than in most cities. In an age when even the rate of change of absorption of electrical currents by sick persons is under investigation by ultra short-wave diathermy as a possible aid to diagnosis, and certain variations in rhythm are noted as caused by cerebral eccentricities, and reverses of electrical flow as resulting from the difference between consciousness and unconsciousness, it would be interesting to obtain data revealing the extra amount of energy available to the average person when in an atmosphere such as prevails at certain seasons on Manhattan Island as compared with those of more relaxing places. The hours of sleep needed to keep in good health are obviously less.

When the unnatural humidity had passed, the air began again to exert its tonic properties. Night became day with astonishing ease and frequency, inducing only a minimum of fatigue at the time. To the Persian Room or Jack and Charlie's, the Rainbow Room, El Morocco or to a number of other pleasant haunts, we went three or four nights a week in merry parties of anything from two to a dozen; especially to El Morocco, which then topped the pinnacle of popularity and perhaps still does. But for real relaxation, there were, as elsewhere, the quieter restaurants: the Continental with its excellent violinist, the little French restaurant over which old Jean—a sound judge of wine—presides, an Austrian place of which I forget the name . . . indeed, there are scores between 50th and 70th streets alone. And nearly four miles away along the East River water-front, down by Wall Street, in a rather rough and ready eating house where the floors slope crazily and a smell of fish rises from the cobbles outside, a friend and I leisurely ate plain broiled lobsters, slightly burnt and quite delicious, washed down by cheap Chablis brought to us by a huge old negro waiter, secure in his old-world courtesy. His name was Bob. He bowed gravely as I said good-bye to him, and his great black paw entirely engulfed mine.

"You come again, Saar," he said softly and smiled. "Jes' ask fo' me—fo' Bob. Goo'-bye, Saar; and ah thank yuh."

I had odd meals in many places in New York, but I do not remember enjoying myself more than on that occasion. One week-end, when all my closest friends were away, and I had refused an invitation to Virginia on account of work, I took what exercise I could by driving down on Sunday to this part of the city, where I dismissed my taxi and explored on foot before walking back.

There is, of course, little difference to be sensed between the business quarter of one city and another on week-days. It is only when Sunday leaves them deserted, and one is oneself almost the solitary intruder on their privacy, that they can be appreciated architecturally and for the individual or national conceptions which they reveal. Wall Street, humming with activity, criss-crossed by hordes of hurrying business men and women all through the week, and Wall Street empty and silent on a Sunday, present entirely two different faces. But it is the features in repose that give a truer inkling of the city's character. The old dark, church at the head of this canyon of masonry is in itself symbolic of how sterile and withered is ecclesiastical leadership to-day throughout the world; and by its own fault. When it recognises the beam in its own eye—and some of the braver, more outspoken clerics are now openly admitting this impediment—a great day will dawn for humanity. The vast creaking machinery of organised religion, intrinsically unsound ever since the Council of Nicea in 325 A.D., will cease grinding out old-fashioned unwanted information, inaccurately framed, and will speed up to the production and distribution of unbiased precepts, more acceptable by reason of being cut with the tools of scientific fact and having upon them the polish of modern realism.

In any event, we originally owe our humanitarian principles of conduct, the sanest code of morals, and much of a like sort, to great pagan philosophers such as Socrates, Plato, Aristotle, Cicero and others (pagan they were, but it is not the term of reproach that the foolish think it!). True, the modern adaption of those principles for better or for worse, is mainly in the hands of warm-hearted, well-meaning men and women who doubtless profess the Christian faith without much that is accurate about its origins—sound enough in so far as they appertain to what is authentic in the ineffably fine example of the Jewish carpenter's son, but which is anyhow a minute part of organised Christianity, now wealthy, almost commercial, and hopelessly out of touch with the needs of the multitude to-day. So each of the churches, outwardly convinced of infallibility, still points a different path to their jointly symbolical heaven, and only when pinned down to hard facts of history are some of their representatives honest enough to admit being "a stranger in these parts."

An intellectual poltroon, preaching in the old way, would doubtless cling to the usual anchorage and liken the mighty office buildings of New York to the forces of evil, against which the gallant little church is fighting the good fight of Christian soldiers. Yet, we know that there is undoubtedly as much good as evil done in office buildings, and almost certainly more genuine Christian soldiers occupy them than shelter behind the pretensions of any church or cringe from the world in monasteries.

In the matter of time, the Chinese as moderately competent astronomers in 2449 B.C. and the Egyptians writing a little on surgery 5,000 years ago and excellently on mathematics 4,000 years ago, are merely the students of yesterday. And for the rest, the worship of natural phenomena such as the sun, to which each religion has owed something, was nothing if not a primitive instinct gratefully or fearfully to acknowledge the conscious blessings of light and warmth.

433

Then came a little knowledge and with it the birth of superstition. Now great knowledge comes apace and before it superstition, ritual and dogma daily retreat. Knowing much, we are becoming simple again. But instead of worship at the dictates of emotions, many of us seek with due humility to know more of the Cosmic Intelligence in Nature, and in mankind as part of Nature. This is the nearest that any of us at present can get to understanding God, for only the ignorant and innocent may feel closer, or the hypocritical claim and preach such knowledge. This is the God who, I consider, promises us eternal life, because I cannot conceive anything so out of conformity with Nature as the complete cessation of any human mind. This is the God whom many of us try, haltingly no doubt, to approach in our work, and in difficult moments when our duty of personal responsibility will carry us no further, with an inner reliance wherever we are.

Many now find great inspiration and a satisfying grace in the New York skyscrapers, and in the swift planes to be seen racing across the sky above them. Both are undeniable testimony to the courage, intelligence and will for achievement inherent in man, direct materialisations of his God-given power to discover and create. One day, religious leaders in greater numbers will cease carping at progressive knowledge, will seize it with both hands and turn it to good account in the function which they themselves should help to perform for our world—that of the sieve letting through good, however new-fangled, and restraining evil, between which they frequently fail to distinguish at present; and the world will greatly benefit. Either the churches will do this or die. A now largely sophisticated and partially educated public is done with Parish Pump interpretations of Genesis, the revelation of John and all the mumbo jumbo that priestcraft has built on Scriptures of undoubted beauty but strictly limited practical value.

Where the business quarter of Manhattan Island differs from similar districts of other cities is in the proximity, the close juxtaposition of its important edifices with the sea. This is magnificent. Stand on the edge of the Battery to look out past the Statue of Liberty towards the Atlantic, and you would think no city existed for miles. A salt-laden breeze causes you to clutch your hat, and there is a sense of invigoration and at times of peace. But turn round, and at once you feel almost pushed into the harbour by the most enterprising feats of building in the world. And no more than two minutes distant on your feet is Wall Street, the financial hub of America. Until you visit offices high up in these immense pinnacles, you do not realise how quiet they are, how the noise of traffic seldom reaches them, or how fresh is the air outside.

Then, back up the East river, you will come upon quiet old-fashioned houses like those in Beekman Place. Yet—just round a corner or two, and almost shoulder to shoulder with them, there are slums. By contrast, a brisk twenty minutes walk will take you right across the island through the thick of the traffic, over the busy thoroughfares and the fashionable ones like Park, Madison, Fifth and Sixth avenues and Broadway, to the docks. Go into the Bronx district, and you will encounter almost another race and to all intents and purposes another language—the accent productive of such gems as "toid avenue and toidy toid street"—which corresponds, I suppose, to our genuine Cockney. Or drive up to Audubon at night and walk back, as I did, through Harlem; which also will be something new. I patrolled several streets before any one would talk to me. The groups of negroes drew together lowering their voices as I approached. When at length a half-caste girl summoned up courage to accost me, I discovered why. She explained that they had thought I might be a

435

detective. Many of the New York detectives were Irish, and she said I looked Irish.

Leaning against a street corner and chain-smoking cigarette after cigarette, we talked for maybe an hour; and she told me freely a lot which is neither here nor there. Among other things, she confessed to a preference for white men when they were nice, because they were often gentler, more understanding than black men: but when they were wrong 'uns, they would steal her money if they could and hit her. What was so pathetic was her surprise that I should bother to talk to her like a human being and give her, for no apparent reason, a few dollars and the remainder of my cigarettes. Still, she quickly threw that off and laughingly said she would sooner have earned them.

Then her face grew dull again and her voice bitter. It was hard, she continued, to be half-white and half-coloured. Her own folk, the negroes, were always a bit suspicious of her, and many of the white would have nothing to do with her as soon as they knew she had negro blood.

"D'you tell them?" I inquired, surprised.

"Yes, if they're nice," she replied simply. "Then it's on the level."

Her honesty would have shamed many people I know, for whom life has been a bed of roses.

She was equally frank in admitting to a not infrequent enjoyment of her way of life.

"After all, if a fella's good to a girl . . . well, it's nice to be nice to some one who's nice to you, isn't it?"

Her fine dark eyes, the whites of them slightly yellow, looked up somewhat beseechingly. She had really rather a delicate face, oval shaped and with the level tint of old ivory. Her lips were full, sensuous but kindly in expression. Only her hair, jet black and with a faint crinkle in it visible on the side of her head exposed by a hat saucily tilted, would have suggested to a close observer that here might be a dual personality, consciously, unhappily at war with her two selves and suspicious of the attitude of others towards her. In this particular case, character seemed to be winning out by sheer good nature, anæthsetised from too much mental torture by the blunting effect of a preponderant physical instinct.

"Back of our minds," I responded, "we never really forget any one outstandingly nice . . . there's always an inner gratitude." But as I spoke, I realised the complete inadequacy of any such short reply to what she had said. My words sounded lame in my own ears, and I hoped that she wouldn't notice.

"I've tried to hold jobs," she went on. "But some men try to take advantage of girls like us. We're looked upon as coloured if we're found out, see; although we're not really. But they know we'd sooner not be with real coloured folk and do most anything rather than be fired and go back to Harlem. I had a good position down town, but the boss got to know about me and wanted me to sleep with him. So I quit."

"Yet, you're doing this," I interposed quietly.

"Well, it's different, see," she explained, "men just chase us mulatto girls any place, and this way I can pick and choose . . . he was just a swine, I guess."

A silence fell between us.

"Maybe," she added hopefully, "I'll meet a fella' who'll understand and not care. Then we could get married. I've saved a bit and I swear I'd make a good wife to a nice guy who was lonely and liked me."

"Of course you would," I reassured her. "But try to let it be a man with blood like your own."

She looked up again, without any resentment. "Sure," she agreed, "I'm not out for more trouble."

When we parted, she shook hands rather convulsively.

437

But I knew our conversation had made me feel more helpless then she. Walking back to the Weylin, I noticed none of the lights, none of the sights. I kept seeing her face—the hurt, nervous look in her eyes, kept hearing the pathos in her remark; ". . . it's nice to be nice to some one who's nice to you. . . . "

Heaven knows, the colour question in any country needs a book to itself: a courageous book. And still more it needs courageous action. In no case do the sins of the fathers and mothers react so hardly unto the third and fourth generation as upon the children of mixed unions. The fact that some white men like coloured women and some white women like coloured men, is not negatived by being taboo as an item for discussion in polite society where greater *finesse* in talking scandal is preferred. Nor will intimate association between widely differing races be stopped in our time except by a form of compulsion, itself unworkable in some instances. If and when it does cease, it will be because of education—a state-inspired dissemination of the facts of ethnology. But at least preliminary steps might be taken (and are infinitely desirable on all grounds) to penalise very heavily those responsible for the birth of a half-caste.

At present, it is the world in general which unfairly penalises the half-castes themselves.

The fact that this girl was a not altogether unwilling prostitute, does not absolve her parents of one whit of their responsibility for her life-long curse. Indeed, it has nothing to do with it; it only points another finger at the ridiculous ideas on the subject prevalent in the minds of the self-righteous in most countries. I seem to remember being taught as a boy that King David (a most uncivilised person), was a good man who stood well with the heavenly authorities. To-day, we would dub him something of an old reprobate, whose hobbies were obviously fornication and the writing of psalms which we

438

have since been forced to learn. And the ex-Emperor of Abyssinia, who signally failed to rule Ethiopia while his barbarous Amharas ravished the indigenous tribes,[1] is held to be descended, so the newspapers tell us, from a racial mis-alliance and arranged *affaire* between Solomon (another fast liver) and the Queen of Sheba. Doffing our rose-coloured spectacles, we see attachment to the old sentiments to be supremely hypocritical in the light of modern knowledge.

Likewise, when every man and woman is living in stream-lined vita-glass houses incorporating submarine and aero-plane properties, and feeding on sustenance pills and with their sex instincts evolved, or devolved, to test-tube birth in a laboratory, then and then only will prostitution, professional or amateur, cease to exist. Meanwhile, to dis-courage it by educational methods as much as temperate police action, is doubtless the best means of keeping it within bounds; but to be brutal about it is to take a grave responsi-bility. And to fail to provide medical centres where such persons can go, protected by medical etiquette and undogged by the thought of police observation, is a crime against humanity. For no one has ever yet put paid to the account of the oldest profession in the world, and to hound its practitioners like vermin is only to drive them deeper underground and prob-ably to increase the incidence of disease.

The police may rightly protect the strolling public from being too openly or frequently importuned, but should not the severest penalties be reserved for those who actually pass on diseases known to be a scourge? It always seems to me a little hard that the woman of the street or the hotel lounge, though many pay her court in private, should her-

[1] The Galla Arussi, the Wallama, the Kafa and the Kimira under-went more than one massacre, and had their cattle taken: The Chara and Naos have practically all been sold into slavery, and the Burgi, two hundred thousand strong in 1895, now number about fifteen thousand.

439

self pay so bitterly and publicly in open court, while notorious courtesans of society, whether simply affectionate or in receipt of money for their dress bills, should be addressed as madam by the constable on patrol duty who has recently heard from their smirking butlers the names of their latest admirers. The difference is simply that of opportunity for selecting and soliciting, and tact in making the approach. For if the latter did it openly, they too would sometimes be arrested. And it is common knowledge among the thoughtful that although the law does not distinguish, as cracked-brained critics say it does, between the rich and the poor, the rich (because they are well known) usually get the worst of it in England.

This is neither a plea for the first sort, for whom honest men in thousands would privately if not publicly seek sympathetic consideration at all times, nor yet a condemnation of the second, whose anonymity all chivalrous admirers would rightly study to preserve. It is merely a re-statement of age-old facts, coupled with a hearty damning of Pharisees of both sexes. Ladies of easy virtue have often done as much, if not more, good than harm—from royal favourites, like Nell Gwyn, founder (among other generous works) of Chelsea Hospital, down to those who comforted lonely drunks shortly to return to the trenches. If they have a chance to return to a better mode of life, should we not make it easy? If temperament and economic circumstances force them to cling to their present careers, should we make it harder for them than it is already?

To license prostitution, is abhorrent, except for certain native tribes in which such practices are still officially recognised by ourselves and for whom any white woman must therefore be put out of reach, because she belongs to the more evolved race now ruling. Prostitutes are human beings, not cattle. But subject always to an unobtrusive guardianship of the public health and surface morals, let us above all be kind to those whose shortcomings, admittedly regrettable, are at least natural and understandable.

It is for loathesome perversion that we should reserve our particular hate. It seems to flourish in waves, and the world and its wife are far too apt to treat it as a joke. Severe penalties, social ostracism and exile are our weapons—none, I venture to think, sufficiently used—and in its incipient stages, at whatever age, a sound horse-whipping would almost certainly prove more efficacious than the psycho-analysis of the sloppy school which holds that these deplorable creatures can't help it. For vice is one thing, and indeterminacy of sex another. Victims of the latter, now becoming surprisingly common, deserve and receive the sympathetic assistance of the medical profession.

Apart from what I have previously recounted, in itself implying enough, I saw little evidence of the colour problem, undoubtedly fierce in America. I did not go far enough south to encounter strong feeling, and so I cannot write of it. Without exception, all the negroes who waited upon me were well-behaved and some delightful. Travelling out to Long Island one night by train to stay with a friend, near Jericho, I saw my only two tipsy ones; a man and a woman. Drink had made them hilarious and childlike, but coarse. They kissed rapturously from time to time, whereupon the woman would drop her lighted cigarette and the man leap rowdily to his feet and laughingly search for it. Then they would settle down again, she with her head on his shoulder; and presently they would start giggling again. Now and again, the man would introduce her in a general way to the occupants of the carriage at large—a long carriage, like those on our Metropolitan railway.

"Meet ma honey," he would announce proudly, "she's ma

441

sweetheart." And turning to her—"Ah, yuh sweet black bitch, yuh!"

Another cheerful guffaw. And another hug.

Their fellow passengers, mainly business men, commuting, took it in excellent part.

"But unfortunately," I thought to myself, "it is not infrequently a case, in the *cafés* of the negro quarters, of 'you sweet white bitch, you,' and doubtless the passengers wouldn't consider that (as they'd say) so hot."

But every one, even three or four women commuters, probably stenographers, were thoroughly amused by these two immensely cheerful negroes. They became quite the mascots of the carriage—a kind of side-show. And every one looked sorry when they got out.

But it made one think. Without entering into causes and Lincoln's great crusade to remove those causes at the end of the American Civil War, or our own abolition of slavery in the British Empire thirty years before, the sober fact obtrudes that a backward race remains a backward race for a long time, however many university degrees its outstanding members may acquire. The veneer is thin. If subjected to certain forces, it will crack in the majority of cases, although certainly not in all. But then the veneer of more evolved people is also thin; six thousand victims, chiefly coloured, have been lynched in America in forty-nine years. And only about seven hundred lynchers have stood their trial for this savagery.

Understanding, trust and genuine affection has often been given by whites to negroes in the past; and many times has been thoroughly deserved. It is still given by the thoughtful. But that it shall in future be given in increasing measure is largely in the hands of enlightened negroes themselves, as the people most likely to raise the general standard of their race and make certain qualities innate in succeeding generations.

442

This, I feel, will never be thoroughly accomplished while the birth of half-caste children continues to take place. Racial history from the earliest days of cross-breeding, thousands upon thousands of years ago, shows only too plainly that the offspring of a union between a human of a highly evolved type and one of a less evolved type, nearly always displays an over-riding of the finer of the normal qualities of the first by the coarser of the normal qualities of the second. More than one mounting civilisation has been halted, set upon the downward grade and dragged to its doom by the merging and losing of its best types among those less advanced spiritually and mentally, and less refined physically. In every way, it would be better for all concerned if serious attention were paid in future to broadly selective regulations governing marriage for the purpose of procreation and to severe penalties for both parties privy to the conception of a half-caste. Meanwhile, the multitude of half-castes themselves, no less worthy than other people of the world's respect, sympathy and consideration, should be allowed to revert to the type possessing most appeal for them; for no other decision to-day could be regarded as humane.

Gradually, over a period of generations, a strengthening of the better traits inherent in each type would accompany the purification of their blood. Nor need it be presupposed, I consider, that internecine conditions would develop on this account. I am optimistic about the future of our world. True, it runs great risks at this moment. But I believe there are sufficient men of goodwill among the leaders of nations to prevent the cataclysm foretold by the pessimists. And our advancing civilisation, if truthful education becomes more and more its life blood, will be firmly enough founded in future to prevent racial strife or even too uneconomic competition.

Take a simple example. New York is to a great extent

Italian; Chicago to a great extent German. Suppose they were entirely so. Is there, or would there ever be, a deadly trade warfare between these two cities? A friendly rivalry, yes. But a cut-throat business campaign, no! Each deals with the other in a score of different ways to their mutual advantage and to the advantage of the United States. The Germans are unbeatable instigators of orderly system, lovers of home, great musicians: the Italians are splendid merchants, creators of happiness, brilliant in the fine arts. That there have been so many gangsters is, as we have previously seen, because the legal system lower down the scale has left many loopholes for corruption. And standing momentarily on a broader platform, it is not noticeable that the preponderant type in the development of American aviation seems to have been Nordic? Why? Surely, it was the adventure once associated with this novelty that called them, as throughout the ages it has always called those of their blood.

What the future holds for the negroes, what the negroes will give to the future, remains to be seen. Certainly, the trend of both lines of development, interdependent as they are, will be shaped in no small measure by great-hearted, open-minded men and women of their own race. The great days of the negroes will come, but not yet awhile. Civilisation as we know it to-day only enlarges our knowledge of nature and its Divine processes, and speeds up some of them; it does not alter them.

So, too, under sympathetic carefully graded guidance by the Federal Government, the native Indians of America, Apaches, Hopis, Navajos, Havasupais, Hualapais and various other tribes, will eventually come to take the part most happily suited to them in the nation's life—a part obviously destined to alter in accordance with their own progression, which in some instances is clearly noticeable, in others scarcely at all.

"Surely, it was the adventure once associated with this novelty that called them...."

[Photo by courtesy of T.W.A. Inc.

But those who visualise American Indians solely as makers of blankets, bracelets and pottery, or as cattle herds, may be interested in the following quotation from a book by Mrs. Margaret Smith of Arizona. She is recounting a talk with a white trader, an old and affectionate friend of his Indian clients:

"He also told of an old Navajo silversmith who ran his car around without oil until he burned out a bearing. He laboriously took the machine to pieces, while the trader looked on with apprehension. He felt certain when the reassembling started there would be any number of stray parts for which Jim would find no home in the machinery. But, to his amazement, the old Indian located the trouble, made himself new bearings of his native silver and put the whole thing together again. For years he ran that car around Navajo land, and when an attack of 'flu carried him away in spite of medicine man sing-sings, the car was traded in by his heirs on a new one.

"Indians have a natural bent for machinery, and the hundreds of Indians used by the railroads are steady, trusted workmen."

And even such an account of the innate ability of an old, largely ignorant Navajo, pales into significance beside the modern piloting achievements of the late Wiley Post, the Indian from Oklahoma, who flew the Atlantic with a co-pilot and subsequently flew solo round the world faster than any one had ever done it before or since. Presenting an entirely different problem from that of the negroes, and having another historical and contemporary background altogether, the Indians also, so their well-wishers prophesy, will now evolve more quickly during succeeding generations. Both they and the negroes have to some extent got over the effects of the initial shock of living alongside white races more evolved than themselves, a number of whose members did not and do not show it.

445

Taking advantage of sunny days that ousted the sultry greyness of my return to the east coast, I joined in a picnic drive up the Hudson. This was the bit of country which a friend of mine had yearned to show me in the early fall when the leaves were turning. Now, alas, the trees were bare. Still, the same drive (minus leaves) was held to be the next best thing.

We took a grey Rackard " 120" over the George Washington bridge on the West Side, turned north along Palisades Boulevard and soon were shifting smoothly up the fine non-skid road that curves gently through woods crowning the cliffs above the river. Such scenery, if not such a suitable surface, belongs to the road which, emerging from our New Forest, keeps to the high ground inland of Bournemouth as one circles behind that town and Poole Harbour. Bright sunlight filled the flanking copses; turning the fallen leaves to heaps of treasure guarded by shadowy bars stretching from every tree trunk. Where we caught glimpses of the Hudson, it matched the sky for blueness. There was no wind. Smoke from the cliffside houses topped the highest twigs with lazy wisps, idly moving. The air, as we passed through it, was charged with the scent of warm woodland earth.

I took over the car and found it, not unexpectedly, to be better than most others in its price class. Thus we swept on round bend after bend towards West Point, the Military Academy; about forty-five miles by the way we had come.

A further seventeen miles along the Storm King Highway, with the Catskill Mountains starting to loom up ahead, brought up to Cornwall. There, we turned aside up a steep narrow lane into the foothills and found a place for luncheon by a small lake. Some grizzled men in red shirts had assembled to shoot. We ascertained the direction of their advance, and chose a safe spot on the ground that they had already covered. I backed the Packard into some trees near by.

"... backed the Packard into some trees near by."

" When the shadows began to lengthen on the water ..."

Loving sequestered places, I have spent days in many. But I shall not soon laze away the midday hours in another place so full of intimate charm. Feathery trees on the gentle slopes surrounding the lake seemed to give it an audible guarantee of seclusion, almost a fairy-like air of being apart from the world. Recent sights, sounds and experiences in New York instantaneously became far removed: things one had once read in a book, which could not, and for the moment did not, belong to life as we have to live it. When a breeze sprang up, causing the woods to sigh, it seemed to apologise for intruding, but bore in extenuation of its arrival a message of peace and help such as we all hanker for at times. Were there not sometimes occasions, places and inner messages like those, the iron tasks of workaday existence would crush more people than they do.

When the shadows began to lengthen on the water, the Packard coughed once and resumed her purring. She crept with us to a neighbouring house not far away, whence I was shown a great view over the valley past Newburgh. Then we made again for West Point, and passed on this occasion slowly through the actual grounds, consisting of large lawns and many trees and wide paths, which surround the dignified grey buildings of the Academy itself. This lies in a bend of the river, where many years ago attempts were made to foul the British naval sloops by stretching enormous chains across. Part of one of these chains is still there as a memento.

West Point was founded in 1802. Cadets who have qualified to go there, do so at Government expense; they receive $780.00 a year and one free ration a day. Their full dress uniform, little changed since Revolutionary days; would seem curious to us, but it is picturesque in the extreme—as delightful to see as some of the old uniforms worn at our annual Tattoo at Aldershot. All was quiet as we rolled through. One day, I would like to see the place in full swing, for naturally the greatest keenness prevails there; and efficiency and beauty together form a rare combination, although there is no reason why this should be so.

By a steep bluff a mile or two south of West Point, we stopped and got out, then clambered over a wall to look down the Hudson which the caress of nightfall was then greeting. Round the next big bend, we crossed Bear Mountain Bridge, so as to drive home down the eastern bank. But thereafter, the road lies farther away from the river. As we started to separate from it, I took another photograph—an attempt to capture what lay beyond the hills. And again, as we crossed a wide adjoining creek, the view became so like an etching that we could scarcely bear to leave. Then darkness came. The double radiance of our headlamps shone out ahead. Through Hawthorne, then White Plains, we gently hooted our way; and so at length into the Bronx and from the Bronx into upper Broadway. Around us once more, the lights of New York were flashing. An unforgettable day had passed into the storehouse of the mind.

About this time, Louis Skinitzero turned up in New York. We lunched together in the Cloud Club, and compared notes as to our respective doings since we had parted six weeks before in Los Angeles. With the adroit air of a conjuror, he produced for me out of his pocket a pass for the forthcoming Motor Show.

"We knew you'd want to go," he remarked, meaning the Chrysler Corporation.

And their inveterate thoughtfulness on my behalf was no whit reduced by the arrival by post next morning of another pass and an invitation to a banquet from the organising body of the Show itself. I gratefully gave the pass to one of my generous friends in New York, but I had to refuse the invitation because I was going to Washington and Virginia for the week-end.

I drove down to Washington with Cy Caldwell, of *Aero Digest*, in his V-8 Ford. He was heading for Langley Field to make up his mind, so he said, just to what extent the interceptor plane had had its nose put out of joint by the modern high speed fighting bomber. It was a poor morning, dull and raining, as we faced the first flatly monotonous part of the run. But Cy, Canadian born, who fought in our Royal Flying Corps, was conversationally in form; and his friends know what that means. Any one passing us, would have thought that we were both simultaneously trying to learn something by heart and repeating it to each other.

In due course, we pulled up at a German-owned eating place, just to show that we had so far nothing against Nazi-type sausages. It was a drive not devoid of incident. Cy refused to hurry, although I told him that I was due at my friend's house in Georgetown at 5.30 p.m., and we had still to see Glenn Martin's aircraft plant *en route*, a visit which Cy had kindly arranged.

"You'd better send your friends a wire," said he.

But for ages we did not stop at a post office, either because we didn't see one or were arguing too furiously. At length, I sent a long wire which arrived some considerable time after I, myself, should have been there. Then a nail relentlessly deflated our near-side rear tyre. Cy removed his coat and got to work with the jack. I kept mine on and wrestled with the wheel brace. I could have sworn that the wheel had been born, so to speak, on the car. All was done eventually, and we proceeded. But weeks afterwards, when I had been back in England some time, Cy sent a message to me by Charles Grey, to say it was a pity I knew so much about motor cars that I had put on the nuts the wrong way round. Only a creaking noise, he declared, traced by a garage hand to that same wheel, had prevented it coming off and causing him to break his neck.

Apparently, the nuts had a rounded side which fitted into

449

an indentation in the hub flange. Whereas we, in England, when we use nuts to hold on wheels, usually have a different arrangement which necessitates their being put on flat side first, with a spring washer. Of course, I ought to have noticed, But perhaps I was sleepy, or our discussion had overtaxed my wits. Anyway, I replied that we Britishers had long ago given up as old-fashioned the custom of attaching our wheels with nuts (a downright exaggeration) and had used knock-off hub caps instead. To which, Cy retorted that as they had no House of Lords for their surplus nuts in America, they just had to go on using them.

One of these days, I shall think of a crushing rejoinder.

We had come by Camden, where my eastbound plane had failed to put down a fortnight before owing to fog. Not long afterwards, we took a ferry across the Delaware, which is notably wide at that point. And by now, we were driving along just inland of Chesapeake Bay and out of sight of it. It was here that we turned off to the Martin factory, probably the finest plant of its kind in America, and situated practically on an inlet of the bay so as to have suitable water for the flying-boat side of its output. It was certainly the biggest aircraft factory that I have ever visited. But dusk was nearly upon us, and we could not stay longer than half an hour. I was just able to walk rapidly through the various shops, to notice the lines of fuselages for the twin-motor bombers and superficially to inspect, outside and in, the second of the Martin "Clippers" which stood in the open. Then we left again.

Long before we reached Baltimore, it was dark. And when we hit Washington and found our way into Georgetown, to my friend's pleasant, old world house, I was precisely two hours and forty minutes late. Cy was full of glee.

"They'll have gone to the country," he chortled. "You'll spend the week-end with yourself."

"That's better than spending it in your car," I replied offensively. "I could kick my hat faster than it goes."

"That's all right," said Cy, in satisfied tones. "I just go my own pace."

"You do," I agreed.

Laughing, we made a date to meet at Langley Field, or, failing that, in New York the following week; which, in fact, it turned out to be. Then he dawdled off, waving, and I rang the bell; wondering which of many excuses I would make first. But, though I had never been there before, I was in a way on my home ground. My host was my oldest friend in America: his coloured butler, who already knew my brother, greeted me like a long lost son: and my friend himself had waited for me, had ordered a splendid dinner of lamb chops, pushed me at once into a bath with a cocktail, and talked to me while I shaved and changed—all as though I had originally been expected at that God-forsaken hour. Afterwards, when I was clean, fed and rested, his coloured chauffeur smoothly drove us forty miles on through a fragrant night into Virginia, to an old converted farmhouse full of mellow furniture and pretty curtains and covers, where his wife had stayed up to welcome me.

When last I had seen them, they had been with me in England a year or two before, so we had much to talk about that would scarcely wait till the morning. But my hostess, seeing me tired, said with kindly firmness that it must. Shown to my comfortable bedroom, I opened the windows wide, letting in the scents of the dark countryside and the murmured intercourse of the trees: I had always wanted to be in Virginia, and there I was. On that contented note, I slept quickly and deeply. The sun was well up, and the household long astir before I opened my eyes to see a dark face smiling good-morning at me and careful hands setting a breakfast tray by my side. Before eating, I went to the win-

451

dow. Yes, there were the rolling, park-like grasslands, the woods and thickets, the soft sky of Virginia in November— just as I had often read about it. I felt no stranger to it. And I was glad.

Later, there were the makings of a new garden to inspect and discuss; also two small adopted daughters by whom to be inspected, and in whose candid eyes and manners one hoped for an approving reflection. There was the news of many months to be thrown lazily backwards and forwards. There was the short journey to be made across the park to luncheon with the gracious owner of the neighbouring big house, to renew most happily with her and one daughter a short acquaintance of years before in far-off London, and to meet a younger girl. From behind its tall pillared portico, this big house has stared placidly for many years over its Virginian domain; a centre of hospitality, of culture, of the kindly sophistication of travelled inmates, of benevolent interest in those around it. Like other calm old houses of its kind, it would cradle cheerful recollections of its various vanished children, as if to say: "While they were here, they were happy and sad as every one is. But often they rejoiced in me; in the proportions of my rooms, the view from my windows, the evening scents on my broad porch, the spread of the lawns around me and the guardianship of flowers. And so they have left the echo of their happiness in this, their home. No one coming here should be sad on their account." All houses of united families speak thus; the happy voices are the ones the mind most clearly hears.

Of Virginia, and of this place in particular, I carried away an impression of a less fenced and ordered blend of Warwickshire and Dorset; a more elemental landscape, as indeed it is; lonely enough to emphasise the ordered shapeliness of garden walks and pleasances, but full of generous hearts. On Monday, my friend and I returned to Washington.

" From behind its tall pillared portico, this big house has stared placidly for many years over its Virginian domain. . . ."

[By courtesy of my friends

One should visit Washington when the cherry blossom is out beside the Potomac, rather than when the fallen leaves, whispering along the sidewalks, foretell the advent of the snow. But it is true that framed by naked branches, the buildings of this modern Paris fully reveal a dignity which trees in leaf might tend to hide. Planned, I take it, to be America's own version of all that is best in European building, it will be one day the marvel of our descendants, as striking in its way as Venice is to us.

Its likeness to Paris consists chiefly in its boulevards; the wide, tree-lined roads driven through it in several directions; long and lovely vistas which frame distant buildings of great beauty or memorials of cold grace, that harbour warm gratitude to famous men. Constructional work appears incessant. Temporary Government buildings of large size, having served their turn, are being razed again when the basic scheme reaches and engulfs them. As one walks, there is often dust on one's shoes and *débris* to be noticed at the sides of the streets. Likewise, the young trees need to grow, and a number have yet to be planted. The old trees, of which there are many, consequently afford a more than usually welcome relief.

Washington is a city in transition. Part of it is now old, and history hallows it. Part of it is comparatively recent, yet already mature. Part of it is starkly new. As an old man, paying my final visit to America in years to come, I shall try to go last to Washington and think back over the years since I first saw it.

The White House is distinctly impressive. As the official residence of whoever is President of the United States at the time, visitors doubtless stare at the building with that fact fore-most in their minds. And it is eminently satisfactory to find that successive first gentlemen of America live in a pleasant, dignified gentleman's house, no more and no less. I spent

453

quite a time one morning walking round the ring fence, and peering over at intervals into the gardens. These look pretty enough; and from the higher ground immediately behind the house, there must be an inspiring view down towards the Potomac—inspiring because it is historical: Lincoln must so frequently have gazed in that direction, thoughtful and worried, during the Civil War. Surely, few lovers of America can study the setting of the White House without thinking of the gaunt, obstinately-courageous thinker from Kentucky, who wrote such golden pages of new human history in an old land. The clarity of his vision becomes more understandable, if no less remarkable, when one remembers that he, himself, is said to have been something of a mystic, and that communion with eternity apparently meant much to him while still labouring on earth.

But a taxi-driver's lurid comments on the traffic jams which ensue when all the Government employees leave their offices in their thousands of cars, drove these thoughts from my mind. He was driving me to Pierre's, a pleasant first-floor place, for luncheon. In the afternoon, the new Supreme Court building enthralled me, a truly lovely example of simple architecture; proportioned inside and out with such infinite pains that the result, harder to achieve than all else, is—simplicity.

New York, whither I flew next morning, had turned cold and wet. But, as days passed, less rain fell and the expected cold snap materialised. A luncheon visit with Cy to the Commandant of the Air Corps garrison at Mitchel Field, Long Island, ended in a minor blizzard. Indeed, at Roosevelt Field, to which we subsequently went on our tour of inspection, it was impossible at times to see more than a hundred yards. Both are fine aerodromes; particularly the first, which also has a model layout.

" . . . the result, harder to achieve than all else, is—*simplicity*."

"More than once now . . . a foreground of powdered snow. . . ."

More than once now, I found a foreground of powdered snow to my favourite views from Central Park. Then the restless days came as they had come in Los Angeles, when I knew I was soon to be gone. Engagements piled themselves on one another like the lines on this page. With one friend and his party I went to *Dead End*, as good a play of its kind as I have ever seen—it should be brought to London. With another and his party, I was present at the first night of *Boy meets Girl*, a satire on motion-picture life which I felt sure would convulse Rupert Hughes when he saw it—we have since grabbed this one. With yet another friend, I went to *Porgie and Bess*, the coloured folks' singing play.

I had been to the main Motor Show. But now Ledyard Mitchell was back from England and took me round the Chrysler private exhibition. He and Mrs. Mitchell were my guests later that night at the second of my three or four little farewell dinners which, for a host, are such a mixture of pleasure in entertaining and regret at parting. Another day, as a guest in the Harvard Club train, I journeyed to Prince-town to see the clash of the respective Universities' football teams. On the way through the grounds to the stadium, my friends insisted on a pictorial record of the temporary resting place of the two unknown gentlemen on the next page. I had to stalk them with my camera to the silent joy of about forty onlookers. My own repressed laughter is responsible for the shaky, out-of-focus result.

No one sat much in the train, either going down or coming back; for two baggage cars fitted out as a bar were attached to the rear of it, and there as many of us as possible congregated like sardines and sang, accompanied by an accordionist. Or, alternatively, three specially engaged negro minstrels sang to us. I realised that I had never entirely enjoyed travelling in a train before. As for the football, it was my first and only experience of the American game. It struck me as rather like a slightly slower and less graceful edition of Rugger, played in an armour of padded clothing. It is very exciting; and the armour is undeniably needed. The individual arrival and massed parade of the protagonists' uniformed bands, lends the whole spectacle an air of a Roman holiday in an amphitheatre. The only feature to disappoint me was the organised cheering parties on either side. We all out-cheered them every time.

Like the next negative on a film, my memory moves to some charity ball or other, similar to such functions in London; overcrowded for easy dancing, and with midnight entertainments by society amateurs who were incredibly comic and quite unconscious of it. Several ladies, magnificently garbed, posed or paraded with a brave absence of professional poise; and a man, dressed as the devil, sang interminably and not too well. In spite of this, I hope the ball made the money which the object of it undoubtedly deserved.

An exhibition came on of Van Gogh's work, and I wandered round it for as long as I could stand a hot, overcrowded room; which is never very long. What a tragedy his name recalls, this man! Unable to earn more than a few pounds for all his many paintings combined, he committed suicide at the age of thirty-seven, having often known dreadful want. Forty-five years later, this exhibition of only ninety-two out of his seven hundred or so pictures was valued, so I heard, at $1,000,000. The famous Sunflower canvas alone is said to be worth $90,000.

For me, there were others of his paintings more appealing: a cornfield glowing in the sun, some windblown pines and a landscape with what was then a prophetic touch to it; for it looked like a downward view from an aeroplane flying through heavy rain, which, of course, he could not have known. Van Gogh's story haunts one.

Another, equally haunting and too unpleasant to be re-

456

" . . . the temporary resting place of two unknown
gentlemen. . . ."

" . . . played in an armour of padded clothing."

" . . . the massed parade of the protagonists' uniformed
bands. . . ."

corded in detail, came to my ears a few nights later. My friends had parties of their own or were going to bed early, so I was taking one of my nocturnal strolls through the city; drifting with the crowds, to watch them and listen to them. Passing slowly along beneath the flashing lights of Broadway, I had nearly reached Times Square when two men reeled out of the door of a small restaurant and right in among the passers-by. They were in a clinch, but the bigger of the two freed himself as the open space was reached and sent the other man crashing to the sidewalk with a right swing to the jaw. He fell about three yeards from me. Those nearest to him went immediately to his assistance, but he did not come round for quite two minutes. Apart from the small knot of people gathered round him, the crowds paced past on either side, unheeding. I, also, soon passed on.

A few yards beyond, a white-faced woman stepped out of a doorway and thrust some sort of a paper or tract into my hand. It was the last she had. I did not read it but let it fall to the ground, for I have seldom seen any one so near as she was to sheer physical collapse. Looking more closely, I saw it was plainly due to hunger, not drink. She was haggard and rocking on her heels, almost at the end of all pretence.

"You're English, aren't you?" she muttered faintly, in response to my opening remark that the weather had turned colder.

"Yes," I said, thinking quickly. "And I haven't had dinner yet. I'm rather hungry. D'you know of a quiet place to eat near here?"

Her hopeless, staring eyes lit up. She suggested a Chinese joint.

"Perhaps you would care to come too," I queried, already knowing the answer. But I wondered if I would get her there.

She took my arm, and we set off. It was necessary practically to hold her up. Chop suey and noodles, she confided, was

457

what she liked best. When an expressionless man brought it to us, she ate hers voraciously and, seeing that I only wanted one plateful, asked with a sort of bold shyness if she could have what I had left in my two bowls. Thereafter, she drank far more cheap brandy than was good for any one, but at least it brought some colour into her cheeks. Bit by bit, she told me a story of foul disaster, patently founded on fact. Then the brandy did more of its work, she even laughed once or twice, her eyes took on a cunning gleam, her voice assumed the wheedling tones which circumstances had forced upon her, and she embarked on a "hard luck" story of the present that rang as false as her previous statements had rung true. Still, the original responsibility for this behaviour was not hers. It was easier to give her on parting the price of another meal than to show disbelief in her more recent revelations. We must all act like mutts sometimes, and hope that the after-effects will justify our actions: which probably they won't.

As I walked back to the Weylin, the theatre audiences (among which I might easily have chanced to be) were leaving. Interested, I hung about. Fortunate people were getting into their cars, just as they do in London, Paris, Berlin, Rome, Vienna. Watching scenes like this, one cannot help having the fact forced upon one that those who rule in the years to come will need above all else the authority of easily recognisable clear thinking, of a shining integrity, of mental asceticism where public work is concerned, and of an iron will; that is, if the balance is to be safely held for posterity between the old order that now rightly changes and mobs in the birth-pangs of the first real education, the first agonised glimpse of understanding ever known to them.

In the next day or two, I started a final round of places that I had grown to like: the Algonquin, where the theatrical folk congregated, old Jean's where the *plats du jour* were so inexpensively good, the *à la carte* dishes so painstakingly dis-

458

cussed, the Continental where all the waiters were one's friends and the violinist every one's favourite. The last after-noon called for three intimate tea-parties, one after the other, three or four people at each, to whom I was really sorry to say good-bye—in each instance, for an indefinite period. They had shown me, like nearly every one else whom I knew in America, such true and exceptional kindness.

My luggage was already in the *Aquitania* when I went in to dinner at the Continental for the last time. The violinist stood smiling by my table for long periods; playing all the Viennese waltzes I like best. The proprietor brought me a note which he begged me to give to Ferraro, the famous *maître d'hôtel* at the Berkeley in Piccadilly, where he had once worked.

"You will be back soon," he said confidently, "you will be back soon."

Even to a fairly hardened traveller, it seemed unbearably difficult to bring to its close a first visit to America.

From right aft on the boat deck at midnight, I watched over the side while the huge liner moved cautiously astern out of her bay into the river. Then we slipped slowly down-stream past the towering buildings with their myriads of windows, and, clearing the Battery, were soon steaming faster into the night towards the enfolding darkness of the open sea. Minute by minute, the great city's illuminated sky-line grew smaller, less and less clear cut. After a time, only the coloured beacons surmounting the tallest buildings remained visible. At length, these too disappeared. At one o'clock in the morning, we were hull down over the horizon. I turned to tread a deserted deck in search of my cabin, and once again I heard the lonely song of the sea air in the rigging of a great ship at speed.

.   .   .   .   .   .

The Solent in December: a ceiling of haze above the Isle of Wight; bright gaps in the gloom at Cowes and Calshot, mist at Portsmouth; seaplanes taking off up-river to Southampton, circle south to Ryde; a liner heading quietly for the docks, is leaving smooth furrows on the glassy water to ripple the lifeless image of the foreshore, sharp contrast to the shoving, chattering throngs and yelling porters soon to assemble at the Customs counters. The level railway lines, linking the coast with London, still traverse old familiar scenes and stations, before darkly burrowing pair by pair into fog-ridden areas well beloved of exiles and bringing to them the wintry smell of England.

APPENDIX

SOME NOTES ON THE COST OF MOTORING ACROSS AMERICA.

Gasoline

The following prices apply to ordinary gasoline and not to Ethyl, which is 3 cents to 4 cents more per gallon.

New York to Detroit	19 cents to 20 cents per gallon
Canada	
(North shore of Lake Erie. A similar grade of gasoline was purchased but measured by the Imperial gallon.)	21 cents „
Nappanee, Indiana	$19\frac{3}{5}$ cents „
Lincoln, Illinois	$17\frac{5}{10}$ cents „
Moberly, Missouri	$17\frac{3}{10}$ cents „
Elk City, Oklahoma	18 cents „
Carlsbad, New Mexico	$21\frac{1}{2}$ cents „
Gallup, New Mexico	24 cents „
(Small, isolated town. Consequently, transportation charges raise the price of gasoline.)	
Flagstaff, Arizona	22 cents „

(Same conditions apply as in Gallup.)

Kingman, Arizona	21 cents	per gallon
Needles, California	13 cents	,,
Los Angeles, California	11 cents	,,

Gasoline wars are periodically provoked in California by small independent refineries. Their gasoline, just as good but not so well known as other brands, can be had at the rate of twelve to thirteen gallons for a dollar. These companies run their own service stations, and erect huge signs the night before they are about to reduce or raise their prices. Such a sign would read something to this effect:—

"FILL UP TO-DAY—PRICES RAISE TO-MORROW
BY 2 cents."

These gasoline wars sometimes take place twice a year and last for three or four months.

Oil

Oil averages 30 to 35 cents per quart for the best grade Pennsylvania brand. This is a fairly constant price right across America, there being very little variation. Other "open" oils, not in sealed containers, can be had at 14 cents or 15 cents per quart, but it is not advisable to use them. In my notes, there is only one reference to the purchase of oil at the cheaper rate of 26 cents per quart; this was at Lincoln, Illinois. That district is a great distributing point for oil, which doubtless brought down the price.

Car Washing

It is possible to have a car washed for as little as 50 cents, or 2s. 4½d. A more usual price is 75 cents, and in the big hotel garages as much as a dollar, or even $1.25 will be charged.

461

Hotel Charges

A small country hotel in Illinois charged $2.00 a night for a double room and $1.25 for a single room. The food was ridiculously expensive. $3.60 was charged for dinner and morning coffee for two persons. A bottle of lemonade cost 50 cents—an appalling price.

The best hotel in Kansas City charged $3.50 for a double room or $2.50 for a single room. This is about on a par with the same class of English hotel, but the food was more expensive. Both types of room would have a private bath.

The rates at the hotel at Carlsbad, New Mexico, were the same as at Kansas City.

At Flagstaff, Arizona, the rates were $4.00 for a double room with bath or $3.00 for a single room.

At Needles, California, the rates were $5.00 for a double room and $3.00 for a single room.

The prices for accommodation at a really good auto camp are approximately as follows: $1.50 for one person, $2.75 for two persons, $3.25 for three persons. A good cabin consists of a bedroom, a sitting-room with a built-in radio set, a kitchenette with a Frigidaire, and a private lock-up garage next door. Dishes and linen are supplied, and the price also includes gas and heat and light. When three persons are accommodated, an extra bed is made up in the sitting-room.

Such camps of good cabins are usually owned by a "chain" company, and are often arranged in a half circle behind a service station. No food or drinks are supplied in the cabins. Motorists either bring their own food or go to the little communal restaurant.

By contrast to the increased cost of hotel accommodation as one nears the West Coast, the actual price of food purchased in the shops decreases—remarkably in certain instances (see pages 235 and 236 of Intermission).

INDEX

ABYSSINIA, Italian occupation of, 400; slave-trade of, 273, *see also* Italo-Abyssinian War

Acoma, the sky city, 353-4

Addis Ababa, false news from, 400

Aerial attack on towns, and defence against it, 309-10

Aero Digest (Caldwell), 309, 449

Aeroplane, The, articles in by the editor, 32, 64

Aeroplanes, American, ventilation of, 376 ff.; four-engined, 301; general purposes, 299; improvement in, anticipated, 304; modern and pioneer, 393-394; noise in, 324; Pressure Cabin, article on, 304; variableness essential in, 305

Agello, Warrant officer, World's Air Speed record made by, 393

Air Convention, signatories to and developments of, 420

Air, The, is Our Concern. (Nigel Tangye), 62

Aircraft, accidents with, news value of, 403; ice dangerous to, 332, 346; re-equipment with during war, 392

Air Forces, British and American, 310

Air Mail, U.S.A., 135, 290

Air-passengers, comfort of, cars designed for, 391; as catered for by T. W. A., 325, 331, 335; co-pilot attending to, 330, 348-9, 362, 364, 370-1, 378; horizon for, 359; reaction of, to weather, etc., 395, 402-3, and reassurance of, 406-7, 410-11; sleepiness of, 370

Airplane Development Corporation, the, 311

Airports, 325; American, some drawbacks at, 228, 240, 361, 376, 379-80; Canadian, 60

Air screws, 317

Air Service Training, Ltd., 64

Air-sickness, miseries of, 39

Air transport and travel, help of, to busy men, 364, 369, when realised, 353; insularity abolished by, 57

"Air Transport To-day" article by C. G. Grey in Tangye's book, 64

Airway beacons, 206, 321, 324, 372

Air-yachts of the future, 415

Albuquerque, by road, 174 ff.; by air, 331, 339 ff., 350, 354, 358

Alcatraz, penitentiary on, 282

Alcock, Jack, and Whitten Brown, first non-stop cross-Atlantic flyers, 393

Allaire, James P., 389

Allan, Elizabeth, 255, 294

Alleghany Mountains, 382

Amarillo, 153; by road, 145-6; grain elevators and aerodrome at, 152, 360

America, air-mindedness in, 364, 403; aviation in, 299 ff.; and Britain, automobile accidents in 389-90; contrasts between, 83; cranks in, 55, 224; culture and political purity in, 231; fast long-distance flying in, 299; national spirit of, 231; West, cordiality in, 153, 159-60, 277; American acumen in making changes, 349; aviation, *see under* Aviation, and British motor car drivers, 89, 99, 131, 390; cities, emerging from, troubles of, 128; determination to keep unentangled with Europe, 274; efficiency, 222, 238, 249, 357, 360, 422, 448; feeling as to England, 153, 274, 277; gardens, 90; gift of humour, 285; hospitality, friendliness and kindness, 14, 75-6, 79, 81-2, 103, 106 ff., 110, 124-5, 152, 256, 265 ff., 280 ff., 302 ff., 451-2, 455, 459; Indians, future before, 444 ff.; local politics; in, 228 ff., 290, 361; motoring, concentration essential in, 80, 101, 102, 146; National Debt, 107; 'plane manufacturers, pleasure of visiting, 315; rangers, 167, 181, 189, 190; specialisation in games, etc., 285; tempo, the, 75, 109, 111, 114; transport co-ordination problem, 424; Transport 'planes (*see also each company under name*), hostesses carried on, 323, 325, 330, 349, 371, 410, 411; pilots on, salaries of, 415 *n*.; speeds of, 330 ff.

American National Automobile Dealers' Association, scheme of, for dealing with used cars, 124

American Public Airlines, 333; sleeper, 'planes of, 381

Americans as hotel-keepers, 176

464

465

467

468

469

Surrealists, the, 53
Susquehanna River, 92, 102, 382
Swinton, Viscount 307

"TALKIES," the, improved films due to, 239-40
Tatra car, 121, 390
Technology, Californian Institute of, 303
Television, 241, 243 ff.
Tempelhof airport, 320
Temple, Shirley, 65
Texas, the drive across, 151 ff.
Tom Sawyer and Huckleberry Finn, a statuary group of, 137
Towanda, 92, 129
Townsend, Dr. Francis, 224
Tradition, 181; value of, 191
Traffic Commissioners, appointment of, 423
Traffic signs, *see* Road and Traffic Signs
Train efficiency, slow development of, 386
Train *versus* motor-car travel, relative cost of, 370
Trains, crack, 152, 172, 387 *n.*; trans-continental, names of, 172
Trans-Atlantic airlines, future, 290
Trans-continental bus, the, 149, 150
Trans-continental trains, nicknames of, 172
Trans-continental and Western Air Line, flight by, how planned, 330, 334 ff.; that of the author, details of, 302, 330, 331 ff., 339, 340, 360, 385; meteorological department, forecasts of, and route, accuracy of, 332-3, a problem in radio reception solved by, 334; schedules of, percentage flown, 333
Transport, all forms, liaison between essential, 421-2; of the future, as largely airborne, 353, 420-1
Transport 'planes (*see also under names*), fast, American efficiency with, 357
Transportation, not motoring, term used in U.S.A., 116; buying of, 241
Trees, in autumn, 19, 66, 91; large, moving of, at Hollywood, 247; in street, U.S.A., 90, 136
Tunkhannock, 91
Twin Peaks, California, 284

UNEMPLOYED, in America, 204
Union Air Terminals, 228; arrangement of, 319 ff., 361
　Daily arrivals at, 1934, list of, 317-18
　Daily departures from, list of, 318-19
United Air Lines, a round trip by, cost of, 316; stewardesses carried by, 317, 322; a tour on, 369-70
Universal "lot," Hollywood, 246, 249

VALLE, General, on flying in the stratosphere, 305

"Valley of Cattle," the, 198
Van Gogh, an exhibition, 456
Vaughn, 169, 170 ff., 351, 359
Victorville, 208
Village welcomes, in Canada, 103
Virgin River, 347
Virginia, a week-end in, 451 ff.
Voronoff, Serge, 63
Voyage to America, 19 ff.; a rough passage, angle of roll during, 36, 67; incident of, 35 ff., 61; end of, 69
Vultee, Gerard, 303, 306
Vultee 1 A 'plane, a flight in, details of, 310-11 ff.; military version of, 312

WAGHORN, Flying Officer, Schneider Trophy winner, 393
Walpole, Hugh, 291-2
Wall Street, *see under* New York
Warner Brothers, film studios of, 232, 250
War-time possibilities of aviation, 392-3
Washington, airport of, 290, 408; a drive to, 449; features of, 453, 454
Water transport, inland, slowness of, 60
Weather, in the British Empire, in relation to air transport, 299, 414; conquest of, 386, 388, 414; foggy, 332, 373, 374, 382 ff., flying through, 383, at San Francisco, 274, 278, 281-2; lightning distant, effect on passengers, 407; snowy, flying during, 372, 407; and speed, on Trans-continental flight, 330 ff.; turbulent, areas of, avoidance of, 333
West, Mae, 258, 275
Webster, Flight-Lieutenant, Schneider Trophy winner, 393
Wells, H. G., Utopia of, 46
West Point, a visit to, 447
White, Jim, discoverer of the Carlsbad Caves, 163
White House, the, 230
Whitney, C. V. and J. H., polo players, 78
Wilde, Oscar, 54
Wilgoos, A. V., 303
Willard, mountains near, 174
Williams, Arizona, 195-6
Wilson, President Woodrow, 273-4
Windsor-Detroit tunnel, the, 104
Wireless, in America, interspersed with advertisements, 225;
Witchita, airport, 362, 364-5
Wolfe, General James, and Wolfe's Cove at Quebec, 19, 65, 66
Working-class apathy as to local politics, 229
Working-class conditions, long-range improvement of, problem of, 218-19
World flying, personal equation in, 386 ff.
World press, post-war characteristics of, 404

472

473